EAST MEADOW PUBLIC LIBRARY
3 1299 00972 5293

East Meadow Public Library
(516) 794-2570
www.eastmeadow.info

D1116818

NO ORDINARY STALKING

a look at organized stalking and electronic harassment

by June Ti

FriesenPress

Suite 300 - 990 Fort St
Victoria, BC, V8V 3K2
Canada

www.friesenpress.com

First Edition — 2016

ISBN
978-1-4602-7139-1 (Hardcover)
978-1-4602-7140-7 (Paperback)
978-1-4602-7141-4 (eBook)

1. TRUE CRIME

Distributed to the trade by The Ingram Book Company

Table of Contents

ABBREVIATIONS

OS	organized stalking
ti	targeted individual
perp	stalking or harassing member of OS
EH	electronic harassment
v2k	voice to skull

Every name has been changed.

To Victims of Organized Stalking and Electronic Harassment

A truck jumped the curb and hit you
You didn't see it coming
You couldn't have stopped it if you had
It's not your fault
Stop blaming yourself
All the same
You're stuck in a nightmare

miss, holding a conversation with his buddy, standing inches from her chair. The jokes about his grandfather's burial service were so disgusting the women had considered moving tables. And now, here he was again on her bumper.

Watching him pass as she parked in front of her home, Jen was glad that the harrowing drive was over. Grabbing her parcels, she hurried along a rhododendron-lined path. After two seasons of gardening, the yard was shaping up. It was not like her to overlook the magnolia she'd planted the week before.

Climbing the porch steps and spinning around, the five-foot blonde squinted in October's sun, scanning the street for men, instead spotting damage to her car. Faint scratches, lots of them, ran along the passenger side of her new silver hatchback. This was not the work of a punk walking along with a key held out. This act of vandalism would have taken substantial time.

"It's that carpenter I wouldn't date. I knew he was a creep," she murmured. Unlocking the door, her mind replayed his wolf whistles. "Macho jerk—thinks he's getting even."

Furious, Jen plunked her purse on the bathroom counter. She hated to be so vain, so materialistic. Still, she loved her car.

"Idiot!" she yelled, picking up her brush like a club. Packed with dryer lint, Jen examined it, dumbfounded.

Dropping the brush into the sink and glancing into the mirror, Jen paled at the reflection of somebody else's blouse hanging on the shower rod. Turning, she fondled the sleeve as if to be sure it was real. Classy, silk, and emerald-green. It was gorgeous.

She recalled the suit-and-tie guy who had stopped her on the sidewalk that morning. "You'd look awesome in emerald-green," he'd said smirking. Thinking him brazen, Jen had kept walking.

To Victims of Organized Stalking and Electronic Harassment

A truck jumped the curb and hit you
You didn't see it coming
You couldn't have stopped it if you had
It's not your fault
Stop blaming yourself
All the same
You're stuck in a nightmare

Welcome To Hell

CHAPTER ONE

JEN'S STALKING

Being stalked by an organized group of ordinary-looking citizens is terrifying. Yet it is a crime that is scoffed by nonvictims. And it does sound odd. Let's begin with Jen and her friend talking outside a restaurant.

"Hey, Marlene, do you see those guys there? I think they're following me."

"Don't be silly, Jen. They're probably running errands same as you."

"But I've seen a couple of them outside my house."

"There's that paranoid imagination of yours again. Let's just have a nice lunch."

The young women did have a nice lunch. Jen was a bit edgy though, scarcely able to ignore the newly familiar faces parading back and forth to the men's room.

Waving goodbye to Marlene then sliding a dead bird off the hood, Jen tripped getting into the car, surprised to see a circle of white stones at her feet.

She was distracted when she ran the stop sign, not even noticing; for her thoughts were back in the restaurant. The driver of the tailgating truck had been eating there too. He'd been impossible to miss, holding a conversation with his buddy, standing inches from her chair. The jokes about his grandfather's burial service were so disgusting the women had considered moving tables. And now, here he was again on her bumper.

Watching him pass as she parked in front of her home, Jen was glad that the harrowing drive was over. Grabbing her parcels, she hurried along a rhododendron-lined path. After two seasons of gardening, the yard was shaping up. It was not like her to overlook the magnolia she'd planted the week before.

Climbing the porch steps and spinning around, the five-foot blonde squinted in October's sun, scanning the street for men, instead spotting damage to her car. Faint scratches, lots of them, ran along the passenger side of her new silver hatchback. This was not the work of a punk walking along with a key held out. This act of vandalism would have taken substantial time.

"It's that carpenter I wouldn't date. I knew he was a creep," she murmured. Unlocking the door, her mind replayed his wolf whistles. "Macho jerk—thinks he's getting even."

Furious, Jen plunked her purse on the bathroom counter. She hated to be so vain, so materialistic. Still, she loved her car.

"Idiot!" she yelled, picking up her brush like a club. Packed with dryer lint, Jen examined it, dumbfounded.

Dropping the brush into the sink and glancing into the mirror, Jen paled at the reflection of somebody else's blouse hanging on the shower rod. Turning, she fondled the sleeve as if to be sure it was real. Classy, silk, and emerald-green. It was gorgeous.

She recalled the suit-and-tie guy who had stopped her on the sidewalk that morning. "You'd look awesome in emerald-green," he'd said smirking. Thinking him brazen, Jen had kept walking.

For that moment, the young woman had no idea what to do. She stood there dazed, trying to make sense of the scratches, the circle of white stones by the car, and the men who seemed to be hanging around. She thought back to how she might have got lint in her hairbrush and if she'd forgotten about owning such a beautiful blouse. She tried to picture the stranger who had complimented her.

"Maybe it isn't the carpenter," she thought. "The loggers at the protest rally—I wish I hadn't spoken to them. They were pretty hostile."

Jen looked from the brush to the blouse. "There were how many coincidences today?" The normally clear-thinking woman was completely confused. "Coincidences happen," she told herself. "Maybe Marlene is right. I do have an imagination. But she called me paranoid. Am I being paranoid now?"

Inching timidly down the hall, peeking into the other rooms, Jen entered a tiny kitchen. It was a small house, and it was all hers. She was proud to be a homeowner. Jen was happy there. "Tea," she muttered. "I'll think about this over tea."

Jen found the teapot teetering on the blender and an opened box of exotic tea packets beside it. It was an unusual box: wooden-slatted, all bright colours with drawings of dancing orange children.

Pulling down a different teapot from the highest shelf, then peeling cellophane off a new box of tea bags—her tea bags—Jen knew she had to call police. As the kettle steamed, Jen practiced what to say. "Sir, someone's left stuff in my house. I think men are watching me. Could you send an officer over?"

Jen's voice was shaky. The officer should have noticed that.

"Ma'am, check with your friends. It sounds like someone you know is taking liberties, someone you've given a key to."

"My friends wouldn't come in like that. Not without asking. They wouldn't balance my good teapot on the blender." Jen was worried she sounded a bit nuts. "Men are hanging around my house. My car's been scratched."

"Ma'am, if you want to report vehicle vandalism, you'll have to come to the detachment."

"What about the men and the stuff I'm finding?"

"Are there any men right now?"

"Hold on, I'll look." Jen returned a minute later, having stood on the porch looking up and down the street. "No, sir. It's the first time in days they haven't been out there."

"It's often the case," the officer said, "when ladies are spooked they think someone is stalking them."

Hanging up, Jen was not only deflated, but alarmed. "Who said anything about stalking?" Needing to talk to someone, she called the friend she had left only an hour before.

"Marlene, my house was broken in!"

"My God, Jen. What did they take?"

"Nothing. They didn't take anything. They left me a blouse."

"What? They left you clothes?" Marlene giggled. "Really? Can you give them my address?"

So begins the end of Jen's world, although the process of evaluating her began the week before. She hasn't been stalker-free for days, yet was right in telling the cop that no men were outside. The moms with the baby strollers talking by her car—she looked right into their faces—they are part of the stalking team.

Soon, conniving lowlifes—the men at the restaurant and the moms—will slander Jen at her nursing job. The staff will treat her with contempt. As well, Marlene will turn uncharacteristically mean, pleased when Jen is wrongfully dismissed. Jen will lose other friends too, and the house. She will lose her career, family, home, car, savings, health, dreams, happiness, creature comforts, and her privacy.

Jen's stalkers know that any crook can get someone fired, bankrupted, and murdered. But to remove a person's identity is to shred her bit by bit. It's eliminating the frivolous things that these miscreants find effective in making the target miserable. And as causing misery is the gang's core ambition, they've made a science of it.

With each loss, the victim is a little less of herself. Be it picnics or petunias, if the victim likes it, it will be erased.

Stripping away the layers of a person is a slow process, a million tears long, which is exactly why psychopathic-types find it entertaining. There's much to do, so much to take away.

The big things have to go as well, but are overall straightforward to remove, and there's no hurry. If it's something a victim really needs, such as eyesight, they'll decide as they go along whether she can keep it or not.

Thinking up insane tricks to permeate the target with dread is the glue that keeps the gang unified. The membership is based on encasing a victim in hell and trapping her there. She can never leave. Ejecting all the people in her life ensures that she is their hostage—in plain sight.

The criminals know that a reliable way to maintain control is to inspect Jen's every move to see what will produce the most anguish. Once they know how Jen ticks, they can unwind the clock.

Right now, they are seeking everything Jen finds distressing (road-kills are on the list), what she worries about, what she treasures, and particularly what she shops for. They are studying her past, her likes, and her dislikes. They will attain so much data on

Jen that her future behaviours can be anticipated. Jen's stalkers will know more about her than she knows about herself.

A fundamental part of their job, a requirement, is to read illegally obtained documents: anything with Jen's name on it, along with records of family and friends. This getting-to-know-you process is so critical that I'm going to repeat it. Amassing information about the target is crucial to the installation of stealthy dozens-on-one disprovable hijinks. Stalk. Interlope. Harass. Intimidate.

While the horrified twenty-seven-year-old nurse drinks tea in her cozy yellow kitchen, the attacking troop is one block down, partying. Gathered in a meeting-living room, on folding chairs around a plywood tabletop, their mandated agenda is serious, despite the hilarity. They are plotting how to decimate Jen's next few months, one day at a time. Many men and a few women must be harassing, stalking, threatening, vandalizing, and inflicting pain without pause.

Jen's perpetrators are dedicated to her psychological, financial, and physical slaughter. The louder the cries for mercy, the more merciless they become. Conscience has no place in this crime. It is absent. The work is intoxicating for those who enjoy it.

Visit Jen's supervisor and say she's making porno movies? Sprinkle glass shards in her slippers? Disconnect the phone? Poke a cardboard tombstone in the flower bed? Re-hang her seascapes upside-down? Charge a patio set in her name? Tell her parents that she's bipolar? Leave road-kills where she's sure to find them? Tell Marlene lies?

At the eight-week mark, Jen's computer will be ravaged, together with the rest of her electronics, and her cat. Yes, they'll maim her beloved pound cat while it is curled up on the sofa wondering why strangers are in the house. Indeed, breaking in and annihilating their quarry's belongings with cordless tools and high-powered lasers is something they find comical. The gizmos are toys to the gang, flipped on and off as if they are three-year-olds with flashlights.

People, pets, or stereos, it makes no difference to the men. It's all in good fun. Their top munitions, however, are radiation contraptions that send noxious energy through a wall to make a person sick. The gang's electrician built lunch-box-sized gadgets that killed the last mark before they were ready to let her die. That's who Jen's replacing. They'll back off this time.

They figure it shouldn't take long to make the nurse too weary to retaliate. With an arsenal at their disposal, they have the ability to dominate. And murder. The best part is that no one suspects. Not one of the weapons is typical. Who ever heard of average-looking folks using lethal energy gadgets anyhow? Or phony cell phones that spray nasty chemicals? For the new guys it's a great assignment. They admit Jen is a sweet woman, a perfect target with the bonus of being pretty and petite.

The key players are experts at their craft. They teach the underlings how to enter a locked door undetected, how to circumvent security, how to install spy get-ups, and surreptitious use of contaminants. A couple of the overseers show handier trainees how to construct the inconspicuous equipment that dispenses harmful energies. Buying the devices is all right; money is not a barrier, and lots of perpetrators have bought their own, but it's the homemades that pack a punch.

With Jen's phone and computer already hacked into, everything she has said, done, or planned in the last week is in a perpetrator file.

Plus, with a pinhole camera they hid in her bedroom, they peep. Naked-exercising is watched by stalkers, rapists, and a few clowns.

Jen has been targeted for the crime of organized stalking. An organized stalking predator who was attracted to her gentle smiles had assessed Jen in the market. He wandered alongside noting what she put in the cart: halibut, lemons, cottage cheese, and baby greens. He liked the way she helped a disabled lady find the newspapers. And because she wasn't wearing a wedding ring, he followed her car home.

Early the next morning he parked down the road from Jen's house and trailed her to the seniors facility she worked in. She seemed to meet the group's criteria, so he rented a house nearby. It's what he always did.

Stalking is going to be just one of Jen's difficulties. The organization's standard harassment and torture are scheduled. For the first couple of years, Jen is going to fixate about why this is happening. She is going to retrieve every bad memory and every suspicious event in her lifetime: every bad person, every bad word.

But right now, Jen's demise is in the planning stages. The gang is having a riot deciding on what disguises and gestures to use, and what to say that will scare the pants off her.

Within hours, stalking men will be wearing "Jesus Saves" pullovers and carrying Bibles. When a new patrol joins in, consisting of women wearing jewellery with Pagan insignias, they try to befriend Jen. The next group of bicycling stalkers wave at Jen like they are pals, and another group posing as tourists won't stop asking her for directions. Throughout it all, various people stand close and shove the number 66 at her, or point, or say, "Me oh my." Whenever Jen thinks she's figured out what the stalkers have in common, they throw in boorish fellows with big gold logos on their hats. Duping Jen is exactly what is necessary to destabilize her.

The target she's replacing got bombarded with bearded males and gory spectacles, and the men found it tedious. For this victim, harassment styles will switch constantly. The goals, however, are rigid. The contract is to derail her. Confusion, fear, isolation, extreme poverty, chronic illness, and pain will be dispensed until Jen is dead. To the perpetrators, she's not human any more, but a creature in a warped kind of hunt.

* * *

Three years almost to the day Jen and Marlene had lunch together, the men leave a dildo and pretend pistol in the beater Jen's ended up living in. She visualizes passersby gawking in the window, shocked at seeing a rotting corpse, a hole in her abdomen.

Jen, thirty, homeless, and emaciated, has her stalkers congratulating each other. She folded faster than anticipated. Her last thousand dollars was spent on a van to sleep in while she travels, trying to shake the pack. Destitute, her hair is falling out, and she's cold all the time. November is coming.

She tries to live in the van all winter, and that makes her perpetrators especially pleased. It was hypothermia that changed things. On a sub-zero morning Jen woke up bone-chilled, and because she was gone all day warming up, the men took the opportunity to trash the engine.

On the street and freezing, the nurse-beggar asked another homeless woman where to sleep and was invited to tag along. With her family trying to have her locked up in a mental hospital, Jen can't ask for any kind of help. Family, friends, and cops have decided she's developed a delusional disorder. The harassment sounds far-fetched.

By age thirty-three, Jen's targeting has become almost impossible to survive. Her life revolves around finding shelters and safe houses with room to take her. It isn't that she's unemployed by choice. The stalkers won't let her keep a job long enough to get on her feet. Either they make her too sick to work or they tell the bosses lies. At the last job, a stalker put a crack pipe on her desk and then told the manager he saw her smoking drugs behind the building.

Jen, though, is a fighter. Every time they have her on her knees she manages to pull herself together. The next job she finds is at a recycling depot where an employee gives her his scrapyard truck and camper so she can run. She is curious how he recognized her silent desperation when no one else could.

Driving to nowhere, Jen is fanatical about turning corners, and racing through yellow lights, and sometimes red ones, trying to throw off anyone following her. As often as she dares, she parks at night outside police stations, hoping the truck's condition won't be noticed. Elsewhere, she stays awake as much as possible, afraid that the melted doll she found on the mattress is a threat of what's to come.

The men keep finding her. Her logical mind says they've put a tracking device on the truck, yet it's a ludicrous idea. It's not like she's somebody important, unless, that is, the plan is to light her into a sacrificial torch. A cult would need an isolated person to do that to. Somebody with nobody. It's an image that Jen can't get out of her head, triggering moments of hysteria.

Flicking lighters in Jen's face, dropping matches everywhere, and leaving melted lumps for her to find—the squad feel they've outdone themselves. Jen is in a state of pure terror. She has no way of knowing that the men have no desire to set her or her camper on fire, that they prefer fictional-sounding crimes, like emitting microwaves to make someone sick.

The gang members sarcastically call radiating a whole person "people cooking," and they can hardly wait to people-cook Jen again. But for now, the organization's leaders have chosen to heat her in small patches, every day or two, with a long-reaching high-tech tool. It's their simplest torture as it takes little effort. If Jen ever finds slum housing, the weapon made just for her will be covertly set up in an adjoining apartment, and she'll be microwaved through the wall like a TV dinner, but just enough to enfeeble her, which is what they did outside the bedroom wall of her cute little cottage in the beginning. (Microwaves flow through walls. See illustration on page 160.)

Jen's death is scheduled to take place in year nine. Her passing is planned to be suicide, watched and applauded by the organized stalking members. Between the bets, and the sly videos they take of her naked, and the rip-roaring videos of her flipping-out—the ones they watch over beer—she is vital to her stalkers' image. She and the other targets are the reasons the members get up every day.

As the woman weeps in her eight-foot camper-home, her heart beats irregularly under a blazing hot breast, a triumph for the autocrat in charge of searing body parts from a distance. If somebody doesn't give a damn soon, Jen's life will end unnoticed, and the goons will go on to the next pawn.

Surrendering, Jen is going to let herself starve. There is no reason to continue, with no one to continue for. Companionship is not allowed. They made that apparent when they dangled a freshly killed puppy from her side mirror.

Listless after deciding to die, Jen walked away from the truck and camper for good. Besides, with no money for gas, she felt defenceless in the deserted lot she'd had to park in. At night the morons peed on the wheels, wisecracking about marking their fucking territory. She couldn't take it anymore.

Moving into a house for recovering addicts, Jen keeps to herself. She's not an addict. She lied to have a roof to starve under. A stalker moving in right behind her keeps trying to enter her room.

"I'm sorry," the woman says ten times a day. "The rooms all look the same."

Feeling safer than she has for years, it is the coffee table brochure *Stress Management for Victims of Violence* that makes Jen angry enough to try again. "Bastards—taking my career and my house," she says out loud as she flips through the leaflet. Back to eating, the nurse realizes it will be a while before she's well enough to scoot. She figures that the loitering posse outside will end up on the bus with her. She prays she can lose them.

Dishonesty is not in the woman's nature, yet to at least try to escape she has to make up more lies, stories to outfox her stalkers. She is sorry that well-meaning people are going out of their way to move her to a place she'll never go.

On the morning Jen has planned to leave she is vomiting, unsure if she can pull it off. She suspects that the stalker up the hall is putting something in the drinks, not caring that everyone's being poisoned. Taking a discarded biscuit package to puke into, Jen leaves her laundry in the dryer, her nightgown on the bed, and a half-empty purse in the drawer. Tiptoeing out a side door, she walks to a bank to cash a government-assistance cheque the recovery house helped her get, and then heads to the soup kitchen, hoping to find crates of outdated groceries. Nauseous or not, Jen doesn't know when she'll next eat. The money is for fare.

Empathy is a trait the stalkers have not been able to remove from this target, and after she asks the sallow-skinned volunteer how he is, he nods towards some bins and hands her a recycled plastic bag so full of holes it is not much good. "Lucky," she thinks, rummaging through oozing black bananas and smushed apple fritters, "this stuff was five minutes away from the pig farmer."

At the bus depot, Jen asks the cashier about schedules to no-such-city and then pretends to make a call from the phone booth by the door. "I'm going to be late," she says a tad too loudly. "There's no bus going there today, so I'm going to ask. . .—unless you want to come and get me. Okay then. I will." Hanging up, Jen's only plan is to set as many decoys as she can, but when she hears a bus start its motor she knows she has to go. The game's too grueling for someone so sick.

Leaning her head against the bus window, glimpsing at the doughnuts dropping through the holey bag onto the dirty floor, the once amazing woman was unrecognizable. Closing her eyes after catching her reflection in the glass, she was reminded of an old battered woman, a wartime prisoner from a photo that stuck in her mind. Rearranging throbbing legs, she couldn't recall hurting herself.

Not seeing stalkers on the bus doesn't mean there aren't any. An ever-changing roster ensures that the victims are suspicious of everyone. They'll let her know soon enough if they're on board. It's the only way to continue the chase.

Trying to get her mind off the leg-pain, Jen ruminates about all the times she asked her enemies what they wanted, asking them what she'd done wrong. "Nothing," a woman said. "We're supposed to watch you kill yourself." Jen didn't know what to think. They said so many things.

The staff at the next women's safe house are more helpful than most even though they discount Jen's tales of dozens of stalking men and women. Still, they persevere in helping her get rooted. They cannot understand what the nurse went through slipping her assailers.

Within two months, Jen has a sleazy apartment and a crummy part-time night job cleaning for cash. She is grateful for them both.

Coming home to stained carpets and a ripped sofa feels like heaven after living in a cold van, homeless shelters, centres for abused women, a scrapyard camper, a recovery house, and on the street.

Being reclusive most of the time is boring, and though used books are cheap, they aren't free. In her third un-stalked month, Jen enters the library as it opens, cases each patron, and hastily approaches the front desk. Watching as the clerk copies her rental-agreement address into a computer, Jen panics. But it was too late. Jen walked out with an armload of books, so traumatized that she had to constrain herself from darting into traffic.

Remarkably, the next few days aren't bad at all. Jen immerses herself in stories, masking sadness so deep she feels her soul has been lost. A bare light bulb dangles over the couch: the long electrical cord threaded through a tall branch leaning against the wall. Jen didn't mind the branch. It's not like she has company.

Finding a used cord and socket for a dollar, with a 100-watt bulb already in it, was the week's high point. Jen's eyesight has deteriorated so badly that without light in just the right position, she cannot see through the cloudiness. The deviants, it seemed, had tried to blind her with chemicals they spritzed, that blistered her face. Or maybe it had something to do with the little box one of them carried. It didn't seem to do anything, yet she got a headache whenever the man held it up.

Nevertheless, Jen was reading and warm. It was puzzling the way her whole being vibrated. She felt "charged" and put it down to being in fight or flight mode for so many years. Even the couch vibrated when she sat down.

The hundred and twenty-eighth day of escape, according to Jen's SPCA calendar, was promising: each un-stalked day leading to another. Carrying a canvas tote of carefully chosen books, Jen entered the corner store.

"Hey, Karen," the manager yelled out. Jen, known as Karen in the store, was friendly with the staff. She had been looking for additional nightshift jobs, and everyone was keeping their ears open, not knowing why she could only work for cash. Today, Jen was dropping off a note, not expecting the manager to be in. The note was embarrassing, asking for outdated fruit and sandwiches. Handing it over to the pleasant woman, Jen beetled it out, wondering if she'd be brave enough to return. She felt like a bum.

Sure, the food banks were great. But she'd not gone back since a man in the bread line had spoken to her: "Kyle's taking engineering you know." Then the man bolted without getting anything, not even the outdated cinnamon buns everyone was grabbing at.

Kyle was Jen's younger brother. He'd always wanted to take engineering. Deciding not to dwell on it, freedom had been too hard-won to needlessly obsess. It had to be one of those freakish things. Still, the comment nagged at her while she went about rebuilding her life, trying to find something to eat in other places.

Hurrying home one morning from the women's resource centre, under an incessantly grey West Coast sky, Jen was full of muffins and thoughts, wondering if Kyle might somehow be involved. They'd never got along.

"Jen! Jen!" a man hollered from across the street, enthusiastically waving. Red ballcapped and jean-jacketed, the fellow was determined to get her attention, no matter how many people rubbernecked. Jen knew him instantly. He was one of the very first. Whirling around and speed walking in the opposite direction, away from her apartment, Jen knows she'll soon be homeless and jobless again.

Within minutes of seeing her stalker, Jen considers prostitution and stealing purses. She needs money for a gun immediately and wonders where to find the scum who will sell her an illegal one, for she has no firearms license. She's relieved to have found a solution.

After hiding for hours in a department store ladies' room, the thirty-four-year-old races through her seedy neighbourhood's dark vacant lots all the way to her door, and completely falls apart.

As a nurse, she knows that her threshold of fear has been surpassed. She wonders if drowning herself in the bathtub would be a good or a bad thing to do but cannot figure out the taps: hot, cold, on, off. It's all too complicated. So is making tea, her old standby. Jen is experiencing brief psychosis. It isn't until she's stuffing raw noodles into her purse for getaway food that her mind begins to engage. What she really wants to do is scream at all the people who betrayed her—who became rivals when she needed saviours.

It took two days of self-persuasion before she could look out the window and another two to go outside. Jen realizes that by eluding her stalkers for four months, there will be a punishing sentence. She admits that she's too weak to skip town this time. Seven years of violence have left her vulnerable. Dying doesn't faze Jen anymore. It's not an issue. How the men kill, is.

There's nothing left she figures, at least until she buys a gun, other than talking to the cops. Her heart tells her it's a dumb idea. Her complaint files say she is a lunatic, but she is desperate.

Pleading with police has never worked, so Jen gets riled this time, demanding protection. "It's true. Why would I lie? These men are trying to murder me." Jen knows she presents a wretched picture and that shouting could sound antagonistic.

The cops check out her worn sneakers, one stained with diarrhea from when Jen was too ill to find a toilet; though they'd never have guessed it was poo. She hopes they don't notice that under her trashy nylon jacket is a sweatshirt with a smiley face: all you can stuff in a bag for two bucks from the youth section of the thrift shop. "If I was rich or the mayor's daughter would you believe me then?"

"Dozens of men following you? And women too? They do what? They leave dead animals for you to find? Do you live near a road, ma'am? They make up stories to get you fired? They spray you with chemicals? Ma'am, I suggest you make an appointment at the mental health clinic. There's one a few blocks from here."

The stalkers, having followed Jen to the police station, listen to her tirade. They knew where she lived all along. It's just that they weren't ready for her to die, having never encountered a target who would starve herself to death. Giving her hope was necessary. The game isn't quite over.

It takes a bit of juggling—this timetabled suicide business. They find Jen less manageable than most. Watching her rebound is beginning to make them grumpy, so they are constructing plans that are practically non-survivable for an already half-dead female. What she endured before will seem like a holiday. To end the torture, she'll have to take her own life, as have several of the others. It's her turn.

To hasten Jen's demise, so many men and women stalkers make false complaints to the police that she is interviewed, arrested, handcuffed, and committed into a psychiatric ward. The perpetrators portray her as a violent schizophrenic, and with Jen's extensive file of weird grievances, she is locked up for weeks, including incarceration in the rubber room. The doctors keep her so heavily sedated that she can't counter their conversations about court appearances.

When Jen is released, she has nowhere to go other than the homeless shelters where she is harassed. So she wanders. The men make her fall on the street, pretending to be clumsy drunks. They shine lasers in her eyes. Finding legal help who understands organized stalking is what needs to happen. But her owners will never allow that. She knows it, and I know it.

The amazing woman is done battling a gang of hit men all by herself. She cannot raise gun money because she cannot force herself to steal purses. And she's too scared to hook, afraid a stalker will torture her. So she can't buy a gun to shoot herself in the head.

Searching on the library's Internet for information on suicide, Jen sees my name on an organized stalking site offering help to homeless and suicidal targets.

Crying, she calls me, "I don't know what I did wrong."

Jen's targeted history is, unfortunately, typical.

CHAPTER TWO

THE FACE OF ORGANIZED STALKING

Publicly acknowledged strokes of terrorism do not include dismantling one human, a sliver at a time. All the same, for years I called organized stalkers terrorists. Some victims call organized stalking a hate crime, without knowing why they are hated.

Organized stalking impedes every action in its quarry's world. From feeding the squirrels to riding the bus, if you are a targeted victim and you do something—anything at all—it will be interfered with or removed altogether.

Think of five things you might do every day: opening the curtains, checking your emails, talking on the phone, kissing someone, and having a private shower. Now, imagine that each of these activities is unsafe, difficult, or impossible. The next five forfeitures are grocery shopping, sitting outside in the sunshine, credit cards, pets, and friends. Keep going.

Long-term victims, whose everything has been deleted, subsist on endless grief. If they didn't, the empty spots would fill with horror. New victims exist entirely on confusion, plus horror. Grief comes soon enough. Rage is common to all.

What motivates me to work with targeted individuals is their unbearable sadness. It is a thousand losses deep. It bothers me tremendously. By the time isolated, homeless, and suicidal victims contact me, they need to mourn their losses and adapt but are incapable of doing either. They are too busy and too traumatized.

There is no stopping organized stalking. If a victim does not eventually learn to adapt, he or she will not endure, though quick elimination may be in the cards anyhow. Asking a target to adjust to the crime is akin to asking a bludgeoned cashier to cover her head and think optimistically, which sounds ridiculous, so I never use the word adapt when counselling victims. However, in roundabout ways, learning to adapt is precisely what I'm suggesting that they do. This is not giving up. Giving up and adapting are entirely different survival tactics. Adapting is halting, modifying, or adding physical or mental behaviours that will allow a person to hang on. As the attacks cannot be prevented, victims must learn to outlast them. Seriously harangued and tortured victims unanimously consider suicide now and then.

What inspires me, awes me really, is the resiliency of human spirit. The condensed history of Jen's targeting presents a small percentage of the buffeting she took. Nonetheless, she and so many others make a conscious decision to trudge on, despite legitimate hopelessness.

What pushes a lot of targets to suicide is forced homelessness and forced isolation. A homeless victim who is hammered with unremitting offences has no retreat. As for isolation, losing everyone you love and know—just everyone—feels like extinction.

You will read that certain stalkers leave feces outside their dupe's home. Yet this is a sophisticated crime using proven techniques until mental breakdown cannot be averted. Organized stalking's psychological thresholds is a subject I've studied, only because I am a target assisting other targets. Isolation, pain, chaos, fear, grief, and demoralizing are brought to precisely plotted peaks and then continue until the situation is mortal without intervention.

As you learn about the crime, you will see that the victims' responses are entirely apart from the responses of usual stalking victims once it is found out that avoidance, deterrence, safety, and lawful measures have no effect.

Also different from normal stalking is that perpetrators demand to be seen as intimidating outlaws even while they are openly engaging with their prey. This is not a display of obsessive or incensed attachment to the target such as what famous people, singled-out women, and people in power experience, or when a relationship has ended where passion or revenge is the objective.

Organized stalking is a job; thus, the hirelings need their handiwork to be linked to them. If a victim misses a trick or a trap, or blames a premeditated problem on bad luck or someone else, an aggressive perpetrator may insist that his target clue in, even if it means coming to the door and telling her (or him) in an indirect way. Around-the-clock collaboration between the hunted and the hunter is unusual, except in this crime, with each knowing the other's role.

Interaction from an organized stalker to his prey involves bullying and manipulating and can be an obvious setup for future offences. Intentions and desired consequences from a misdeed might be backhandedly revealed to the victim beforehand, during, immediately afterwards, or even weeks later; for example, Jen's pursuers put a melted doll on her mattress prior to burning her breast.

Fear is an important resource for organized stalkers, and they do all they can to exacerbate it. Overall, fear and anxiety are excessive for OS (organized stalking) victims due to the number of assailers, overwhelming harassment, sincere threats, the use of energy weapons, and not knowing why this is happening.

Before we go any further, I want to briefly tell you about energy weapons since I just mentioned them. An organized stalking energy weapon is any article of any size that emits energy to cause harm. It can be inches away or a very long distance away. Consider the damage that heat can do and consider that sound waves can kill. For instance, in extreme circumstances police and militaries use either heat-producing energy weapons or knock-you-flat sound wave (energy) weapons to disperse crowds. Both types are lethal when used improperly.

Energy weapons are responsible for organized stalking's electronic harassment and are used with the intent of incapacitating, sickening, injuring, torturing, and killing. They can be as low-tech as illegally adapted laser pens and as high-tech as illegal transmitters that scramble a person's thinking or cause him to be drop-dead tired.

It might help you to understand if you think about an energy-emitting apparatus in or around your home that has the potential to be detrimental. Some folks think about the controversy over radiation from cell towers and other folks recall when they accidentally seared their head with a hair dryer. Energy sources are vast, as are the troubles they can cause.

So why does organized stalking use electronic harassment instead of sticks, stones, and guns? Because energy, even when it's deadly, can be undetectable by onlookers. That's why. Moreover, maiming people with energy sounds made-up. I want you to pretend that Jen joins you on a bench at a bus station. You can't help but notice that she's a mess. She's having problems walking and seeing, and ooze is spotting her blouse, just like the ooze from when you burnt your wrist on the stove. It's obvious that she's unwell, injured, and in pain. "It's electronic harassment," she says. "Energy weapons. They're killing me." Chances are you are not going to believe her. You might change your seat because you don't want to sit next to a nut. Electronic harassment, in its many forms, is usually invisible, and usually unbelievable, and always terrifying. It's perfectly suited to commit perfect violent crimes.

That's all you need to know about electronic harassment for the moment. I've given you a start-up definition because I personally find it annoying when an author casually mentions a little-known subject (in this case energy weapons) and then leaves me hanging.

We can now get back to talking about the perpetrators: the men and women whose ambition in life is to destroy a life. Maybe yours. Certainly mine.

Although a victim may know one or more perpetrators, perhaps from social circles or from work, the majority are strangers. For me, they are all strangers.

As you've already discovered, stalkers work in groups. A single perpetrator may follow or harass his prey, but you can be certain that his partners are waiting for an update, watching, or listening.

The felony is called organized because the perpetrators organize themselves to commit structured preplanned offences.

None of the stalking studies I researched were helpful in understanding this crime. Almost every article and book examined dyadic (a pair) stalking. In each report, prototypal motives and how a victim is chosen did not apply.

The similarities between conventional stalkers and organized stalkers are limited to the acts of following and watching, a mishmash of vandalism and harassment, sexual voyeurism, and the stalkers' flawed character traits.

In my domination, there is a preponderance of gang members with personality disorders, a known factor in many dyadic non-psychotic stalking cases. I suspect this is likely in other targets' cases as well and is not unique to my own. Because perpetrators permeate our lives every day, for years on end, we get to know them.

Each targeted victim has invisible masters—office managers—who dictate how far mental and physical torture should be exacted by the stalkers, and when. The masters decide when a target should die, be it by an electronic weapon, disguised accident, extreme poverty, or the preferred suicide. Homicides are recognized by other victims, but not by the populace.

I should mention that stalkers, harassers, perps, perpetrators, hunters, and predators are different names for the same miscreants. Victims, as you've already learned, are referred to as targets, and also as ti's (pronounced t.i.) which stands for targeted individual. Organized stalking is often abbreviated to OS.

Having covered the basics, let's look at how easy it is for organized stalkers to commit silent, slow murders; the fun they have doing it; and how they get away with it.

CHAPTER THREE

A CLOSER LOOK

A lone man in black coveralls, camouflaged under no moon, hides one eye behind the rough bark of his regular tree. Thrilled with a fleeting window glimpse of his prize, he scurries away, leaving only his disgusting thoughts behind.

This man is not an organized stalker. Organized night crawlers have to make their presence known at that moment or by leaving clues that they were watching. A member of OS (organized stalking) might have thrown a stone at the house, made noises, or left something odd in an equally odd place. If he's been watching the same house for months and knows that the victim no longer calls police, he may scrape a stick along the walls or pass under a window laughing, coughing, or jingling keys.

If the victim's house has attentive neighbours, or she lives in an apartment or condo, meaning a stalker can't intimidate up close and personal, he'll sneak around in the dark and plant something interesting where she's bound to find it: door, hall, foyer, mailbox, entrance, walkway, vehicle, or wherever she is known to go. He might make a design out of rocks or bottles, or dribble her usual rose nail polish into an X. Should he have watched her buy a pink lip gloss that day, he might have bought one himself and put its package or its receipt on her windshield. After finishing the hijinks, he'll probably still laugh, cough, or jingle keys intermittently throughout the night near her apartment window or door, or on the street outside her house.

If his prey was an apartment-dwelling mom with preschool sons, he might hang a broken plastic fire engine on her door or car. If she's in a house with a yard, he will hang the toy on a branch or a fence. If he's fulfilling an arsonist theme, he'll drop matches underneath.

A retired logger who is targeted may find that garbage bags of woodchips were dumped in the middle of his lawn, in the middle of the night. And if logger Tom's pickup has firewood in the back, he may wake up to find his alder neatly restacked—right beside the truck. If Tom is a heavy sleeper, the grandkids' swing set may have crossed the yard. Organized night stalkers move belongings. They muddle with everything that's outside. Big stuff and little stuff. From apartment door numbers to logger Tom's tractor. Even a cow.

That galvanized steel gate you blew two hundred bucks on? With a little help from cordless power tools, every second screw, bolt, and rivet will be on the ground long before your rise-and-shine coffee. At least, that's what happened to my gate. Disassembling things is a favourite. If it can come apart, it will.

Nothing's off limits. The birthday bike little Mindy's all smiles about could be tomorrow's trash. Night vandalism causes just enough damage that the item is ruined. Oftentimes, it is not obvious until you go to use the thing. That includes security equipment.

The objects a stalker leaves behind, which I call tokens, are cryptic indications a sleuth is watching and studying the target. The crime is intelligent, even if some of the perpetrators aren't.

To create suspense, without fail, intruders and night stalkers leave miniature doodads around, quite unlike the highly visible articles. These diminutive tokens are dollhouse or board-game size. They will also leave minute cut-out words or pictures from magazines and wrappers that only the victim sees as significant. The same applies to leaving miniscule graffiti or stickers, pieces of fabric or string, and bits from nature such as sand, petals, and seeds. To ratify alarm, the teeny items are often placed where they would never ordinarily be; a potato peeling or toothpaste cap might be placed on a car dash. New targets can find tiny tokens outside or inside their homes, vehicles, or jobs most mornings for the first few years.

A greenhouse grower may discover teeny artificial flowers in his wheelbarrow. Or a daisy-shaped button. A baker may find cake sprinkles glued to her barbecue utensils or chocolate chips on top of her Welcome sign. Mouse skull necklaces may adorn a jeweller's shutters, and a fan of king crab will need pliers to extract a crab claw fragment that a night dastard crammed into her garden hose. Common to burglarized single women are the charms made for charm bracelets and the half-inch weapons that accessorize warfare figurines and ornaments.

High on the creep meter is when a ti (targeted individual) finds remnants that were taken out of his, or his loved ones', curbside trash-can weeks, months, or years before. It could be the receipt from little Cuddle Bun's dolly; or a terrible recipe that was discarded, along with one of its terrible gingersnaps; or something personalized, like a postcard.

Encountering one of these items is no big deal. Happening upon them all the time is unsettling. The larger items are, actually, easier to contend with as the victim has absolute certainty a stalker was around. Wondering if something got stuck to your clothes, or if you are having memory lags, or if you are becoming paranoid or daft confuses a ti who is trying to find excuses to believe nobody was nosing around when in his heart he knows somebody was.

Long-term targets continue to be gifted with tokens, big and small, even after a dozen years, but by then the perps are onto new fear tactics and tokens are left only to fill a specific need. When a target gets used to a maneuver, it is replaced.

Vandalism is forever. If a target starts out with a lot of night-time vandalism, he will be battling to keep his possessions intact for the rest of his life. Conclusively, the blackest hours is playtime for the stalkers.

Leaving Rover outside for protection is futile. Though he might bark or attack in the beginning, he will be made to shut up. Perpetrators are as quick to kill a dog as they are to befriend it. They will do whatever it takes to keep Rover quiet, be it feeding, stealing, kicking to death, poisoning, or a lethal discharge of electricity. Having assessed both the locale and the target, then being given instructions from a criminal boss, it is a stalker's job to overcome obstacles. For Rover to survive outside, he would need to silently stay out of the way.

An OS (organized stalking) night prowler, unlike a neighbourhood tree peeper, would not scurry away alone. His comrades would be spying from different trees and bushes, or loitering behind nearby buildings and fences, or feigning to be occupied at street corners and phone booths. They may be walking a dog or a baby, or dressed up as a couple of homeless guys with a shopping cart, even at 3:00

a.m. Others more would be driving back and forth, or waiting in cars, lots of cars, to pick up the trespassing stalkers, to watch for police, and to watch for problems. Lookouts would be posted blocks or miles away.

Communication between these idiots is instant. They use expensive handheld and head-worn technology with push-button alerts. At close range, they use hand signals, physical gestures, and codes. They can scatter or amalgamate in seconds.

Should a young lady in a lacy nightgown look out the door after hearing a rock bounce off her house, her stalkers would not be thinking, "Oh-oh, she's on to us. We need to warn the others and run." They'll be thinking, "Great, let's wait an hour and do it again. Maybe we can get her to come outside." Because the rock throwers have reliable direct interactions with guardsmen, they can take advantage of every dark hour to unsettle the beauty. Indeed, with so much uninhibited time, her fear level would be noted in detail while she investigated the banging on her walls. As with all young women, her attractiveness would be described, photographed, and discussed as if she were part of a perverted inquest.

When logger Tom discovers woodchips in his yard, his reactions, too, are recorded in his very own stalking file.

Perpetrators depend upon seeing and hearing reactions to their pranks in order to set up further pranks, ones that carry the biggest punch. Manipulating a target's emotions is critical to achieve domination. Perpetrators must know their victim's weak spots. And trigger spots. Afraid of spiders? Worry about paying the bills? Have allergies? Hindered by dyslexia? Recovering from knee surgery? Recently divorced? The distinctive ways a target handles life's ups and downs are examined and then incorporated into tactics that will cause maximum mental distress.

A target who is kindly towards garden snakes and tree frogs will never see them within her harassment schema. On the other hand, a target who goes bonkers over stepping on a slug is going to find slugs everywhere. What's more, a ti (targeted individual) caught crying over her mother's death will be swamped with calls and conversations about dying moms. A grieving ti will unquestionably receive perp-sent *accidental* mail and messages meant for the deceased loved one.

How, you are asking, do stalkers know their prey's reactions? How do they know what victims are feeling? Do they really watch around the clock? Yes they do. And they listen. And they read. It's a big organization. Members work in shifts walking, driving, hanging around, prowling, following, and eavesdropping. With a victim's phone and computer hacked, if logger Tom throws a fit on his cell, expressing a get-even attitude towards the jackasses who dumped woodchips on his lawn, his stalkers will definitely hear.

Let's consider the young nightgowned beauty who emails her brother: "Something's been thumping on the house for the last few nights. It's scaring me. Could you stay over?" Because her emails are read by the stalkers, they become motivated having learned how skittish the woman is alone at night. Far more frightening noises will be added, for instance, men talking, growls, or the commotion of someone trying to enter. This tearing-down, fear-making strategy will never happen when the brother is over, and he'll eventually tire of protecting his sister from nonexistent bogeymen. The cops, too, will stop believing the woman after finding no source to the ruckus, assuring her that it's in her head and that she's hearing normal night sounds.

By intercepting the woman's phone calls and emails, then relaying news to each stalker simultaneously, whenever the panicked woman summons help, the gang members vanish faster than cockroaches under a light bulb. Frustratingly, and suspiciously, both security cameras the brother installed are faulty.

Now that the young woman's quiet bedtimes have turned into an inescapable nightmare, she will definitely suffer from serious anxiety and insomnia. She's also going to feel hurt and angry about being left to fend for herself, certain that rape, kidnapping, sexual slavery, or murder is inevitable. Keeping safe will become a priority, for she is justly petrified. She doesn't know what the men want.

Organized stalking's abuse of emotions is so intrinsic to a target's demise that it's worth repeating: as soon as a target expresses fear, confusion, despair, or rage over a particular harassment, trick, or life occurrence, notes are made and the singled-out emotion, along with its causation, are induced repeatedly to mentally rip a victim from his or her foundations. Targets' reactions are easily witnessed because victims are never left unattended, whether it's by computer hacking, phone tapping, skulking at night, or stalking by day.

Burglarizing is also productive in information gathering. A knife stuck in each plant pot or an opened roadmap reveals a victim's state of mind. Perpetrators always know when their prey leaves home, even if it's just to jog down the block and back. They don't require much time to break in, get busy, and get out.

Some stalkers are kept on twenty-four-hour standby. They are prepared to tag along with those already on shift in case the target has unexpectedly gone out. The stay-behind stalkers who can get inside undetected will plant tokens; vandalize; and taint drinks and food. Obviously, glove-wearing stalkers who raid homes and vehicles do not want to get caught while they are actually there. They do want the victim to know it was them and not the garden variety of intruders.

If stalkers are relegated to staying outside, they will pretend to be salesmen or repairmen when their prey is away and leave a path of tokens and disrepair to the door.

Then there are the lookouts, even when a target is gone for the day, in case visitors come by. Remember, this crime is roaringly successful because a committee of riffraff uses insignificant details of the victim's life as a process to derailment. When you get two wrong numbers for someone named Greta as soon as you get in, along with someone at the door looking for lost Greta the cat, you wonder what's up with all the Greta references. After Aunt Greta calls and says she's sorry she missed you, you're bound to feel a mite unsettled. You can brush off these uncanny occurrences the first few times. But not dozens.

Occasionally, victims catch a perp vandalizing or using an energy-emitting device as a weapon and get him sentenced in court. Organized stalkers are, after all, human. But there are too damn many of them, and though justice is important, a follow-up blitz ensures a target is formidably dissuaded, or out of the way altogether, being dead.

Organized stalkers can be the new neighbours or the canvassers at the door. They can be the ladies who walk their dogs behind you every evening when you walk your own dog. Furthermore, they can be parents who are affectionately engaging with their teens or preteens. They'll flash their "I love my kids" smiles at you, and you'll admire the wholesome scene. But in truth, the youth are being trained to stalk and harass you and whoever else the parent is targeting. It's sick and it's standard, and sometimes it's done in the victim's face.

On-your-heels stalkers are sometimes volunteer Citizens on Patrol who are told lies about the target. Many of these city watchdogs are seeking excitement and will relentlessly stalk and pester someone even after they find out the person is innocent and harmless. There is no shortage of stalking Citizens on Patrol, and I imagine it is often under-trained volunteers who act like buffoons. For these bozos, who often stalk and harass in droves, ruining an honest person's day is brainless recreation.

I feel like I need to apologize to the city watchdogs who are honourable. If you are a genuine peacekeeper, please don't believe everything you hear. The crumbs among you are killing my friends and me.

The stalkers, as you can see, are as diverse a crowd as their victims. They just happen to have a penchant for cruelty. And though they usually look like ordinary folks, it is their disturbing view of victims as worthless that sets them apart. Choral ensembles, actors guilds, yacht clubs—pretty well any formed group—can be craftily approached to widen the stalking circle. Private investigators and motorcycle gangs are prompted to join in as well.

Indoctrination is often through setting up friendships and vilifying the target during passive conversations. To clinch the coercion, false but convincing paperwork which portrays the target as scum who needs to be kept in line will be offered. Like the city watchdogs, some of these folks end up as full-time perpetrators. Harassment becomes a vocation instead of a hobby.

So who are the sharpest visible members of this organized death squad? Let's start with educated professionals, cops, leaders, businessmen, and electronics wizards who are caught up in the crime. They do stalk, but most of their crimes come from within their positions. They change documents, lie on documents, and create false documents. They hack into their target's finances, generate disastrous slander, ruin careers, and distribute date rape drugs to the others. If they are in a profession that enables them to insidiously mentally or physically injure a target, it will definitely occur. High-level perpetrators get their victims into jail, or the loony bin, or the morgue. Going to university or cop school is no guarantee of decency. Neither is being a trusted leader.

You must be asking why this crime exists. What the point is. Victims don't know, for sure. Every targeted individual (ti) has a theory. The basic questions of who started the crime, who continues to make it grow, who finances it, and its purpose are not answered well enough to put before a judge.

The sprinkling of folks whose targeting began when they were engaged as environmental activists, whistleblowers, or human rights activists believe organized stalking has been implemented to shut them up. They're probably correct, yet there is no difference in harassment between them and the lion's share of victims who are randomly picked.

Contrary to what you might think, targeted whistleblowers and activists cannot name their individual day-to-day stalkers. Neither can they prove why the group they fingered wants to take over every trifling aspect of their lives. Confusing matters even more, some of these justice-seeking folks are led to think that the wrongdoers they exposed are responsible for their country's, or the world's, organized stalking. In looking at this situation broadly, targeted whistleblowers and activists are harassed by different corporations and different government agencies that utilize organized stalking and electronic harassment.

It appears that these ti's are tapping into pieces of the puzzle, perhaps even big pieces; yet OS's source (absolute ruler) remains an enigma.

Targets are told that if they can't provide legal proof of why they are attacked year after year and can't name specific harassers then they must be imagining the whole thing. That's unreasonable.

Compounding societal disbelief is OS's premise of implementing crimes that are too outrageous to be considered true. This is how the conversation would go should I report the latest vandalism: "Honest, officer, I took my lunch outside and found big goose feathers sticking out of my picnic table. Somebody must have drilled a bunch of holes in it last night and brought feathers to poke in. You see, Canada geese nest in my yard, and I was collecting the feathers yesterday. So because I'm watched by an assassination gang, the guys who sneak around all night thought they'd play a joke to prove my day stalkers were watching. What? Am I on medication?"

It can never be a victim's fault for not knowing who the perpetrators are, what gang they belong to, or why they commit the crimes. This is what is required of OS (organized stalking) victims.

Let's assume your home is broken into by the district thief. Your laptop and a valuable oil painting are taken, and the robber made himself a sandwich. People you tell show empathy. They will not call you delusional even if it happens three times, though they may call you careless for not beefing up your security. If during the third break-in the robber steals a TV and makes soup to go with his sandwich, then does something flaky like replace the stolen painting with a crayon special, you still won't be called crazy. Nevertheless, because organized stalking crimes are void of normal components, such as intruders consistently leaving things instead of taking them, it is the victims who are called delusional, instead of the perpetrators.

Being poor doesn't help. Targets are forced into poverty quite quickly. Poor, sick, and traumatized people tend to be ignored.

Speaking to targeted people who started out financially secure has been interesting. They fold slower. Backup finances means they can replace or fix vandalized belongings and secure their premises with top technology. They can keep a stable address for a while after the thugs have destroyed their career, credit, and health. These folks are in a better position to endure. Simply, they can't be rushed into homelessness.

Demanding police involvement will not stop the harassment. In the beginning, a strongly assertive appeal for lawful protection might slow the stalkers down for a week, give or take. But that's all. Naturally, targets repeatedly ask for police help in the first couple of years while they are learning how OS operates. Almost all these despairing ti's are called mentally ill by policing services, thus receive no aid. Once a target has a psychiatric label from the cops, the perpetrators can get increasingly violent with little chance of the victim being rescued.

Retribution for seeking police help cannot be understated. The few cops who start out well intentioned, but mishandle or drop OS cases, can get people murdered.

I have worked with targets from all over the world; however, the majority who contact me are Canadians and Americans. I am Canadian, living on British Columbia's West Coast. Targets who move from country to country trying to lose the crime become stalked foreigners.

I worry that when this experiment, or game, or whatever it is, ends, the victims will all be dead, and no one will be held accountable.

CHAPTER FOUR

JOURNAL

As we go along, I will include a day here and there from my current stalking journal and incorporate narratives of explanation. Most ti's chronicle their stalking, harassment, and torture in videos, logs, and letters, or by telling other targets.

My situation is ordinary for a victim with themes of violence and isolation.

Monday, Nov 28

This morning I went out. I was supposed to go tomorrow. With the phone and computer hacked into, errands must be kept secret or vague, so I switched days. Being eavesdropped is a nuisance as calling ahead about store hours, items in stock, or prices is impossible. If the stalkers know my plans, they get to the stores ahead of me and kick an imaginary bug off the back of my leg, making me fall. When they are careless and someone sees, they fawn all over me, shouting apologies and pointing to a beetle they dropped. It doesn't look like an assault, so they keep getting away with it.

If they have time to organize, they put on a skit, called street theatre, where they repeat back to me a conversation I recently had on the phone. Sometimes they put on a play that includes names, locations, and events that precisely portray parts of my life or a loved one's life. I don't care about the street theatre, not after so long. But falling down sucks.

Leaving home is stressful: a lost civil liberty. Having been outgoing, adapting was slow. Begrudgingly, I've come to accept feeling trapped, at least, most of the time. It's either get accustomed or get depressed. With no private communication, handing the cab driver a note of when I next want a ride doesn't ensure a safe future trip. It's the best I can do.

Owning a vehicle is out of the question. Tampering is unsolvable and deadly. In the first five years, a substantial portion of my savings was wasted repairing and safeguarding my truck. In my mind, back then, a wheeled escape was the best way to save myself. I was wrong.

Living on this little island is better than the other places I tried, except when the perps have advance notice that I'll be out for a while. Then they come over in a boatload. They are exuberant when they get together and hold a jamboree: a sadists' happy reunion. Their antics make me question their maturity, having watched a group shrieking with exaggerated glee, staring and pointing and copying my actions as they rehashed their plans to ruin my beach stroll.

Two or three times a year I pretend to be free and go somewhere nice: maybe to the petroglyphs, or the lookout where swift tidal currents are spectacular, or the sandy peninsula where my gang collects along the seashore to defeat my peace.

Besides a camera and a voice recorder, two duffel bags have to come everywhere with me. The bags are heavy, loaded with this book and anything that pertains to proving organized stalking. Although very few OS intruders steal pricey belongings, preferring theft through bank and credit accounts, all of them steal evidence and appliances that would prove the crimes. They'll burn a home if it means destroying evidence.

To further complicate sightseeing, aside from carrying cumbersome packs, there's the transportation problem, the being followed and harangued problem, and the effort of fortifying the house. There's nothing free about going somewhere nice. Or going anywhere at all. Even so, sometimes I try to act like being owned doesn't matter.

This morning when my landlady phoned, I carelessly mentioned tomorrow's plans to run errands, so I was forced to re-arrange my ride. There's no pretending that is normal. Really, just how many other situations require average people to outmaneuver a structured mob whose purpose is to make trips to the mailbox a critical risk to life. War? Genocide? Discrimination? Is hunting humans a new sport?

Seconds after calling the island's only cab driver, asking if he could pick me up immediately instead of tomorrow, one of the phone tappers goofed and called me by accident. "June is leaving right now!" she blurted out.

"I'm June," I said. "I'm the one you're stalking." What I wanted to do is call her a loser, but that never goes well. The punishment last time was a night of the screaming meemies thanks to the window rattlers. I was concentrating hard on her blabbering string of excuses, listening for information leaks, when she was cut off midsentence. No doubt, another phone tapper ended the call for her. This low-IQ perpetrator uses a prairie-province phone number and lives in an ancient forest up the road. It's improbable she was alerting the other stalkers. Stalkers do not communicate one call at a time. It seems that she uses my plight as shared entertainment among friends.

In her initial attempt to be a nuisance, she giggled at the door, feigning to have found a Scottie dog, asking if it was mine. The entire time we spoke, she lovingly stroked the little dog's head and called him Angus. If kissing his nose wasn't a final giveaway, her partner's expressions were. Seeing the mistake, stalker number two looked positively horrified, ran back to the car, and tried to disappear in the front seat.

Curiously watching her accomplice's exit, it occurred to my rival that she was supposed to ask to use my phone, for stalkers follow strict directives. I was elated. Humour is exceedingly rare for targets.

Strutting through the living room, delighted with thinking she'd put her scam over on me, my enemy reached for the receiver and froze. Having forgotten the number and knowing she had to call somebody, she sighed and looked like she needed a chair. I pointed to the phone book, even opened it for her, and waited for the show to continue.

Pages ruffled, tension mounted, and with a mighty cognitive breakthrough the much relieved woman managed to contrive a couple of names, who she faked finding, followed by long, long stories of why calling these people was useless. "Would you like a piece of cake?" I asked, hoping to hang on to her. Eventually, my stalker dialled, speaking like an android: "I was on Triangle Mountain. Found a dog. My number is ——." It would have been difficult to call that number, all eights and nines and too many of them.

Swaggering back through the living room, Ms. Super Spy looked over her shoulder at me snickering like she'd pulled the swindle of the century. She practically danced to her car. It's almost an insult to have such a nitwit assigned to me.

It's common for stalkers posing as folks in need, or passersby with questions, to try and enter targets' homes. Every other time I've said no or scared them off with a camera, but this, clearly, was not an opportunity to be passed up. Nevertheless, I was attentive, for perps are instructed to dispense toxic chemicals and other nasties.

Pleasant looking, under twenty-five, and physically fit, this twit is in a position to do great things with her life. Yet she chose a job as an organized stalking perpetrator. Whenever she hurts or inconveniences me, her lips press together in a freak-smile. Most of my stalkers do that, and I assume they are told to.

Okay, back to the difficulties of running errands this morning.

Mercifully, the taxi picked me up right after I called. In fact, it arrived so quickly only one visible perp had time to organize himself and hassle me, and that was when I dropped off my books at the library. This stalker is a handsome, husky fellow and looks at me as if he'd like to rip my head off. I cheerfully greeted him and, as always, engaged him in an amicable conversation in front of the library lady. He hates me for this. He can't knock me down, and he can't be rude when I have him in the public eye, being all friendly. I then got my mail at the post office, which includes mail-order library books, and went home, a forty-minute round trip twice a month.

Living in the back country has advantages. Conspicuous malice and other diversions from predictable island etiquette are discussed at the coffee shop and the grocery store. Moccasin telegraph here is the real deal. Regardless, like all targets, my home is monitored, and the husky stalker had to have been on duty for him to get to the library ahead of me. He seems to be my primary male perpetrator here and is a dangerous intimidator, quite unlike the irritating jokers who outnumber him.

Yes, the island is good. Houses are spread out with woodlands and coves and meadows between them. Off-island, a dozen perps as hostile as my husky guy would have been hassling me at the library. And the post office. If perps can dawdle around a ti's neighbourhood, or trespass, or drive up and down the target's street, all without attracting public attention, or can live nearby, there's zero chance of running errands as easily as I did today. Should I be living in town, a swarm of them would have been a couple of hundred feet away, eager to harass. It's an uncomfortable feeling, being surrounded.

Returning home this morning went smoothly but was not conventional by mainstream standards. I have forgotten what it's like to step inside relaxed. I never know what to expect. One deranged OS intruder equals one dead target. It has crossed my mind that writing this book will bring me further trouble.

Furniture blocks two of the doors, and the sliding-window tracks are blocked with dowels. This morning I put plant pots, shovels, and bags of potting soil in front of the main door when I left so it would take them longer to break in, and I stretched transparent tape across the jamb.

Organized stalkers use professional crime tools, so deadbolts won't keep them out. As soon as the taxi dropped me back home, I headed straight for the bird cage, for perps love to mutilate pets. My dear little lovebird was fine. Cautiously grateful for an unusually successful trip, my uneasiness continued. Stalkers do weird things in fridges and cupboards. And I'd forgotten to take the book's latest draft with me.

By noon, I was working on Chapter Five, finding my left hand too burned to type. So it's one handed. The husky guy could have been holding a small, indistinguishable electronic weapon. My guess is the burn came from somewhere else.

Today's intention was to write for long stretches, now that my skin-peeled spine and feet are finally healing. It is taking weeks to recover from a doozy of a weapon's attack. Hundreds of writing hours have been lost because of it.

My perpetrators spent the first thirteen years trying to drive me to suicide through psychological torture. Because I'm still here, they are baking me a piece at a time, banking on me to give up. I have to die, and by their mandate my only relief from the torture will be suicide. Outright murders occur, but speaking from experience, suicide is undeniably what they have planned for me.

Extending assistance to victims gives me a reason to persevere, granting that as many phonies as targets ask for help. This afternoon an American perpetrator couple called posing as victims. They asked if they could stay in the suite I used to offer to distressed ti's, before beginning this book project, for I lease a big old beach house. The couple said they wanted to fix their motorhome in Canada and needed somewhere to stay close to the border. I said my place wasn't near the border, and they got grouchy, instantly deciding that their motorhome could only be fixed at my town, despite not knowing where it was. I would have hung up, but again found my enemies amusing. With one mom and pop gas station, where groceries, mail, gifts, booze, banking, and the only pay phone share the same small building, I wondered how I might have missed this internationally renowned repair shop. I asked for its name. They got mad at me, so I asked for the mechanic's name, offering to call him for them. Gees, they didn't have to yell. Is it just me getting moronic perps?

A long-term target from Los Angeles, California, called soon after the motorhome pair. She also wanted to stay. I know her. She believes that the crime can't be as bad in Canada. Many Americans think if they travel north they'll get a break from the harassment.

Organized stalking is as bad in British Columbia's Pacific Northwest as it is in New York or California. Canada, overall, is rife with it.

There are also a lot of wrong numbers today, same as yesterday. They are perps, for a ti (targeted individual) friend six hours away is getting the same calls. We compare.

My pressing problem, other than my hand cremating, is a letter in the mail from distant relatives who want to stay for Christmas. My heart says yes. I love these people. But embarrassment at how far the harassment and torture have caused me to sink is engulfing. Impersonating the inspired woman they remember from eighteen years ago is impossible now. Revealing why I can't cook a turkey dinner or decorate a Christmas tree is not something I am willing to do.

Far worse than fretting over my own state—what if my controllers are seeking new prey? A holiday here could destroy my loved ones' lives for hours or forever. How do I explain that? How does anyone explain slow selective extermination for no apparent reason? It's better to be considered inhospitable and say that now's not convenient, knowing that the word convenient has been omitted from my existence.

I am a hostage in plain sight, randomly chosen.

It's 7:05 p.m. and my left hand is so thoroughly mangled that I fear permanent damage. The pain is making me nauseous. My palm and thumb are swollen and flaming. Electronic torture destroys tissue and organs. It's supposed to.

Unlike the beneficial instruments used for energy-beamed procedures on medical patients, organized stalking's energy (electronic) instruments are employed to maim. Such an instrument, now a weapon, can maim a target's whole hand in one go. Or the whole target. I need to write faster.

Except for the hand, it's been a better day than most.

CHAPTER FIVE

STALKING, HARASSMENT, AND REACTIONS TO THEM

Organized stalkers are required to pressure their victims into as many of the following emotions, behaviours, and defensive actions as possible.

- Confusion
- Disbelief
- Nervousness progressing into unremitting critical stress
- Dread
- Fear
- Anger
- Irritability
- Insomnia
- Hypersensitivity to sounds and sights
- Intense awareness of surroundings
- Bouts of rage
- Aggressive actions to identify and combat stalkers
- Many complaints to police
- Many complaints to others
- Many doctor's visits

Remember, a victim's negative responses confirm which breaking-down tactics are the most effective.

- Staying inside if being out feels particularly unsafe
- Closing window coverings in daytime and covering exposed windows
- At night, keeping home lit inside and out: may install extra lighting
- Installation of security systems at home or wherever target is staying
- Purchasing weapons, audio recording devices, cameras, and spy gear
- Sneaky or illegal conduct to stop the crime
- Setting homemade traps to ensnare or dissuade vandals, trespassers, and intruders
- Refusal to answer phone, door, or emails
- Missing work, school, or obligations
- Quitting work or school
- Depending on others for necessities
- Hesitancy to stay alone in own home due to fear of being assaulted, held captive, or kidnapped
- Asking to sleep at others' homes
- Flat refusal to be in own home at any time
- Inattention to finances
- Blaming self for being stalked and harassed
- Unrealistic reasons why this is happening
- Running
- Hiding
- Isolating by choice (avoiding contact with the outside world)

You may have noticed that isolating by choice, as mentioned above, is the opposite of notwithstanding aloneness. Isolating by choice, which is different than hiding, tends to occur after initial attempts at resolution fail, and the victim is bewildered, tired, and disappointed at the lack of assistance.

Offensive actions, also listed, oppose shutting down, shutting out, running, and hiding.

Each target tackles the crime individually through various stages. A brawny fellow who boldly sits in his vehicle for a night, ready to protect his property from vandalism through a physical brawl, may be overcome with anxiety the next night. Despite hearing the vandals at work under his jeep, he cannot summon the wherewithal to confront them. Shifts in behaviour like this are entirely typical for both male and female targets.

Size, age, and muscle power have little bearing on either turning tail or charging ahead. Men should not be judged for backing down, and ladies should not be judged for becoming fiercely scrappy with an "enough is enough" attitude, particularly when loved ones are endangered.

The big, strong fellow who listened idly while his jeep's undercarriage was ravaged knew he had to save himself from falling apart by relegating this one raid to defeat. He's not chicken. He's battle-weary. Battle weariness is in part due to keeping pace with the crimes. For example, if a ti succeeds in reducing nighttime terrorism, which, by the way, would take monumental and continuous effort, a new infraction will replace it, and the struggle begins all over. With the new development, the obstacles may be practically unsolvable, and the ti will invest umpteen hours and possibly hundreds of dollars trying to ax it. This happens time and time again and is exhausting. An uninterrupted succession of minor ordeals has the same grueling effect.

Keeping up with the violations is just one reason targets intermittently crumple, meaning dormant periods of discouragement or respite are standard. However, ongoing inaction to self-protect is abnormal and may underlie perilous despondency or physical decline. This target needs immediate intervention.

Ordinarily, when it's safe to, long-term targets wind down their defences and construct lulls, for peace becomes unnatural or absent altogether. I create artificial moments of peace. Lots of us do. Sometimes we only get a few minutes. Sometimes longer.

So it's confusing for lookers-on to watch this inconsistent behaviour, the highs and lows of saving oneself, especially since the masses are unable to witness what the target is going through.

Ian is in this predicament. He wonders about his targeted friend, who we'll call Edgy Jim. They'd made plans to meet for coffee on Friday, and when Edgy Jim didn't show up, Ian found him pacing in his locked office jabbering insensibly about a menacing client and refusing to leave. On Saturday, Edgy Jim, oblivious to the fact his phone is tapped, called Ian: "Stay away. Don't even come in the driveway. The bastards were in my garage again. I'm going to teach them a lesson they won't forget." Edgy Jim's weekend is spent bundled up on a lawn chair holding a golf club, peeking around the corner of his workshop. He's there night and day, waiting for a stalker to get caught up in his fishing-line trap. Come Monday, Edgy Jim's worn out and making mistakes at work, consumed with how the culprits knew to back off. Unable to face another tense evening at home, he drives to his friend's to shoot pool and blows up when Ian calls him a weekend warrior.

The same emotional mix up goes for targeted Candace who is watching TV with her boyfriend. Jumping up after seeing the fourth stalker loiter under her apartment window, she's saturated with pestering and is stomping out to end the nonsense that minute. "If I die tonight, I want you to know I love you," she tearfully tells her boyfriend, ignoring his pleas that they enjoy a quiet evening at home. After all, it's a good movie, and he hasn't a clue what's going on. When he tries to calm her, telling her to be reasonable, she screams, "You fucking don't get it! Those men want to hurt me!"

Bursts of frustration are as unavoidable as stints of paralyzing fear and fatigue.

Overt displays of strain can be exhibited in excited speech; arguing; swearing; overlong commentaries about organized stalking and electronic weapons; purchasing and carrying articles for protection; unstable emotions; alcohol or drug binges; setting beastly stalker traps; chasing stalkers; impulsive departures; reckless or illegal undertakings; undue suspiciousness; intolerance to loud voices; intolerance to specific sounds, sights, and settings; and conspicuous nervous exhaustion. Cravings for solace can lead to overmedicating, thoughts of "doing away" with the stalkers, or thoughts of "I'd rather be dead." Sad to say, intermittent explicit indicators of despair are common to most ti's during the first few years and are almost always vehemently projected in the beginning.

Whether a ti (targeted individual) photographs a pawing perpetrator upon leaving yoga class or vanishes at 3:00 a.m. to an undisclosed hideout for a month, the responses are appropriate. So are fluctuations between begging for help and continually fleeing. It takes ages, research, and experience to partway figure out even one element of OS (organized stalking). New tactics are perpetual, and all of them are either insane or inhuman.

A ti will go to extremes trying to learn what is wanted from him and why he's hated, believing the answers will set him free. His life is devoted to finding a solution, undeterred by what people think of him. Therefore, minimal time is available to go through the motions of normalcy since it no longer exists. He's doing everything he can.

Simply put, victims are forced to evolve. This evolution always means transformations that others may find unacceptable and that might be regretted later on.

I am no different and have exhibited self-absorption, explosions, and flashes of idiocy. There's no getting around my mortifying and rash breaches. It seems to be something new targets have to go through while ticking off a checklist of drastic measures to save their hides and homes.

Cornering a monster-sized biker on my old farm was just one impetuous folly in my second harassed year, trying to prevent the horses from being beaten again. No one could have curbed me from rushing through the front door that night after hearing the livestock gate rattle. By sunrise, I was shaken, realizing that the crime had driven me barmy; for who in their right mind challenges someone three times their size, in a dark shed, in the woods, with no chance of winning, and with no one else around except other OS members who want you dead anyway? Every seriously harassed target can tell similar stories.

I've allotted significant text here to discussing changes in behaviour. Seesaw emotions and gambits get interpreted as fruitcake traits. This is never good. With a crazy-label, no one will help.

Worth mentioning, too, is that not everyone gets the whole terrorism package. This is why I refer sometimes to seriously harassed victims. Seriously harassed targets' reactions are exemplified because, for all the right reasons, they believe their stalkers are capable of murder.

As each ti is harassed with personalized tactics, meaning Shirley won't get the same harassment as Pierre, some folks feel safer at home, whereas others intuit violence if they stay in their home, even if someone is with them. The places a target assesses as livable can change in an hour if the perpetrators reverse their strategy, which is likely. The crime is designed to upend stability in every area of life.

Severely harassed or threatened targets are safe nowhere. It's just that some situations seem more secure than others, for a particular ti, at a particular time.

Women targets, especially if they feel sexually threatened or vulnerable, are disinclined to be alone in or out of the home in phases throughout the crime. After staying inside for weeks, a woman may be mistakenly deemed agoraphobic. In doing the opposite, if a woman's home feels like a deathtrap and she refuses to live there, she is deemed dotty.

Petrified females may ask for help with day-to-day chores such as buying baby needs, groceries, and pharmaceuticals; or they may ask someone to fill up their car with gas, too afraid to unnecessarily get out of the vehicle. A seriously threatened woman will miss work or be unable to tend home life. If she is ridiculed for being nervous, she may pack a bag and hole up somewhere, often at a hotel where she can tell the desk to keep watch or perhaps at an undisclosed safe house. A mom who believes she or her children are about to be held captive at home, or raped, killed, or kidnapped, may take desperate measures that others consider farcical.

After targets have begun displaying some of the transformations on the list (beginning of chapter), such as the ladies' vagaries just mentioned, then it's indisputable that the gang has taken over.

This produces the processes of keeping highly detailed records and itemizing crime-related articles. Stashed in a closet or escape-bag may be a box of tokens (items left by stalkers to disturb targets) and videos, snapshots, or voice recordings of perpetrators, along with proof of their misdeeds.

An angry ti will ask his stalkers who they are, and what they are doing, and scheme to see identification. By necessity, targets become excellent evidence collectors and at first relinquish irreplaceable material to the police, certain that a mountain of clues will be appreciated. These clues include license plate numbers, names, addresses, photos, videos, items with fingerprints, phone numbers, proof of phone tapping, proof of computer hacking, tampered documents, repair receipts from vandalism, audio recordings, harassment logs, broken objects, tokens, and proof of credit card or other financial transgressions. (As all targets' confidential records are in perp hands, including security passwords and codes, financial tinkering is excessive; financial theft is less so.)

In the beginning, victims imagine that by naming the stalkers and gaining information about them they can make a legal case. If a ti has already unmasked and investigated a perp or two, he will continue to accumulate facts, prospecting for leads that could explain why he's fixated on.

When a target is working hard at evidence gathering and self-preservation, even if he's taking a breather, there is a mindset of having some control: that there is hope in stopping the madness. Letting your world fall apart, sighing, "Oh well," could never be right.

With most police refusing to acknowledge organized stalking, targets are indebted to collar a formidable gang by themselves. They go after the perpetrators single-handed for the purpose of nabbing them in the acts of vandalizing, trespassing, breaking in, following, harassing, contaminating substances, and electronic-weapon use. If a fired-up ti does catch a perp doing something illegal, he may refrain from calling the police. Unheeded grievances have taught this contender to take an alternate course. Even a milk and cookies grandmother will throw a well-aimed rock when she spots the scab in her yard who put out his cigarette in Ginger's eye. She'd rather rely on police. But she can't. Nevertheless, retribution from injuring, insulting, laughing at, thwarting, tracking, cornering, exposing, or prosecuting a perp can be grim or mortal. Ti's do it anyway.

A problem with proving crafty harassment, unlike a blatant felony, is that on the surface it can appear just a mite off or even humdrum. This is no accident. Persecution in public is calculated to be psychologically destroying without attracting witness attention.

For one, stalkers in public places often shout their conversations. Or they stand too close, bodily pushing the target a step or two over. A stalker might drop an umbrella three times in a line-up, gushing with loud, elaborate apologies, begging his dupe to pick it up. Playacts share exaggeration and insistence. Perpetrators cannot risk being ignored and will do anything, and I do mean anything, to make their charges feel dominated. They can be sappy-polite or obnoxious.

When affronts are seen as a single irritation, such as having a door slammed on your face, the incident looks like one of those things that can happen to anybody. Nuisances carried out in clusters also appear insignificant. Complaining that lots of people are bumping into you in town will not give rise to pity. Add that other shoppers buy the same things and keep asking where the jelly beans are and you'll get raised eyebrows. If you hand over the obituary notices stuck to the front gate every morning saying that they are deliberate, folks will think you're cracking up.

Each of these trivialities should not be an issue. So what if newspaper clippings are blowing around? And if shoppers are bumping into you, buying the same items, and asking questions, that's what goes on in stores.

Telling a friend to "come with me and you'll see" invariably ends up with the ti looking like a fool. Obvious harassment usually happens when a target is alone. Cat and mouse games still occur when a ti is with someone, but only the ti will recognize it, as in a known stalker stepping on the target's heel. Saying, "I told you I was harassed," while putting his foot back in his shoe makes a ti look silly.

Cunning gags are just as frequent at home. A letter in the mailbox that erroneously thanks the ti for being an organ donor will not rouse anyone else's alarm.

Should you be the recipient of twenty different forms of harassment of which several are performed every day, well, you can see how this goes.

The intention is to make the prey jittery around the clock, without pause. It is the tally of irritating and creepy moments that determines effective nonviolent harassment. There is no getting away from it. It's in the kitchen, the hockey games, little Andrea's ballet classes, and at the ski lodge. With every stressful minute and every hectic task, the enemy gains more control.

Dale is a fellow whose stalkers shadow his every move. One of the harassments includes knocking food out of his hands at fast food restaurants. Dale now insists on a big bag even for a small packet of fries, for he needs a firm grip on the thing. He has stopped buying the chocolate milkshakes he loves. The stress of getting them to the table isn't worth it. Dale wasn't overly upset the first time a meal tray ended up on his feet. The third time, at the burger joint near his welding shop, Dale grabbed his stalker's shirt with one hand and made a fist with the other. As often happens, it is a retaliating ti who is penalized. The troublemaker would have walked off grinning after hearing the manager deliberate whether to call police. When Dale told his friends, grumbling that his food always ends up on the floor, they wisecracked about his beer drinking.

Having for years enjoyed lunch-break hamburgers and shakes so close to work, it's a freedom that this target misses. He's defensive now when it comes to carrying food. Moreover, he's become defensive in public about carrying anything at all. It's not something he'd ever thought about before.

Dale's life will not be sunk because of this. It's the other nineteen harassments, and the next nineteen, that will take him to the bottom.

To combat the losses, Dale is integrating new and sometimes unusual habits that his buddies find unsettling. Organized stalking harassment is strategic. Dale is supposed to look like he's lost a few screws.

With a victim telling incredulous stories and making inexplicable changes to his routine, none of which are correctly interpreted by others, it's challenging for him to get anyone to believe he's in danger. Yet believing is precisely what is necessary or the target is, quite honestly, doomed.

As I mentioned, my own behaviour in the first years was irregular and undoubtedly misinterpreted. Complaints to police went nowhere, so I was getting the proof myself for analysis by whoever could help me. I drove half the night. I led my stalking parade down dead end roads and into parking lots where the drivers would have to turn their vehicles around, allowing for good evidence collection.

I used the same baiting ploy while walking. In my reasoning, proving repetitive following might summon backing, and I was desperate to do just that.

Luring thugs is not viewed as normal. My family knew why I did this, for strange men hung around our property all day. And the night terrorism was savage. But the household was upset over my ventures. They did not see how threatened we'd become—that their lives were in jeopardy.

A family can be gravely impacted by attempts to permanently separate the target. Splitting families and relationships and annihilating employment are vitally important in OS's strategy to disconnect an individual from society. Segregated, a lone ti is set up for teamwork violence.

To pressure a targeted parent into leaving home, his children, being his love and his weakness, are used as leverage. I'll illustrate this with a few of the intimidating practices used on my own family, as my history of bullying campaigns is emblematic.

Stalkers were swerving on our country lane, sideswiping my children while we rode the horses or walked the dogs. Other adults were not allowed to see these assaults, and shockingly, the cops didn't care. In addition, the phone threats were for my ears only: "Hey, is this Valley View Cemetery? My niece just got run over." The warnings in town were the same: "Can I jump ahead of you in line? I'm late for my grandson's funeral." No one but me understood the dark implications in bones and carcasses we were finding on the property or why a strange lady parked beside the corral at the same time every day to watch my daughter tend her sheep. The longer I sought a solution, the more endangered my kids were.

What you, the reader, must keep in mind is that organized stalkers have no limits of what they will do. Empathy does not exist.

Maximum grief is sought. If repeatedly burning a ti's toddler with electronic weapons is necessary to drive the ti out of his home, that's what is done. The child will display welts, redness, blistering, abnormal crying, and ailments which cease when the parent leaves the toddler with someone else for a few days while seeking safer housing or justice. If the parent doesn't catch on, he will be told, circuitously.

A large number of ti's declare that disguised pack-around electronic (energy) weapons can be aimed by a nearby perp to burn, shock, tire, inconvenience, or disorient a loved one; or burn holes in his clothes or purchases; or induce health, eyesight, or hearing irregularities in him.

In conjunction, as we have already briefly discussed, inexpensive energy-emitting devices that are effective through walls can cause terminal or lingering radiation sickness.

A magnetron is necessary to construct a homemade through-wall microwaving device that will induce sickness. Magnetrons are easily obtained.

Let's clear the air here. Although I've mentioned the stalker's through-wall radiation equipment several times, I'm betting you, as a nonvictim, still think the concept is hogwash—that it's a goofy way to assault someone. No worries, I did too. Regrettably, anyone with a defective conscience and a few tools can build and use through-wall radiation equipment. The defective folks who don't have tools can buy or rent "can't get caught" energy weapons from a catalogue. Yup, I said a catalogue. Nope, I'm not telling you any catalogue names.

Then there are the exceptionally high-tech devices. High-tech long-distance electronic weapons send invisible deadly energy directly to targets and their loved ones. How does long-distance energy know who to strike and when to strike? That's the high-tech part. For now, it's enough to know that a target cannot prevent his spouse or child, even a newborn, from all burns, radiation, and other energy-caused afflictions. The only way the assaults on his loved ones will stop is if he severs all contact with his family.

I should add it's probable that some handheld or worn perp-gear, as innocuous as cell phones, link to the gang members who run the far-off weapons. In that way when Ms. Stalker-Behind-You pushes her device's red button in the cafe, Mr. Liquidator, who is nowhere near, knows it's a grand time to send a long-distance burning beam to the child who's enjoying a butterscotch sundae with his targeted dad.

Ms. Stalker-Behind-You has then coordinated a disfiguring injury to the tot's face with no chance of arrest. It appears perp-to-perp energy attacks like this are commonplace, yet until OS's practices are criminalized in a courtroom, it would mislead you to declare that victims are clear about everything that handheld, worn, tabletop, and remote contrivances are capable of. Mind you, some of the electronic harassment tools are fully understood.

If you want a quick overview of a few of the "easy to buy or build" tabletop and handheld energy weapons, refer to the pamphlet published by the now inactive group called C-A-T-C-H. You can find the pamphlet by typing "Citizens Against Technological and Community-Based Harassment pamphlet." The weapons are listed in Examples of Technology on page 8. An OS info-site will tell you how dangerous energy weapons are. A shady company that's selling or renting them, won't.

When a child dies from radiation or is put into foster care, or a spouse is disabled from the weapons, the perpetrators' evaluation of their deed exposes triumph and incentive. Jubilation is openly expressed during and after a heinous operation.

There are no barriers to cruelty used to isolate a target. We've just learned that one way is by covertly harming, or threatening to harm, a loved one until the target leaves. Then there's the dilemma of family riffs due to a victim's new habits and astonishing stories. Slander and altered documents which make a ti look disreputable are other isolation methods.

No matter what tactic is employed, maximum psychological decline is the objective. A heartsick tormented target who has been isolated for a while has suicidal thoughts. The strategy is to make death the only release from incursions and sadness.

Perpetrators savour their subject's deterioration, and organized stalking bosses are accepting when it takes a long time for a lone ti to die. I imagine for psychopathic-types it's much the same as leisurely eating a great steak.

To clarify forced isolation a bit, not every target has an isolation theme, though it appears many do. Most of the victims I work with are isolated, tortured, suicidal, or sick and homeless; thus, the bulk of my data and studies stem from life and death cases. I, myself, fall into the category of isolated and seriously tortured from electronic harassment (EH). Pretty well all isolated cases are life and death situations.

It does not matter what a target's station in life is in order to be chosen for an isolation and suicide theme. The only requirement is to be breathing. An already homeless person will be further cut off from necessities. Falsehoods will ensure he is banned from shelters and soup kitchens, and slander will destroy friendships. To clinch collapse, electronic harassment will be trained on legs and organs. Racked with pain, the fellow gives up and dies in the gutter.

Students living on or off campus will be isolated through perp-caused expulsion and social ostracizing. Isolated students could be homeless, gravely ill, or dead within a few short years. Or a few short months.

Psychological torture and electronic torture are not nearly as effective if a target has companionship, a stable home, a job, or assistance. Unfortunately, when a ti has been forced to leave his home, job, or campus, he may be ostracized or abandoned by family, friends, and associates, having left under extraordinarily taxing circumstances.

Some ti's face isolation attempts from the get-go. I am one among thousands.

Let's examine a rising targeted professor with this detachment theme. At risk of losing her job and credibility, she will go to great lengths to ensure that it doesn't happen. Slander, false evidence, and false documents may label the professor as a fraud, thief, child molester, or drug addict. She's also contending with ghastly harassments that focus on anything to do with blood. She's scared half out of her mind but needs to save her career and is determined to do whatever it takes. Some of it may be illegal. She's going to break into confidential files, record conversations, install security products, accuse colleagues, sneak around, and tell her superiors that she is being set up. She may ask for police and lawyer help or hire a private investigator.

Because the professor has no enemies, no one believes her claims of being framed. They find it easier to believe she is the rotter that the perpetrators convincingly portray her to be. After all, the perpetrators have invented and presented a stack of verifiable evidence.

With the professor suddenly acting suspicious, even eccentric and paranoid at times, staying home for days and refusing to answer the phone or the door, the perpetrators have gained considerable ground. What onlookers don't see is that because the crime is peculiar, defence and coping mechanisms match.

In the beginning, most people don't realize what they're in the middle of. They have never heard of organized stalking, nor have they heard of electronic harassment.

If you accede tit for tat, victims respond appropriately to the absurdities inflicted on them. If the crime's intentions could be understood at the start, the person's responses could be understood as well, and perhaps restructured. A target's misconduct, no matter how evasive, cutthroat, or erratic it looks to others, reveals a desire to survive.

It's like crawling behind a signboard after seeing a gun-waving candy vendor. Until your shouts are heeded, everyone looks at you, the crawler, as if you're loopy because they don't understand you are trying to save yourself.

Naturally, people respond according to their personality; but they are affected by full-blown anxiety, confusion, horror, and anger, whether they outwardly exhibit all the symptoms or not. Plus, they have no coping skills to draw on that are relevant to organized stalking.

I'm going to jump in here and mention the state totally controlled targets are in; however, we'll be covering this extensively later on. It's important to know that completely dominated targets, who are often isolated, are conscious every waking minute that they can be wreaked with near non-survivable electronic-weapons torture or be murdered anytime, anywhere. The most disparaging long-term targets are often the most non-complaining. Subdued ti's will never hop up and down bawling, "They're killing me!" They're silently facing their fate alone. On observation, a subdued ti's lifestyle says it all.

A thoroughly oppressed target, whether he is mute, howling, or drooling, is never going to be okay. He is never going to act like he used to. He could be a hermit; or a firestorm of resistance; or be trying to live like a free person, which never lasts long because it is impossible for someone in a hostage-like situation to live normally. A thoroughly oppressed target could also vanish without a trace.

I strongly suspect that some of the missing ti's have been kidnapped or coerced into a situation and then executed after a specific need was fulfilled. Because targets are separated and isolated from loved ones, after a few years it's a perp free-for-all. For certain, not every disappearance is from bolting or suicide.

One instance is a young New York ti who went missing. She trusted the person who told her about a low-rent ti-run apartment complex in Texas and, as the offer sounded better than homelessness, fell for a perpetrator's con job. After she conveyed entrapment in a short mumbled call to a California victim, who then contacted me, it took three months and a Texas doctor to get her out of a gated complex where she was drugged and raped every night. So, though the crime fancies psychological and electronic operations, there is proof that capture, bondage, and rape occur.

Ti's who have turned to a cult for protection and then are relocated by the leader to a sequestered site, which could be urban, may or may not be alive and well. Nobody knows.

Some disappeared targets have shown up, but it's not them. Perps will take over a ti's identity.

Most troubling is the high number of targets' children who die or go missing, including adult children. In my circle of a dozen close targeted friends, seven young children died in the parents' first three years of the crime and a twenty-nine-year-old has been missing for over a decade.

My introduction to the missing and dead children crisis began when I met a ti mom whose three children died in an arson fire. She took to the road and vanished in her third year of mourning.

Let's sum up this chapter. Organized stalking is incredibly complicated, so we need to step back and look at what we've just discussed.

- High numbers of wily and threatening harassments, inside and outside the home, push targets into changed behaviours and emotions.
- Targets are then compelled to alter their lifestyles and conversations in an effort to do the following: make others believe, save their own and others' lives, collect evidence, stop the crime, psychologically cope, recover from electronic-weapons attacks, and sometimes recover from physical attacks or contaminated beverages or food.
- The target's new and often unusual behaviours and conversations are viewed as unacceptable because others don't see what's going on. This misunderstanding cements a target's vulnerability.
- If the target has an isolation theme, the perpetrators are making an extremely strong effort to quickly separate him from family, friends, home, job, school, and associations.
- Losses begin, but more slowly for someone who does not have an isolation theme: family bonds, job, schooling, financial stability, enjoyments, and all things social are being removed or hindered.

- The target may be unwelcome at others' homes or in society due to misconstrued behaviour and conversations.
- If the ti is forcibly isolated, unbearable psychological and physical torture will commence.
- If the ti is not isolated, psychological and physical torture may still occur, but due to support, or hope of support, the target is better off.

CHAPTER SIX

IMPACT OF HARASSMENT AND UNCONVENTIONAL WEAPONRY ON BYSTANDERS, ACQUAINTANCES, LOVED ONES, AND RESCUERS IN A TARGET'S LIFE

Have you wondered what happens to the many people who cross a target's path? Could a ti's (targeted individual's) dog groomer suffer miserably because she gave Muttsy a bath? Why, yes. But not necessarily.

Let's begin this chapter with what some stalkers do to the diverse population who are in their target's radius, as many ti programs require luckless others to be inconvenienced, confused, frightened, vandalized, harassed, injured, disabled, made sick, made to lose money, made to feel threatened, or murdered.

In these programs, a person calling, emailing, or so much as sharing a park bench with a ti could receive the same harassment as someone who shares a bed with him. In other words, it doesn't always matter what the connection is. What matters is that the target recognizes that when he interacts with people or animals, they might be picked on.

Unless there is a sexual component, harassing others, at first, is done only if the target is likely to see it or hear about it. With organized stalking capers being camouflaged, it can take time for a ti to link harassment—say, towards visitors at a gallery, to his presence. Most targets carry lifetime guilt for not catching on sooner.

Harassment to non-targets is a cornucopia of tribulations, just as it is to targets. The action can be heinous, like elbowing a target's jogging competitor into traffic. Or it can be a time-waster, as in a perp asking a target's business partner to draw detailed directions to the hotels across town.

Some stalkers bother assorted people around their target several times a day. Then again, harassing others could occur infrequently. Every few weeks, a prowler might burn paper alongside the home of a target's parents.

In many victims' themes, stalkers observe and harass bystanders who are close at hand. This means if you are sitting in a restaurant booth across from a target who is chowing down a plate of rigatoni, you could find that his stalker does something to you. He could bug you with incessant demands. He could pace back and forth and add to the conversation. He could blow his nose over your food, and he could smoke the back of your head with a high-powered invisible laser beam. If it's annoying or painful, he will definitely do it. His duty is to disrupt your meal. You're wondering what the point is. The point is power. Displays of bullying and power in front of a target are as vital to organized stalking as they are to all organized gangs. It's very controlling.

This is what bystander harassment looks like when it's deadly.

Stuttering from stress, a stalked grandmother approaches a ticket seller's booth: "The, the kids are small. Do, do you have any seats for Saturday left? Close to the front?" The once poised woman is momentarily pleased. She's pulled it off, and the kids are going to be thrilled. Disappointed that she's not taking her grandsons to see the performing dogs, she is grateful that her daughter-in-law is. Granny is too harassed to make plans for anything.

Passing a family on her way back to the bus, the woman suppresses a gasp. Ten minutes before, she'd paused to compliment the sweet toddler about his teddy bear. Now, he's red-faced and screaming, pulling at his shirt with a tiny hand, the bear dropped. While the parents check his chest for a wasp sting, the grandma hears their panicky voices, for it's not wasp season. She tries to reject the thought that he's been struck by an energy weapon, but when a college student jolts at the busy bus stop, and then her ankle is zapped, she knows that her presence has caused two innocent people to be injured. Limping up the bus steps, she feels responsible for insisting on buying the tickets in person.

By midafternoon, the grandmother is sick from remorse, loathing herself for having spoken to the toddler. She worries the strike was lethal to his little body. She doesn't want to go out anymore.

In this instance, a stalker carrying a concealed electronic (energy) weapon, or who has requested a long-range weapons operator to discharge harmful energy, or who is a long-range weapons operator acting alone is responsible for wounding bystanders he knew the target would see. A different perp could have done something else. He might have pretended to trip, knocking the child down as the grandmother passed. He might have said something disturbing to the parents, same as to the college student. Whatever is done, it has to be something Granny Target understands is perp caused.

There are various reasons why OS goons harass bystanders. It might be to stop the ti from going to a place he enjoys. Or it might be to stop him from going out at all. And if the ti has angered his stalkers, it will be to punish him. It can also be a demonstration to show off a fearful, inconvenient, painful, expensive, or embarrassing tactic so that the ti will fret endlessly that he is next. No matter what message the stalkers are trying to get across, as you know by now, the goal is to maintain power.

Bystander harassment does not appear to be part of each target's package: a little over half. I know darn well that some targets might not yet recognize it or will not admit to it. Bystander harassment could be more widespread than what I'm hearing about.

Alrighty, what's next? We discussed in the last chapter that loved ones can be tormented until the ti deserts them. Therefore, we know those people are affected. But what about acquaintances and friends who interact day-to-day with a target whose theme includes harming others. Whether you are this ti's babysitter, acupuncturist, bar buddy, stockbroker, biology tutor, veterinarian, or personal chef—because you have participated with a ti who has a theme that includes menacing others, you can be knocked about physically, psychologically, or financially.

An analogy can explain this better than I can. When a shotgun's shell disperses into a spray of pellets, it's hardly a targeted duck's fault that others in the flock are hit, yet by being a hunter's choice, the duck's companions were wounded. This is what targets face, and it's a mortal problem, which is not an overstatement. Suicides and serious depressions occur from the guilt of involuntarily causing untold anguish to others.

So, if a ti has a theme that includes the ploy of dishing out harm to his acquaintances and friends, what happens to his apartment manager? And the receptionist at the office? They are most definitely scrutinized when they are engaging with this kind of target. There's no doubt about that. Even a regular courier service man or woman is noticed if chatter is exchanged.

What rigors are these folks submitted to? For starters, vandalism and preplanned accidents (which could affect others) such as slippery-coating a porch. Add to that strangers saying or doing things that cause unease: copycatting or a coughed "You pig." Then there are the evils of stalking, slander, break-ins, online theft, poisoning, and electronic-weapons attacks. If it's despicable, they'll do it.

Anybody who catches a stalker's attention, from babe-in-arms to wizened elder, can be used to hoodwink, intimidate, or destroy a target; and the unsuspecting innocent is going to have a few cruddy minutes. Occasionally, the cruddy minutes go on for hours or days. If the innocent remains useful to organized stalkers, the days turn into years.

Again, an analogy explains this best. People in some targets' lives are used in the same way a key is used to scratch a car.

Let's clarify acquaintance-harassment by looking at condo-dwelling Tess who doesn't know yet that she's a target.

Generally contented, Tess puts aside her crocheting, turns down the TV, and hesitantly answers the door. She's a bit nervous, certain someone is following her. A man she's never seen before greets her as if they are pals: "How are ya? Wouldn't you know, I've an extra tin of Smith's Coconut Cream paint if you can use it. Isn't that what you bought last month for your hall?" Tess is baffled. How would a stranger know that? Well, the stranger knew that because a stalker recorded the information in Tess's target file. The paint was used to spoil Tess's evening.

The next week a different perp-stranger approaches Tess Target in the condo lobby: "I've got coupons if you want them for Looking Good Hair Salon. Sally's back. She's your favourite isn't she?" Tess, as a new ti, is startled that the man knows how she adores what Sally does with her hair. She doesn't, however, understand the conversation's ramifications. If an experienced ti heard this remark about Sally, she would be perturbed, not so much because the stranger knows her business, but because she realizes that Sally is on the information list.

Having Smith's Coconut Cream paint on a victim data list is no big deal. Having Sally on the list is. In the perps' eyes, people and paint have equal value, so it's no surprise when Sally is used to confound Tess, just as the paint was.

After bogus drop-in clients tell Sally that a windbag named Tess is trying to have her hairdressing license revoked, she seeks the advice of a lawyer. Sally is a ready for a fight. A week later when the target calls for an appointment all hell breaks loose. Sally is threatening to sue, and the target doesn't know what she's talking about. Sally, like the paint, has been used as a tool to further deteriorate the target's sense of normal.

An experienced target would not have called Sally, and a confrontation might have been avoided unless the two bumped into each other. Sally, though, will never forget about the expensive lawyer and being so stressed that she missed work. She perceives Tess as wicked.

We know that Tess's life as a target will speed downhill, all the way to the bottom. But we don't know what's to become of Sally, so let's go through the possibilities. If OS knaves find Sally vulnerable and attractive, she could be stalked, peeped on, videoed naked, drugged and raped, or terrorized at night, all by large groups of men. If reviling Sally develops into a hobby, she will find sexual and grisly tokens (things) left around her home: perfume bottles, blobs of pretend blood, or condom wrappers. Should the men find her too enticing to let go, her life will be in shreds until they do. Just as easily, following her usefulness in the scheme to trash Tess, Sally could be left alone.

No matter what Sally's destiny is, because she believes Tess Target damned near had her hairdressing license falsely revoked, she got Tess blacklisted from every salon in the city. Sally will never accept that she was set up no matter what the ti says. Perp-slanderers are thorough. By drawing on Tess's data files, they configured a mass of fictitious yet convincing evidence to make-believe she has a malicious side.

Scenarios like this are so common for OS victims that they learn to expect them. Relatives of a ti, along with employers, landlords, colleagues, neighbours, and friends, are used in the same way as the hairdresser was.

Let's explore the impact another new target had on others, for her Saturday shopping spree began a series of disasters.

On her own for the first time and excited about creating a personal décor, a young woman fondles a stack of fuzzy bathmats, chiding with the stalker-stranger beside her who is shopping for towels. "Hmmm . . . mauve or beige?" she asks him, smiling.

Decorating an apartment and treating herself to teriyaki wings every night is all the eighteen-year-old dreamed it would be. When Josie told her mother that men and women were trailing her, her mom said, "Relax. No one is following you. It's natural to feel jumpy after leaving the nest."

Josie came home from work twice to find her mauve bathmat had been moved. Once it had been switched with her flowery welcome mat. Another time she found it on the kitchen table with a vase of daisies on top. With no sign of a break-in and nothing missing, she didn't quite know what to do and called her minister-friend. "Did you say someone keeps breaking into your apartment?"

"Yeah, but they're only moving my bathmat around. And leaving flowers."

As a subscriber to altruism, the minister, even though he thinks Josie's having girly qualms, suggests that she tell police, and he offers to counsel her through the adjustment period.

Poor Reverend Spauld. For being supportive, he's ended up replacing his car motor, had his poisoned dog put down, and been in Emergency with inexplicable chemical burns on his palms. All within a couple of weeks of speaking to Josie. Of course, like everyone else, he concludes that he's hit a rough stretch.

Lamentably, it doesn't stop there for the minister, for Josie has an isolation theme. Every time she leans on the fellow to talk about the stalking and the break-ins, something happens to him. If she didn't have an isolation theme, he could still be browbeaten for comforting her, but perhaps not as drastically.

Like the bathmat, the minister is an instrument that is handled in diverse ways to upend Josie. To organized stalkers, the minister and the bathmat have equal value while performing different functions. Reverend Spauld's job is to teach Josie how her isolation theme works. The bathmat is just one of many objects used to create fear.

It took over a year before the young woman made the connection between the fellow's mishaps and her victimization. By then the reverend was on medication for wobbly nerves and was a lot poorer. If the perps decide to hang on to Reverend Spauld, even after Josie moves to a faraway safe house, they'll attack his reputation.

Josie's brother, nonetheless, who drives her to choir practice on Thursday evenings, only ends up with a hoodlum at the door dressed as a phony janitor. For the most part, he's escaped the perp's interest. If they need to abuse him, they will.

Targets' neighbours are often broken into, and Josie's next-door-man was no exception. He found bleach dribbled all over his antique chair and pink polka-dot stickers on the fridge. Feeling watched, he applied for a job transfer.

* * *

Let's confirm who in a target's life gets harassed, and why.

- Anyone can get harassed if he or she is needed to hasten the target's isolation, or decimate part of the target's life, or disembowel the target's mental equilibrium. Assaults can be mental, physical, financial, or all three.
- Trivial harassment may be all someone around a target gets, as in being smashed into by a stalker's supermarket cart or receiving an unsettling phone call.
- Severe harassment can be deadly, such as prowlers tampering with a relative's propane tank line or tainting a home's water supply.
- Victims' helpmates and close loved ones are commonly harassed, although they are unlikely to recognize that their unusual problems and unusual occurrences are OS caused.
- The incidents can continue until the ti has no more contact with that person and sometimes even after that. Either way, a target's acquaintances, friends, and loved ones can be harassed daily or just once in a while.
- Except for females who the stalkers find sexually rousing, people around specific targets are ignored and left alone because they are not useful in fulfilling the ti's program or because ignoring them fulfills an ulterior motive.

- People who are aggressively assisting a target and cannot be coerced or scared away, along with right-fighters who are trying to expose organized stalking, can be beaten physically, mentally, or financially, and often all three. They can be killed.
- Lastly, a few selected people around a ti can become targets.

* * *

Innocents who bring happiness to a target can be penalized. A smitten bagel vender who hands a free cinnamon special to a ti every morning could find a bag of dog feces in front of his kiosk shortly afterwards, day after day. He's unlikely to see the connection, and realistically, it doesn't matter what he thinks. Sooner or later the ti is likely to hear about it and wonder if the poop is OS dirty work. Her harassment is so outrageous, anything is possible.

If this ti is not resigned that joy is forbidden, both the target and the vendor could have identical defacement done to their homes, workplaces, or cars.

Being handed a free cinnamon bagel is not at the top of everybody's "whoopee" list. That's plain to all of us. It's a piddling nicety that provides an opportunity to further decline the target's sense of normal, and to erase a small bit of pleasure, and to further erode the freedom of social interactions.

Perps who are destroying one or more parts of a ti's life, such as cheerfulness, employment, career, housing, or finances, regularly cause trouble for a ti's pals, casual acquaintances, landlords, neighbours, teachers, associates, employers, relatives, or community leaders, and then blame the target for causing the trouble. A perp will purposely dent a city councilman's parked Mercedes and then claim to have seen the target do it. Or, using a ti's email address as a contact person, post beware literature of contrived pedophile charges against the ti's medical school dean. Because stalkers are assigned a task, there is nothing they won't do to people around their target to get it done.

With fear, confusion, despair, and anger being the only acceptable emotions in organized stalking, people who supply a ti with housing, employment, education, help, comfort, joy, orderliness, or an opportunity to achieve are often harassed until they are no longer contributing to the victim's well-being.

We'll go through a couple more cases and then move on.

A violin teacher who is driving home after a ti's lesson is run off the road. The next teacher is afflicted the same. The ti gets the message and foregoes lessons altogether. Though it is of no interest to the perps, one of the instructors crashed his car and was injured.

The final case is a target who is a keen player at the Bingo Palace. Every time she puts her cards on the table, the nearest volunteer coordinator is stricken with sudden abdominal pain. Most of them double over and leave. The ti concedes that witnessing so many churning bellies is not a fluke. She knows all about electronic weapons, having suffered the same stomach blows.

As you'll recall, targets are made to know what's going on, notwithstanding that it takes a while for an unseasoned ti to connect his presence to others' misfortunes. This ploy has colossal clout. That's why pursuing innocents in a target's life is often more effective than pursuing the target himself.

Once a victim discovers that people around him are being abused by perpetrators, he has no option other than to withdraw. From family reunions to the bowling league, social activities have to be curtailed. If a ti is determined to stick it out, hoping that innocents will stop being harmed, he's mistaken. He'll end up having to shoulder the consequences of knowing what his presence was responsible for. Since electronic strikes and accident-causing perps can, and will, break a bystander's bones, a ti may have to live with the knowledge that the friendly fellow sitting beside him at the hockey game is now in a cast.

Okay, so we know that anybody around a target can be used to prevent that target from having enjoyment, employment, housing, education, possessions, freedom of movement, help, and to isolate him. Also, to remove a sense of normal. It can never be normal to know that a person can be hurt because you exchanged small talk at a gym, sat next to someone in a theatre, or attended a wedding. As long as a target sees or hears that someone (or an animal) has been distressed, and understands that it was OS caused, the perp's mission is accomplished. We know, too, that if people around a target have become interesting to stalkers, they can be harassed even after the ti has moved away.

By design, organized stalking is multifaceted, and so far we have discussed the impact the bulk of ti's have on others. For now, let's change pace and check out the smaller percentage of ti's, those who appear to have little immediately discernible impact. (There could be repercussions later.)

It may be that the OS program a ti is on *initially* allows or requires the social connections that boost his standing. Business people, wealthy people, popular people, celebrities, politicians, and professionals can fall into this category. With these victims, the crime's lead perpetrators are infiltrating, skillfully spreading slander, and then manipulating the duped people's reactions. Lies against a prominent target are often told under the guise of good intentions—of informing employers and the public that the ti is unworthy of his or her position.

Although the pliable folks in this ti's circle are usually unaffected by palpable physical and financial assaults, or vandalism and harassment, they will be convincingly influenced to think badly about someone they admire, namely the high-profile target. This will be the central impact, for no doubt, the friendship will soon become strained or in some cases irreconcilable.

We can all agree that psychologically managing someone falls into a category of having impact. However, it is expertly executed and is unlikely to be noticed as having evil intention, except by the target.

Integral to a high-profile target's downfall, besides slander, are crafty ruses that portray him or her as dishonest, crazy, prejudiced, coldhearted, immoral, or addicted. A targeted doctor may be slipped drugs and then asked to give a urine sample. A politician could be listed as a supporter of anti-Semitism on a widely distributed flyer.

Limelight targets are forced into becoming diligent guards of their status and assets as they appear to be in a program that is exclusive to career, reputation, financial, and health (mental and physical) decimation. Hence, they bypass the violence-towards-others intimidation and retribution ploys that force total isolation. Despite occasional worriment of being in grave danger from stalker-caused attacks, worriment about physical attacks on loved ones is uncommon and usually unnecessary. Limelight targets are not often among the homeless ti crowd, in spite of severe harassment. Yet when it comes to stress, confusion, coping, and compromised health, every target is on equal ground.

Should notable ti's speak openly of the tyranny—of cataclysmic slander, document tampering, ruses, gang stalking, and electronic weapons—it could spell the end of their profession. The crimes always have an unbelievable quality, and this group cannot risk being laughed at. They are careful who they confide in.

High-profile ti's do not escape to public safe houses. They are disinclined to ask experienced targets for OS information, support, or tips on how best to handle stalking and electronic attacks. Declaring themselves as OS victims is not something most are willing to gamble. Thus, the information here has been compiled from the few brave souls who have come forward and been candid with me.

To review, in situations where eminent social connections are initially allowed, a ti's devotees, friends, employers, colleagues, and family may be urged to dislike him, but they are otherwise unimportant to the plan. Subsequently, they are less likely to find a puddle of oil on their terraces or have their windshield wipers snapped off. They probably won't have their homes burgled.

Targets who do not significantly impact others are a minority. Nevertheless, there are other small pockets of ti's in this class that we need to peruse.

People around the targets who are on a strict course of lethal bodily attacks are not always harassed, but as you will see, when rescuers and certain witnesses are struck, they are struck hard. This operation is designed to slowly exterminate the target by assaulting him with electronic weapons and once in a blue moon by poisoning him.

One atrocity is the continual use of a high-tech device that emits unstoppable noise into the victim's hearing. This device, along with its noise, is called voice to skull or v2k. Voice to skull is an important part of OS to understand because sound torture is used extensively in this crime.

Voice to skull's sound is as silent as a cell phone call travelling through the air until it reaches a receiver that in this case is the target's head. We all know only one person's cell phone rings when a call is sent, even though there might be twenty phones nearby. It's the same with a piece of equipment that is intended to call up and put noise into one person's head. No one else will hear the sound; only the targeted head can.

Crude short-range voice to skull instruments, of tabletop size, were recognized by 1961. The original intent was to send conversations, oral information, and music into deaf people's noggins, bypassing their anomalous hearing structures. The equipment has come a long way since then.

Here is a quote from page 8 of the declassified 1998 U.S. Military report *Bioeffects of Selected Nonlethal Weapons*. It discusses using (microwave) voice to skull technology as a weapon.

> **Application of the microwave hearing technology could facilitate a private message transmission. It may be useful to provide a disruptive condition to a person not aware of the technology. Not only might it be disruptive to the sense of hearing, it could be psychologically devastating if one heard "voices within one's head."**

When voice to skull (v2k) is emitted as a ti's extermination scheme, electromagnetic waves silently travel through the air, undetected, until they reach sound-triggering mechanisms seated inside the targeted person's head. The head will hear whatever was sent, and for an extermination scheme it's going to be an excruciatingly loud or rankling noise, or a fault-finding commentary, sometimes all together, none of which can be stopped. Panic, depression, physical collapse, suicidal ideation, or suicide always results.

Military sound torture, in various forms, is emitted to suspected terrorists and can go on for days, weeks, or until death is imminent. For single-torture OS targets, the v2k device is turned off when the victim is deceased and not a minute before. The patent for voice to skull technology is in the appendix on page 463.

I'm going to get right to the core of remote energy torture, for we can't continue without you having some understanding. Remote energy torture greatly impacts the people around some targets. Voice to skull isn't the only kind.

The following list explains how long-distance weaponry beams, including voice to skull, could be remotely finding the heads and bodies they are hitting, even when there is no line of sight. There are many possible ways. This is one and it involves brain wave tracking. Bear with me, in a flash you'll be the sharpest person in the room.

Brain wave tracking theory

- First, you must understand that interpreting, recording, and collecting an individual's brain activity is a common medical and research procedure. For example, a person undergoing surgery has an anesthesiologist interpret his brain's electrical activity in order to monitor his well-being.
- Second, you must understand that every person's brain has a unique and identifiable brain-activity (brain wave) pattern much the same way as every person has a unique and identifiable fingerprint pattern.
- The remote brain wave tracking theory says that OS is scanning and recording a targeted person's unique brain wave

pattern, along with scanning and recording the unique brain wave patterns of selected people who connect with that targeted individual.

- This means that a target's (and others') brain output could be coded and put into a database, like a fingerprint is put into a database. However, because brains are electrical, this database is comparable to the one used by a cell phone provider.
- To grasp how easy it is to access brain activity, consider that ordinary folks are buying brain interpreting headsets as a mental health aid ($100 and up) and that interpreting brain activity is necessary in some medical fields. So, is it not reasonable then to consider that advances in the equipment have led to reading, recording, identifying, and tracking brain waves (heads) from a long distance?
- "Yes," according to the brain wave tracking theorists. They say targets can receive OS energy transmissions (like voice to skull) wherever they go because each targeted head is a separate channel, or code, on OS's electronic equipment.
- In other words, it's deemed possible that furtive technology tracks (stalks) a specific head because the person's electrical brain wave pattern (brain signature) is a receiver for OS electronics.
- It is further theorized that senior OS staff operate computers and high-tech electronics that send energy (like voice to skull) to a targeted head, and to the body under it, as smoothly as a transmission is sent to your cell phone or satellite phone, granting OS's equipment is much further advanced than what a mobile phone-service provider uses.
- With zero doubt, disregarding how it happens, targets are like a radio station on your stereo. Except that only the enemy has

the off switch. It's all about the transfer of energy; frequencies; and like a cell phone, being encoded into a database.

- The fact that OS interprets brains has been proven, yet the equipment that does the interpreting has not been proven well enough to get into court. But all that could change by tomorrow. Ditto for the out-of-sight equipment that sends harmful transmissions (like voice to skull) over a long distance.
- No matter what the source, all energy beams that are emitted to do harm, including voice to skull, are called electronic harassment, covert harassment, electronic torture, energy harassment, and energy torture. Electronic harassment is the term targets often use, and they abbreviate it to EH. The weapons are called energy weapons, electronic weapons, directed-energy weapons (DEWs), or covert weapons.
- "Remote" in this book refers to being stalked *from* space (satellite) or *through* space (over land and sea) and to being energy assaulted from or through space, all by high-tech equipment that is a long distance from the target. The words "**space**" and "**via space**" simply denote energy travelling a great distance.
- Note please that satellites, as they are known, are incapable of reading and tracking brain waves or directing energy at a single person. As theories are all ti's have got to go on, references in this book about from-space transmissions connote some folks' theory that advances in satellite technology enable covert tracking and assaults. Through-space (over land and sea) technology is also considered.
- The terms "energy weapons," "electronic harassment," and their variations are sometimes used interchangeably in this book. I understand that each term has its own definition and that my word-vacillation can offend science-types. Be that as it may,

the victim community's flexible lingo is essential for you to see, bearing in mind that organized stalking and electronic harassment is a historically new crime that needed a new vocabulary to describe it. Internationally, there are pockets of victims who use the name "covert harassment" to represent the whole shebang of offences.

Please be mindful that while I'm writing this there is no courtroom proof of how ti's are remotely stalked. Targeted academics have done extensive research along with interviewing the scientists who invented people-monitoring technologies. Thus, concepts in the book about how remote stalking and remote harassment are done are the most popular and well-researched theories.

We'll be discussing remote energy transmission in detail later (don't worry, it won't be boring), for although short-range electronic weapons are used to cause injuries, cause radiation poisoning, send sound, and assassinate, most of the energy injuries and deaths are committed by long-distance ware that sends lethal energy directly to a target's brain and body. The murderer (alternatively, a few blame artificial intelligence) is sitting in front of a panel that is assumedly linked to ultra-progressive far-reaching transmitters. Some (definitely not all) of these transmitters (weapons) may very well be illegal adaptations of inventions that are useful to people, or are illegal tagalongs: misused cell towers for example.

You're probably already aware of many governments' satellite programs that watch and keep tabs on adversaries. That's old news. Targets are trailed from or through space second by second, but it's not because a satellite camera got lucky in finding them. Targets are trailed by technology that is not common knowledge.

There is definitive evidence that targets' brain waves are scanned and recorded, yet there is no evidence that this is how OS's remote stalking occurs. There's no way to know. The underworld bosses aren't revealing what equipment they use.

If you find it confusing that each person has unique brain waves (brain activity) that can identify him, consider that each person has unique irises and DNA, as well as fingerprints.

My head, your head, the Queen's head, and every other head has what's called a brain wave signature.

In two steps here it is: (1) Targets are watched, stalked, and monitored by long-distance ware, and then harmed by directed energy anywhere on earth they go. (2) Remote stalking could be by tracking brain waves, or it could be by something else.

A number of targeted scholars who have studied OS presume that brain wave stalking is the only feasible way one scanned and sought head among millions can be found and followed, seeing as each brain emits unique electrical activity. There are other theories, and we'll get to those further along.

How a person is remotely stalked is irrelevant right now. Soon enough, you'll discover that it's a new fact of life. Think of it this way. Cell phones, GPS devices, and Internet-enabled computers all operate because energy finds them through or from space. So, it comes as no surprise that related technology has been adapted to find and then harm or annihilate an electrically-conductive human. OS victims aren't the only people showered with deadly energy. Progressive governments' militaries use the same classification of weapons on supposed enemies and threats. Undoubtedly, militaries and intelligence agencies developed the remote stalking technology OS uses.

Phew. It's uncomfortable to write about remote stalking and killing seeing as it's me who is under attack. Way back in the book, I mentioned that my hand had been mangled by an energy beam. It was probably a remote beam. Remote beams, of one kind or another, hit ti's day and night, which is how OS victims got the name targets. Knowing a target, or being near one, is all it takes to be hit by remote beams as well.

You've just learned that victims are stalked via space (page 84), resulting in them, and sometimes others, being attacked by energy via space. It's a lot to swallow, but I had to tell you here. You needed to get the gist of remote harassment and torture in order to understand the extent of a target's impact on the people around him.

Let's get it over with and establish what remotely sent energy torture is. One kind is crippling pain or crippling wounds to internal and external body parts. Then there are persistent voice to skull transmissions; internal and external burns that appear out of (apparently) nowhere; sudden, inexplicable eye damage; internal heating (cooking); and mounds more. We'll get to the others later.

Once you've digested that knotty section, we can get back to OS's practice of sending noise through a target's skull, right into his noodle, termed voice to skull or v2k. The equipment used to send it can be up close or far away.

I know what you're thinking. Why don't the victims stick in earplugs? Earplugs don't work. You have to get rid of your head. A voice to skull transmission, such as a song or the words "We see you," seeps through a skull so that it can engage with a brain, as well as enters ears. This is why it works on folks whose hearing structures

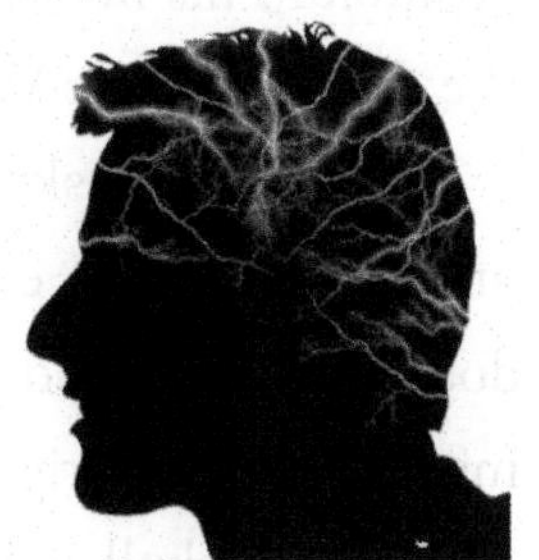

Voice to skull transmissions seep into a brain.

do not receive sound properly. Voice to skull's sound is constructed right in a noodle, into consciousness.

Here's a bit of homework: memorize the fact that a victim's whole brain is the receiver for OS electronics, which is how voice to skull noise flows through one head. Your brain is electrical.

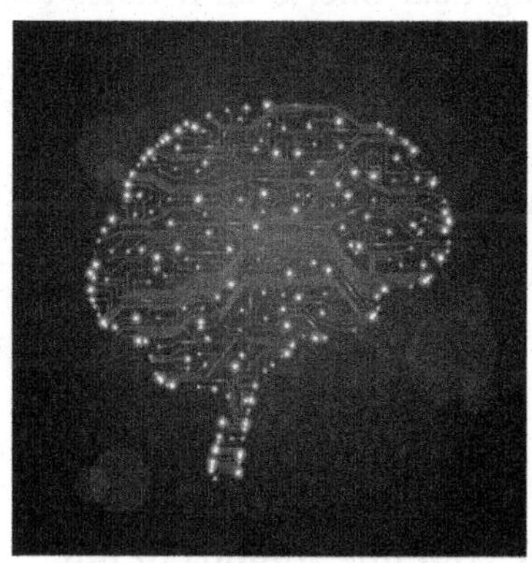

Your brain is electrical.

This next scenario of OS's methodology is hypothetical and considered correct by many: let's say that you're shoveling snow when OS decides to scan your brain waves. You didn't see or feel anything. Regardless, your brain's unique waveforms have been recorded into OS's electronics as an ABCD code. You are a "thing" with an electronic serial number, like a cell phone. Now, which code do you think OS will use to connect with your noggin and follow it around? Take a guess.

When organized stalkers transmit energy waves (such as voice to skull) to your ABCD-coded noggin, no one else is going to be affected. No one else on earth has the same ABCD electrical composition in his noodle. Only you. Papa Peter's might be HIJK. And the dog's might be WXYZ.

Most voice to skull (v2k) transmissions come from afar. On the other hand, some equipment is used quite close to a target and doesn't need to find his head from miles away. Short-range transmission was the original invention for deaf folks.

Voice to skull is homicidal when it is emitted in an unceasing clamor. The few condemned souls in a v2k murder scheme often have little impact on impassive others.

The majority of victims' v2k is not intended to kill them, but to grate and impair. These victims, being the mainstream, have perps and programs that include hurting innocents.

Voice to skull equipment can emit any sound on earth: thunder, barking, screaming, heavy metal music, swearing, a children's ditty, insults, the victim's voice, the perpetrator's voice, tinnitus-type ringing, anything at all. It can be ear-splitting loud, or a whisper, or subliminal. The array of sounds is hardly mysterious. An OS employee downloads, for example, squealing machinery, and then plays it back, but not to himself. He sends it silently through the air to a defenceless targeted head. The person wearing the head will hear squealing machinery until the maniac at the computer turns it off. *If* he turns it off. Other people around the head will not hear squealing machinery, not even traces of it.

Voice to skull transmissions permeate a skull, then engage with a brain's electrical system to produce sound no one else can hear.

If you're a non-ti reading this, I suggest you look up voice to skull, HAARP, and military satellites, to begin with. Biased material will declare their value and not their nefarious uses. You know better now and can explore publications and documentaries that reveal a dark side. (I suggest Dr. Nick Begich's books, articles, lectures, and websites.)

We're going to take an infinitely necessary crack at exploring how v2k affects others. Rescuers of those with an upcoming murder or suicide can be sorely impacted. Most often, however, v2k aimed at innocents is short-lived.

When the target's recorded voice is transmitted into a person's head, a rift always follows. The target hadn't said a word, yet the person heard him speak.

I'll use my own skirmish to explain it better. A relative enjoying an ocean swim came back to shore huffy at me for incessantly yelling questions that I apparently expected him to answer. It wasn't me. I was reading a book on the beach quite a distance away. All the same, it was my prerecorded voice that was causing trouble, transmitted into his head by voice to skull equipment. There was no convincing my relative that he could not possibly have heard me, especially when he swam out of sight into the next cove. I had to drop the argument and put up with him being miffed at me for lousing up his swim.

He doesn't know it, but because he is a loved one, he's been targeted on a lesser scale for nearly two decades. Otherwise I'd never have let him visit. Estrangement from this fellow is futile. He's already been chosen. Still, I keep visits down to every few years, not wanting to motivate our shared perpetrators. For this man, voice to skull and other electronic-weapons tortures are a "pushed button" away for as long as he lives—for as long as all targets' loved ones live.

Voice to skull can be aimed at anyone near a target, even a stranger, for seconds, minutes, or hours. If he is uneducated about OS's sound weapons, he may think he's experiencing an episode of psychosis or believe a deity is talking to him; for the voice, who is a criminal sitting in front of unorthodox equipment, is saying or playing a script to disorient him. Rather than voices, day-to-day noises are regularly sent to bystanders who will look for and never find the nonexistent source. Wall banging, door banging, window plinking, sirens, animals, a ringing phone, a crash, footsteps, and heavy furniture being moved are standard transmissions to both non-ti's and ti's.

I'm supposing that you, as perhaps a newcomer to OS, would consider transitory v2k transmissions as having impact. You are unlikely, as has been proven, to recognize the madhouse you were so hastily introduced to. A single voice to skull transmission or a single energy-caused burn that is sent to a rescuer, loved one, or anyone else around a ti will never convince him that this form of torture exists.

Logic rules. And the use of electronic weapons on the general public is illogical.

When a spouse or other loved one, or a rescuer, is sent a life-changing voice to skull message, even though he discredits electronic weapons, he might still be shaken: "This is the devil talking, and you're going to smolder for eternity," sounds stupid on paper, but when it is said into a head, or even over the phone, the response is revulsion.

People around targets do not receive continual v2k torture unless they are assisting a ti or have figured out what's going on and are exposing the crime. Then, v2k is used as punishment.

The ten percent or so of victims receiving nonstop voice to skull all consider suicide as it's the only way to make it stop. Some victims suffer for years before their thresholds are exceeded. Homelessness, extreme poverty, aloneness, suicide, and slow self-destructive deaths in this one-torture group are in exceptionally high numbers.

Most (or all) victims hear voice to skull from time to time, and some hear it quite regularly. It is torture when it interferes with accomplishing a task, including sleeping and thinking. It's homicidal when the noise is eternal.

Voice to skull transmissions cannot and should not be confused with auditory hallucinations. They are entirely different from one another. Labelling a voice to skull torture subject with schizophrenia is like putting a morgue tag on his still-warm toe. Targets cannot cope or save themselves when they have been forced to take psychiatric drugs that exacerbate the problem. Misdiagnosed voice to skull ti's often bolt, not to escape stalkers, but to escape doctors; therefore, they are unable to access urgent medical care. An improperly treated ti would rather risk sepsis (blood poisoning) from an infected energy-charred leg than ever again speak to a doctor.

Coping with unending voice to skull transmissions requires total commitment to inner strength. When this inner strength is removed through mind-numbing medications, the ti always considers suicide.

Let's look at some more extermination drills, for as I said, although single-torture targets have less impact on others, when rescuers or justice seekers get in the way, their retribution could be the same torture or another that's just as wicked.

A different one-torture program, quite unlike sending a racket into someone's skull, consists of an energy weapon that is aimed to damage small sections of the ti's innards, such as what has happened to my hand. The skin may stay intact. The innards, however, are pelted. Just like with voice to skull devices, the weapons can be nearby or yonder. If there are no abrasions, people around the victim may not recognize how serious the wounds are, in spite of the victim's obvious pain. Internal bleeding, organ failure, and broken bones are possible.

Over half of the ti population are regularly banged up this way or are completely incapacitated every few weeks, remotely. When the attack is perpetual, night and day, it is often a one-tactic stratagem and eventually becomes non-survivable. Other aggressive harassments may occur only sporadically. Non-interfering people might suffer no consequences.

Radiation poisoning from extensive energy-weapon use is another ploy. A ti in a one-weapon program can be getting thoroughly radiated for weeks or months. If he doesn't die, he will require a year or more to partway recover. A radiated victim can feel he will vomit to death and may never again be well.

Another single-torture method is to mete out the same chemical or drug over and over. A water system or personal item may be tainted. Breaking in is not a hindrance unless ti's have educated themselves about the perps' break-in tools.

A one-torture method I cannot confirm but have heard whispers of is worth bringing up for the sake of caution. In situations with a shared wall, such as an apartment or duplex, pure carbon monoxide or an alternate toxic gas could flow into the target's home from a cylinder hose that a perp-neighbour has poked through a hole he drilled. Perps, using false ID, often rent a unit that adjoins their target yet have no intention of living there; that's an established fact.

To straighten out this poisoning business, so that you don't become fixated, poisoning a target for the sake of making him sick for the day is not all that usual, but it happened to me, only once for sure, when a watermelon slice in my fridge had been tainted during a break-in while I was at a police station appealing for help.

When you see the word "poison," don't think strychnine. Think date rape drugs, laxatives, sedatives, eye drops (poisonous when swallowed), ordinary medications, energy boosters, pesticides, and anything at all that can cause unpleasant symptoms when used incorrectly. Perpetrators do not want to get caught, and they do not want medical testing to reveal foul play. They do want to make a suddenly ailing target wonder if his food or water has been tainted.

Deliberate poisoning occurs just often enough that it should be included in the book; there are documented and proven cases. Yet I hate the word "poison." It dredges up unnecessary paranoia, for almost all OS-caused illnesses are from electronic harassment. For this reason, I only vaguely mentioned poison in my first drafts, then decided to be more forthright by referring to tainting (poisoning) as need be. What can I say. It happens.

Slow poisoning, sometimes by a tainted water system, is a means to deliver long-term retribution to a target who is always seeking legal help and also as a way of making someone too ill to keep a job. Or even to kill him. Poisoning or drugging for the sake of forcing sleep, confusion, or weakness, often as preparation for a sexual or other assault, is routine for a very small number of targets. So is spritzing chosen target's faces with chemicals that cause a skin, eye, or respiratory reaction. Radiation poisoning, which does not involve tainting food, fluid, or personal belongings, is a different matter altogether and is something I consider standard, overall.

By my observations, most or all heavily harassed ti's are seriously poisoned by radiation or chemicals at least once.

The process of incapacitation from being continually poisoned, maimed by directed energy, or full-body radiated is as drawn-out as you would expect. After weeks, months, or years of pain, vomiting, severe nausea, dizziness, weakness, diarrhea, dehydration, starvation, sleep deprivation, an irregular heartbeat, digestion failure, eyesight failure, disabled legs, or difficulty breathing, a ti is unable to function. These people are habitually disbelieved and misdiagnosed.

Victims whose foremost harassment is one disabling tactic are still stalked, as are all targets. Their phones and computers are interloped, too, as that is always mandated. In addition, they may be exasperated from time to time by vandalism, pranks, and other kinds of energy strikes, but not to the extent that it impedes everything in their lives. That's the primary weapon's or chemical's job.

Advocates and rescuers are hard to find in a one-torture group, in small part, because done-in, one-torture victims can become unreachable. If these victims can't find help within six months to three years, depending on their torture type and their resilience, they can't last and often become suicidal and reclusive or are dying in private. They can also be homeless and unavailable, or running if they are well enough. It takes pluck to help someone in this group. It's much like racing into a flaming building. Be that as it may, we're going to examine what happens to these caring folks.

The first line of defence to thwart would-be advocates is to fabricate slander and scenarios that "prove" the ti is a nutcase and should not be believed. This still impacts the advocate as he will be bombarded with realistic appearing evidence by perps who present themselves as professionals and friends who want what's best for the *delusional* target. This advocate will be submitted to an intense and coordinated brainwashing process, and he may not take time to think the situation through. He's going to be overwhelmed with authoritarian people who insist that the only way to help the *delusional* target is to commit him to a mental hospital or to ostracize him. Unless the advocate is an independent thinker and wonders what's up with the snow job, he's going to do a great deal of harm if he pushes the target into the enemy's awaiting arms.

During this period, or shortly afterwards, through increased use of the immobilizing weapon (or poison), the victim is going to be kept at death's door for several weeks to discourage him from seeking help again. An experienced target skedaddles when he sees an advocate being successfully bamboozled.

Conned advocates do not get off distress-free despite sidestepping harassment. Emotional repercussions can occur years past the original situation either when the advocate realizes he was deceived or when he wishes he'd been more helpful. Undoubtedly, the poisoned or electronically attacked target he considered assisting will be in very poor shape, dying, or dead. If the ti dies soon after a prospective guardian turned his back, the guardian may feel responsible.

Monitoring protectors and every other person around a target is critical to organized stalking's success. With perpetrators not about to waste their time trying to con a helper who exhibits a strong predisposition to defending the target—who is not going to fall for the usual "delusional" ploy—explosive cruelty is usually successful to deter interference, particularly when the rescuer's or target's family is threatened. A child might find a rigor mortis pet under his bed sheets. And a teenager's stolen brake light bulbs will be a message that only the parent understands.

Death threats made to either side, advocate or target, must never be misconstrued as hollow. Gang members kill when it comes to securing their ownership over a target and kill to avoid arrest.

Rescuers, naturally, seek police help. It's often a useless exercise.

You can see that sometimes this is a no-win situation. A possible rescuer can be harassed or snuffed out, including his family members; and the victim he's rescuing will be doubly tortured for accepting help. The victim's family members can be attacked as well. A conned rescuer will be left alone, but again, the victim will pay an ungodly price for seeking protection.

On rare occasions a concerned loved one gains knowledge about the offending weapon or the likely chemical (poison) and learns how it is killing the target. Universally, people around targets are for the most part disbelieving. But when it does happen—when a single-mode tortured ti gains an informed advocate—the advocate can be tortured as well. It may or may not be the same torture. Whatever is done, it will be deterrence and punishment whether the support person recognizes it as so, or not. The goal is to get the advocate out of the target's life. (A covert near-lethal or lethal energy-weapon or chemical attack is often misidentified by non-ti's.)

Murdering an advocate is a last ditch solution and done when a persistent helper is exposing the crime. In this case, an informed rescuer could be murdered before a ti is. A supporter can be more effective than a target in drawing attention to organized stalking and its use of lethal contrivances. He may be a witness who holds sway and will be a lot healthier (in the beginning) than the tortured target; thus, he will have a better ability to investigate. More importantly he won't (yet) have a *kook* label and has a better chance of moving a target through the justice system.

When a ti has been tortured unmercifully and is close to suicide, or death from the torture itself, stalkers may be unwilling to finish him off, even when he or his advocate is troublesome. Stalkers invest substantial time and money into commandeering a ti's decline. Watching a suicide or the last breaths from a long-drawn-out slaughter is the reward for their hard work. They'd rather not miss it. And as targets are monitored by through-wall surveillance from remote stalking inventions, and even by in-home spy cameras, all with computers that record, the macabre scene can be watched again and again.

Accidental kills happen to rescuers when a stern warning has been carried too far. Being hit by a car; being injured because of a tampered surface, vehicle, or machine; and being incapacitated by an energy strike to a heart, stomach, or brain are stock OS exercises to teach a rescuer to back off. Targets can be informed of a rescuer's death or injuries by a detailed backhanded message given in person or over the phone, or by a concise statement sent by voice to skull into the ti's head. Organized stalkers need to be credited with their crimes, and targets are not allowed to think a death or injury was faultless when it was caused by perpetrators. No opportunities are missed that might create a fearful reaction. Frightened people are controllable.

In fact, oftentimes these frightened controllable people are loved ones who blame the victim for bringing evil into their lives, for undoubtedly, if loved ones aren't seeing the crimes, they're sure to be hearing about them. Presumably, an upset spouse is going to eventually distance himself from who he perceives is the source of the morass, being the target.

Remarkable, to me anyway, is how fast spousal desertion is when one partner is complaining about endless one-weapon torture, or is complaining about stalking and harassment, or if they are both crumbling under regular night terrorism.

If the target is determined to continue living at home, the spouse, in all probability, will try to kick the target out. If that is impossible, the spouse may hightail it to what he perceives is a sane new residence. Either way, the spouse is likely to become backbiting if the ti continues pleading for help, outraged at whatever his partner has done to turn home life into a snake pit.

An angry spouse has decided that the ti is lying when she says she doesn't know who the stalkers are or why they are attacking. He almost certainly thinks she is lying or exaggerating about being incapacitated by the weapons or by being poisoned or radiated at work. This spouse doesn't know it, but by showing timidity or hostility—enough to abandon someone he loves—he could be in for a rough ride until the stalkers are finished playing with him. Strong reactions from a loved one are too provocative to skip.

It's not unheard of for a sulking spouse to idly watch at a distance while his mate is stalked, harassed, assaulted, tortured, or killed. It's more common than you'd suppose. Spouses of heavily harassed ti's who are determined to stick it out year after year as full-time guardians are atypical and often end up as full-time targets themselves.

When implications about a rescuing spouse's (or any rescuer's) upcoming execution or torture are disclosed to the target by clever stalker-to-target comments, or through actions, or by voice to skull messages, the ti may flee, or tell the rescuer to stop, or tell the rescuer to leave. This target might commit suicide believing it would save the rescuer's life.

All stalkers get off on the terror and hysteria they create with their sordid messages and in-action threats. The more cowardice a rescuer or target shows, the more terror he will receive. Fundamentally, pretending not to be cowardly is a tall order. The bus is headed for the cliff, and there's no getting off.

Now that you get the drift of single-weapon-tortured ti's and how their rescuers are affected, let's return to the limited impact these victims have on indifferent families and friends. Single-weapon extermination programs do not regularly impact undisruptive and unconcerned bystanders, acquaintances, friends, and non-spousal loved ones. The folks at the coffee counter are (probably) going to be left unscathed as long as they stay disinterested in Tory Target's tales of woe. To sum it up, other people are not used to wipe out assorted areas of the ti's life. Homicidal electronic weapons and tainted air, water, and food do that.

Overall, it's primarily rescuers, investigators, and justice seekers who perps go after within a one-torture group. Why I have been allowed to live despite assisting these targets is murky. My hunch is that I am part of OS's research, for learning how to curb agitators would be an operation unto itself. Not that I get off scot-free. Near-lethal attacks are so familiar that they've become normal, if that makes sense. My handlers always let me go when I am imploring skywards. If my stalkers wanted me dead, I would be dead. Ditto for the activists. They get half-killed, recover, and do it all over despite the slaying of their comrades.

Ti's, like me, who are intermittently electronically injured, or fully radiated, or infused with voice to skull transmissions, or even drugged or poisoned are not on a single-weapon protocol and get a bit of everything.

I will never declare good news within this crime, but thankfully, besides the one-torture group and the high-profile crowd, there are other ti factions where non-interfering innocents receive little duress.

Because victims are assigned varying themes and tactics, a few actively harassed ti's manage to share their homes indefinitely with minimally pestered spouses, parents, or roommates. These ti's are, for the most part, harassed in all the usual ways, every day in many cases, but may be receiving a toned-down mixture of pandemonium; for living as an ordinary person during full-blown terrorizing, even for a day or two, is impossible. This is not said to diminish what moderately harassed targets go through. Daily OS turmoil on any scale fractures a target's life and that in turn affects family members' and friends' lives.

People who are weathering organized stalking's continuous disruptions cannot offer stints of uninterrupted affection, or pother-free stints of time, or long-term attention to goals. Neither can they offer reliable stability, security, or financial aid to loved ones. Although they'll certainly try. Goals, plans, and present achievements entail maneuvering through mazes of zigs and zags and dead ends, and more dead ends.

Targets with minimal impact who are allowed to remain in close relationships are often sent remote energy blasts that are aimed to cause disabling head and limb aches, as well as heart, eye, and other organ irregularities. Plus, slander and gossip for these folks are excessive. Defamation will be so widespread that they will have trouble finding or keeping employment, and spouses and parents get fed up. This can go on for years. If these targets belong to a church, tennis club, volunteer association, or anything else, they may no longer be welcome yet are unlikely to ever find out what lies were told.

Once in a while, when this ti is out with his partner or parent, stalking may take on a daredevil flair with perpetrators flaunting their irritating routines right in front of the two. Nevertheless, the shared-home loved one and other folks around these ti's are less prone to be seriously injured or harassed.

We're going to take a second look at this flaunting behaviour as it is remarkable. Every blue moon, perpetrators want an unbelieving loved one to see their public hijinks.

I don't know why they do this because witnesses of flagrant stalking are usually forbidden. Maybe it's to muck with a target's psyche—the crime is designed to confound. Or it may be that some stalkers are playing outside of the rules. Anyhow, it happens to most targets, and it happens to all targets who have an unbothered house-mate. As a ti, I can tell you that flagrant stalking is extraordinary, particularly when a witness persists that OS is a fairy tale.

This conversation actually happened: "How can you say I'm not stalked? That guy with the red beard has been following us for hours. When he got his hand stuck in my hair, you laughed!"

A fleeting single attack on a non-targeted housemate has no influence, either, in convincing him that the crime exists. A targeted wife and non-targeted hubby may both be burned by directed energy on their foreheads and the hubby . . . Well, you know the rest. He'll insist on blaming the soap or some such thing. Perps count on OS-ignorant folks to claim they have been unaffected, ascribing that an errant illness, burn, labour-intensive snafu, or aberrant breakage is chance or their own poor judgement. As for inane occurrences, such as strangers saying "Happy Birthday" to the loved one, the events are considered one of those things and are forgotten.

To top it off, perps will pull a stunt in front of a ti and his unbelieving housemate that is sure to make the ti look less credible. This is another form of the street theatre I mentioned earlier. A ti may look to his wife and say, "Look, there's my stalker pretending he's choking again. He always does it in a crowd and then motions for me to help him. I hope he does choke." Whenever a stalker plays a trick in front of a skeptical or mocking loved one, the target always ends up looking like an ass. This has purely a psychological impact and works to deteriorate a ti's relationships.

Victims find that not being believed is insulting. Which it is. Yet, a non-targeted spouse or housemate sees and receives so little obvious harassment, it's easier to think that the ti is losing it rather than pursue the matter.

Let's take a gander now at another thoroughly twisted area of OS—at individuals who never get an inkling of wrongdoings.

When specific possible rescuers are around a ti who is asking to be believed or protected, the harassment can slow to a crawl or stop altogether. This is not happenstance. Should a headstrong ti come close to finding a headstrong ally, such as a relative, colleague, friend, private detective, or lawyer, the crime can come to an abrupt halt as long as that ally is watchful and open-minded. It's tough enough for dubious onlookers to recognize covert violations, but in this case a diligent investigative ally who is trying hard to see them won't see them at all, for they've disappeared.

After weeks with no hint of harassment, the ally concedes that the ti is delusional or lying and may offer to get the ti psychological help. Or he could tell the ti to get lost. This hoodwinked person, who was willing to believe, will never see a scrap of OS trouble.

With the ally now out of the way, the ti, who is mistakenly jubilant that the crime has ended, will be mentally persecuted and literally taken out of circulation. False psychiatric detainment or criminal imprisonment may be this ti's future, or he could end up dying on the street or dying by suicide.

Remotely transmitted voice to skull or other remotely sent electronic barbarisms will be used on this ti, even during mental hospital commitment or imprisonment, yet are unlikely to be an immediate cause of death, for headstrong ti's are skillfully pushed beyond the psychological bounds of humanity as punishment. Due to non-compliance, the fellow (or gal) will be made to reel between suicide and murder for months, years, or forevermore.

If he is not imprisoned or committed, he will be disallowed from having employment, housing, shelter, money, assistance, companions, pets, and appropriate medical care. Stalking, slander, physical assaults, electronic attacks, poisoning, intentional accidents, and vandalism, along with concocted psychiatric and criminal charges, will ensure that the fellow cannot keep so much as a bag of peanuts in his possession.

When this victim knows he will probably die soon, he is likely to return to the earlier hoped-for ally and try again. After pleading one more time for relief, a refusal could produce suicidal helplessness. Don't forget, the ally received and saw zero harassment and feels reassured that the ti is having mental problems, or is an alcoholic or drug addict, for in the space of a year or two he has become homeless, jobless, streetwise, unhealthy, and is talking so outlandishly he sounds rabid.

If perps allow this ti to remain alive and wandering, he has no alternative but to subsist as a misunderstood dejected soul, all the while suffering unyielding attacks. He may panhandle and live out of garbage dumpsters while his loved ones at home shake their heads at how he could have made such a mess of his life. Somewhere between the turkey and pumpkin pie, poor Uncle Henry might be remembered as the raving relative who prefers now to live as a bum.

Let's change pace here and discuss the fate of people who are around sexual victims. Targets who are raped, secretly filmed naked, naked peeped, or watched all day for sexual reasons always impact others. This is a hard group to access as the repercussions to witnesses and rescuers are somber.

You, the reader, probably think I'm referring to young women. Mature women and a target's children and grandchildren can be sexually viable to stalkers, as well. Please keep these other vulnerable people in mind as we discuss OS sexual crimes.

Peeped and videoed victims, like raped victims, are rapidly forced to disconnect from their families while perpetrators coerce or intimidate loved ones out of the way. Raped and, oftentimes, videoed women and teens are pressed into threatened conditions that prevent interference. Peeped, videoed, and sometimes raped targets—because they are sexually entertaining the perpetrators—may be allowed to keep a sexual partner, perhaps a boyfriend or husband. This is confusing to would-be rescuers and is a temporary situation as the woman is unable to maintain a relationship.

We can all agree that trapped, or raped and trapped, targets are in a grim circumstance. Even should escape seem possible, they are often too drugged or afraid to save themselves. Overlooked are the videoed and peeped women who are not initially drugged, raped, or trapped. They are in greater peril than you might imagine. Spy cameras may have been installed in various rooms of the woman's house, and an indeterminable number of her stalkers could be masturbating while she's slipping her panties off. Add to that a sizeable group of viewers after the video has been sent as amusement to other perps in the vicinity.

Because so many assigned degenerates see the already trailed woman naked or having sex, she is going to be stalked by packs of men, and sexual harassment will evolve into sexual terrorism. This disbelieved woman fears she is slated for rape, kidnapping, or sexual slavery. It's just a matter of time.

From what I can tell, only selected victims are viewed naked from cameras that are hidden inside their homes. A small percentile of ladies, aged teen to mature, receive sexually explicit (personally detailed) calls from diverse men, signifying widespread sharing of certain photos and videos. It should petrify all of us that these targets' young daughters, sons, and grandkids are filmed also.

Hidden camera

Even ti's find it difficult to comprehend that an intruder would use a burglar's adapted key (called a bump key) to enter a locked home and then install hidden cameras for peeping and filming. Think about it. Miniature spy cameras are cheap, ready-to-order, simple to install, and scarcely detectable, and a voyeur-ogled woman is available. This is quite unlike watching Missy Feelgood on a porn flick. Some perp-voyeurs manage to install live-stream spy camera systems that allow ribbing their ti about the lacy bra they saw her put on minutes before, describing in roundabout language how she started out with the plain one and then changed her mind. I can't begin to tell you how insecure this woman will feel. Naked-spied victims are a sport. They are hunted, appraised, interacted with, and sometimes assaulted.

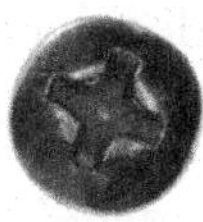

This is a normal screw head. Or is it? Screw heads that conceal a camera lens are easily bought. Here's an ad, copied with permission.

Phillips Screw Head Pinhole Camera Lens

ML-SCREW

Be the first to review this product

Indistinguishable from a conventional Phillips screw

OUR PRICE: **$19.95**

Women who are sexually watched outside of their homes are also much revered. They are enthusiastically critiqued, and they are incessantly followed by OS men who exhibit panic when they lose sight of their plaything.

Stalkers can become obsessed, and a fixated-upon woman who is not naked-peeped is still in serious danger, as are all sexually targeted women. They are, in effect, owned. Anyone who tries to assist, protect, free, or shelter a sexually pursued woman is going to get threatened or coerced.

Tragically, the destiny of a trapped, raped, videoed, peeped, or stalked woman or teen in this targeted group rather depends if anyone has paid attention to the victim's backslide into obscure living conditions. If somebody is uneasy about the woman's or teen's transformation or disappearance and makes inquiries, he will not understand that as a friend of the prized female his phone may already be tapped and his computer hacked. He is oblivious of the war zone he's about to enter.

Witnesses and rescuers of sexually useful targets (women, teens, and young children) can be suppressed by intimidation such as butchered pets; references to murder; and preplanned accidents from tampered brakes, steering, hood catches, brake lights, and tires. Tampered staircases and being *accidentally* tripped or pushed are other favourites. Preplanned accidents may be the most popular "we're warning you" exercises because alarm, injuries, or death are the only outcome. A rescuer and her baby daughter will be sent tumbling down a steep footpath or an escalator. Or bumped off a wharf. Deeds like these are performed as if people are litter. Ecstasy is openly exhibited and I, personally, find this very, very disturbing.

Stalwarts trying to liberate owned targeted ladies may find that toxic chemicals, which may or may not be found on drug store or hardware store shelves, are snuck into their foodstuffs and drinking water. Their undergarments, outer garments, shoes, cosmetics, and toilet paper may be dusted, smeared, and sprayed with chemicals or irritating substances.

For an immediate result, an electronic weapon discharged from afar will ensure that a possible rescuer will be dead in minutes, or incapacitated, from an apparent cardiac arrest.

Nonviolent schemes can be employed too. Aggressive brainwashing that the raped or otherwise sexually exploited victim does not want or need help is the typical nonviolent method to keep saviours away. Police officers who are working as OS outlaws always assert that a sexually threatened or sexually abused ti is delusional or lying to gain attention. If a perp-cop has done his job in convincing others that the woman has a mental disorder, she will likely say, write, or video a gloomy farewell and take off despite knowing the crime will follow her. This woman is certain that her future lies in being gang raped to death, and she would rather die alone than die where people are treating her as if she is deranged. Moreover, they are making it impossible for her to take the necessary steps to lessen the danger.

This kind of exchange is representative: "Honestly, Sue, if you can't walk by yourself from the parking lot to the restaurant, then I'm going to have to agree with that nice officer. He's really gone out of his way and has assured me that no one is after you. It's in your mind. If you're worried about the dark, take a flashlight."

"But, Mom, the cop lied. The men will follow me."

"Your brother's excited about his graduation dinner. Be there."

A targeted woman who has accidentally and repeatedly appealed to a perp-cop is apt to seriously contemplate, attempt, or commit suicide within four years of the cop's lies. She will have begged officers, counsellors, relatives, and legal advisors for help in ever-changing towns, finding that because the corrupt cop wrote "delusional" on her complaint files, he has given her a death sentence. Spurned by everyone despite unyielding violence, this woman has tried everything to set herself free and inevitably becomes too weak to defend herself. Unless she can find a rescuer, her situation is hopeless, and she knows it.

Complicating efforts to help this woman, she may develop an automatic fear or anxiety response around all men, including masculine voices on the phone. Thus, a genuinely concerned male, be he a neighbour or perceptive onlooker, may be rebuffed until the woman feels somewhat comfortable speaking to him or being around him. I suspect most continuously threatened ladies feel or exhibit an involuntary stress reaction towards unfamiliar men after years of the crime.

If you're a man trying to help a harassed, stalked female, please be uncomplaining of her possible slowness to accept your goodwill, for it's easy to misinterpret her outward behaviours. On the inside, she's afraid, she's tired, and she needs time to weigh a proffered encouraging turn of events. Now jaded, this woman may have been terrorized by dozens upon dozens of OS-hired men who, for sport, may have enlisted their bar buddies as well.

A terrorized woman may not even be able to talk to other ti's: male or female. It's not unusual for heavily harassed targets, especially women, to not want to speak a word to anyone, due to being socially restricted by PTSD symptoms or for fear of engaging with the enemy. Heavily harassed ti's become so accustomed to being treated badly that anyone who is nice to them, maybe a store clerk or old school chum, feels out of place. Prisoners of war experience this.

What you, as a non-ti, can't fathom is that a victim is in constant dread of her (or his) life getting worse. It happens regularly, just as it's supposed to, which is how a victim is driven to suicide. Targeted women, in particular, are by necessity very cautious.

Having said all that, a woman who is certain she is going to be raped or killed within the next few hours might accept help from a total stranger. I've done both: rejecting well-intentioned help and leaping on it the second it was offered. This is not an example of confused thinking. Targets with violence in their themes save their skins according to what's going on minute by minute. What seems like a good idea one day could be dangerous the next. Plus, there's the dilemma of sometimes being hampered by reflexive stifling nervousness from overlong extreme anxiety, in conjunction with being hampered from nightmare experiences and perhaps from PTSD. Taking no action for a week or two may be a well-thought-out decision. So might be quickly accepting help or bolting. Taking no action could also be symptomatic of fear-paralysis.

As a white knight (or knightess), deliberate again the risks to yourself and your family, and then, as you wish, ask for a second or third time, "What can I do to help you?" Any measure of assistance is significant, whether the offer is denied or not. Knowing there is someone who cares and believes is huge.

A target is a target, meaning a man can display the same intimidated responses as a threatened female, minus the factors of being cowed through the sexual vulnerabilities of rape, sexual slavery, human trafficking, and being swiftly over-powered.

Anyone, of either gender, who tries to save a threatened woman (or man), besides being enduring, has to be strong, not in muscle as you might think, but in grit. The delusional label will come up again and again, and a rescuer will be under concerted brainwashing to walk away, followed by fierce and harrowing intimidation to send him running.

The reasons why both violent and nonviolent methods are used against would-be rescuers are dependent upon several things. As we discussed, coercion will be used if it looks like a samaritan can be easily swayed. Certainly, though, if a helper is getting too close to the truth, attempts will be made to eliminate him, and that usually means hurried, intense fear tactics and injuries to himself and the target. Murder, disguised as an accident or a sudden health disorder, is possible.

A rescuer must never forget that organized stalking is a savvy crime and that his personality and his relationship with the victim influence how he will be treated, whether coercion, intimidation, or violence will work to get rid of him. A rescuer, to save himself, must recognize that he and everyone interacting with the target are studied. This is no fools' game. Perpetrators closely analyze a rescuer so that they can anticipate his next move to free the victim, whether he is pleading with police, offering the victim advice, safety-proofing her home, trying to get her into a women's shelter, or trying to move her into his own place. The rescuer will be stalked night and day, and his phone and computer will be hacked into at work as well as at home. He's going to have to be ingenious with every move he makes.

When it comes to helping an owned woman, or any target, the perps' personalities factor in. Some victims end up with perpetrators who far prefer to inflict hair-raising terror or agony on a target and a target's could-be saviours. Others—not so much. These less violent perps stay in the shadows. They may bankrupt a target's witness. Or utter death threats over the phone. Even though perpetrators have bosses and follow directions, it is apparent that the targets who are saddled with insatiably vicious stalkers have more impact on others.

Samaritans have a better chance of saving themselves and the target if they learn about organized stalking before they get involved. A few hours of watching YouTube videos, listening to radio broadcasts, researching, or reading is imperative. With me, you are learning the bare bones, and no doubt you will gain much from inquiring further. Recognizing OS's motives and tactics could permit a spot-on maneuver that could save a life, including one's own. A sloppy rescue, despite heroic intentions, has potential for going sideways. Organized stalkers kill.

Talking to the victim is vital so that a rescuer can hear what's really going on. When that's impossible or unwise, the rescuer had better double up on his homework and that could include talking to verifiable targets. Contacting OS-educated targets is a good idea anyhow.

Oh-oh. I've hit a nerve in almost every long-term ti. It's accepted decorum that non-targets should never educate themselves by direct communication with victims they don't know. This is because targets' ardent opinions will come out in a casual dialogue. Subjective, often unbending, interpretations about OS are molded by how the ti is victimized, along with his view of the world. Some of the interpretations are eccentric, but not necessarily wrong. A ti who is hounded by Satanic-type terrorism may believe Satan is running the show. Another ti will blame military scientists, a secret society, or a religious group.

The viewpoints of ti's you contact are not important right now. Your mission is to save a ti, perhaps her children, and yourself. A shaken ti who you are driving to a hotel might have no knowledge of brake and steering tampering, or the habit of perps burning rescuers' babies with energy weapons, and could be too distracted to warn you if she does. Veteran targets are well-versed on retribution whereas retribution is seldom discussed in books, documents, radio broadcasts, or online.

To find helpful victims, you could begin by checking out the sensible-sounding websites of target associations, and view their lists of recommended videos, research papers, info websites, books, and ti support groups. Where possible, contact the authors, video-makers, and groups' directors for advice. By doing so, you'll find that there are a number of sympathetic and supportive targeted professionals and other OS experts who, besides assisting folks, are speaking out in public. A few will have strong opinions you don't agree with, and that's perfectly all right. It's their knowledge and pluck that are important to you. Listen well and think for yourself.

You'll find a resource list in the appendix on page 465.

As you'd expect, perpetrators have posted a ton of disinformation, and panicking ti's have posted without forethought, so please don't choose an online name willy-nilly. Worth remembering is that a lot of heavily tortured and heavily harassed ti's have posttraumatic stress disorder, and if you catch someone in heightened disarray, despite his or her intellect, the conversation might not go well unless you are patient. It's possible that for the first few minutes you'll hear about pending blindness, Felix the cat's perp-shaved tail, and a glued-on gas cap.

What's more, considering the number of perps posing as targets, and considering that as a novice you don't know who's who, or how to tell the good guys from the bad guys, you'd better be smart about information gathering. A perp pretending to be a ti will get you and the ti you are rescuing into a lot of trouble no matter where he is stationed. Confiding in an imposter in the Florida Keys, U.S.A., when you live in Victoria, Canada, is the same as confiding in an imposter next door. The crime is called organized for a reason. That also means an expert in a foreign country will be as helpful to you as an expert close to home. Organized stalking's refined intelligence of pushing a victim into irremediable repression does not change over the globe. A cook in a Pacific Coast logging camp and a businessman in Paris can have the same crushing agenda. I'll say it again: please seek verifiable OS-educated targets for support.

Of course, their phones and computers are interloped, so use communication systems and language that won't lead back to you or your home. It can be done, but is a Russian roulette crusade when a potential advocate is unsure about whether or not OS is keeping tabs on him. A non-harassed person on the watch list has no privacy, yet will detect few, if any, indications.

When you do connect with an obliging ti, state your objective without delay. If you are hazy, you will be brushed-off. Targets can be bombarded with perps pretending to be this and that, so you need to be direct. The fact you are saving one of us will gain you favour. You will get all the help you ask for.

Worth repeating is that every victim receives different forms of harassment. Some ti's get a lot of mob stalking, others get mostly slander, and so on. A ti you contact may not have personally confronted the dilemma you are trying to solve but could still be proficient in the subject, and other subjects besides. Whatever you learn could come up later and save your life, even if you think your research was nonproductive.

Don't be deterred by your inevitable confusion over masses of conflicting information. All us targets are confused, and we are the wretches stuck in this nightmare.

Never lower your guard when you are rescuing a ti. Stalkers look and sound like you do. The discrepancy is that you are bent on saving the same person they are bent on tearing apart.

Notwithstanding what a perp's score is on the carnage meter, be he an extremely violent or less violent perp, sexually managed women, their videoed children, and all other targets are commodities in this crime, so anyone who gets in the way is dealt with by bold or subtle handling.

Leaving an OS life and death situation up to police is a personal decision. Most cops don't assist targets and their rescuers even when a child is threatened with murder as either retribution or intimidation. Pleas to either a good or a bad cop can leave one family member dead through a planned accident or an electronic weapon hit. Connecting with a cop who assists OS victims—who knows his way around stalking gangs—is exceptional, but I've seen it happen.

I'm going to take a moment to explain what it means to rescue a target because it doesn't always mean sneaking into a gated property and sleuthing away a trapped victim. Although it could. Rescuing someone runs a gamut. Believing a target or assisting him to find help is a rescue. So is giving a penniless ti a few dollars so he can split. (Targets will never outpace the crime, but some situations are safer than others.) Arranging respite housing may give a ti enough of a break that he will decide to live. Installing security devices and burgle-proof door and window locks on a home may prevent contents from being tainted and may prevent evidence from being stolen. Hiring a company to check for hidden cameras, radiation levels, and gas could save a life.

You could consider giving or sending a cell phone, prepaid phone cards, an escape bag of necessities, a video camera or voice recorder, anytime bus tickets, an address book of emergency shelters and food banks, a handbook on self-protection, a carbon monoxide detector, information about organized stalking and electronic harassment, organized stalking advocates' contact information, and even a small thoughtful gift—these are all forms of rescue.

I cannot speak for other parts of the world, but many Canadian crisis centres, or crisis lines, sell (or give away) pamphlets of local and national resource contact information for every possible emergency or dire circumstance. A ti and a ti's rescuer would benefit from owning such a pamphlet. Each call-in crisis centre has an office. Just call.

Don't offer an illegal weapon to a ti. A found-out weapon, even a legal one, is an opportunity to frame a target, and you don't want to be any part of that. Offer a camera. Stalkers hate being filmed and audio recorded. I am not saying that ti's shouldn't defend themselves. I am saying that cameras have advantages and are safer to give.

Don't offer booze or drugs to help a victim calm down unless you are going to be with him. If he gets into trouble or commits suicide because his resistance was down, you will feel accountable. In the beginning, booze and drugs are inevitably used by targets to ease the tension. If incessant over-analgizing is a victim's only release, he'll end up worse off. I recommend other stress reducers. Connecting with other ti's, researching the crime, and calming exercises won't stop OS, just as booze and drugs won't, but an informed clear mind is a ti's best armor.

When a runaway ti has nothing, truly nothing, having lost all freedoms and possessions, a small blessing is an absolute rescue. Should such a ti contact you, ask which post office you can send something to. Address it to the person, General Delivery, and the post office's address. Don't ask the ti to get you the postal address. Do it yourself. He may have PTSD. If he does, everything is hard. Keep in mind he'll need to show photo ID.

Don't take for granted that a moneyed ti doesn't need help. Fear, PTSD, threats, depression, radiation, and energy wounds can paralyze anyone.

Asking a ti what he needs can prevent suicide or imminent murder. Remember, using public communication systems is no guarantee of safety if you're unknowingly on the watch list, as when remote and on-your-heels monitoring are in effect, what should be confidential, isn't. Watched or not, it's best to withhold personal information and to begin a written or verbal conversation with "Don't say (or use) my name. I know you know why." Plan your questions ahead of time to avoid slip-ups.

Anonymously sent parcels may not stay anonymous, but they could be lifesaving. Any initiative that offers safety, information, legal assistance, love, food, or hope is a measure of rescue.

Please be cautious. If you are a close loved one, your phone and computer are probably interloped. If that's the case, there's an OS file on you.

Now, you are asking, "Why will a stranger smear caustic paste on the car's door handle the day after I take my sister in?" The answer is this. Targets are owned. Anyone helping a target evade his owners and anyone helping a target cope or stay safe are organized stalking's adversaries.

We're going to switch here to a pathetic group of casualties: a mixture of folks who crossed paths with a ti and have been chosen for consistent permanent harassment. These folks bear angst-riddled and disappointing lives.

Called lesser, secondary, or part-time targets, they do not get around-the-clock persecution. Exceptions are those who are being upgraded to full-target status and those selected for sexual service, whether it is rape, naked-videoing, peeping, or being sexually stalked outside the home.

Although secondary targets seem to be randomly picked from a ti's circle of contacts, if perps have collected information on someone, perhaps a relative or colleague they have already harassed, then that may be a deciding factor in singling him out, for they've come to know him quite well. Being chosen as a sexual victim also supersedes random picking. Everyone around a victim, however, is fair game in being pegged as a lesser ti, right down to the ninety-year-old a target gardens for.

A ti's paperboy might be fine for two years and get picked for ongoing hassles on the third. Or the ti's mechanic who is hit in the back by a weapon on first contact could be elected right then and there for lifelong drawbacks.

An experienced target will listen in dismay while her oblivious father, a lesser ti, rants about the latest mystery woman. This time the woman knew that he was out shopping for Howdy the parrot's favourite treat. Last time, in the hardware store, a woman reminded him to buy putty and to hurry up because his daughter was bringing over a homemade meat pie. The dad is more amazed than concerned. It's not like his stalkers blab an outright statement. They don't.

The stalkers' conversations sound like this: "My gosh, I don't know why I bothered. The cashiers here are snails. I didn't want to come out today, but my parrot was out of pistachios. Oh yes, Howdy always comes first. Spoiled brat." Or, "Don't you just love hardware stores? I could spend my paycheck in an hour, but I'm only here for putty. Do you have the time? My kid is bringing dinner over. A homemade meat pie. No one should be late for that."

As with all secondary ti's, the dad's phone and computer are encroached. Perps for miles around are recording everything, even catalogue orders. If the dad is a victim of mob stalking, several stalkers could hold a detailed conversation among themselves that he is sure to hear. Howdy, putty, and meat pie would be small pieces of an eerie discussion that includes the father's intimate affairs. Because the dad is a lesser ti, he's predetermined to live in a fuddled and oftentimes pessimistic state. Rehearsed conversations and actions that mimic him, his daughter, or another loved one will regularly occur, forever. Each time the senior leaves home, or answers the phone or the door, he's going to anticipate that something mind-boggling could happen. He might never link the dozens of mimickers to the vandalism. (A primary ti harassed this way, will.)

A different secondary ti, just as naïve, will spout off about workplace slander that portrayed him as a racist, his credit card being wrongly cancelled, child pornography a hacker snuck onto his website, what looked like vomit on his trunk lid, seared eyeballs, and a hard-to-fix bank error all in a month. Lesser ti's experience so many agitating cycles, they get worn down.

They also have unending landline and cell phone problems. If someone who knows a target begins getting excessive numbers of dropped calls, white noise, clicks, beeps, echoed voices, unusual calls, dead air, an inability to dial out, or a phone that won't ring, along with irregular and numerous computer breakdowns, in my view, this person is likely being harassed and could be a lesser target.

Sure, everyone has phone and computer problems, but not numerous times each month, every place, with every company, with every new device, especially phones, year after year. Too, phones, computers, or other personal devices that behave like someone is using them when no one is may signify a snoop.

Perp-caused electronic problems are often odd. They're supposed to be. Simple problems can be simply fixed which is why perps create enigmatic, complicated, or unsolvable snags through hacking and signal blocking. (Signal blocking, or jamming, is called a

The white box with the five antennas jams (blocks) cell phones and other electronics.

denial-of-service attack.) Breakages, adjustments, and interruptions in service are premeditated so that it will take part-time and full-time targets hours or days to remedy the problem and possibly a lot of dough. Some perps' contracts are geared to fouling up personal electronics for the purposes of wasting their victim's time and money, of creating a frustrating situation, of impeding communication, and as retribution. When these perps are not busy breaking, blocking, or re-formatting a phone's, computer's, or printer's functions, they are reviewing online and phone activity, then erasing and changing data. Yes, it's a real job. Perp-caused problems with service providers can often be resolved by filing a complaint with The Commissioner for Complaints for Telecommunications Services (CCTS).

Public phones, public computers, and borrowed devices can also be sabotaged by signal jamming, and by far-off directed energy, and perhaps by hacking, not that it matters how. My point is, if perps want you to have communication problems, you're going to have communication problems. Period.

Texting a friend, ordering take-out, sending flowers, online banking, emails, printing out directions to Sticky's Diner, and dialing 911 will be obstructed or altered.

Secondary targets persevere with the same recurrent, unsolvable document tampering that primary ti's get. Enrolling into university may take a disappointing three years' worth of mix-ups. Transcripts, programs, course grades, entrance exams, payment, transfers, dates, names, signatures, addresses, scholarships, prerequisites, wait lists, registration, student loans, housing, and acceptance will never be right. Plus, the documentation will be lost repeatedly.

Whenever the wannabe student thinks he's making headway and hands over what he was assured is all the right paperwork, he'll find out he was given all the wrong (meaning tampered) information, or find out his personal files have been changed, for the zillionth time. Infuriated, he tries to enter a different university, one that isn't inept, and encounters another series of brick walls. He will be told he's lax and should have invested more effort into getting things straight, in spite of being bright and methodical.

Computer and phone hackers are ruining his dreams. The fine fellow is not supposed to get ahead. He is not supposed to achieve his goals, make a decent wage, or be happy.

Obviously, more than university files are mucked with. Any important record can be used to drop a secondary (or primary) target to his knees while he tries to remedy one swindled form after another.

Deleting, altering, blocking, and adding to confidential facts, figures, and communication in hacked computers and tapped phones of homes, corporations, financial and educational institutions, associations, small businesses, and government departments make electronic interloping one of OS's most dictatorial tactics. Lola's online preschool schedule will be in the hands of perpetrators. So will a lesser or primary target's personnel chart at work. And his finances. You can see how critical this is. Being fired, evicted, and bankrupted are now in the enemies' hands. There is no stopping it, and each and every primary target and secondary target have horrendous errors to unscramble, constantly. A tremendous amount of money and a great number of opportunities are lost this way.

Loved ones, acquaintances, and witnesses may also suffer from document tampering and like lesser targets never understand it was OS caused. Rescuers can get the brunt of it. Pre-authorized payments to a known, unknown, or bogus company will be withdrawn with, apparently, the right approvals. A bank manager will tell you it isn't possible—that your account is secure—and I'm telling you, with proof in hand, that he's wrong. A perped withdrawal doesn't always mean OS took your money. It could mean they are playing with it, shuffling it around to confirm that you have no control over your finances. It could also be the first step to a sizable theft.

As a victim's and his significant others' account numbers, account histories, PINs, passwords, answers to security questions, and signatures are stashed into countless crooks' files—good luck is all I have to say. Taking accounts out of your own computer won't help. Not one bit.

Because perps are average appearing, they often get office jobs, so more than computer hacking is involved here. Coerced, paid, or threatened non-perps also falsify documents. One criminal office worker can financially or professionally level a lot of full- and part-time targets, rescuers, witnesses, and loved ones. As hard as victims try to sort out the mire, sometimes it is impossible.

As a long-term ti, I can tell you that data breaches and data erasures are a royal pain. But it doesn't end there when it comes to OS's habit of discarding stowed information. Directed-energy weapons, besides frying people, can also fry expensive electronics, along with anything else that uses electricity. Poof—there goes the laptop and smartphone with all your business dealings. Poof—there goes the house alarm, vehicle wiring, Nana's electric wheelchair, and the TV, all invisibly toasted from near or far. Constantly replacing and fixing everything is stressful and can put a ti into debt until, that is, he owns nothing.

The few ti's with an overriding theme that focuses on frying electronics cannot keep a new camera working for very long. They end up with a closetful of broken ones, hoping to find a model that can hold up to electronic harassment; for filming perp activities offers priceless evidence and protection. Read on. The lowlifes are pretty inventive.

Illegal signal-jamming gadgets, accurately aimed, are quite capable of preventing a perfectly good keyless remote from opening a car door whenever a perpetrator feels like it. It's a matter of blocking frequencies. This and other perp-made breakdowns occur at either an inopportune time or when there is a convenient stranger (usually a man) insisting on giving the stranded ti (usually a woman) a ride or other form of assistance.

Perpetrators can be sugary benevolent, and a secondary ti is never the wiser having given the lout gratitude for helping her when he caused the calamity in the first place. Through impromptu chitchat, the lesser ti will have provided the perp with additional info; and if he finds her attractive, a few photos will have been surreptitiously taken for the monster to fantasize over. This, regrettably, is real, real common.

This 7 1/2 inch (190mm) signal jammer is easily concealed and blocks many electronic devices.

Sexual stalkers will block (jam) a woman's car door remote and her cell phone.

If your car or garage-door remote and other electronics work fine shortly after a malfunction, without doing any repairs, and it happens to you more often than to anybody else, perhaps question if you or someone around you is a target.

As this chapter is committed to explaining OS's impact on the people in targets' lives, we're spending considerable time on what happens to folks who become secondary targets (also called lesser or part-time targets). Had they not associated with the principle ti, organized stalkers might not have noticed them.

Besides electronic invasions, lesser targets can be emotionally and financially devastated by relationship invasions. It is standard practice for a perp to attach himself (or herself) to a lesser ti, claiming love. As planned, the couple almost always ends up living together.

Perps do not behave characteristically for someone in love. A lesser ti can wake up with wounds after a night with her beloved, and in the beginning, she'll blame imagined mishaps. She may be sick a lot, likely from rape drugs and other chemicals. Or she might experience sudden weapons-caused problems with her heart, eyesight, hearing, lungs, bladder, stomach, and limbs, for starters, despite being in great health. Inexplicable immobilizing lethargy and severe headaches are also hallmarks of living with an OS contractor.

Perp-lovers may spend an awful lot of time and money away from home, usually because they have a double life on the go. They are employed to mistreat the lesser target and have no sentimental investment in the union. Displays of romance may fool the ti and her friends just some of the time, for there is a lack of sincerity. The relationship is a sham, riddled with gifts and promises, and is never good for the target even though a few good times are shared.

These OS degenerates set their patsies up for grief every which way they can. They may buy a pet and then make the target get rid of it. They may buy plane and concert tickets for a shared holiday in Las Vegas, Nevada, and then cancel it after two months' anticipation. They might go so far as to plan a wedding. A perp-lover may coerce his victim to move away from family, friends, and employment and then terminate the relationship before they've even unpacked.

Perp-lovers dissolve the courtship only after mangling a central part of the ti's life. Family and friend dissension, depleted finances, deferred education, a destroyed career, a long-distance move to an undesirable location, or poor health due to slow poisoning or electronic-weapons attacks are setbacks that the ti will have to rectify by herself. After causing a final heartbreaking or insurmountable hardship, the perp-lover will invent a lame excuse for leaving and then quietly and hastily slink away with little or no apology. His assignment is finished.

A different formatted relationship is when a lesser target's non-perp boyfriend, girlfriend, husband, wife, relative, or friend is coerced into becoming a perp. This person is getting lied to, or brainwashed, or paid. Maybe threatened. This doubly confuses the target. The rapport may have started out genuinely wonderful.

Though primary targets can find themselves with perpetrator lovers, relatives, and friends, it seems to predominantly occur with secondary ti's. This is undoubtedly because lesser ti's are ignorant about organized stalking and make excellent suckers. (Primary targets are more likely to have colleagues, classmates, business associates, and neighbours who are perps.)

I truly pity secondary targets. Bedraggled, they struggle hard through life. Because they will not acknowledge OS, the multitude firmly believe their prior indiscretions are being redressed. Some even say they deserve an inferior existence. It concerns me when these targets, who don't know they're targets, blame God, karma, the devil, poltergeists, a vengeful deceased person, a past life, or that they've been jinxed or cursed.

Steamrollered intermittently, what secondary targets endure borders on psychological and physical torture; for they spend half their time upset, doggedly righting wrongs, or they are unwell. Crises, anxiety, hopelessness, and health disorders run rampant in this group. They lead distracted lives in a constant battle to overcome some pretty big obstacles, year after year. With barriers to happiness occurring in concentrated spurts, they can forevermore be stuck on a teeter-totter of despair and relief. They may ponder suicide from time to time, morose about their futures.

We cannot skip a small subgroup of lesser ti's who every day or two, for months, receive slightly annoying OS trademark botherations, along with rare surges of physical or psychological torture. The full-time target who is linked to a lesser ti in this group will quickly recognize the symbolic signs and should weigh the pros and cons of ending the relationship. Keeping it going could add to the lesser ti's troubles, and ending it could result in withdrawing soon-needed support. This lesser ti may be on a step-by-step path to becoming a primary target.

Still and all, secondary ti's are not usually forced into homelessness or isolation, and they are not stalked and harassed around the clock in the same way primary targets are. Exceptions are sexual victims who get followed oftener, and the few part-timers who are increasingly bullied while being raised to full-time target status.

Lesser ti's don't get pommelled to death with weapons. Yet, electronic weapons and noxious substances are definitely used on these folks, and they initially blame unrecognizable ailments on whatever syndrome, "bug," or over-activity fits the symptoms. Customarily, these victims go through periods of tracing their own health histories, along with the health histories of blood relatives, trying to find out what's wrong with them as electronic-weapons-caused eyesight and heart anomalies, and various other internal and external enigmas, including radiation-caused illnesses, are not diagnosed by unenlightened doctors.

Poisons and sneaky drugging are rarely considered because, as a rule, secondary victims are not in the least suspicious in spite of questionable acute and chronic health conditions.

They are as off-guard as lambs being led to a merry butcher, unable to fathom that a partner, friend, or stranger would tamper with their food, never mind their phones, computers, and documents. The vast majority cannot accept the existence of electronic weapons and will not under any terms believe that outsiders could be gang-employed to condemn and conquer them. If they were tormented or tortured into the screaming meemies, they would think differently.

A knowledgeable target who tries to convince a lesser ti that he's a victim will likely be told to quit talking. Almost all of the time, secondary targets flatly refuse to believe in organized stalking and electronic harassment.

Part-time targets are surprised when they have a smooth two or three week period, harbouring trepidation over whatever trial is coming. They are vocal about their dilemma: "I'm just waiting for the next thing to go wrong. I'm afraid to make plans anymore. My last two vacations to the rodeo finals were spent in local hospitals." If they could accept that organized stalking exists, they could at least try to work around some of the traps.

There's something else about lesser ti's. They impact innocents in the same ways primary targets do, be it stalker harassment or electronic harassment.

I don't know why some people around targets are turned into secondary ti's. So let's go through the theories. Making someone miserable might be experimentation to see how far a person can decline, yet still function reasonably well. Or maybe secondary ti's are assigned to perps in training and need to be kept alive. I've also considered that they could be recreation, that maybe all targets are recreation.

A significant number of primary targets surmise that secondary targets are vital for OS to slowly gain dominance over huge populations and that primary ti's are a core group from which others are chosen. These ti's believe that a powerhouse cult or government is attempting to weaken and overthrow developed nations by accumulating more and more secondary targets. Surviving primary ti's like myself would, naturally, have to be threatened into silence, or forced to commit suicide, or killed, as we're protesting the crime from our soapboxes whereas secondary ti's don't even believe in its existence.

Knowing a ti does not mean you will be chosen for a lifelong sentence. It just means you can. Including bystanders, of the hundreds of people I've connected with since my targeting began early in 1998, nine for certain are secondary victims, thanks to me. Two of those, I believe, are presently being promoted to full target status. Furthermore, a third or so of everyone I've directly interacted with has been attacked: some for seconds, some for months. Many have been ignored. Living as a recluse now, I cannot account for the long-term fate of most of those who I have affected. The numbers I've presented could be much higher.

Off-shoot harassment and off-shoot energy-weapon strikes are somewhat dependent upon whether a ti falls into the heavily harassed category and if he has an isolation theme. A particularly hard hit ti, such as myself, will affect a lot more people than a secondary ti will.

Veteran targets promptly realize when others are under attack, even for a jiffy, and not riding normal ups and downs. Aside from developing a sixth sense about the crimes, targets learn to detect harassment patterns. It's more than uncanny when numerous people in the ti's life are limping and just as sketchy that every neighbour is asking, "Are you hearing things at night?" When several cars a ti parked beside that week get a flat tire, well, that's not coincidence either.

If a new ti doesn't eventually twig that by association he's hurting others, he is shrewdly told, such as a stalker-stranger using calculated words in an implicit conversation: "Hey, did you see the ambulances in front of Elda's Dry Cleaning last night?" If the ti still doesn't clue in that Aunt Elda has to stop dropping by, Elda could be lambasted until he does.

Ti's, once they master the rules, are made to feel responsible for someone else's life being trounced whether it is for a moment or a lifetime. This is one of the prevailing ways to keep isolated targets, isolated. And to keep potential helpers from being helpful.

Mercifully, most greenhorn ti's soon recognize torture and premeditated breakneck accidents aimed at loved ones or rescuers. Obvious weapons burns, attempted murder, agonizing or potentially lethal cruelty, and death threats cannot be mistaken as anything else. The target is often meant to witness the loved one's or rescuer's trauma, and if not, he'll certainly hear about it. He knows that to save these souls he must go but is unlikely at first to understand that the goal is to isolate him so that a slow suicide program or a slow murder program can begin.

It takes way longer to sort out acquaintances and side-shoot people who are experiencing health complications, breakages, and aberrations and tie them to the crime. This is not due to inattention or indifference. The crimes are unbelievable. They make no sense until long-term reoccurrences are established and extensive research is done. After all, acquaintances and bystanders are not pivotal in the victim's life. At the start, a target might think they are new victims in their own right, as I did.

Low-impact targets have perps who only occasionally harass others, so they are apt to socialize. High-impact targets, like me, have no intention of creating problems for others, yet we are seen mingling in the public because as reclusive as some of us become, we cannot avoid everyone.

In my world, answering the door to kids on a bottle drive is selfish. It's not that every person around me gets abused. But what if my controllers are in a bloodthirsty mood? Or needing to razz others to hasten my psychological demise? What if others are attacked as punishment to me because I pretended I was free for an hour? Ghastlier still, what if my controllers are scouting for primary or secondary targets? A person talking with me on any of those days could have his toes roasted by a remote beam right on the doorstep, or he could have a totally destroyed life.

Most ti's contacts are not attacked as viciously as some of mine are. It just happens that I am on a regime that uses preplanned lethal-type accidents, energy weapons, and excessive vandalism towards others and myself in order to sustain control over me and to fortify my isolation.

Besides the guilt of being alive, problematic for ti's in my situation is saying no to invitations, friendships, community involvement, family events, conversations, and company. Classroom education, belonging to an association, most jobs, and lending a hand cannot be considered for ti's in my OS program. With outsiders not recognizing the crime, high-impact ti's have to be okay with whatever ill will, cross reactions, or unwarranted judgements their aloofness creates.

My best friend from pre-targeting life just lost her son in a car accident. I called her though I knew it was wrong, and we cried together. She wants to be here with me, for she has tried hard to revive our friendship after finding me online, yet we must never see each other again. There is no way to explain that. Targets hurt people's feelings in order to save them, a sad state of affairs for all.

Let's streamline this chapter.

- Most high-impact targets limit their socializing and public interaction in an effort to protect others.
- Anyone near a target or interacting with a target can get harassed if he or she could be useful in a scheme.
- Initial harassment to others is done to control the target in some way.
- Initial harassment to others is often a single momentary strike, but in some cases progress into long-term terrorizing.
- Bystanders, acquaintances, friends, loved ones, witnesses, and rescuers who become lifelong part-time victims do not get around-the-clock harassment unless they are eventually upgraded to full-time target status.
- Infrequently, someone around a ti is chosen on the spot to be a secondary or primary target.
- Rescuers can be murdered.
- Some people interacting with a target will never get harassed.

Assisting a target is an exceptionally personal resolve and may be dependent upon factors such as whether the helper has children, which is why a potential supporter is a lot better off if he takes time to learn about the crime. To help or not to help may be the most serious decision a person ever makes.

Believing a target, without taking action, can be enough to deter suicide. When zero people believe in a ti's psychological and physical torture, he has an honest understanding that there are no prospects to being freed and is prone to give up. Realistically, he has every right to feel that way. One undermined person cannot repel a large organized gang of thugs and assassins. What a target requires is help in coping.

In places throughout the rest of this book, I will be mentioning people who have helped a victim, and who have refused to help a victim, and who simply know a victim, for in my opinion people close to targets are affected in one way or another, even if harassment is seemingly absent. Subsidiary exposure to energy weapons, being posted into OS's computer files, and emotional aftermath all may be invisible, but intercept a life.

CHAPTER SEVEN

JOURNAL
AND
ELECTRONIC HARASSMENT

There's something tapping the windows at night. At first, I was telling myself that big bugs were bouncing off. Then I convinced myself that holly-climbing raccoons were eating the bugs, their claws striking the panes. Last night, realistically, the tapping could not have been raccoons or bugs; so I'm sleeping on the couch as usual, but under a pole lamp. It's disappointing to need the light as I try to live normally and feel like a dope. As for sleeping on the couch, over half of the heavily harassed target population cannot, or do not, use a bed or a bedroom, for reasons of trauma, vulnerability, and poverty.

Checking outside for tapping men is a bad idea. If they think their strategies are working, they get motivated. I'll set up my night-shot camera instead, placing it in a barely open window for a few minutes, between houseplants where they can't see it. Videos of prowlers are only good for use down the road. Showing them to the cops, or to someone who cares, ensures that a week later terrorizing will commence until I'm demented. When the night terrorists caught me taking pictures last time, they scattered into the dark, returning with vengeance.

To be miserably candid, I'd rather not make the effort, not even on video, to see the morons crouched under the window like naughty boys, pane-pattering sticks in hand. It's essential for heavily harassed ti's to disregard as many fear tactics as possible. Night terrorism for me has been going on since early 1998. Collecting proof and engaging deterrence measures have become onerous.

Outdoor security you say? Are you suggesting mounting infrared cameras and spotlights on the house? Do you have any idea how long it takes my crew's signal jammers, lasers, pellet guns, wire cutters, and remote energy to knock out lights, cameras, and hardware? Click. (A few ti's can keep security equipment operating. I'm not one of them.)

Tapped phones and hacked computers, as you know, are worse than ineffectual to summon help, owing to the revenge factor. Yup, targets are whooped when it comes to self-protection.

Night terrorism used to put me in fear-based shock that would upend me for days after a particularly vicious attack. I spent years sleeping upright in front of the door. Now it just gives me the creeps.

In order to stay calm tonight when the tap tap tapping begins, I've decided to tell myself that voice to skull audio equipment is to blame, which it very well could be anyhow. In case this is the only chapter you plan to read, voice to skull technology is the process of electronically sending sound into a person's head and was originally invented to send words and music into a deaf person's noggin that only he can hear.

Because OS uses voice to skull contraptions, targets hear whatever perps want them to hear. On any night, a victim can listen to glass breaking, doors splintering, or voices and be terrified that men are busting in. Except, no men are there. They'll be watching the target's reaction from a safe distance. The noise was a recording sent from outside the house into the victim's noodle, by way of a far-reaching transmitting device. Predictably, new ti's get posttraumatic stress disorder from these antics, firmly believing they are about to die, not knowing enough about the crime to consider ruses.

On to other news. A delivery service is picking up and dropping off my mail now, which is a huge relief as errands are stressful. All the same, it drives me batty knowing the pleasant entrepreneur could be punished for our brief exchange. I try not to talk to her, making our twice monthly contact no more than ten minutes. Islanders are renowned for their warmth. She finds me rude. Going myself endangers the cab driver and the postal clerk, plus the stalkers are a nuisance. Asking someone else to make the trips for me isn't the answer either. It's hard to be alive.

With communications infiltrated, mail can be a target's lifeline. I say this with trepidation as the Canadian Security Intelligence Service (CSIS), United States' Homeland Security, and other countries' security agencies examine mail of citizens who are earmarked as interesting, be they whistleblowers, activists, business people, criminals, or folks who express rowdiness against the government. No, it won't be noticeable that someone's read your letter. X-ray spray makes the contents legible without opening the envelope and leaves no trace. Yes, you can buy X-ray spray online. It's about twenty bucks. The less magical techniques of rifling packets and parcels are revealed in books that fed-up CSIS employees have written. Intelligence officers are supposed to have a judge's permission to open mail, but they go ahead without it.

Along with letter snooping, there's innovative remote surveillance that invades a citizen's right to keep his affairs to himself. The spaghetti you slopped down your front is an abracadabra away from being filmed and recorded into national archives. If you think these discrete observation toys are exclusively used for military reasons, you are wrong.

When an OS target needs to communicate, his best bet is to write a coded note, in invisible ink, in a dark closet, and cast it out to sea in a bottle. Okay, so I'm being melodramatic. There are moments though when ti's are entirely defeated in finding privacy. Did you forget? Organized stalking extracts all freedoms and rights.

Postal service for me is more than a precarious safety net. It's my main connection with the world, for international research and pastime material is sent for free from a postal library service. As you'd expect, hackers add items with unsettling titles to my online orders, like *Enemy at the Door* and *Essential Killing*. They subtract what I want and write the librarians notes. Please don't tell me to change my library password. They see whatever I'm typing as I'm typing it. No, there's no way to get rid of perp-hackers. Their expertise and resources are beyond what most targets can contend with. So I send my book orders through Canada Post now, having explained that a hacker can't be stopped and that emails saying "I miss you!!!" or "Love is Dead!!!" are not from me. Perp-hackers overuse exclamation marks. Their enthusiasm for the job is boundless. Undoubtedly, OS is trying to have my inter-island library membership suspended, especially since the local library closed. Pleasure is not allowed, and Books By Mail gives me a daily diversion.

For the moment, I am going to elaborate on the pitfalls of everyday tasks using my own sundry chores as examples, though we superficially explored this in the last journal entry. It's an important part of OS to understand as victims are browbeaten by others who don't appreciate the predicament.

When it comes to perfectly mundane responsibilities, targets are as edgy as whipped dogs and may exhibit odd behaviour, crankiness, or resistance over endeavors like answering the door, putting out the trash, tending mail, or dashing out to buy aspirins. Mom's cross-town prime rib Sundays may require a Hollywood performance to get through. Those who ordinarily mask their fear, trauma, and grief may momentarily and uncharacteristically cry or erupt; or make a questionable alibi for a new self-saving behaviour; or hastily take off when faced with a standard but last-straw request, unable to keep up the façade a minute longer.

I was as nervous as the rest at first and, before becoming segregated, made lame excuses to wiggle my way out of tight spots, knowing that explanations were useless. Admittedly, I've learned to ignore much of the harassment. Although it took years. Refusing to sit in a restaurant window, which is where my elderly dad wanted to sit, is abnormal. Let's-have-a-nice-lunch does not include, "Dad, the gang who shot a BB at my windshield might drive by and shoot me." So, I didn't say anything. Instead, I acted like a selfish daughter who wouldn't let her aged dad enjoy a scenic view.

Thoroughly isolated now, awkward situations are scarce. Still, things have to be done, and as hard as I try to live like a regular person, it simply cannot be. Letters and library books—getting and sending them—is a substantial strain in my world.

As you might recall, unsolvable vehicle tampering means that now owning a car is a pipe dream. The three miles to the post office would be walkable if electronic weapons hadn't ruined my health or there wasn't the likelihood of a perp plowing into me. On these twisty woodland roads there would be no witnesses. Even if I could walk there, leaving for so long would give intruders time to get past my traps and steal the book's drafts. They're getting too heavy to carry very far.

With the phone tapped and the computer hacked, pre-arranging an outing gives stalkers time to organize group harassment. Giving the cab driver a note of the next pickup date can work except when he calls to re-arrange the time or forgets. Half the time he forgets.

When we manage a trip, leaving the heap of manuscript papers in the locked car or trunk is not an option. Neither is asking the cabbie to stay in the car with them as he insists on getting a doughnut at the store that shares the post office. With island theft being rare, people here don't understand my cautionary ways and are uncooperative, assuming I am insecure about the community's trustworthiness. I'm tired of others huffing and puffing at my insistence of lording over my belongings.

The cabbie, an otherwise good-natured fellow, is definitely at risk of being targeted. So is the postal clerk because everyone around me is an OS candidate in an effort to reinforce my isolation and suicidal ideation. Twice now, the taxi has been vandalized when we stepped away. The driver was more disappointed than angry, for he feels safe here. Those are the only times it's happened in his sixteen years on the island. Hiring the local errand lady to get my mail is the best option, but she has preschoolers. The responsibility of OS causing her and her family hardships rests on my shoulders. The postal clerk has children too, teenagers, meaning there is no possible way to avoid impacting a family should my handlers feel that doing so will further isolate me or if new prey is being sought. If you think I'm being overcautious, you are correct. Sort of. Reckoning after-effects on innocents is conventional for a target with an isolation theme.

A ti, even without an isolation theme, especially in the first years, may have from one to a squadron of stalkers waiting for her to get the mail, even if it's just to step out the door to her mail box. They will be in the apartment lobby, or outside the house, and will make certain she recognizes them as stalkers. If she needs to go to a postal outlet, it's conceivable that she is too traumatized, harassed, or ill from electronic harassment to walk or take public transit as, by this time, she may not be able to afford a car or keep one un-tampered long enough to use it. Targets who can keep cars running may elect not to drive when they are exceedingly frazzled or because of being strong-armed into accidents. Those with violence in their themes find that bicycles and motorcycles are deathtraps.

For the sake of a few, I must add that selected victims find that public transit and public transit waiting areas are where their stalkers intimidate en masse. A couple of my own bus rides ended with my legs buckling from fear as I exited.

And so it is that monkey wrenches are thrown into every basic pursuit including, of all things, trash removal. That's right. This morning was aggravating; it was garbage pickup day. Big deal you say—garbage day. For an average Canadian, my life couldn't be more defective. I am owned.

Nevertheless, a lime-green sticker has to be put on or in the trash container to prove prepayment for the service: no sticker—no pickup. My stickers, naturally, get stolen only to turn up days later crumpled and tossed in the driveway. Sticking the sticker on a sheet of paper inside the can and covering the paper with rocks and then covering the lid with rocks doesn't work. Neither does standing guard as businesses here run on island time, a lovely, relaxed way to live, but unhurried and inconsistent. Leaving a hidden camera running outside might catch the vandals if, that is, the camera was not remotely fried.

To me, retaliation over identifying mere sticker thieves would be counterproductive when a letter and prepayment to the garbage company might settle the matter. I cope better by letting some of the harassments slide. Conversely, the oppressed who have a bulldog never-back-down approach think nothing of investing sixteen-hour days into trying to catch their vandals. Thus, they live in a constant state of reprisal. These bulldog victims consider any complacency as defeat and are disgusted with themselves when they are too ill, scared, or fatigued to defend the fort.

I, on the other hand, consider complacency towards petty pestering as winning by not letting the enemy take all my time and all my mental might. Time and might are my last combative angles—my last reserves. I refuse to waste them.

Garbage day hiccups are not a major concern. In fact, talking about garbage and mail is boring. Still, because every transaction in a heavily harassed target's life is foiled, what looks like one small hiccup transgresses to an inability to draw any air at all.

Victims get worn down trying to maintain groceries, mail, garbage, laundry, banking, a phone, and a computer. Keeping a home and income so they can have these things to worry over is a titanic achievement for many. My situation is far from the worst. Actually, it's pretty good for a heavily harassed ti. Nonetheless, these renditions of mail and garbage glitches represent the treadmill of daily hassles.

So, what else? I might have radiation poisoning again. It seems to have snuck up. Radiation sickness has always been a part of my theme and has made me decrepit.

Diagnosing myself as radiated feels wrong even to me. But, as there are no local doctors who assist ti's, I've made a deduction based on symptoms, known energy weapons, other victims' input, and the fact that energy weapons burn, cut, and internally hurt me daily. I think I'm correct and would much appreciate a doctor who is educated about electronic harassment to give me his opinion. Radiation sickness, proven and unproven, makes many a ti's life hardly worth living.

On my first targeted day, and every day before that, I was riding horses and chopping wood and was strong, athletic, and in topnotch health. Since then, my stalked self has been too compromised to swing a saddle or an ax. I miss that lifestyle immensely, being a country girl to the core.

I was (probably) hit with energy weapons at the crime's onset. Each day revolved around whether I was vomiting nonstop or vomiting every hour or so. My hair fell out, my face swelled grotesquely, my head hurt, and my nervous system was so out of whack my body quivered like quaking aspen leaves. I was a textbook of radiation symptoms yet was too new a target to know what was going on.

Stalkers were approaching me to make comments. "You're sick," they'd cheerfully say. They intently studied my grossly swollen face and my vibrating body. Two showed apprehension—a faux pas. Empathy has no place in OS. One looked aghast when I collapsed while throwing hay to the animals. And an always-present blond perp looked ashamed at a medical clinic while he watched me tremble my way down a hall to the heart-testing room.

By the sixth month, stalkers pretending to be salesmen strutted up and down my walkway as ecstatic as lottery winners to see me crawling on the living room carpet, too weak to stand. I was grievously ill for years. Here I go eleven moves later on another round.

With the first (unconfirmed) energy poisoning, I believe night stalkers were streaming a form of harmful energy through an outside wall. My partner had the same symptoms until I abandoned the bedroom. Night terrorists have gear that detects what room someone is in, and I've no doubt now that the shrub rustling and wall scraping was them setting up an energy weapon and then retrieving it during their unvarying 4:30 a.m. departure.

At the house I live in today, atop a knoll, it is implausible that the stalkers' radiation weapons could reach the second-story couch I sleep on. The energy is likely coming from afar, making it indefensible. Long-reaching transmitters are what retired ti military experts are declaring. I am, after all, remotely stalked as well as gang stalked.

HAARP antennas in Alaska can potentially send disruptive energy to widespread populations, but not to a lone person.

Man-made energy from space can be beamed to earth by satellite and by bouncing a beam off the ionosphere. (The ionosphere is a layer of atmosphere about thirty-five miles from earth. HAARP is an ionospheric project.) From-space energy occurs when an antenna on earth sends its intentions (in waves) to connect with the ionosphere or a satellite, and waves are shot back to a predetermined area. Energy going up and down in space is integral in the present world. My phone is called a satellite phone. Some targets believe satellite adaptations can direct harmful radiation to one person. Yet satellites as they are known to the pubic cannot do so.

A proven approach to radiate someone from a respectable distance, and also nearby, is to use on-ground equipment that is pointed in the target's direction. Never, never, never forget that OS workers are immune to how many people they hurt while converging on their mark.

On-ground units as big as a truck and as little as a radio emit a slew of harmful energies. What is used depends on what kind of injury is desired. The fact my home is in an uninhabited area, meaning neighbours and passersby aren't to blame, I believe my current radiation is beamed from far afield, perhaps with satellite assistance, straight to me. Night stalkers, as I said, can't radiate where I sleep, so high up. Anyhow, if the room were radiated, my lovebird would be sick or dead.

Former military surveillance-development personnel and weapons-development personnel are warning the public about the deadly technology they were involved in refining. One covert weapon is said to send damaging microwaves to a human, or a lot of humans, or even to huge agricultural tracts. Microwave beams that are sent with criminal intentions can weaken, damage, or annihilate living matter.

As you learned in the last chapter, the perpetrators who use remote energy weapons can instantly single out anyone who has been installed into their programs. Remote stalkers can in due course single out anyone at all. That's right, I mean you.

If you have ever located a geographic site on a computer, say your ex-wife's new mansion, then you've already completed Nosiness From Space 101. If you haven't, it's just a matter of having place-finding software (Google Earth) on a computer and typing in 123 Pine Rd., Hickville, or some other spot. The street and house will be shown and can be magnified. The picture won't be live-stream.

Remote stalkers, however, use furtive live-stream equipment that can find people as well as locations. Jane Jones, a ti's best friend, can have her OS code typed in and be immediately seen, presumably on a screen, whether she's picking apples or running a marathon. When it comes to full-time OS targets, the monitors are never shut off. Targets are thought to be surveilled perpetually by multiple armchair stalkers.

Let's assume your computer is like OS's purported computers and has software that is linked to gussied-up remote spy ware. Now type in your address or OS code. You might be XY9. Or, ABCD. Guess what. Instead of seeing your roof on the monitor, you can see through it. You'll be looking at yourself. Off to the left you can see the swallows' nest in the garage. Broaden the screen's image and, my gosh, the neighbours's kids are having a food fight.

Along with using your hypothetical super-duper computer to spy, you can use it to send remote hazardous energy beams to whatever you select.

Now, pretend you are an OS employee who is spying by satellite (humour me), or other ware, on a Newfoundland, Canada, grandpa. Your focus will be on a grandbaby the senior is cradling, for today's assignment is to send a beam that will toast the top of the infant's head.

As an OS sadist, you will smugly watch the grandpa on your screen while he's inside a doctor's office with the screaming child. Your remote telescopic cameras are so powerful that when the pair are back home you can see a pinkish blotch on the baby's head where a directed beam heated him. You can see Grandpa's fidgety fingers drumming his coffee cup.

Other workers at the monitors are ruthless and want to finish the baby off. But that instruction wasn't given. This particular job is psychological and physical torture. Not murder. The next week, OS bosses command you to toast the grandpa's head, and you are happy to comply, sending a beam into his skull while he's eating dinner with his family. It amuses you that the old fellow was rushed to the hospital believing he'd had a stroke. And it frustrates you, for you want your work to be recognized. You need him to catch on that he is watched and played like a puppet in his own home.

The old fellow did nothing wrong, and you know that. He got chosen at a political meeting, being outspoken for all that is right. Injuring the baby was an effective way to devastate the man as he cherishes the child with all his heart. His retriever is scheduled to be next: poisoning by on-heels stalkers.

As a hired torturer, your task is to watch the grandpa on your computer screen and record his stress. The plan is to see if he can be pushed to kill himself.

Analyzing his reactions to the crime and to life in general, second by second, will dictate his demise. His vulnerabilities will be targeted. That's why you burned the baby. And that's why you'll continue to burn the baby. That's why the dog will die. Replacing all loves with despair is your most useful tactic. On-heels stalkers are important. But many suicides would not occur without the high-tech intrusions into subjects' homes, minds, and bodies.

Let's get back to you being you and talk about seeing through walls. It's a topic that makes ti's and non-ti's cringe alike. The hand-held devices some night stalkers and perp apartment-neighbours use have a screen that displays where in a home their sleeping, hiding, or moving quarry is, including kids and pet. Such a detection device allows for goofproof radiating and terrorizing. Anyone with a big piggy bank can buy a good (radar) through-wall detector. A little piggy bank will soon get you one that's low-grade. They run on standard batteries, usually AA.

Nonetheless, what we're talking about here are the space (from-space or through-space) stalkers. They use what is thought to be military remote see-through-wall technology. What everyone asks is, "Can these far-off stalkers see me naked?" You're not going to like the answer. Whether remote surveillance is done by satellite or something else, the people operating the equipment can inspect your genitals. If pain is on your day's agenda, these same people will send invisible burning energy to your genitals, besides.

As soon as female victims realize their most intimate moments are viewed, they change their behaviours. At first, they might dress, bathe, and bathroom in the dark whenever possible. Grooming, vomiting, scratching, crying, binging, menstruating, and idiosyncrasies are suddenly excruciatingly embarrassing even when no one is around. Looking vulgar, vain, or silly to the remote stalkers is a genuine concern. Women who have just discovered they're being remotely watched tend to curtail matters of sex, sexy undergarments, personal hygiene, and personal medical needs. Being erotic and exotic and being attentive to their bottom half are off the menu, for now. In time they will adjust, a little bit.

Self-conscious women find it difficult to shop for certain personal items, and with good reason. Remote stalkers, along with on-heels stalkers, will use a sensitive, emotional, or intimate purchase to tailor-make vile harassment.

Men, of course, are terribly affected by their remote stalkers. But as for being viewed naked or having sex, or doing anything else that's personal, it seems to be a mortification that is discussed man-to-man or not at all. A male ti has never brought up the topic of intimate viewing with me. Females, though, mention lights-out bathing and other personal remote-surveillance worries constantly.

Having someone remotely stare at you around the clock produces a sense of being vulnerable. And owned. Having someone remotely hurt you with energy produces the same feelings. There's no getting away and no forgetting who's in charge.

The Newfoundland grandpa, once he clued in, would be reminded of his remote watchers every time his head was struck. He would be aware at all times that his controllers were staring at him and choosing where to strike, when to strike, and what to strike with.

If an energy-strike pattern evolved and Grandpa's head was penetrated with pain whenever he was with his family, this is hypothetically what happened. (1) He stopped attending family gatherings. (2) His explanations of energy harassment were disbelieved. (3) He felt upset and disappointed with his family. (4) His family slowly withdrew. (5) He died from energy harassment, brokenhearted.

I know you understand that remote surveillance is possible, as on a less intrusive scale it's already being done by militaries and intelligence agencies. What you don't know is how seriously it impedes a life, so we'll be talking about this again.

Each type of energy, whether it's sent from afar or the guy beside you at the news stand, is discharged with the same ghoulish intent. Yet, the classes of energy feel poles apart on impact. I suppose the best comparisons would be the variations of being popped in boiling water, oven-cooked, electrically shocked, sunburned, branded, impaled with a red-hot poker, squished, punched, baseball batted, stung by bees, pricked by needles, deeply scratched, or singed by flying embers or machinery sparks.

Other strikes cause or simulate a broken bone or two, a stroke, and heart or other organ failure. Eyeballs and skin can feel as if they are on fire or that acid is eating through. Muscles hit by God only knows what kind of beam can go into spasms that would make Hercules cry. When respiratory tracts are struck, targets suffocate. There's also a sudden or gradual sensation of losing consciousness, described as if from blood loss, brain trauma, asphyxiation, or exhaustion.

Deep baking, which may or may not char skin, can debilitate a person for a week or more due to unbearable pain. The breast or other area may stay so hot that the victim will feel nauseous and faint. After two or three days the ti usually goes into shock. When that happens, I suspect that the beamed area may be under continuous remote assault. I mention breast-baking because it is done excessively. Head, feet, legs, hands, and genitalia are runners-up for roasted anatomy.

Whole body radiation, such as what I might be experiencing, feels like poisoning and not at all like the flu, though some of the symptoms sound similar, except for the hair loss and an out-of-whack nervous system. Remote energy also causes unsolvable itchiness and rashes. Beamed razor-looking cuts to feet, upper thighs, bottom, and genitalia may be a ti's primary via-space (page 84) electronic harassment for months. Usually less than an inch, these cuts are incapacitating. Walking, sitting, bathrooming, and wearing undergarments or fitted clothes may be unmanageable.

Harsh remote and close-up energy assaults to the brain cause extreme pain or stupor and are mind-body life-force draining. Beams directed to impair digestion and bowels, from near and far, are so commonplace I almost didn't list them, forgetting that not everyone has to live like this. All ti's suffer bathroom, or wish there was a bathroom, episodes that involve projectile vomiting, prolonged retching, cramping, diarrhea, incontinence, and intense abdominal pain. Onset is rapid and often follows a victim's attempt to find help. An attack on a target who insulted or caught a predator will be quick as well. Ditto for a ti who has found a moment of happiness.

Loved ones, secondary targets, and acquaintances often suffer remote stomach strikes when they are with a ti, which forces the person to go home or to the hospital. What's more, it happens to people who have made plans with the victim and always results in cancelling their get-together. Rescuers can count on recurrent stomach aches and bathroom bouts. The pain can be staggering.

Targets who cannot ascertain remote energy harassment often think their food is being poisoned. Food poisoning does occur, particularly in beverages, but perhaps not nearly as often as some victims believe. A victim who finds himself in pain and running for a bathroom every time he eats or drinks outside of his home may believe that stalkers are one step ahead, sprinkling toxic chemicals. When he gets sick at Uncle Jeb's feast, he'll decide which family member is a perp. The next day he'll drink pop right in the store, still get sick, and make a cockamamie excuse for how the poison got in the bottle.

Victims who are slow to catch on to remote energy strikes end up offending relatives, friends, store clerks, restaurant workers, colleagues, and passersby. Rationality dictates that people, not long-distance energy, are at fault. These ti's know that their health anomalies are caused by the crime. They've got that right. They've simply misinterpreted the source.

Having said all that, perps have been caught red-handed poisoning their prey. Some get their noses broken and some get jail time. I recommend that all ti's be cautious of what they stick in their mouths. A ti living with a perp shouldn't eat anything at home that he didn't carry in and watch.

Despite knowing that food tainting happens, for those who think they are poisoned every time they go out, they might want to consider that an unavoidable beam is responsible.

Targets who refuse to accept that remote stalkers are in control end up as psychological messes. If they could do a bit of reading, they'd understand that far-reaching man-made energy is in effect not just on them, but on all manner of things.

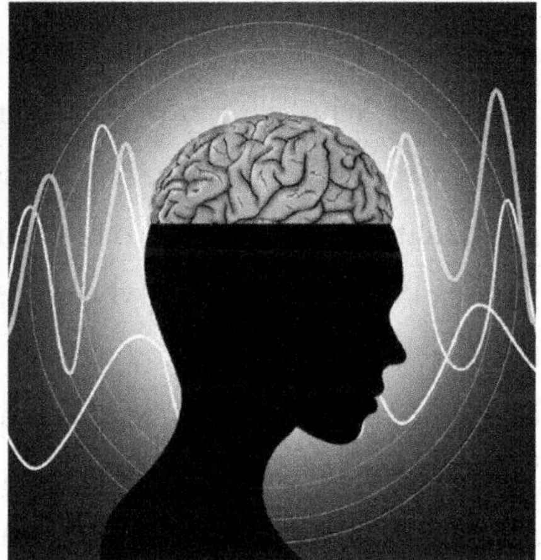

Transfer of energy with an electrical object and transfer of energy with an electrical person

I suppose the discerning factor here is plausibility. It's unlikely that every cafe has a perp behind the counter with a vial of thallium in his apron or a deadly nightshade berry in his sock. It's just as dubious that every peach a ti buys was perp-sprayed with toxic chemicals seconds or minutes before. Persistent gastrointestinal strikes occur because the remote stalkers know what will cause the most anguish and when.

Once a ti catches on, he can usually distinguish between energy harassment, food tainting, and normal illness. Energy beams that attack digestion, as mentioned earlier, can be obviously retaliatory or obviously sent to ruin a joyful moment or occasion. They are also sent to augment a downward spiral. In all cases they can be split-second spontaneous.

A beamed stomach ache often has different qualities than the usual maladies, aside from the sudden "punched in the gut" symptom that some ti's convey. The telltale sign can be the person's perplexity. He wonders what brought this on. And so fast. Other than pain or a disorder where the energy struck, which could be critical, he feels fine.

In public places, unforeseen incontinence or projectile vomiting, or discomfort or piercing pain in a bottom or belly, or a blocked airway causes some remote-beam disbelievers to assume that a mini energy weapon is close by. Indeed, there could be handhelds with all these capabilities. It's an impossible accusation to substantiate. The bad guys are closed-mouthed about their unorthodox contrivances. Notwithstanding ignorance about some of the handhelds, nonstop energy harassment comes from afar.

One ti I know refuses to consider remote electronic harassment. She grabs strangers' phones, cameras, packsacks, parcels, and purses when a beam hits her gut, positive that the nearest person has a disguised weapon. She is constantly talking her way out of arrests. I understand why B has gotten aggressive as stomach zaps render her so nauseous, cramped-up, or incontinent that she has to line up rest spots and bathrooms before she goes out.

Stalkers do carry disguised offence and defence weapons. There are scads for sale online. They make their own. But not every phone, pocket, or shopping bag is one. If my friend carries on refusing to believe in remote harassment, she's going to end up in jail or committed to a psych ward. Furthermore, when remote stalkers are getting a kick out of their target's reaction from a particular assault, they will repeat it until the person is half-dead or half-mad.

Loved ones, acquaintances, secondary ti's, and rescuers are unlikely to recognize a beamed energy attack. This is because they have no history of them to draw on, or disbelieve in organized stalking and electronic harassment, or they are not aware of mobile and long-reaching electronic weapons. Most every ti can recount loved ones' hurried trips home or to Emergency because of inexplicable agony in his or her stomach, bowel, brain, or heart, or because of difficulty breathing. Ti's with high impact see this all the time.

Energy strikes feel like energy strikes. They cannot be mistaken for anything else once the target knows what's happening to him. The most common complaints, other than cooked body parts and ailments that affect a brain, stomach and bowel, are feelings of being baseball batted, skewered, and of each leg being squeezed in a vice. Yet the pain is somewhat different from bashes, spearing, and squashing and typically leaves no abrasions. There are exceptions. From time to time, and don't ask me why, skin patches look (and feel) as if they've been sunburned, set on fire, chemically burned, badly bruised, grated, or sliced. Most heavily harassed targets get remotely pelted day after day; however, for many, the injuries are usually internal and invisible.

Damage to clothing is limited to small smooth-edged holes, and I suspect holes made in fabric or any other material is done on purpose, just as it is to flesh. A person's new jeans can be covered in little holes and his skin may be untouched. Most victims do not find energy-made holes in their clothes, and those who do say that like the rest of the harassment types, clothes-holing is done in phases or as punishment. They're absolutely correct.

As I type this, my clothes are unscathed even though my right side and back have been getting stabbed, compressed, and clobbered by energy for hours, and my hair is unscathed even though my left ear is getting what feels like a pencil shoved into it. A few minutes ago, the area above my left knee was struck. You'll have to take my word for it. There's absolutely no trace of harm. What I can show you is the result of last night's attack: deep three-inch bloody cuts on my shoulders. To be blunt, I've been carved like a ham.

Because I am alone most of the time, obvious torture is more prevalent on me than on non-isolated ti's. Telescopic lancing energy weapons were designed for militaries and can cut someone in half. Ongoing attacks, such as what I am experiencing, are routine for heavily harassed targets. Unless they've been disabled or are dying, they don't bother to bring it up, not even with other ti's.

Very nearly every victim experiences sleeplessness from remote weapons. I'm not implying that weapons' strikes sometimes keep targets awake. I am declaring that imposed sleeplessness is a fundamental ploy in organized stalking to create weak people. Some ti's get phobic about sleeping, allowed only fitful catnaps. Such a reaction is reasonable.

Remote beams can wake up a ti at predetermined times. Last year for me it was every fifteen minutes. For the last few months it has been at 12:18 a.m., 1:00 a.m., and three times between 2:00 a.m. and 5:00 a.m. This isn't bad at all compared to what many targets put up with. Nighttime wake-up energy hits are often strikes to the brain which are always a bit startling. Targets do not get blasé about brain hits. They get used to them—but head strikes are always unsettling.

Have you ever opened your eyes at 3:00 a.m. because you felt something was there? Only to find little Janice or Queenie the spaniel inches from your face, silent as the curtains? For a second your thoughts are jangled. You are surprised. This is the closest I can come to explaining what an energy-caused inner-mind wake-up is like when it's painless. You've heard nothing, yet you know that someone has entered your thinking space.

A target waking up like this has the enemy in his head. An armchair hit man is sending a beam through his captive's skull as if he were shining a flashlight through tissue paper. There is no dismissing this night intruder. It's not like shooing little Janice or Queenie back to bed.

Remote energy wake-ups are easily distinguished from waking up normally. First, targets are made to know that the enemy is in charge, which is why wake-ups can occur at the same time every night, be it by a subtle, startling, irksome, painful, or voice to skull (v2k) emission. Second, the sensation of having your body or head infiltrated by a destructive beam feels somewhat alien, in a familiar kind of way. Like vanilla ice cream that's been spritzed with pickle juice. The peculiarity of energy infusion, actually, is the giveaway, for the person begins questioning what is going on, for even when he's experienced insomnia and physical ailments, they were never like this.

Classical waking methods, aside from subtle mind strikes, emulate the sensation of being electrically shocked or pricked with a pin, often on the limbs. The keep-awake antagonisms are more creative. One is an energy type that causes intense itching. I'm talking about needing to scratch until you bleed. Then there's the travelling beam which gives the impression that a bug or a mouse is in bed with you. Or a whole family of them. This can result in undressing and taking apart your bedding every few minutes looking for nonexistent critters.

If the perps want to veto any chance of you dozing off, the remote energy weapons are programmed to cause unremitting and unsolvable harassments and tortures of which some are muscle spasms, body-part cooking, baseball batting, brain squishing, brain skewering, electric shocks, itching, crawly things, or raking of genitalia or anus.

Nighttime genitalia strikes are a chronic problem for many targets and frequently for loved ones. Age and gender are not factors. An eight-year-old, eighteen-year-old, or eighty-year-old of either sex can have a meticulously focused remote beam sexually manhandle him or burn or cut his genitalia.

On some nights, the impression of encircling compression waves causes a ti's brain to feel as if it's getting constricted into a small ball. On other nights a brain can feel as if it is getting flattened or bored straight through by a rod. The same kind of pressure wave is in my ear right now. A friend has it on her eyes. I'm telling you, pressure beams are brutal. There is no stopping them. They lock on.

Brain squishing and brain skewering are usually wee-hours capers. When a victim will display agony, the torture is reserved for when he is alone or when he is around people who won't believe that his predicament is an emergency. A rigorous brain blitz is iffy. If the victim survives, he will be disabled for an indeterminate period. Walking and talking can be lost for a while. Vision, the other senses, and clear thinking may be impaired, too, for minutes, hours, days, or forever. One fellow compares his wee-hours assaults to broken glass swirling around inside his skull. It is so painful, he says, that he wishes it would hurry up and kill him.

An acute night strike to the brain or genitalia can generate a primal fear response. If the pain or trauma threshold is exceeded, the ti may feel he is losing his mind. No matter how well he weathers the attack, for the next few weeks he will likely choose to sleep for as little as possible, and sometimes not at all, hoping to avoid another session, for highly specific night-only strikes often occur in batches. It's one thing to be awake when your brain and genitalia are hit. It's quite another to be sacrificed when sleeping.

Voice to skull (v2k) sounds that are discharged to jar someone awake is, well, jarring. Used excessively at night on skittish ti's, it can sound like there's a clumsy burglar rifling the cupboards. A ti who's not skittish could wake up to the reverberating banging of a hammer on sheet metal.

When a victim is scheduled to be sleepless or harried for days, weeks, or years without pause, it will occur. There is no avoiding day-and-night tracking and harassing beams that emit the most effective spine-chilling or keep-awake energy for that victim. If a ti is terrified of insects, he's going to feel insect-simulating energy scuttling up his chest every time he nods off. If he is terrified of hearing doors banging in his locked home, he's going to hear them via v2k every time he thinks he's safe.

Last year, for me, nighttime v2k was occasionally employed to emit ferocious growling, seeing as I live in the wilds. It was a daffy attempt to scare me and failed its mission as I had become insensitive to animal sounds after I figured out that crows couldn't be living upstairs. So the v2k'ed bears were replaced with machinery noise that wakes me up only once a month. Voice to skull equipment can download sounds and emit them into their target's noodle. Any sounds. Any time. Anywhere.

Many targets are awoken to v2k'ed whispers, which isn't really a big deal compared to bomb blasts. Last night the whispers woke me to a chorus of, "We're all here." They weren't. I think they are in the United States. I have requested that whale songs replace whatever v2k they've planned next, so we'll see what happens. My sarcastic appeals never go well, but sometimes playing dead gets monotonous.

You can build a v2k transmitter if you are intelligent. The workbench variety, as far as I know, has a short range.

A few ti's swear that their stalkers have pack-around models. Other ti's say ground-based computerized v2k systems are in their vicinity. I envision a more prolific long-distance system, likely through (or from) space, with portable and workbench units for the stalkers' amusement. Hundreds of thousands of folks worldwide hear v2k regularly. It might be millions.

Please note again that in the confines of this book, long-distance (remote) energy is depicted in the following two ways. (1) Energy travelling "through space" means energy travelling over land and sea. (2) Energy travelling "from space" means energy travelling from satellites. As it has not been proven where all the electronic harassment comes from, it is prudent to mention both "through" and "from" space as sources. Overall, energy in "space" is defined here as energy moving in an expansive range. Not that it matters to a victim when v2k is destroying the last vestiges of his life.

I once heard a rabbit screaming as a raccoon was killing it. Now, that's a sound I wouldn't want to hear over and over. Neither would I want to re-hear a child sobbing after a much-loved pet had died. If v2k sent either of these sounds, rabbit or child, into my head, I would not be pondering the "through" or "from" space question. I'd just want it to stop. Yet finding the source of the v2k could mean just that: stopping it.

Unfortunately, though, as you well know by now, the remote equipment that is sending words into a lone fisherman's cranium has not been verified. Targets know technology exists that transmits v2k great distances, but they cannot name what method OS is using. This is why I cannot say how a fisherman hears, "Put me back," whenever he reels in his dinner.

The tabletop v2k models that were intended for deaf folks are well defined. So are the directed sound systems that galleries employ. Any of these devices could be responsible when a ti hears annoying v2k-type noise nowhere but at home or at work. This is a problem for those whose day-to-day perpetrators broadcast their own recognizable voices via v2k to make threats and personal insults.

People, like me, who live alone in the boonies are definitely hearing remotely sent v2k. I'm wagering that most v2k comes from afar whether someone lives in a sailboat, a penthouse, or a vehicle.

Because targets can't get their hands on the far-flung voice to skull weapon, they have constant scraps over its source. M thinks she's proven it's this and P thinks he's proven it's that. One thing ti's agree on is that organized stalking's classified technology of latching on to one skull and then stalking it around the globe for eternity cannot be reproduced in Ralph's Repair Shop.

I only hear daytime v2k a time or two a week, although in the beginning it was more often, not with voices, but with birds, explosions, and footsteps. Nighttime v2k is frightfully common for targeted women who live alone, and for targeted women who have unbelieving housemates, and for female rescuers. Also, brand-new victims. In all these instances, unless v2k is being used as torture, it is generally transitory, as in the sound of a doorknob being rattled or of heavy furniture being dragged along the floor. Sometimes v2k'ed conversations are sent to someone who will mistakenly believe that two stalkers are talking right inside the home or are talking outside a door or window.

My v2k is in tune with remote surveillance as is all ti's v2k. After I put the groceries away, it can sound like a dozen cans have tumbled out of the cupboard and are rolling across the floor. It's one of those rackets you can't mistake for anything else.

I can't think of a better way to make someone look crazy than to use voice to skull and other invisible forms of electronic harassment. Crazy-labelled people have no say. This allows for ongoing crimes until an inevitable suicide or murder.

In understanding the potency of OS's unconventional armaments, you must accept that your brain is an electrical organ. Your entire body is electrical. Therefore, it's unarguable know-how that a brain and body can be abysmally impacted by man-made energy designed to do them harm.

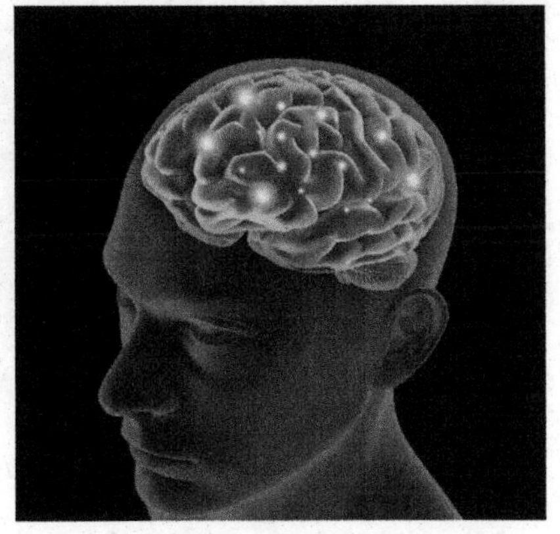

Electrical impulses in a brain

Any old energy transaction can be misused, but electronically tinkering with the brain's natural impulses, the ones that operate visual, respiratory, hearing, nervous, and heart systems, is serious stuff. Targets suffer from left-field maladies.

The consequences of electronic harassment (known as EH) on hearing, eyesight, brains, and bodies are the same in spite of the energy's category or intention; psychological shake-ups, modified behaviour, injuries, pain, physical weakening, mutilation, and incapacitation always occur, followed by a disability, a slowly imposed death (murder), isolation, abject poverty, suicide, or rapid murder.

As many targets blame microwaves for their injuries, we'll take a look at microwaves next, beginning with the mobile weapons that emit them, granting that other energy forms disbursed at targets are also sent with little ado. (Microwave harassment will be cited in following chapters.)

Picture a microwave oven. Mentally remove the door, fiddle around with its components, and plug it in directly behind a partition or wall so that it's out of your target's sight. That's one weapon. If one or more are in continual use, illness is likely. At close proximity, over time, death might occur.

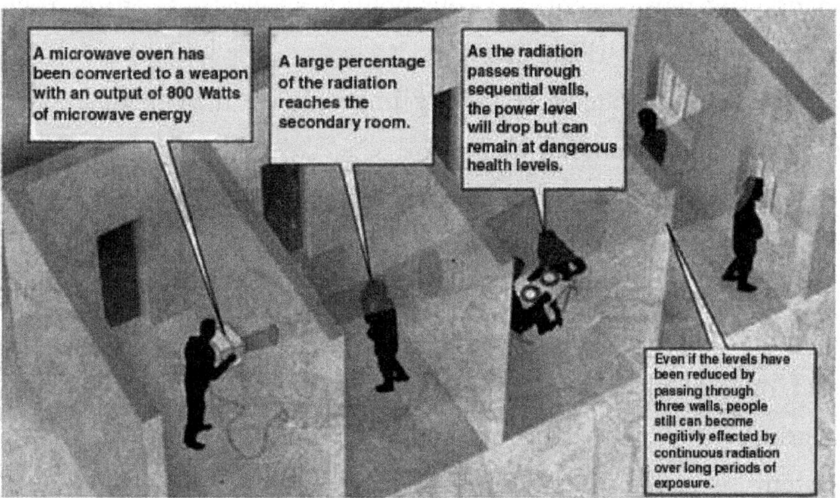

Microwave oven converted into a weapon

Next, imagine metal tubing (size and shape depend on usage), for a microwave weapon only needs casing to direct the beam and somebody to construct the innards. Directions on the Internet show how, for a few dollars, to make one that fits in a lunch box. Or you can buy a kit. Or one that's ready-to-use. Page 59 shows a magnetron that produces microwave radiation, such as what's in your microwave oven.

We have to stop here and get something straight. We all know that the slang term "nuke" is a misnomer as nuke refers to a nuclear weapon. Yet, to hear Mom say she's going to nuke her coffee is normal. In a lot of targets' and perpetrators' minds, nuking food and nuking people are one and the same, although no one is actually locked into a microwave oven. Instead, as has already been explained, an open-ended microwave device spews energy out to make someone sick.

If seeing the word "nuke" offends your appreciation of proper English, scratch it out, write "microwave" or "electronic harassment" overtop, then call me names. Now on with the chapter.

Because microwave implements are easy to build or obtain, and because microwaves flow through non-metal structures, nuking is a popular short-range stratagem. That means a perp can plant a lethal disguised box and spew microwaves at a target through his home or job walls. Most of the successful EH (electronic harassment) court cases have been by targeted office workers who proved that their perpetrator colleagues were using any one of a number of through-wall EH weapons, usually microwave weapons, to beleaguer them with health disorders.

Although nuking through apartment walls is rampant, it is harder to get into court. The perp, after using false ID, will rent an apartment next to his victim, set up the microwave equipment, and take off.

We definitely can't overlook night stalkers who, with or without gizmos that detect where someone is in a house, will bring a power source if need be to energy-harass children and other loved ones through the house's bedroom walls in an effort to separate the target from his family. Until the target gets informed enough to make drastic changes, or amscray, the people in his home will likely continue to suffer from some form of EH, although a scarce few selected loved ones are electronically harassed forever. Nothing will stop eternal EH, and ordinarily, nothing will convince selected long-term secondary targets that they are being nuked or impaired by energy weapons. A target's grown kid who has become a lifelong secondary victim will generally not believe a person could, or would, be microwaved, certain that nuking humans is bunk.

Night stalkers, rather than microwave a human, meaning you, your child, or your spouse, will set up their behind-the-wall equipment and merrily nuke a pooch as he dreams in his doggie bed if it will break the victim's heart, or a child's heart, to see the pet die from failing organs.

The supposed slave-maker weapon shoots microwaves through (or from) space to a predetermined object, maybe you.

To rehash, a victim's naturally electrical head and body make up a stalkable antenna. I believe this happens after the person's unique brain waves have been externally recorded and filed into computer ware, but am open to other theories. Externally recording brain waves is a present medical, research, security, and military procedure.

Whatever method is employed to shoot harmful energy to the correct head and body, it's as infallible as your favourite radio station perpetually transmitting music to your stereo. Conclusively, each targeted individual is a receiver. If you'll recall from the last chapter, the only proof that brain waves are necessary for remote stalking is within academic research. None of the OS bosses have fessed up, so the academic targets have had to do a lot of homework. Lots of victims disagree that brain waves are central to remotely finding and following someone. However, everyone except for the fringe theorists agrees that electronic harassment is in his head, whichever way he is tracked, and that his mind's activity is analyzed by remote ware.

Reading a brain's electrical output is not the laboratory science of the past. It has become so simplistic that the United States Department of Homeland Security has built trailers outfitted with scanners (called MALINTENT) that detect a state of mind. Slated for use at events, corporations, and airports, Holy Hanna can be directed to walk inside a MALINTENT-rigged trailer, where she will have her thought process scanned for signs of bad intentions. Nothing will be connected to Hanna's head. No wires. No touching at all. Just nondescript wall-mounted sensors that read Hanna's thinking process. The results show on a computer.

Should Hanna be having an off day and is thinking about swiping her boyfriend's yardful of pink flamingos, an employee will have to make a personal decision: good person or bad person. The employee cannot read her thoughts; he can only read that her thoughts are sinister.

Depending on a security firm's intent, Hanna's way of thinking (that day) could be permanently recorded into federal files. Trial-run brain-readers have already been mounted in high-traffic airport queues.

Homeland Security has a name for the project: FAST (Future Attribute Screen Technology). Project FAST has eluded journalists for a while, and I have to wonder if it's gone underground like the rest of the unethical government projects that are used on regular folks. In my opinion, a government that reads its citizens' brains has gone too far. Mind intrusions, as ti's know all too well, lead to zero privacy, maximum harassment, destroyed lives, and murder.

You can see how trivial it is to file someone's brain activity for use later on. The only requirement is money for offbeat gadgetry. Of course, OS's brain wave reading equipment is a step above the norm, beyond what medical practitioners and security firms use.

For each electronic device that is directed at a ti, whether it's to read his brain, melt his rubber duck, laser his eyes, or send v2k, and whether it is sent from a stalker's improvised candy tin or a satellite, the upshot is the same: control.

My apologies. I got off-topic. We're supposed to be talking about microwaving. I get so darn worked up whenever mind-reading is mentioned that I tend to rant, even when it's me who mentioned it. So, let's get back to microwaves.

High-intensity microwaving is just one form of energy that causes total physical decline and advanced ageing. Even at moderate levels, it creates a sluggish person. When a loved one or helper is getting a dose intended to cause temporary minimal impairment, he will be tired enough to speculate about medical anomalies and ambiguous stressors. This can last days, weeks, months, or years.

A person being continually microwaved will seemingly grow old even when he's young. It may take a year or two, but his face will develop a worn-out look. Fun and ambitions will dwindle, perhaps indiscernibly. A loved one under a continual moderate dose may have become an electronically harassed secondary target. With all vim gone, he will make a poor rescuer for the primary ti in his life. He could also be adding to the enemy's data about the effects of microwaving or be getting used as a tool to isolate or punish the primary ti.

I'll explain this further. A smattering of secondary (part-time) targets are bypassed when it comes to pestering and vandalism. In replacement they receive electronic harassment through (or from) space, or from nearby. It could be microwaving; intermittent voice to skull; baseball-batting-type beams; energy-caused skin wounds; energy strikes on a brain or other organs; energy strikes to impair breathing, digestion, or eyesight; or strikes to cause intense itching. Though the individual may not be aware of wrongdoings, he is managed. Everyone who is in organized stalking's clutches will have some degree of freedom removed. If his harassment is exclusive to electronic attacks, areas of health will be removed, unless, that is, his

EH (electronic harassment) is exclusive to voice to skull. Voice to skull removes a person's freedom of owning his hearing.

As mentioned, microwaves appear to be occasionally discharged to people who are in regular contact with a ti. I base this claim on accounts of my and other ti's loved ones, helpers, and acquaintances who go through periods of the same malaise as targets. I agree with you that everyone has ups and downs. Microwave illness is different. A healthy twenty-year-old should not be experiencing such exhaustion he misses work every time he checks in on his targeted sister. Unless they are partying or wrestling tigers, the young soul is probably being remotely nuked.

It's implausible that I need to tell you this, but I'm going to anyways. Microwaves have a wide range of applications. Cooking is one. Communication is another. You're undoubtedly aware of the debate surrounding microwave-emitting cell phones.

What I do need to say is this: proof of targets being microwaved from afar does not lie in a courtroom. It lies in a stockpile of research that includes medical and scientific tests that appear, on some ti's, to display indicators of radiation. So there's still wiggle room here. Yet, because hundreds of thousands of targets declare they are microwaved, and because many expert scientists and medical doctors agree with them, we'll continue to speak of microwaved humans rather than speak of humans injured by microwave-like weapons. If I could get away with writing about thingamabobbed humans and thingamajig weapons, I would; for discussing torture methods that have not been discussed in court, such as from-afar microwaving, is asking for trouble.

One more thing, you should know that microwaved innocents do not usually feel heated. But when they do, their insides or outsides, in sections or in entirety, are uncomfortably warm. It's not the kind of warm that's felt on a hot day, or during a fever, or from a sunburn. It's unsolvable, uncustomary, and unexpected. During acute radiating of this type, a heavily hit victim is certain he's being cooked alive.

Ti's who feel as weary as they look have to push themselves through each nuked day. Their loved ones, helpers, and acquaintances are doing the same on occasion. Certainly, rescuers are nuked.

As several nations' governments are thought to microwave citizens for experimentation, and as militaries already use microwave defence weapons, it's possible that large populations can be unknowingly nuked into becoming despondent, for nuking does more than wither our insides and deplete pep. Over time it makes us glum. In my opinion, microwaving is a mainstay daily OS operation to dis victims' physical and mental health.

Upon moving here at just over fifty years old, the landlords assumed I was around seventy. Targets age quickly anyhow due to extensive fear, worrying, grief, pain, and often poverty. Add EH, and Prince Charming will evolve into Prince Frowzy.

Energy-based sicknesses in targets can appear as ionizing radiation or non-ionizing radiation. Targets can be harassed by several kinds of energies at one time.

Undoubtedly, you've figured out that electronic weapons produce a changed person, animal, or object and that damage is from the inside out or vice versa, depending on the energy's aspects. However, you must be wondering what a radiated person's life is really like. Without exception, every target who is receiving extensive electronic-weapons torture looks terrible, is sick or dying, and is depressed. On his worst days he could appear corpselike and may have to pee and upchuck into a bucket from his chesterfield. This can go on for weeks. He may not be able to keep down water. On the victim's best days he might totter to the store. If you can recall film footage of Hiroshima atomic bomb survivors whose internal injuries were explained as radiation sickness, you're on the right track. Extreme weakness and hollow emotions are predictable along with no appetite, nausea, vomiting, or diarrhea.

A target bedridden from radiation is apt not to care about usual concerns. He is, after all, at death's door. If he was already mourning over lost loved ones (including pets), or is a long-term ti, or has been mislabelled as mentally ill, he may refuse hospitalization and focus on a precious photo, object, or memory during his decline. This person may be hoping to die and should not be scorned for an unwillingness to accept help. Psychological and physical torture that no one else recognizes has exceeded his threshold. Homeless ti's in this condition die on the street.

Some ti's, like myself, slowly deteriorate from incurable internal trembling. Our (electrical) bodies vibrate like vibrating cell phones. When the quivering is felt by others through sharing a couch or by hugging, the target is thought to be shaking from nervousness. Though nervous shaking occurs, a fine uninterrupted internal buzzing (vibrating) sensation is produced by being infused with infrasound, perhaps ultrasound, or another energy type. Distinguishing vibrating from shaking is unsophisticated. If the person feels plugged in, then he was or still is receiving lethal-bearing

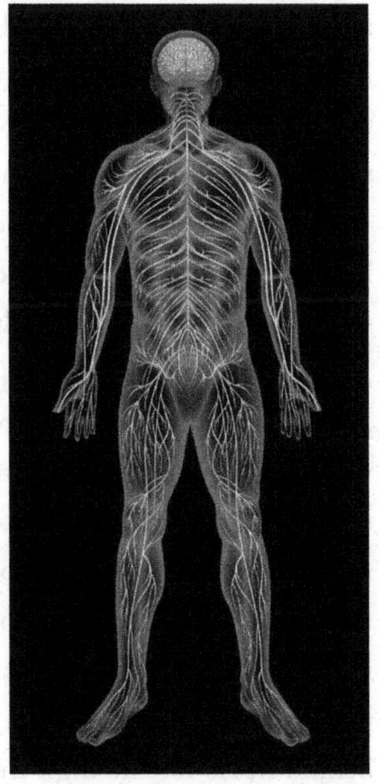

Electrical nervous system

energy waves. A target can quake without pause for a year or two and intermittently after that for a decade. At its peak, assistance may be required to eat, bathe, and dress. Sleep and rest may be unachievable for long periods despite conspicuous exhaustion.

Let's sketch over sound waves that are transmitted to do harm. When certain inaudible sound waves, being high or low frequencies, are fed (beamed) into a person's head, his physiology and thinking are disrupted. Emitted from a voice to skull or other weapon, often in beats, these high and low frequencies upset a body's natural rhythm. In other words, frequencies that aren't supposed to stay in humans are steadily transfused into a victim with the intention of malfunctioning his nervous system (especially his brain), and his heart. Dizziness, headaches, lethargy, nausea, vomiting, diarrhea, an odd gait, irregular heartbeat, vibrating, incoordination, overall aching, and incapacitation may occur. The mind injuries are disastrous: memory erasing and overall mental jumbling. A ti may have a torture-designed frequency beating into his skull every day.

It's feasible that my years of vibrating were not caused from ionizing-like radiation. An inaudible sound wave with a low frequency (infrasound) could be the culprit. I expect never to know.

Pulsing objects with frequencies is elementary school science. An example is music. It's hardly silent, yet certain frequencies rattle windows and pictures—as moms of teens can attest to. Do you remember how Beethoven composed music after he went deaf? He felt the piano because it vibrated differently for each note. Some targets' furniture and whatnot quiver or rock without the music, so it appears that beaming inaudible low frequencies is standard OS practice, for a single kitchen stool doesn't shimmy without science behind it. As for the high frequency range called ultrasound, we're all familiar with its use to repel vermin and loiterers. In the wrong hands it, too, is lethal to humans.

Comprehensive radiation poisoning and inaudible sound wave infiltration cause overall frailty and melancholy, and sometimes total prostration, as they overload a body with noxious energy. Along with the electronic weapons that ail a whole person, there are the trajectories that cause highly specific injuries of which internal bleeding, shattered bones, blindness, scalp wounds, and organ lesions are just a few. It depends on the energy form and where the perpetrators want to cause damage. Obvious abrasions are only a small part of EH.

If you're finding electronic harassment difficult to grasp, compare radiation deaths to carbon monoxide deaths. Both munitions are absorbed into a body and are invisible. As for pinpoint energy hits, such as a focused beam puncturing a person's lung, compare it to a bullet.

Targets receiving incorrect treatment for illnesses caused by sound wave torture and other types of energy, or incorrect treatment for strikes on internal organs, are often made a lot sicker as their health is already in peril. Energy illnesses in people and animals are misdiagnosed in stereotypical medical fields, including in autopsies. People who tell doctors that they are dying from electronic harassment are laid to rest as a fruitcake.

The bizarre nature of attacks by electronic weapons leaves victims stranded and alone with their injuries. A victim can be ill for years with no one believing his accurate renditions of why he's flagging. Instant EH murders are labelled as death by natural causes, usually heart failure. Heavily hit EH'ed targets experience heart hits on occasion to keep them in line. I experience heart strikes once or twice a year, which is average. Some of us don't survive them, and some of don't want to survive them.

Had I been smart enough in the beginning to accept that suicide is what's planned for me, and that EH is the preferred killing method, my life would be better right now. I wouldn't have wasted every penny trying to lose my stalkers. Messy murders occur. But I'm on to them now. If they want you dead, there is no getting away.

Some ti's are inundated with EH, and some are inundated with other things, like slander. A few of us get it all, and I'm rather glad to have had, with a few exceptions, the profuse array thrown at me. Otherwise, I wouldn't fully understand what the other targets are talking about, and writing this book would be impossible.

If you find that torturing folks off the street with invisible far-off energy sounds too strange to be true, you have plenty of company. Most targets felt the same way. It is beyond accepted limits of science and humanity.

Victims need to publish more books about living with energy torture. A personal account, actually, requires an entire book as medical, psychological, and social effects are complicated and devastating. The technology is another issue altogether. Plainly, few EH'ed targets have the strength for such an undertaking, and that includes me. My tenacity is good, but my health is sagging.

Next on my docket, providing I can holdout, is to compel a documentarian. Only when the public reacts to the crime will it stop.

To be honest, I did turn down an offer from a big film school because of their offhand attitude. While telling them that my harassers could cause them trouble, they replied, "Bring 'em on. We're not scared." It was an ill-informed, cocky answer I couldn't let slide. Naïve and arrogant people are eaten alive in this crime. For everyone's sake except mine, a book is a safer medium, although a film would reach more people, which is precisely why I'd like to compel a documentarian.

I'd not planned to write a book. If I had, it wouldn't have been about something incomprehensible. Subsequently, I'm finding organized stalking challenging to explain.

OS's hundreds of criminal actions need to be broken down into an encyclopedic format, followed by corresponding consequences to the target, along with the impact on people around the target. As helpful as that would be, and somebody needs to do that, it would skip the entire reason for writing this book as the despair cannot be conveyed without commentary. Nevertheless, with OS largely unseen by non-targets, my work's cut out.

It's pressing, too, to portray mundane-looking stalkers as evil even though they happily use mental breakdown techniques that Nazis, MKULTRA staff, and other depraved autocrats mastered and recorded.

It's probably a good idea to explain Project MKULTRA for those who have not heard of it because, like OS, it seems unbelievable. MKULTRA is just one of a number of government-sanctioned mind-control programs on non-consenting citizens that happened to get exposed. It involved mutating brain functions and behaviours in thousands of uninformed folks. I'm not suggesting OS is a government test. It's just worth recognizing that large-scale illegal experiments on humans occur, in case OS is one of them.

MKULTRA was a secret CIA (Central Intelligence Agency) research project in the United States and Canada that began in the early 1950s and was supposed to have halted in 1973. There is strong evidence that this experiment is active today under a different project name.

Some of the present-day torture practices used on suspected terrorists were initially tested on unsuspecting MKULTRA victims—people like you and me—to see what would force mental chaos, information extraction, submission, and the loss of abilities.

MKULTRA experiments included isolation, personality restructuring, memory erasing, electricity, hypnosis, blinding lights, sleep deprivation, deafening noise, sexual abuse including rape, emotional degradation, radiation, lies that loved ones had died, and dozens of other perversions. Drugs and poisons were routinely used for the purpose of causing paralysis, ageing, anemia, memory loss, eyesight loss, hearing loss, lesions, well, the list is endless. Most experiments were brain damaging, at either end of the scale. Deaths were masqueraded.

A single MKULTRA misdeed became notorious when the CIA said that a scientist fell or jumped from a thirteenth-story window after they'd slipped him LSD, declaring he had a bad reaction. The duped fellow had been one of the many CIA employees drugged in a quest to compare altered-state compliance in individual setups. An autopsy and court case publicly declared that the man was probably murdered and tossed out the window after expressing concern over the CIA's unconscionable projects. He'd been slipped LSD nine days before. This legal face-off, thankfully, widely exposed MKULTRA's trickery in exploiting subjects in over eighty establishments.

One swindle involved folks who were unaware of the real reasons doctors were sending them to hospital, often for minimal or non-existent health concerns. Many were already in hospital for routine procedures, and a substantial percentage of MKULTRA subjects were students and staff attending universities. Then there were the pharmaceutical employees and prisoners. To broaden the testing, doctors in rural areas and in children's centres were commissioned.

Vague whitewash consent contracts were offered in cases where subjects were more likely to sue or die. Uniformly, these human guinea pigs had no idea what they were agreeing to: the university students and the professional folks believed they were taking part in a frivolous exercise, and the medical patients believed they were signing a standard consent form.

The folks who were just going about their lives, such as stay-at-home moms, blue-collar workers, white-collar workers including CIA staff, prostitutes and their customers, and homeless people signed nothing because no one told them that their free will had been hijacked. They were repetitively slipped LSD and other drugs, then stalked and watched, sometimes for years. These subjects went insane temporarily or permanently either because they felt they were losing their minds or because of brain damage. Needless to say, many lives were destroyed. (In the appendix on page 461 there is a CIA memo that discusses drug slipping and other trickery.)

Testing, despite it being painful, scary, or debilitating, could continue on a medically treated victim, such as a postpartum depressed mom, a chronically sick child, or a hospitalized cancer patient, until radical behavioural or physical changes were confirmed and maintained. This could go on for months or years under the guise of a patient requiring systematic care.

Each subject suffered lifelong repercussions as all of the experiments were designed to alter mind function. All were unethical.

Compliance, robotic behaviour, memory erasing, and brainwashing were, and still are, the required results in such tests. This is what mind-control experiments are for: to figure out the most effective ways to control minds. Organized stalking is all about mind control, too. The number of MKULTRA victims killed is unknown. Almost all of the records vanished after the experiment was disclosed. The number of OS victims killed will be unknown as well. (In the appendix on page 459 there is a CIA memo that discusses MKULTRA's cover-up.)

Following is an illegible original MKULTRA document, with its transcript. Full-sized MKULTRA documents can be found on a myriad of websites. Or you could check out the CIA's Freedom of Information site: https://www.cia.gov/library/readingroom/search/site/mkultra You'll still need to type "MKUKTRA" into the search box. If the file you want is not clickable (most aren't), make a request on the form provided.

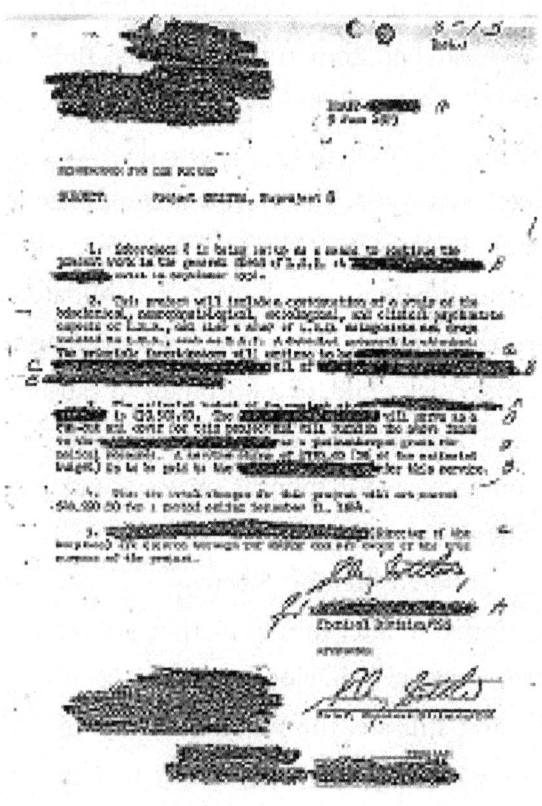

Here's the transcript, declaring Dr. Sidney Gottlieb's approval of a top-secret CIA LSD experiment on citizens.

DRAFT - [deleted] 9 June 1953

MEMORANDUM FOR THE RECORD

SUBJECT: Project MKULTRA, Subproject 8

1. Subproject 8 is being set up as a means to continue the present work in the general field of L.S.D. at [deleted] until 11 September 1954.

2. This project will include a continuation of a study of the biochemical, neurophysiological, sociological, and clinical psychiatric aspects of L.S.D., and also a study of L.S.D. antagonists and drugs related to L.S.D., such as L.A.E. A detailed proposal is attached. The principle investigators will continue to be [deleted] all or [deleted].

3. The estimated budget of the project at [deleted] is $39,500.00. The [deleted] will serve as a cut-out and cover the project for this project and will furnish the above funds to the [deleted] as a philanthropic grant for medical research. A service charge of $790.00 (2% of the estimated) is to be paid to the [deleted] for this service.

4. Thus the total charges for this project will not exceed $40, 290.00 for a period ending September 11, 1954.

5. [deleted] (Director of the hospital) are cleared through TOP SECRET and are aware of the true purpose of the project.

[deleted]

Chemical Division/TSS

APPROVED:

[signature of Sidney Gottlieb]

Chief, Chemical Division/TSS
[document ends]

Okay, so now you know that, historically, OS isn't the only prearranged mind-control crime to use average folks as if they are disposable junk. Thus far, you might not have considered OS as a mind-control crime. Any organization that forces isolation, despair, and pain to unlivable heights in order to achieve a suicide quota is fanatical about controlling the victim's mind.

Unlike me, most ti's do not believe that OS has a suicide quota, although they are acutely aware of the suicides and firmly believe OS focuses on managing their actions, which can only occur by trying to manage their minds.

Because I work with the victims who are pushed beyond what humans are built to survive, my assessment of the crime might be darker than other ti's. Witnessing so much brutality has convinced me that nonstop lethal-bearing psychological and physical torture is exacted on selected individuals in order to analyze the specific elements that will cause a suicide: the elements being the harassment and torture types and the responses to them. I'm also convinced that selected individuals are cleverly kept on the brink of suicide for months or years.

You might think I'm talking crazy. Consider this: MKULTRA's cruel experiments were efficiently and excruciatingly analyzed, so it's obvious that data collection was pivotal, just as it must be to

OS. Perhaps, just perhaps, pushing someone to kill himself could be a doozy of a data-collecting opportunity, necessitating a quota, or body count, for statistical reasons. Being able to keep someone on the edge of committing suicide for long periods would be equally statistically significant. With ti's having insect status, there is no limit to the barbarity. For that, I am certain. Unquestionably, targets are checks in a box.

Let's put aside any ambiguities and collectively affirm that the MKULTRA and OS cruelties we've discussed are all about control, whether the cruelties are EH torture, mind experiments, life-ruining enterprises, or life-ending enterprises. We can also affirm that in these types of secret projects, only two results are sought: making people into puppets and putting outspoken people in the ground.

Anyhow, for what it's worth, you should learn that some MKULTRA victims were transitioned into becoming organized stalking victims. Through age and abuse, many have passed on, but not all. In my opinion, these doomed folks form a subgroup only because their responses vary from victims undergoing surveillance and torture for the first time. Undeniably, OS bosses understand that these folks have already undergone mind-control experimentation. MKULTRA survivors are among the hardest hit of all OS targets.

Project MKULTRA perpetrators presented themselves as doctors and people with authority, and other than drug slipping and sexual assaults, much of the testing was done on citizens in sequestered supervised settings. Organized stalking perpetrators, as we know, have the same thought and behaviour changing agenda as MKULTRA had, but can appear extraordinarily ordinary, harming their targets out in the open.

Hence, in this book, trying to paint stalkers as players in torture procedures and stockpile slaughters is vexing. Moreover, the OS perps with positions of authority, being leaders, cops, executives, and academics, are polite and welcoming, so it's hard to depict them as assassins, as well. To make organized stalking even more confounding to explain, it is not possible to name powerful bosses or why they started an annihilation program in the first place, making OS sound like a whodunit thriller, and that has to be avoided. The only way to examine this crime is with horror.

At any rate, the writing is pricking away at my soft underbelly, the sissy bit that knows I'm cornered, and it's mentally shoving me ahead in the death-row line. I want to yell, "Can't you see that my fingers are typing the fate of condemned innocents in a worldwide atrocity? And that while you are reading, scores of souls are fine-tuning long-contemplated suicides, savouring relief. That my friends and I are begging you to hear us."

With no hesitation, I admit that organized stalking is a remarkable crime and hard to accept as credible. Until someone hears the whole of it, it sounds downright ditzy. Other than in novels, where else would a villain recurrently interact with his stalked acquisition, with each knowing the other's role?

It's this communication factor that unequivocally separates OS criminals from society's cliched criminals, in that stalking murderers don't normally tell their quarry ahead of time that in one way or another a racketeered death will occur, even if it takes decades, so as to keep the hunt going. I'm writing a new version of Roman savagery—the days of killing slaves for sport.

Also odd is how entrapment unfolds. Captives are told and taught that by defending themselves; insulting, cornering, or identifying gang members; seeking justice; finding help; or finding moments of pleasure, they or their loved ones will be tortured and perhaps slain in an unverifiable homicide.

There is no category for organized stalking. It does not fall into the definition of mass murder which typically involves one location and one victim group. Neither does it fall under serial murder which takes breaks between deaths. Nor is it revenge, political, or prejudicial. Defining OS as a spree crime doesn't work either. Killings and forced suicides are implemented by a structured global group whose members are assigned prey-specific roles as torturers. OS is a one-of-a-kind holocaust and, thus, uncharted.

That's why in trying to avert terrorizing, victims have only their personal wherewithal to draw on. There are no confirmed methods, meaning there are no records, on what might and might not work. Even so, some responses, particularly withholding emotions, seem more favourable for staving off attacks. Excitement over power—of having made their victim cry or scream—incites further viciousness that will surely send these swine to perdition.

And speaking of responses, those who are not heavily harassed or fully dominated are apt to speak of weakness in the defeated ti's whose owners want them dead. If this is you, knock it off.

For exhausted or sick ti's, submission becomes a reasonable or necessary response to cope with both remote and on-heels abuses, and even the feistiest of victims go through periods of surrender. Yet, living a life unfit for rodents motivates the healthiest of the lot into the busyness of justice seeking. If their families are not at stake, which is the case with ti's whose loved ones have been estranged for years, they've little to lose.

Many of these crusaders believe organized stalking is a pilot mind-control trial, based on combining new electronic weapons with old psychological breakdown strategies. These folks use MKULTRA and other covert mind-control programs, such as the CIA's Project Monarch, Project Bluebird, and Operation Artichoke, to prove that human experimentations are standard government operations: that OS is not a game. Another sector of activists believes that experimenting is long over and that OS's bosses know exactly what to expect from their crimes. This group believes that OS has the goal of eventually commandeering humankind, remotely.

Below is a partial MKULTRA document that mentions activating behaviour by remote means. What exactly the remote means are is a mystery as the CIA destroyed almost all of the "telling" files. You can see this document in full on page 460 in the appendix.

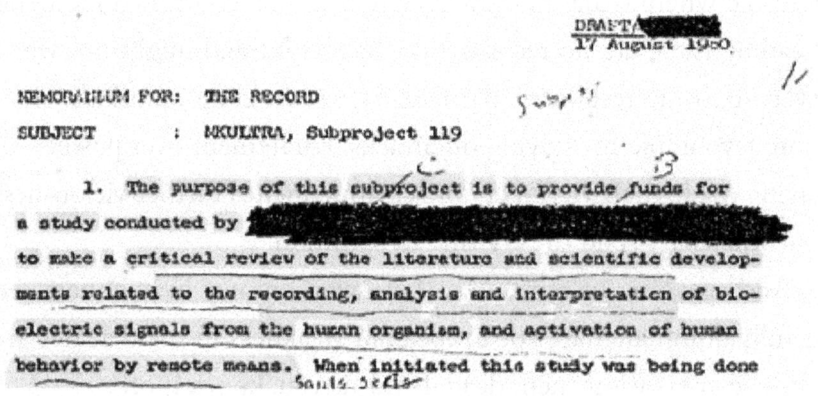

DRAFT/[redacted]
17 August 1950

MEMORANDUM FOR: THE RECORD

SUBJECT : MKULTRA, Subproject 119

1. The purpose of this subproject is to provide funds for a study conducted by [redacted] to make a critical review of the literature and scientific developments related to the recording, analysis and interpretation of bio-electric signals from the human organism, and activation of human behavior by remote means. When initiated this study was being done

We can all agree that OS uses some of the same prisoner-making tactics that Nazi and MKULTRA staff used by replacing various freedoms with domination. How I tend mail and garbage, and OS's control over my sleep and communication, are examples of being dominated. The variance here is that OS integrates dozens of atrocities and harassments all at one time, on one hapless free-roaming subject, while implementing remote electronic weapons to reinforce authority. Victims are held hostage psychologically. There's no historical equivalent. The fact that it costs gazillions . . . What do you think?

Indeed, I have forgotten that this chapter was supposed to be a journal entry. Yet, it's probably just as well to tell the nitty-gritty of OS piecemeal. An earlier draft explained each topic in separate laborious chapters. It may be the right way to write. But it was textbook-like. I had trouble getting through it, and I wrote the damn thing.

OS is so interlaced that in mentioning one element, clarifications are needed. Add my habit of trying to cram as much information as possible into your noggin, and the dialogue does go on. When diverging or racing through topics occurs, a sense of urgency reigns. My ti friends cannot hold on much longer.

Targets slated for suicide understand that every twenty-four hours must be so hellish that they embrace death. And those who are terminally ill from ongoing EH just want it over with. A third group that exist minute by minute are the ti's stuck with the most fiendish of the stalkers.

It's not surprising then that increasing numbers of targets are telling me about pill stashes, the best bridges to jump off, and getting lost in the woods where no one will find their bodies. Yesterday, a local ti admitted for the second time that she'd waded into a harbour with pockets full of rocks. The last few days have been rife with suicidal confessions, so my writing can become disposed to tell it all in one go to make you understand right now. This book needs to be able to tell families what happened to their loved ones, and it worries me that something will be left out.

To my knowledge, I am the only Canadian, other than the enemy, who is scrutinizing OS's psychological effects. A team could do a much more thorough analysis. Nevertheless, as my theme of violence-toward-others disallows non-ti communication and any form of activism (I tried), assisting victims and taking stock of their countless situations is the best I can do. Thank heavens for brave activists. Organized stalking's ramifications take a back seat compared to shutting it down.

I couldn't write this book living anywhere else. A rural home pacifies me, making me so much better off than most targets. I'm not better off because my home is rural, but because it suits me. In my view, if life is going to be awful, it might as well be awful in a tall forest on the ocean's edge, where I belong. The expanses of blues and greens get me through each day; however, the seclusion allows night terrorism from the perps who live here or take a boat over.

In spite of trying to stay positive, the crime has gotten me down lately. The days are nonstop remotely pounded ribs, sides, ears, limbs, and back; suicide calls; other kinds of trauma calls; hearing about deaths; dealing with possible radiation sickness; and stalker harassment. The nights are nonstop baseball batting beams on my legs, radiation sickness, brain beams that hurt, unnerving brain beams that wake me, prowlers, and window tapping. Target-life is never good, and I've adjusted to it as best as I can. Still, there are periods when it's all too much.

A day of fresh air would boost my resistance, but I am afraid to leave the house for very long without the book, which has become cumbersome with its numerous binders and folders. The beach is a short, gentle slope from the door; and last summer I was out every day with a carriable manuscript for hours at a time, exploring low tide and studying OS at the picnic table that looks over the cove. So I miss that.

It's not that I think my book is more special than any other book. It's a matter of not losing the great amount of time I've invested. Some of us ti's guard quantities of time like non-ti's guard quantities of money. And for good reason. Targets are under constant threat that their time is running out.

As a non-ti, you're wondering why I don't store the work on discs, USB flash drives, and other data savers and just take them with me. Well, I do, but because remote energy can (and will) destroy handy gadgetry, paper copies are ever so necessary.

As paranoid as my stronghold over the manuscript sounds, I am one of the few people who hears about dissenting ti's whose paperwork and evidence are stolen, or whose houses have been burned down, or who are *accidentally* incapacitated, never mind dispatched.

My controllers know I'm writing, so it's disconcerting why they've let me get this far. It's probable that a lollapaloozer round of EH torture is coming. The last heart strike dropped me to the floor, and I've had an unstable heartbeat ever since. When a person is under continual fire, it's not always possible to tell if a strike is retaliatory.

Shutting down my computer with the black screen routine has only minimally slowed the writing. Same with deleting chapters, locking me out of my files, wiping the computer clean which they did again last Saturday, breaking the whole laptop, and altering what I've written. A previous day's writing, or a particular chapter, can be a hodgepodge of changes. In my last reread, all the double "l" words were changed to "lll" words, which caused me to develop a dillly of an "ll" hang-up that took weeks to dispelll.

Couple the scab's handiwork with my inevitable grammar and punctuation mistakes and it's possible this book could look like Dumb and Dumber wrote it. Paying for a professional edit would allleviate some of my apprehension, but like most ti's, I am not all-lowed to be anything but poor. Okay, enough with the "lll's." Do you wanna hear how they're deleting the word "not"? So, you do . . .?

A trusty 1950 manual typewriter is a permanent fixture on my work table, a gift many years ago, and would solve the hacked writing problem were it not for being spoiled by the delete button. Still, the typewriter is vital when the computer is down. I wrote my first detailed observations of OS on it between 2003 and 2005, plunking away until my fingers ached: over 2,000 pages. And because communication is my weapon of choice, there's another typewriter wedged in the back of a full closet in the event night terrorists get in and wreck the first one. Bags of hard-to-buy typewriter ribbons are hidden, enough to plunk away for eons.

I'm trying not to stew about the probability of being suppressed soon. Perhaps because my stalkers have invested so much work into my suicide they are unwilling to kill me until it's absolutely necessary. Or maybe reading my findings buoys their beer, carnage, and pizza nights, though that can't be right. To them, my intellect is worth less than a toad's. That I'm part of a study to standardize rebel-purging makes sense. Developing an efficient formula to mute mutineers would be imperative for OS's success. Whatever the reason they are letting me write, I'll try not to dwell on it. Pick and choose our worries. That is what targets have to do.

I'm going to end this chapter with a veiled threat that has everything to do with the book. Please don't be fooled into thinking that this person is concerned about my well-being. She is a notorious Mexican perpetrator and her only interest is to scare me. This is the first of several letters that was sent to hundreds of targets, many of whom wisely advised that I not engage with this enemy. I've substituted June Ti for my real name.

JUNE TI, where is she?

Have you heard about June Ti? Do you have some news about her? If you know about her let me know, or tell her to get in touch with me. URGENT!!! Is she OK? WHERE IS SHE??? I'VE

AN URGENT MESSAGE TO GIVE HER. SHE IS IN RISK. PLEASE HELP ME LOCATE HER. Thanks (name withheld)

CHAPTER EIGHT

JOURNAL
AND
ELECTRONIC HARASSMENT
AND
REMOTE STALKING

I want to say that an old friend dropping by was the best thing that's happened in a year, which it definitely was, yet being around people is selfish. Isolated from her for a decade, she's visited twice since. Unfortunately, Nameless became a secondary target shortly after my own targeting began. Seeing me could exacerbate her harassment.

Our friendship has spoiled her life. Not just a month or two, but all her life's aspirations. My legacy is a trail of offshoot victims. Admitting what I've inadvertently done to others, and am still doing, is morally paralyzing.

Nameless doesn't understand the crime, and so for the first time in weeks I left the house for a full day, unwilling to explain why I shouldn't. It's summer, after all. We went to a typically desolate West Coast beach, its rocky shoreline offering only driftwood, and caterpillars, and seagulls. I had to carry such heavy sacks of paperwork that after falling down in my depleted state I couldn't get up. She had to help me. What could I possibly say? "Hey, Nameless, imbeciles are shooting lethal energy at me and making me sick, so looking for agates with you is hard. Leaving my pounds of papers at home is non-negotiable as they will get stolen or burned in an arson fire, and the data-saving doodads get busted." Who talks like that? So, I said nothing.

For precious hours, my holistic being recalled what togetherness means. There is nothing better than women-friends sitting on a sun-bleached log yacking as women-friends do when they are gazing at water and mountains. Listening to her encounters with nosy wolves and dawdling bears and how to make Chinese soup felt foreign. And sad.

She kept turning around, hearing men shaking the bushes behind us without being seen. She was suspicious of the cars following us everywhere: the dead ends and the private driveway we absent-mindedly drove down. Her alarm when they parked behind us at the deserted beach was transparent. She'd been stalked before. I wondered what she told herself—why she figured she'd be followed.

"They're probably curious to see whatever sights we want to see," I said, determined not to let harassment mar the day.

We talked on the phone this morning, recapping our visit, but as usual, our call got disconnected. I came close to telling her again that she's a target and not jinxed, if for any reason, to make her mindful of avertible snares. "Nobody else has these problems," she said. "I'm trying my best to get ahead, and all I do is go backwards. Do you know I've had to move and change jobs ten times in ten years? You wait, my new phone will cut out before I've finished telling you about the weekend's disaster."

My friend, who would thrive on wilderness treks and career goals if she were not a secondary target, spends half her days fixing OS's symbolic losses, snags, and breakages. Often laid-up with all-too-familiar ailments, I'm certain she is being intermittently radiated, maybe microwaved. The thugs drag her down and down, let her take one step ahead, and drag her back again.

How does someone tell someone else cursed news for which there is no solution and no end? Am I obligated to? Am I obligated not to? I haven't brought it up for quite a while as she dismisses OS as baloney. Because Nameless is pleasant and law abiding, she cannot conceive having an enemy without having made someone mad. My thoughts are consumed with my friend's sorrow, dismayed that her future will be devastated in unimaginable ways.

Last summer I sat on a different barren beach with a different secondarily targeted loved one. There's been no one I love, in between. That means my socializing with (targeted) loved ones is down to a day or two a year. Socializing with non-targets is out of the question, and during the writing I can't let ti's stay for respite as they often have trauma-based problems and can require gobs of attention. Plus, they bring their manic perps and life is turned upside-down. When they leave there's a penalty. To put it mildly, respite care and writing don't mix.

Well, this is interesting. Just this second, I got hit with a weapon that's bored a hole in the back of my left hand. That's a shame. I just started using it again after the last hand-fry. My early-days response to this kind of EH was to tear around outside with a rock in each fist. Now, as a long-term better-informed ti, I refuse to spend day and night standing sentry or taking defensive actions. Been there, done that, and it's a cruddy way to live. Catch one and three more show up. Anyways, given that my window looks down on the cove and that there is no one around, this hole must have been burned into me remotely. There'd be no finding the idiot no matter how many times I circled the house.

Ignoring as much as possible is how I cope. It's not everybody's method, and I am ridiculed for advising others to do the same. However, targets fall apart when they are possessed with witnessing their stalkers and their stalkers' misdeeds. A ti existing with around-the-clock harassment loses himself if he doesn't fabricate lulls. Ceasefires don't happen. Non-harried moments are manufactured.

Energy-beam punctures, like the one in my hand, are as perfect a hole as you'll ever see and vary in size from pen to pen refill. This one is closer to pen size. In my case they bleed for days, so there's no seeing how deep the penetrations are. It's possible that targets' health is so compromised that blood clotting is protracted. It's also possible that the beam is encoded to remain in one spot.

I don't bother with medical care anymore, not even when they burned my breast to a crusty crisp last winter. Can you imagine the conversation if I went to get my hand treated? "You see, Doctor, directed-energy beams are on me all day. I know you don't believe me, but one night I saw two through my ceiling over the couch I sleep on. Side by side. They looked like white stove-burners. We don't usually see them. Actually, that was the only time. They toasted my head. But this is just a little hole. Just a little beam. Not the kind of energy emission I could see."

Gees, I shouldn't have blabbed about the stove-burner beams because now I have to explain them. A highly visible through-roof (or through-wall) beam is practically an impossible occurrence under normal conditions: the light source would have to be incredible. Yet, ti's have taken videos of laser-like beams that flow through their car and house roofs. This can't-happen phenomenon could be a harm-free scare tactic that we'll get to later. The best I can do is to tell you that one dark night, in a power outage, I saw coiled stove-burner-shaped lights shine through the ceiling, and then my scalp was broiled. Every other time that my head has been burned, the energy source was invisible. Don't tell me you're not bewildered.

In short, remote electronic harassment does not always follow the accepted science of energy transmission, which is why ti's are desperate to get their mittens on the technology.

I understand you, poor reader, are getting bogged down; and for me to pile on uncharted phenomenal EH is a mite unfair. But I'm not going to write two volumes: one for believable crimes and one for science-defying crimes. Though I considered it. Shifting gears to gross unfairness, now there is a long streak between my boobs, from neck to naval, which appeared while I was writing the last sentence; and they've just struck my left cheek with energy that feels like a hard punch.

Looking in the mirror, I found several red lines on my throat and one long scrape down my front, like a rough screwdriver blade was raked over, breaking the skin. It's my cheek and jaw that are aching, and they have no sign of attack.

It's remarkable what targets put up with. If scratches, a hole, and a punched-in face suddenly happened to you, assuming you are not used to EH, you'd be perturbed. Heavily harassed targets have to take such things in stride. Being shot at—akin to shooting fish in a barrel—is a new normal.

I mentioned before that victims can be receiving various forms of energy harassment. My situation is representative. A beam just wounded me in several spots on my body. The other day my ear and hearing were pressure-treated; all the while my leg, back, ribs, and side were pounded, jabbed, and squished. Plus, I've slices on my shoulders and am quite sick from possible radiation poisoning.

OS's technology is so precise that the employee who just tore into me, who is assumedly snickering from a comfy chair in front of a console, could have etched his name in my hand. He could have cut it off or cleaved me in half. Without hesitation, it's these "could haves" that are the most unnerving. You can bet his desk set includes the incapacitating weapon that gloms an energy stream onto someone's eye. Or heart. We are talking about probable military inventions that appear to use computer programs rather than provable torture, provable deterrence, bullets, and bombs.

When a beam is programmed to latch on, there is no way to lose it. Twirling, sprinting, driving, and hiding are futile. Full-time v2k victims say the voices (or noises) in their heads can be periodically fooled for a jiffy when they jag right or left but that the sound takes under a second to catch up. Energy beams are calibrated to bull's eye.

Should a ti inhabit or sleep in a Faraday cage (enclosure that blocks electrical fields), the beam, of course, will still be there waiting, if the cage worked at all. Only a scant few folks say their homemade Faraday cages are effective against EH. Most energy buffers do not work in this crime or, at least, do not work for long. It may be that as a profusion of advanced electronics and energies are used, a ti will never successfully repel them all. A handful say they've found a total cure-all that anyone can apply, often an expensive item, but it habitually ends up ineffective for others. My hunch is that these supposedly blessed people are not charmed or extra resourceful and are mistaken, or are perps, or are conning salesmen.

Ninety percent of the ti population say there is no relief, or very limited relief, from using any one of a hundred shielding materials thought to repress painful or internally disruptive beams. Aluminum and other metals, magnets, mirrors, humidifiers, gel packs, and outputs of energy are a few of the tried EH barriers. On a positive note, a small number of folks claim that listening to binaural beats through headphones or earbuds slightly dampens remote mind invasions, including v2k, for a short time. (I haven't tried it yet as I don't have the right equipment.) No one has been able to successfully block out all v2k, although some victims try to drown it out with music or radio talk shows, again, through the use of earbuds or headphones.

Multiple layers of metal insect screening are favoured for obstructing microwaves, yet until hardware cloth comes into vogue, it will never be acceptable as caps or vests. And, yes, I can tell you stories about ti's with cookie-tin hats and aluminum-foil pants. I've spent days with fridge magnets strapped to my fingers. And one night when it seemed I was being energy-killed, I took the screens out of the windows, went back to bed, and piled the screens over the covers. It only sounds funny until you realize that you have a great deal in common with the tuna casserole you're microwaving for dinner.

For information's sake, the "cooking" pain in my fingers stopped as soon as I attached the magnets. The EH dial might have been turned down so that I'd spend considerable time and expense magnet-shielding. I didn't. I'm on to them. As expected, relief was erratic and ended entirely on day three. Remote stalkers play games with their prey unceasingly. Magnets have never worked since.

Victims who are trying to save themselves from directed energy often do the reverse. For instance, when I covered myself with window screens, my owners increased the pain. I was not only radiated through or around them with a higher energy level, but I was uncomfortable. The Mylar blankets that are recommended seldom work for me, even in layers.

Though many learn to live with the attacks, feeling physically ransacked is guaranteed. When EH'ed targets make no attempt to lessen the agony on their noodles, limbs, and organs, they are claiming defeat. I used to worry over this crowd. Now I get it. Learned helplessness during specific EH'ed tortures is a viable brief transitional measure when all else has failed. Calling uncle has its place, for a spell.

Unlike most ti's, I stumbled upon a successful method to momentarily sabotage brain beams. The retribution is grim, so I no longer consider it viable. We'll be discussing what EH does to heads at various points from here on. Brain infiltration is vital to OS's resounding success. It's a form of mind control.

Once a person is logged into a state-of-the-art tracking system he becomes a mobile antenna. I've mentioned this before, yet it's going to come up again and again as (presumably) pursuing someone through airwaves permits untraceable assaults by unseen weapons.

A remotely watched ti who is stomping up a courthouse library's steps can be getting his eyes and feet zapped to prevent him from reaching the top. There's a good chance he'll say "ow" and continue on, for an industrious victim expects a thrashing. Half-blinded and hobbling, this fellow will feel triumphant as he peruses the shelves of legal books. However, he might elect never to go to the courthouse library again. It's possible that while he was flipping through the Criminal Code other people's organs and bones were ravaged.

When remote stalkers are angry at a ti, the dismal truth is that his brother, kissing cousin, and best friend could all be struck within an hour or two of each other, in the same way, whether they are inches or empires apart. Their laptops could fizzle and pop. Their eardrums could rupture. Three of a ti's loved ones could break an ankle on the same day, each wondering how he managed to trip over nothing. What they don't know is that a beam shattered a bone, causing the fall. If a ti is estranged from loved ones, then bystanders and acquaintances will be struck. The helpful courthouse librarian might have spent the afternoon in Emergency. We discussed how others are impacted in Chapter Six.

Anyone can do this stuff if he has a key to the drawer where secret tactical guidebooks are kept and another key to the money drawer; for OS, in my view, is predominately a logged collection of free and expensive war-development sciences and intelligence-agency sciences, some of which are psychology, engineering, energy, space, and computers. It seems the wrong guy got the keys, unless OS really is a government experiment.

You already know that stalking, harassing, and isolating are domination exercises that any disciplined gang can carry out if it applies proven mental breakdown techniques. Combine those exercises with the nefarious mobile energy-ware that governments and their militaries admit to employing on ordinary folks—the same ones OS appears to use—and the word control takes on a new dynamic. Now, tack on covert remote EH, and the victim is in a death trap.

Most targets trust that due to whistleblowers, former secret keepers, targeted professionals, indicted perpetrators, extensive research, and evolving militaries, a smattering of the from-afar energies have likely been identified. Too, some of the government and military weapons emit microwaves, laser beams, and incapacitating sound waves, all of which are popular energies in OS, meaning victims know in part what's out there. Nonetheless, not everybody is in agreement about energy types and high-tech stalking methods. These widely varying views deserve attention because I suspect some of them have merit. We'll take a gander at these views, here and there, throughout the rest of the book.

One notion I strongly agree with states that radical beyond-university physics and radical beyond-university brain discoveries are responsible for expediting OS's airborne torture and mind control. Defence and intelligence agencies with vast budgets are disposed to find ways to one-up everyone else. Hence, it may be that the futuristic extermination and brain-encroachment weapons OS engages were originally developed in backdoor labs for Hitler-ish leaders.

That is why it's probable that under-wraps weapon-enhancing physics is why the extremely well-educated ti's cannot understand all of OS's remote shenanigans, for a goodly number of precisely aimed beams are incredible. Their effects are understood; the types of energies are not. I should explain this better. The energy that can tap noses, make it feel like varmints are scurrying over tummies, and fondle hair is exotic. That's the only word I have for it. It's conceivable that beams are focused on infinitesimal brain centres that make individuals feel and do things. In fact, that makes utter sense. Yet, brain-beams can't atone for stunts on non-living matter—stunts that are beyond appalling.

Aside from up-close and elusory beams that purposely malfunction anything electrical, like TV's, computers, cameras, crock pots, and batteries, there exists other beams that change or damage property, large and tiny.

One is a black (clandestine) operations energy that is apparently capable of pulverizing a car into powder. And a house. And a row of apartments. Targeted academics have identified this defence weapon, who invented it, and why. One fellow I know, who signed a gag order, worked to successfully develop it under the guise of U.S. national security. Naturally, the U.S. government swears that their attempts to build the energy weapon failed. We'll have to wait for the details about this space-based annihilator, for every time a prominent scientist tries to publicly discuss it he is threatened or dead within a week or two. Believe me, this supposed mammoth eliminator isn't the only black ops (covert) weapon. We are living in a society of invisible arms that have the capacity to decimate most anything, from human embryos to miles-wide landscapes. (Black operations, also called black ops, are covert illegal exercises that are undertaken by a government, military, or private agency.)

I've brought up black operations weapons because it's important that you realize I'm not being deliberately vague about EH. Microwaves, lasers, radio waves, particle beams, ultrasound, infrasound, ionizing radiation, and v2k are energies targets believe are used on them from near and far. It's the black operations mystery energy that stymies as its capabilities are extraordinary. And it's used plenty.

There's another muddy issue and that's of the different OS equipment which produces the same result. It's like soup. You can make soup on a campfire, woodstove, gas stove, electric stove, solar cooker, or in a microwave. The heat sources are dissimilar, but the soup still gets made. Voice to skull (v2k) equipment is particularly variable as several technologies can produce the same outcome. Two of the technologies are well-known and the others are not.

To complicate v2k, there's also a sound relay system that engages with specific electrical appliances. Even running water in some cases. Imagine turning on the ceiling fan or the faucet and hearing

"Patty, do the dishes." Nevertheless, voices and noise sent directly into skulls is by far the most common.

Categorizing remote energy types and the weapons they come from is high on the roster of what targets disagree on. Naming beams and weapons will not stop the assaults. Naming the assassins will. Still, it's always nice to know what's exterminating you and your family.

This is a typical quarrel:

"No, Jay, it's the clod next door v2k-ing the Bugs Bunny song into my head. It's coming from a big box on his porch. When he v2k's me to drown myself, I recognize his voice."

"You're wrong. I heard that satellites can send the guy's voice. Maybe even drones that are linked to satellites. You're being paranoid. The neighbour wouldn't put a weapon on his porch. He'd hide it."

"Yeah, just like he hid the laser he blinded me with."

"Did you see him?"

"He pointed a cell phone thingy at me, and then I went blind."

"That could have been a satellite laser. Your handlers want you to think it's the neighbour so that you'll get a crazy label when you sock him one."

"It's him alright. I caught him in the backyard last night."

You get the idea. It's taken me years to come to grips with being felled by electronic weapons. My life is so unimportant. I couldn't be more of a nobody if I tried. Why would an elite clan whose forte is remote lethal energy pick on me? And my loved ones? And leagues of other citizens?

As compelling a question as any of those, can someone tell me how police get coerced to be perpetrators? Are they paid? Are the leaders of front-line countries rallying for OS lawlessness? Or did a radical cult cook up this crime? Or maybe OS is run by a group of global politicians and billionaires who think they can rule the economy if they can control everyone. Could this be genocide? Or, could an insane science research institute be trying to modify people into non-free thinkers? Is it possible that victims are right in believing OS is an illegal experiment in mind control just as Project MKULTRA was? Is it a sport as I initially thought? And what's this talk about transhumanism? And an apocalypse?

A scarce few targets, the one percenters, are certain they are live-stream computer games that are bought, sold, and wagered on, on a high-end black market. As wayward as this sounds, every few months the remote stalkers are replaced. Targets can tell. A new staff, along with holiday and relief staff, are excited and use a profuse mixture of energies. They try out new configurations—tortures that are not on the ti's list. They turn up the dial. I imagine a lot of ti's are disabled or die from overzealous first-time slaveholders.

For the sake of folks around the ti's who think they might be computer games, being knowingly surveilled by OS is altogether separate from the exceedingly rare disorder called the Truman Syndrome, where a mentally ill individual believes he is the trapped star in a secretly staged TV show. A person with the Truman Syndrome believes that everyone around him is an actor and that all of what happens in his home and community has been planned for the show.

OS's regular, new, and relief staff are not actors, but people with criminal jobs. I should mention that the Canadian victims who receive voice to skull around the clock hear new staff make telltale comments into their noggins: "You're Canadian, eh?" or "Jeff's visiting Disneyland, so they asked me to fill in." Canadians are quick to inform others when v2k employees have American accents or admit to being American, for a lot of Canadians believe OS is run by the United States government.

Together with employee changes in the remote staff, there are changes and additions within the on-heels harassment team. There have to be. Otherwise the street theatre pranks would fall flat. Harassers accumulate in number whether a ti stays put, runs, or moves to a new town. A recently moved target may feel he is free of the volunteer and paid part-time perps who stayed behind. He's not. They will be bullying from a distance through slander; hacked and infiltrated accounts; false complaints; and odd or threatening calls, emails, or postal-service letters. If each last-city stalker commits one irritation per month, the victim will be completely overwhelmed with both new and old enemies.

A victim's core group of hunters will follow him across the seven seas. He gets used to seeing the same scabs and immediately notices if one is absent. I'm still wondering why my two blond shadow-men disappeared in year five. Being gang stalked is less complicated when the regulars are always around as their known stalking patterns and behaviours can be anticipated and sometimes skirted. On the days my blond men weren't tagging along I was fretful, expecting a surprise attack from an unknown. When they withdrew altogether, I vigilantly sorted through faces.

It's the same deal with v2k. It can be easier to listen to familiar voices all the time rather than re-adjust coping methods to appease strange voices who are giving new instructions and reconstructed put-downs.

Some ti's develop the Stockholm syndrome with ever-present v2k voices and stalkers, believing that certain predators are sympathetic and decent. (Stockholm syndrome is the term used when someone develops good feelings towards her or his abuser or captor.)

A Stockholm-syndrome-afflicted target is initially reticent, or unable, to admit that her well-acquainted, maybe even welcome, "good" perp is a paid or volunteer member of a hatemongering gang whose intent is to inflict terror and perhaps a slow death on her.

"You look pretty in yellow" may be the only kind words a ti will hear in months, and the fact a stalker says it, or that it comes into her head via v2k, is immaterial.

Besides disparaging remarks, certain victim's v2k'ed voices offer helpful hints and praise, followed by excruciating EH which the voices say they have to inflict. The voices then conclude by apologizing or expressing concern at the person's distress. These v2k-ing perps' itinerary is to schmooze and control. Anyone who mistakenly married a psychopath knows that.

You can see how confusing it is for loved ones and other ti's to hear "I know he doesn't want to hurt me" or, "He's not a bad person" or, "We're getting to be friends" after the ti has been begging for help. Perps who emit v2k and perps who are stalkers—it doesn't matter which—have induced the Stockholm syndrome in more female ti's than I'd like to let on. A male OS victim has never admitted this paradox to me, but that doesn't mean males are exempt. In non-OS crimes, studies of both sexes who develop the Stockholm syndrome are ongoing.

Most folks presume that an ever-present stalker could, in a peculiar circumstance, engender at least a nominal relationship with his worn-down prey. Nevertheless, that a relationship could be formed with a voice in one's head is dismissed as malarkey.

With no help from the outside, an unintended emotional connection with the enemy may be a victim's instinctual chance at survival; therefore, a regular v2k voice or a regular stalker who is intermittently cordial can prompt a self-saving response in the same way a beaten wife might say "Thank you" when the beating stops. There are various self-preserving reasons why someone who is in a bad circumstance unconsciously develops this disorder. Look it up. It's fascinating.

Drat. I wasn't going to get so thoroughly into the Stockholm syndrome. Bringing it up makes those who have it, and those who have had it, uncomfortable. In the long run, it's just as well that I did. Fostering fondness towards a person who wants you dead seems backwards, but it happens. You needed to understand that.

The original point I was making is that victims get to know their enemies, learn what to expect from identified foes, notice when new staff are introduced, notice when old staff leave, and occasionally form a bond with a v2k-ing or stalking perpetrator.

In case you're wondering, I have no proof of what full-time perp staff are paid, or even if they are paid. But paid they must be. Full-time stalkers can afford houses, vehicles, and niceties yet spend their days and nights, month after month, bringing down their prey.

During my first seven or eight targeted years, there is no possible way that any of my full-time stalkers held down a normal job, and there is no way they could have held down a serious relationship other than the one they had with me. Other heavily stalked ti's have the same opinion. And yes, I call it a relationship. My full-time stalkers know me better than I know myself, and before I became sequestered, they spent more time with me than anybody else ever has. If they weren't getting well paid, they would not be so dedicated.

Just so you don't get the wrong impression, the word "relationship" in this instance describes a hunter's bloodthirsty obsession with, and knowledge of, his prey. In turn, the human prey (or animal prey) is constantly looking for the hunter's weak spots, trying to figure out how to make a clean escape. From my point of view, that is a one-to-one relationship, but of the worst kind.

Let's change topics and analyze v2k's roles, and also compare v2k to directed audio systems. You're thinking, "Not v2k again. Give it a rest." Nope, I'm not going to give it a rest. It's crucial to victims and their v2k'ed loved ones that I don't. Anyhow, you've opened this book to learn about the crime.

Remember, silently sending voices and sounds into somebody's head is child's play. Perps aren't geniuses, and they manage it just fine. Sales companies and public buildings transmit directed audio recordings every day, which is considered by a minority as a primitive form of v2k. You've probably heard the directed sound systems that museums and galleries use for practical reasons. One is called Audio Spotlight (https://holosonics.com). Obviously then, marketed directed-sound transmitters are well-established, particularly in big cities.

The directed sound in this ad cannot follow a head as v2k can, nor does it have v2k's trauma-causing technology. Sound that is directed in places like museums and entertainment establishments provides a positive experience.

(Ad copied with permission)

And though they may be marketed and widespread, directed sound's commercial use is somewhat shushed, which is why vacationing Hayseed Clancy who's never heard of this invention is going to wonder if he's schizophrenic, for every time he walks towards Main Street's dairy billboard he hears "You there! Drink more milk." The promotional words went straight to Clancy's head because a device on the billboard is emitting a narrow beam of sound, and he happened to walk into it. The guy beside him didn't hear a thing.

If the beam were a bit wider, the guy beside Clancy would have heard the message too. Yet directed sound systems can only send sound to small areas, meaning that just a few of the parents sitting in section D at Junior's baseball game would be hearing "Buy a hot dog." This audio apparatus does not need to know or scan the spectators' brain waves as they are not remotely stalked and surveilled. It only needs to be aimed at the skulls in section D so that the people owning the skulls will buy hot dogs. Commercial directed sound systems cannot go through walls.

With the decidedly different through-wall long-distance voice to skull equipment, OS perpetrators send sound **into** a particular head wherever it is because the head is remotely stalked. A stalked person's head that is labelled B6N will have the database's B6N sound waves sent to it. There is only one head per OS label. Only one B6N. Brain waves are like fingerprints.

What's more, unlike a company's or a museum's directed audio message, the v2k messages and noises that are sent **into** OS victims are personal. This includes clearly audible, barely audible, and subliminal OS-brainwashing messages and noises, all of which can be repeated every few seconds, minutes, or hours. Exceptions to the standard personal messages are extended periods of torturous ringing, clicking, popping, fizzing, static, muffled talking, or prerecorded "blah blah" prattle that is emitted in a never-ending loop. Otherwise, every word and sound has been tailored for each followed and controlled head. A ti who hates operas could hear v2k'ed opera performances all day, and a ti with a lisp could hear the voices imitating his impediment.

There's something else special about OS's long-distance voice to skull equipment. It receives everything a target says. It's two-way. Like a phone. Just when you thought this crime couldn't get any more surreal.

Office-working top-dog perpetrators who are using high-end v2k equipment hold two-way conversations with their dupe. The voices comment on what a ti said to his cat: "You told Fluffy you'd get him a flea collar and you didn't." The people behind the v2k equipment often admonish the ti's criticisms against them: "Why did you tell Bob that my voice is annoying after I complimented you this morning?" or "I heard what you said to the lawyer about me, so I'm going to send Halloween howls into your head." Long-term ti's respond to the voices and get to know the people behind them, for the voices are OS perpetrators sitting in front of illegal audio systems.

OS's portable v2k devices may or may not hear the victim's words. Some ti's say yes and some say no. The equipment is so variable, both could be correct. Portables do not watch the head they are bothering.

Please consider this: a ti who does not think he receives v2k is still in an invisible two-way communication system, for each victim is remotely seen and heard. Whether seeing and hearing someone are done by different energy types that are working together or are done as an all-in-one is unknown. What is certain is that while directed energy is braising a target's eyes, the computer-operating perpetrators will watch the victim writhe; hear him beg for mercy; and if they wish, they'll tell him via v2k, "You don't deserve to see. You're shit."

Alrighty, you are aware that OS's beams take information back to the operator. Talks with rescuers, talks with your dog, dirty-talk in the bedroom, singing to yourself, fibs, farts, and fights are instantly recorded in OS's logs. The target is under total control as everything he says and does is critiqued and used to terrorize. The same goes for secondary targets, loved ones, and allies who are being surveilled and intimidated, but on a minimized scale.

What bothers me most about being heard is that a ti's, a rescuer's, and a close loved one's prayers are used against him and those he prays for. OS psychopaths crave to learn what someone's weakest areas are in order to deliver maximum cruelty, so pleas to God or Guru will ensure that the worst will happen: "God, you know how afraid I am of the dark. If I can't pay the electric bill I'll die." Even if this ti pays her bill, her fuse box or utility pole will be remotely fried again and again. She'll be in the dark in her next place, too.

A crying ti who hears a whopping bang after begging God for a sign of hope won't know whose bang it is: God's or v2k's. Targets with unshakeable faith claim that only God can hear prayers said in private. I disagree, and so do a lot of others who have grudgingly, and with great sadness, stopped all their spiritual and religious practices, repulsed by, or afraid of, eavesdropping vengeful sadists.

Whispering or writing things down makes no difference. I tried. Targets who have not caught on that they are remotely watched and listened to, always, and I do mean always, tear their homes and cars apart looking for pinhole cameras and listening bugs. I even took down the shutters that were outside the house. We won't talk about what came down on the inside. (Note – some phones can be activated as listening bugs, even when not in use.)

Perps do install pinhole cameras for naked peeping and videoing, and listening. If you suspect one, for Pete's sake look for spyware or, better yet, hire a professional. But, other than for sexual exploitation and maybe to keep an eagle eye on gung-ho activists, hidden cameras are extraneous. A non-rabble-rousing retiree is unlikely to find one.

* * *

Let's shrink OS.

On-your-heels stalkers and harassers force a target into a state of hopelessness and a state of being unable to move freely. They do this through gang stalking, general harassment, life threatening harassment, and the use of spy gear and mobile energy weapons. Long-distance (remote) energy weapons are deployed by another OS division. The target lives with around-the-clock fear, confusion, problems, physical ailments, and pain.

Each target is located, surveilled, followed, and assaulted—remotely. A remote transmission to a person is speedy; consider how fast your electrical cell phone gets a transmission. People are electrical, also.

After the target is noticeably intimidated or weakened, often after he has been considered delusional due to his claims, remote energy use is increased to inflict insufferable pain, injuries, disabilities, fear, confusion, and death at a button presser's discretion. The murderer at the computer is miles and miles away.

* * *

Nevertheless, there are several possible ways to invisibly track and energy-assault a target.

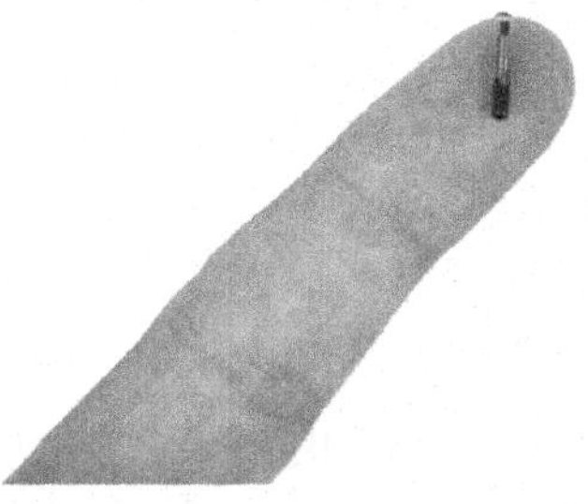

A radio-frequency identification (RFID) chip can identify the human, animal, or object it's put into, as well as provide confidential data.

Other than remotely stalking someone by perhaps following his brain waves, some targets believe a person can be traced because a microchip has been implanted into him.

Implants that can be put into people and pets for long-range or GPS tracking are near completion, according to a company that is designing them, but are not yet saleable or legal. A goodly number of targets believe that the design phase was finished long ago and that GPS implants are on the black market and used by OS.

There are different kinds of microchips and microchip implants, and each of the kinds has its own purpose and appearance. They can be put on boxes in a warehouse so that the staff can find that galdarn missing box of rubies, and the identification-type of microchip can be implanted into horses' necks to prevent a switcheroo at the racetrack. A microchip is called an implant (or a microchip implant) when it is put into a person or animal.

Close up: one type of microchip implant

The United Kingdom's Prince William is said to be implanted in case of kidnapping. Boris the researched grizzly has a tracking tag, same as the leather coats in a ritzy storefront. UK's Nestle candy company put tracking chips in select wrappers so that they could find and then surprise the candy eater with a helicopter-delivered prize. The prize is not debated, but the promotional slogan sure is. Campaign "We Will Find You" has a menacing feel.

The public agrees that corporate use of chip tracking is unethical for promotions or surveys that infringe on folks merely going about their day. Some people don't want to be found or bothered. No one wants their goings-on monitored. Plus, on-product microchip tracking can lead to stalking from personal electronics and stalking in person.

A proposal to produce GPS chips for implantation into vulnerable people, just under the skin, began as a lifesaving idea. A GPS chip the size of a rice grain could have saved an Alzheimer's-afflicted lady who was found frozen in a ditch close to my old farm. As it stands today, some care facilities put GPS bracelets on their wanderers. This kind of a device sends out an alert signal when the person has wandered too far and can also locate him. A GPS device like this needs to be charged, so it is only useful outside a body. It won't work inside of you, or your cat called Scram, not unless it has a built-in power source. It's the power source that, apparently, is still in the design phase.

But hold on, non-GPS microchip implants are definitely in use today in people like you and cats like Scram. These legal inside-people (and inside-animal) implants contain identifying and personal information about its wearer, but as stated, do not support GPS tracking. So that you're clear on this, picture a veterinarian holding a handheld scanning device over a lost pet, checking for an ID implant.

Companies producing under-skin information-storing implants, like the one in the two previous photos, declare that nobody can access the information without permission. Studies and criminals repeatedly show otherwise. If the wandered-off Alzheimer's lady had been implanted, she (meaning her implant) would have been coded into a system that linked to a database of her confidential records that would not have been immune to misdoings by a techie punk or a black sheep relative.

Should a criminal uncover an implanted chip's access frequency, which is elementary with the right gizmo, the person's lifestyle becomes someone else's affair. His identity could be stolen. Someone else could pretend to be the implanted guy because the one-of-a-kind chip now has two *hosts*.

Maybe I sound hyper over the implant debate. Microchip implants are supposed to be useful. Given that the outfall from being tracked by electronic harassment has driven myself and many thousands of other targets to suicidal ideation or completed suicide, I cannot be objective about a potential stalking system. The tracked murdered people wouldn't be objective either.

Implanting a target by drugging him and then inserting the chip through minor surgery, minor enough he may not notice, is done just often enough to grate on the whole ti community. "Am I chipped?" crosses most every ti's mind at some point.

Whether the plan is to implant or rape, rather than being whisked away and assaulted, it's far more commonplace for perp-strangers to establish when an in-home drugged beverage has taken effect before commencing their deed. As well, perp-strangers pretending to be door-knocking Bible thumpers, police, or distressed folks are guilty of doping. In all of these situations, the home is illegally or deceptively entered; and the sedated victim is raped or implanted, or his belongings are rigged, tainted, damaged, or stolen. Perps who have shrewdly befriended their prey don't have to finagle their way in. They spike a drink and wait.

Proof of OS's orchestrated assaults have most often been collected soon after rescuers installed spy cameras or voice recorders, before all the on-heels staff have been updated and before the equipment could be broken, if, that is, vandalism is on the victim's program. No one has solved why selected targets' cameras and paraphernalia suffer no harm.

Unless there is an unqualified video, a ti who has a crooked cop or who has been labelled delusional could expend his last pennies on seeking safety and proof of harm, trying to get someone, anyone, to believe his assertions.

Other than new and affluent victims who are not yet broke, targets ordinarily don't have the money to buy or replace lifesaving cameras and other fixtures. Those who do are often too sick, stalked, or traumatized to make a purchase, install the device, or follow the booklet's instructions. A video is hard for police to ignore when it's presented by a rescuer who felt compelled to set up security cameras. Also hard to ignore are food and blood drug-test results that a rescuer has procured. Keep in mind that a rescuer and his family can be threatened, injured, harassed, tortured, or killed. They can become lifelong targets.

A person certainly knows when he has lost daytime hours due to drugging and is unlikely to report an incident to police who've already called him delusional for complaints of being gang stalked and electronically harassed. A crazy-labelled ti who does present evidence of lost time can expect police to reject his claims or do a "take and toss." If this person shows an incision or lump to an officer and says it's probably an implant, he'll be written off forevermore.

Apart from drugging ti's, mentally suspending them with a remote-EH brain hit is so standard that resigned long-term victims aren't all that concerned when they come to, wondering what the heck happened when they were taken over. A few believe this is a hypnotic beam.

Losing time from an in-person encounter results in far more distress. Both of these mind-numbing attacks, in-person and EH, are wretchedly invasive, and in both cases time and memory are lost; nevertheless, the responses vary. In small part this might be due to up-close fear-fanning, especially by violent perps and night stalkers.

When memories are stopped by an energy strike, the effect is total. Brain beams that are intended to erase present memory do exactly that. It's like the victim is absent from his own life. Every once in a while I hear a click in my skull and think, "Oh, they're turning me off again," and then I lose time. Brain beams are unavoidable, so ti's learn to adapt. Going berserk ensures the attacks will happen more often. Not everyone hears a click. The mainstream learn to detect a split-second channel change in consciousness. A narrow sector say they feel droopy beforehand.

To accept that a person can be implanted and not know it, because it must sound har-har preposterous to non-ti's, we need to cover that a victim's memories, every other brain function, and his time are under OS rule. The condensed version is to appreciate that a target can be immobilized and never be the wiser.

A brain strike that causes unremembered lost time is different from a brain strike that physically paralyzes a victim. A person waking up paralyzed is fully conscious of his surroundings and will exert a tremendous, unsuccessful mental struggle to get his eyes open. Aghast and expecting to pry them open with his fingers, he finds he's inert—alive in a dead body, for not even a pinkie can be persuaded to wiggle. His (and my) only thought after a few minutes is "I wonder if I'm being murdered—left to rot." Ti's cursed with this type of brain beam claim it as part of their general torture package and not a means to implant or rape them.

In my opinion, a remote brain-beaming perp is inducing the condition called sleep paralysis, or a similar condition, and then is keeping the victim in an immobile state, which some ti's report could be up to a half hour or more. (Brain-beamed states are often distinguishable from non-brain-beamed states. There are differences.) Sleep paralysis happens naturally to about a third of the global population at least once, whereas almost all heavily harassed ti's begin experiencing it, mostly in concentrated spurts, by their second or third targeted year. In OS's sleep paralysis, hallucinations are absent, whereas hallucinations are the norm for naturally occurring sleep paralysis. The only thing in the victim's mind is trying to get his eyes open, move, and speak. Several victims who experience OS's sleep paralysis say that as soon as they are allowed to move they are forced back to sleep, with the process cycling until dawn. They say that although it doesn't happen very often, they hate going to bed each night, knowing it will happen again and not knowing when.

There's also a state of not waking at all, even when repeatedly shaken or moved. It happened to me twice at a trustworthy relative's house, and only when an ambulance was discussed did I awaken feeling fine, but groggy. If it had not happened to me, it would be easy to brashly assume that ti's complaining of this, each of who claims not to have been drugged, but brain-EH'ed, are off-track, drunk, over-medicated, or ill, the reason being that OS generally keeps victims sleep deprived.

Targets who regularly cannot be woken worry that a brain beam will put them in a permanent coma or murder them; thus, they take measures to try and wake up every hour or two, be it by multiple alarm clocks or, when possible, by being physically roused by another person. Several of these ti's have corroborating witnesses who have said, as have my witnesses, "There's something wrong. She (he) just can't wake up." When this tactic is employed recurrently, it's probably a scare tactic.

Here is as good a place as any to tell you about a transmitter that can put folks into a deep sleep and that can be regulated to keep them there. If its technology has been picked up by OS, and I think it has, it could for some ti's explain why they have no recollection of being implanted or otherwise assaulted, but bear undeniable proof. This transmitter is a 1950s medical device called the Lida machine, and it was invented to alter brain function.

A quote from Dr. Ross Adey explains the intended use of the Lida machine.

> It looks as though instead of taking a valium when you want to relax yourself it would be possible to achieve a similar result, probably in a safer way, by the use of a radio field that will relax you. . . . The manual (for the Lida machine) says it is a 'distant pulse treating apparatus'. . .

Below is an excerpt taken from a targeted academic's summary.

> The Lida Machine: . . . a pulsed 40 watt, 40 MHz radio transmitter which can be used to make a target exhausted on the job when pulsing at the rate consistent with sleep, and with a pulse rate increase,

> deprive the target of sleep too. Certain ham radio transmitters can be configured so as to duplicate the Lida signal. The Lida uses the repetitive stimulus principle, and its pulsing radio signal is what makes this a through-wall capable weapon. Very slow stimilus induces drowsiness, rapid stimulus induces wakefulness, all done silently. U.S. Patent 3,773,049 describes the operating Lida principle.

There you have it, folks: a machine that was designed for medical use, from which its technology can be used for nefarious purposes. In fact, to prove the Lida machine's effectiveness, it was used to put an auditorium full of people to sleep, although they could just as well have been put into a trance state.

Whoever is operating the little Lida box can do as he pleases with anyone's brain, through a wall and at a distance. Could this or a similar technology have been adapted to affect targeted people from miles away? Victims say yes.

Brain-struck or drugged ti's who come to with noticeable cuts or bumps that turn out to be implants are scrimpy in number, yet these ti's constitute a predictable smaller-than-small part of the victim population. Unscrupulous medical and dental practitioners, along with on-heels stalkers, are all guilty of inserting microchip implants.

Writing about intruders, strangers at the door, perps pretending to be friends, and medical people who zonk-out and implant honest folks sounds made-up. In the beginning, I thought ti's who said they were implanted were mistaken. Legally recognized cases show otherwise.

In California, a ti had five implants surgically removed. Each microchip was expertly identified in Supreme Court as being responsible for the target's hellish years of suffering from at least one of OS's well-known physical tortures. The fellow's preschool sons' proven microchips, as of this writing, are awaiting removal. The lawsuit is groundbreaking.

A riveting book could be written about a different American fellow who was granted a protection order in an "I'm implanted and someone is controlling the implants" court case. He went loud and he went public, publishing his doctor's letter that describes implants that are remotely activated or activated by his own nervous system. What this target endured is horrifying and substantiated. His case, and many others besides, can be seen online by typing "targeted individual implant court case."

Groups of targets, in pretty well all impacted countries, hire specialists to detect implants in them, just as animal shelters scan lost pets for ID chips, except that the human scanners are snazzier. Videoing the scan is essential.

Personally, I do not believe implants are necessary to organized stalking. Saying that does not diminish the impact on people who have them, for microchips result in lifelong transformations. When illegally inserted, they do other things besides offering data: revolting things to a body and brain. Depending on desired goals, they can be built as teensy message senders to reroute thinking and physical functioning. An implanted ti will look at a five-year-old's remote control robot and think, "I'm like that."

Legally planted microchips must be approved by a nation's health care department and, hopefully, do no physical harm to the wearer. I think we've all heard about office workers whose voluntary hand-implants grant them access to confidential files, locked rooms, and photocopiers; such implants are considered an improvement in security. Yet chips have no business being implanted into people who have not given consent.

Whether OS implants track the wearer's distant travels is debatable, as was mentioned a few pages back. A couple of notable scientists state GPS implants are in covert use, and the lion's share of notable scientists say GPS implants are still being fine-tuned in laboratories.

Whichever way OS implants impinge on their wearers, I think the real purpose is to alter physiology and thinking, or to make the wearer irrevocably sick or dead. Underhanded implanting is the express route to disease.

An array of ti's believe they are implanted, or could be implanted, all by imperceptible procedures. Fueling alarm are the media-rousing people who have had illegitimate chips removed from shallow insertions or who have had them erupt out of their skin from infections. These folks are aggressively claiming, as are so many others, that everyone will be chipped in the future, voluntarily or not. You can be sure that following the extraction of an illegal chip, a person will forever wonder about residual repercussions. He'll wonder if there are more.

Quite often, a suspected implant cannot be identified in medical imaging. When disparate matter *is* imaged, straightforward retrieval might be unachievable. I do not think there is an implant in me.

It's worth noting that OS victims whose implants are removed are still remotely stalked. It appears that anything with a heartbeat can be globally surveilled and managed.

Every mainstream-thinking target who has figured out the crime as best he can will tell you that technology tracks him. Some blame brain wave reading, with or without satellites. Others say they are followed by implants that, again, may or may not be linked to satellites; and a newer idea is that microscopic feedback sensors inside of victims betray their bodies' goings-on. Then there are the minorities who speculate on being tracked by artificial intelligence, specially equipped drones (unmanned planes), or by having their DNA remotely read and tailed. Those who think technology is not involved consider professional mind readers or non-human entities.

With today's sciences, locating and following things, animals, or people can be done, or plausibly be done, a number of ways; so in spite of how breezy a stalking-chip would be, other systems may be more reliable. Locating and following someone through computer-registered brain electricity or by detecting ingested particles would be failsafe. We seldom lose our heads or torsos whereas targets have had microchip implants removed.

Nanotechnology's in-body or on-body sensors are under development as a human tracking method. Nanosensors are dust-sized materials with jobs.

Experimental in-body nanomaterials, of which nanosensors are just one of its many kinds, are breathed in, ingested, or injected and do whatever they were built to do, and that can be internal medical repairs such as destroying bad cells, rebuilding damaged cells, or dispersing beneficial matter. Topical nanotech particles are sprayed or smeared.

Dust-sized sensors (nanosensors) for covert tracking on surfaces were developed years ago and respond in complex ways when they are engaging with the signals that locate them. It's easier to get the gist by telling you about the California company that has made silicon sensor dust. Their plan is to sell it to corporations, terminals, and governments for unnoticeable spraying (powdering) that would allow short-distance monitoring of dubious items, packages, and perhaps people.

If nanoparticles or medical-type nanorobotics are deliberately and secretly put into a ti, my belief is they have diabolic missions. As medical-use nanorobotics are designed to change cells, heaven only knows what organized stalking's nanoscale systems would do to a brain and other parts of a nervous system. Targets who hold the nanorobotics theory regularly detox their bodies with either non-toxic or dangerously toxic substances. What they use reflects their level of desperation.

I'm going to go out on a limb here and declare that I am a tad nervous over what's in the chemtrails. Chemtrails are the universal jet-sprayed solutions that are covering our blue skies with white fuzzy lines. They are entirely separate from the vapour trails that jets leave behind. Chemtrails are top-secret chemicals sprayed from canisters that are mounted on government jets. Are we headed for another DDT-like affair? If chemtrails are okay, why aren't citizens allowed to know what's in them? And why are chemtrail activists being threatened, or being turned into OS targets, or dying in their sleep?

I asked a world-famous environmental sciences advocate about chemtrails, and all he said is that conspiracy theorists have it all wrong. I don't know why he brought up conspiracy theories when all I did was ask what the spray is for; but darn it all anyways, what's in it besides the barium and aluminum that activists have identified? The goo was so thick over my bay one day that I scraped enough of it off my laptop screen to fill a tiny vial. Is it barium and aluminum that are causing the nosebleeds and bloody coughs for folks under the spray? Or is it the secret particles? "Dr. Environmental Scientist, your reply led me to think you know what chemtrails are for, but are hesitant to say."

For good reason targets are suspicious of chemtrails. As millions of people worldwide can be simultaneously EH'ed, there has to be a higher technology than conscripting, following, and defiling one person at a time.

Nanomaterial sprayed from jets would infect everyone, though acting alone they would be ineffective in monitoring individuals. One theory is that when these particles are inhaled or ingested they interconnect with a brain, just as any chemical does. We know non-medical nanosensors have beaconing properties. That's what they are manufactured for. If the two are combined—brain and sensors—could our noggins' one-of-a-kind electrical waves flash "Over here, pick me"? Could this allow for automated beams (through or from space: page 84) to assign individual tracking codes to masses of people at one time? And then monitor and energy-beam masses of people at one time?

I've always pooh-poohed the nanotech tracking idea. I am not a science fiction fan: never have been. It seems far-fetched that a population would be forcibly infected with nanorobotics and nano-sensors. Furthermore, nanosensors for tracking people over long distances display kinks in development that are supposed to be difficult to overcome. To boot, OS/EH was reported long before the creation of nanoscale systems.

Yet, nanorobotics have been designed to make changes in people, and chemtrail spraying is clandestine, and governments do underhandedly deploy hazardous technology, toxic chemicals, and sterility agents on residents. As much as no one wants to believe that chemtrails are designed to control the populace, because it does sound daft, many folks cannot find a more reasonable theory for how a monumental number of ordinary citizens are tagged and tailed on any one day.

Declaring that all of mankind could be put in a tracking system is extravagant until you remember that files are already kept on each resident in a developed country. As a long-ago government employee, I had access to these record books. Most workers looked up hoped-for husbands. I didn't want a husband (yet), felt confidential files should be kept that way, and looked up my dad when goaded, not realizing the significance of the government having detailed columns on the planet's kindest man. Vital statistics are one thing. This was another. I recall searching for the name of my dad's boyhood horse, wondering how they could miss Diamond when they seemed to have everything else.

Having a tracking code for each citizen would mean that remotely controlling and silencing dissenters, moral alliances, and regional populations would be efficient and improvable.

Silencing people is what COINTELPRO (Counter Intelligence Program) was all about. COINTELPRO was a U.S. Federal Bureau of Investigation (FBI) program that was formed to cut-down human rights and anti-war advocates. The illegal harassment and intimidation practices it used on good people, such as speakers for women's rights, were identical to what OS uses.

COINTELPRO tracked a great number of citizens, worried that they might say or do something to benefit mankind rather than submit to unfair self-serving government agendas. It makes you think, doesn't it? I'm not saying chemtrail particles are used for tracking folks who speak out. I'm saying that some governments do a lot of terrible things to their citizens, and as chemtrail spraying is a wide-scale government-backed covert operation, it gives rise to theories, of which tracking is one.

A splinter group of ti's have an alternate theory about chemtrails that does not involve tracking. They believe that the barium and the mystery contents cause anomalous electrical impulses in people, setting off a chain reaction, like a spark plug does. Barium is a toxic heavy metal. They think people worldwide are being re-wired.

Those who think chemtrails contain infertility agents back up their suspicions with the U.S. government-funded development of genetically modified spermicidal corn. Spermicidal corn has the potential to sterilize the men who eat it. As the U.S. government refuses to mandate the labelling of genetically modified food, citizens are bound to speculate if national or global infertility is the goal. Smaller populations are easier to domineer.

I've considered that chemtrail spraying is done to fix the climate. Conversely, if that's the case, why are enquiring folks lied to and told there is no such thing while they are watching the jets from their windows.

"Ma'am, you say you're looking at them right now. They are jet vapour trails. Aviators call them contrails. Or maybe you're seeing clouds. If you can recall watching the clouds as a child . . ."

"Nice try. Chemtrails look entirely different from either clouds or vapour. Anyways, the jets and the spray have already been confirmed, so you can't even begin to argue their existence. My question is, 'why'?"

There's one more chemtrail theory. Some folks believe that barium is a medium that enables space-sent energy to do a better job in reaching and injuring us.

No matter how—I am tracked. So are all my loved ones. So are the unfortunate folks who cross my path and are abused, usually by remote means, to further my despair and isolation.

I know. It's exhausting trying to get your mind wrapped around it all. OS sounds outlandish to me, and I am the wretch who has to be rational under circumstances that have bright, sane people asphyxiating themselves by taping plastic bags over their heads.

At this moment, a memorial is being planned for a Canadian ti friend who intentionally starved. Her twelve-year-old son had already succumbed to the crime. He shot himself.

Let's briefly look at why I agree with targeted academics who say brain waves are mapped and accessed via long-range technological achievements. Not everyone supports this theory, particularly when satellites are mentioned, given that satellites are known to have limited functions.

My bias began with research, attempting to learn how to stop a nighttime brain-squishing beam. While asking around, a targeted anesthesiologist, empathic to my plight, took the time to help me. After explaining how an EEG works (recording a brain's electrical activity), he asked me to do a mind exercise the next night my head was attacked. "Send your mind's electricity back," he said. "Make changes in your thinking."

The exercises seemed absurd, but when you are tortured with electricity, you'd chew wood if you were told it would be useful. Mustering every ounce of mental power, I tried to emit my brain's electrical impulses during the next episode. I visualized them as white specks pushing against my skull and out—pushing the lethal energy away.

When the ability to talk, walk, and see returned three days later, I phoned the good doctor. "I did what you said, and they almost killed me. Calling you is the first thing I've done since the attack. The stronger my concentration got, the higher they turned up the dial. I didn't know that level of agony existed."

"Well, it worked then. You bounced their intentions back, and they had to stop you from fouling up the program. The beam is two-way."

He's right; brain beams, including v2k, are two-way, something we touched on a few pages back. Operators send directed energy to a noggin, and the mind's responses are returned. Normally, I sent my operator a stream of frequencies that displayed pain, dread, and surrender. But this time, I fought the process.

It's true that energy harassment involves reading a mind's electrical impulses. Sad, worried, grumpy—all emotions give off different frequencies in a brain. Tracking beams assess these frequencies. That means mind-reading apparatus is trained on a victim's noodle until he dies. Targets often know their moods and thoughts are interloped because of stalkers' comments or because v2k messages tell them outright. Mostly though, EH coincides with thinking, and that's the real giveaway. Targets do not own their own noggins. If you are close to a target, you don't either.

The following 1974 United States patent explains brain intrusions rather well even though advances since then have been astronomical.

US Patent 3,951,134 (Public Domain)
Apparatus and Method for Remotely Monitoring Brain Waves
Summary by inventor Robert Malech of Plainview, New York

> **The present invention relates to apparatus and a method for monitoring brain waves wherein all components of the apparatus employed are remote from the test subject. More specifically, high frequency transmitters are operated to radiate electromagnetic energy of different frequencies through antennas which are capable of scanning**

> **the entire brain of the test subject or any desired region thereof. The signals of different frequencies penetrate the skull of the subject and impinge upon the brain where they mix to yield an interference wave modulated by radiations from the brain's natural electrical activity. The modulated interference wave is re-transmitted by the brain and received by an antenna at a remote station where it is demodulated, and processed to provide a profile of the subject's brain waves. In addition to passively monitoring his brain waves, the subject's neurological processes may be affected by transmitting to his brain, through a transmitter, compensating signals. The latter signals can be derived from the received and processed brain waves.**

While I'm at it, I may as well tell you where you can find a list of one hundred patented subliminal-suggestion and mind-control technologies: rexresearch.com/sublimin/sublimin.htm (Internet sites come and go. I'll take my chances.) A patented mind-control invention does not mean that the invention made it to the public market or that it works well, although it could have done both.

Remote neural monitoring (RNM) is what some folks call EH's mind reading, with or without mind-brain alterations (the definition of RNM is variable). The U.S. National Security Agency (NSA)

is thought to use RNM. Getting into somebody's head psychically (using ESP) is called remote viewing. Terminology isn't important here unless you want to do independent research. You only need to appreciate that ordinary citizens' brains are under attack.

Referring to ordinary, an ordinary person enduring an EH brain attack does not feel ordinary at the time. Imagine being snuggled under your patchwork quilt. Your dream of lollipops and rainbows abruptly stops. An intruder is bonking you on the head. It hurts, and although you know you are a typical Hickville resident, you feel anything but typical and ordinary at the time. I guess I shouldn't speak for you and should depict only my own responses: I do not feel ordinary during an EH attack on my brain. I feel chosen without knowing why, as would a member of a herd that is being culled. Or should I say killed.

Anyhow, let's get back to the ways I've tried to thwart painful EH attacks, allowing that each hammered ti has his own approach, of which many will be better than mine.

Weeks after my near-lethal brain-squishing experiment, the crisis was still forefront, so I began a battery of tests. This time, rather than trying to mentally overpower the directed energy, I began changing my brain's frequencies in a less dramatic way. Whenever a beam hurt, for instance, a limb or a rib, I concentrated with all my might on focusing on the pain, but as a good thing. I visualized that a lost loved one had accidentally hurt me. Glad to have reunited, the pain was trivial and even welcome. Refocusing pain is hardly innovative. Folks with skills in controlling their own minds do it automatically.

Interesting was how fast the pain would disappear and pop up somewhere else, say, moving from elbow to heel. The fact I could make this happen over and over implied more than positive thinking was at work. I played other games, recognizing when my brain was being managed and then opposing the control. I continued to experiment, research, and talk to ti's.

There is zero doubt that a target's always changing brain frequencies are read and acted upon. It's just too easy now to scan a noggin.

Thus, in my opinion only, long-range brain wave tracking seems probable, mostly because it's deemed possible and, also, because it's the best way to control someone. A beam that brings data to a head and then takes data back to a computer operator is about as simple as it gets. For example, when an OS operator receives a targeted brain's happy frequencies, maybe the memory of a romantic dance, a beam can be immediately sent to wipe out the good emotion.

I am not allowed wonderful memories or wishful thoughts for more than a minute or two. Invariably, they are replaced with pain or with a frequency that activates dreariness. This is not a woe-is-me statement. This is what happens to all heavily harassed targets. It hastens giving up and is a hardline form of mind control.

The story you're about to read is an instance of how this type of mind control can affect a person, namely me.

In my fifteenth year of the crime, I was running errands and popped into the island's quaint cafe for lunch. It was a spontaneous (and selfish) decision after a long time of not considering such an endeavor, granting that it's natural for a controlled isolated ti to take on the traits of a long-time hostage. Moving about freely begins to feel strange.

On that day, I hated being stalked and feeling owned. Really hated it, and I was determined to try to feel normal. Pre-targeting, I had been outgoing. I had loved life.

And so in I popped for lunch, hoping to shake the emotions that accompany a captive. For a minute, I felt rather good and ordered tea, which the friendly server brought with a pot of honey. "It's local," she said, and we began a conversation about bees, a subject that's dear to me, as my daughter and I had been beekeepers together.

While the server was chatting about her tangy grilled cheese sandwiches, one with honey, she gently laid her hand on my shoulder and kept it there. This was not unusual, for islanders are incredibly warm. But it was unusual for me to experience the warm and fuzzy sensations of kindness for several minutes. In other words, the woman's gentle gesture evoked an emotion that I'm not supposed to have: that which comes from the compassion of others. I cried. Not out-loud boohooing: just a silent meltdown of tears.

You see, through both EH's mind-control and isolation tactics, a heavily harassed victim loses touch with feel-good emotions, sometimes to the point of forgetting what they feel like for years at a time. That's what happened to me. I'd forgotten the emotion that's involved with receiving an act of kindness. As much as I'd like to say it's because kindness is rare in my life, which is a fact, I can't. It's because I am not allowed (am afraid) to have wonderful memories: specifically, remembering loving relationships and acts of kindness that once meant the world to me.

It's a terrible thing to have your mind controlled in such a way that pleasant thoughts are cause for punishment. Should OS have allowed me to fully re-experience comforting moments in my mind, the emotion from feeling a comforting and kind hand on my shoulder would not have been so unfamiliar as to be astounding. And heartbreaking.

Lately, I've been trying to slip in a happy memory every once in a while, hoping to restore forgotten emotions. My success rate is low, in large part because of the punishing consequences and in small part because my feel-good emotions are often buried. I worry that they'll disappear as they have for others. Lost emotions is a serious and common ti problem.

You wouldn't know it though, for victims on the whole are a blessedly thoughtful bunch, and this brings us to a mind-control paradox that requires an explanation. Most victims are especially thoughtful people who prompt their fellow hostages to survive. But mind control from directed energy, along with isolation, discourages or obliterates the feel-good emotions that occur with thoughtful acts, both in the present and in remembrances. Yet, victims adapt and continue to be kindly as it's in their nature to provide comfort to the others.

Let's change the subject to something else, like revolutionary physics, although you probably need a break about now.

* * *

I mentioned earlier that victims know cutting edge and illegally used black ops (covert) science discoveries are involved as something they can't finger produces phenomenal events to and around them. They say, "It felt like someone behind me was fiddling with my hair, but no one was there." They say other things.

There is an energy that can slide your plate of bacon and eggs to the other end of the table. It can slide, or transfer, the clothes hamper into the next room right while you're doing laundry. You'll pull bloomers out of the hamper, put them in the washer, turn around, and the hamper has taken a little journey. You're alone in the house and you wonder. You're not a crackpot. And the house is not haunted.

I've considered that the bone-smashing or table-rocking energies are possible sources, yet they don't quite fit.

There are suggestions that remote harassment is beyond directed energy, reckoning that it is not as simple as tracking Freddy through his noodle then honing in so that a lethal beam can pierce his liver. One proposal alleges energy strikes and mysteriously moving objects are black ops experiments in a novel scholastic field which combines quantum mechanics with parapsychology.

This theory presumes that remote torture and remote marvels are performed by physics-savvy parapsychologists (scholarly psycho-kinetic spoon-bending ESP experts) in laboratories that send the incidents directly to a person or article. A to B. This idea terminates my thesis that electronic weapons are the main source of abominations against ti's. Has a black operation discovered a straightforward technique of bugging people from afar?

It's a tough question, which is why a lot of targets still suppose that energy beams watch, listen, injure, and send v2k, even if they are sure they are implanted. We all know that typical directed energy has limited capabilities and that the accepted facts of energy transmission are supposed to be unambiguous. Yet because much of the electronic harassment supersedes the fixed laws of science, you will never hear me say that satellites, cell towers, or anything else in this crime are constrained by accepted principles.

Regardless of a person's slant, the hair-on-your-arm-stands-up stunts result in "Jumpin' Jesus what was that?" No one can account for whatever causes an art easel to spin around just as the artist is about to dab. I think black ops physics breakthroughs are relayed with tracking beams. However, the implausibility of it being so simple begs a different theory: that a beyond-university research bureau tapped into a primo sixth sense to recreate supernatural events, and OS got the recipe.

Targets discuss quantum physics, scalar waves, particle theories, parallel universe (interdimensional) travel, teleportation, out-of-body travel, demonic interplay, artificial intelligence, cloaking, aliens, parapsychology, oh, the list goes on. Sure, some of the ideas seem goofy. When you've fallen down Alice's rabbit hole of weird, it's often the weird answers that come to mind.

This is important. Victims should not be ridiculed for their guesses about how phenomenal incidents occur. Their guesses are based on their experiences, not yours. Your two cents' worth, which could very well be wrong, must be offered tactfully, if at all.

I got told off yesterday for asking a clique of targeted professors if v2k beams can be incorporated with tracking beams. After all, remote v2k and remote tracking work in synchrony. The response from one professor was, "That is impossible, and I'm surprised you are still pursuing this given more likely theories. You are obsessed and should stop trying to figure out how it's done." Then the lecture began. This academic believes that physicists have tapped into a hostile spiritual dimension—that evil-genius physicists and demonic entities are working together, which is why no one can figure out the phenomenal happenings.

To be sure, I cannot prove what kind of energy pushes ti's off their chairs, so you won't hear me criticizing others' positions. In fact, what sounds like kookiness could very well be spot on. Thus, I am willing to be wrong in believing that covert advanced physics are solely responsible for the incredible areas of remote harassment.

Overall, it's the mixture of puzzles and crimes that confounds the hypotheses. Not everyone receives the same forms of on-heels or from-afar hijinks. Gillian may never have had her salad bowl travel three feet to the olive bottle and is liable to call those who have, nuts. Gillian might trip at board meetings and is thought to be drunk.

But she knows darn tootin' that it's electronic harassment. There are as many viewpoints about quirky remote EH as there are targets.

About five percent of ti's put up with a steady succession of object-moving, sometimes every day and sometimes every week or so. They get as used to it as anything else and are generally appeased with whatever principle they use to explain the unexplainable. The majority experience it from time to time or in concentrated outbreaks. Those who say object-moving is hogwash pretend not to have witnessed it or actually haven't—yet. I suspect every ti is subjected to object-moving even if it's employed only once to make a showering ti think a burglar rearranged the bathroom.

I've a message for the nay-sayers. Stop telling frantic ti's that intruders are always in the house with them shifting stuff around. By misleading these victims, they become so spooked that they engage in dangerous behaviours and are afraid to be inside. They sleep in their cars or drive all night. Some would rather sleep on the street than at home. Worse, women who are trying to avert being murdered by absent sleuths are known to latch onto any man who will get them through the night. Many of these ladies carry weapons that get them into trouble. It's bad enough coping with real-life stalkers, night terrorism, and v2k that sounds like prowlers are in the house. Believing men are jumping out from their hiding places to rearrange the fireplace mantle can exceed a threshold and result in extreme self-harm. Nay-sayers of quirky EH are scaring these targets quite literally to death.

Once a ti figures out that electronic harassment is why her maple croissants crossed the counter, she can settle down and learn to live with it. She'll be safer and calmer.

This is not to say that intruders aren't a genuine nightmare. As a ti, I'm telling you that because perps believe they own their prey, they break in and do as they please, when they please. Again though, it's a matter of rationality. If a perp is regularly in a house shuffling around shoes and comic books, even carving knives and chesterfields, he's going to be seen. To boot, the victims of object-moving have never caught anyone doing it. A perp's job is his life: his identity and swagger. He's not going to risk it all to slide a bauble across a dresser when the occupant is only a room away.

Gees, I wasn't going to get into the freaky parts of OS until the end. Targets will want to choke me for bringing up this hocus-pocus. It's what turns the non-targeted population against us and what makes us sound like escapees from a communal banana ranch. Well, think of the invisible, spoof-charged energy as wind-like. You can't see the wind and it moves stuff. With object-moving, it's just an irregular science application.

Let's return to less extraordinary topics.

Targets are sensitive to being watched, examined, encroached, and altered by whatever theory they ascribe to. When I say ti's are sensitive, I mean for survival sake they fine-tune their intellect and five senses to notice when their scrutinized actions and brains are being remotely acted upon.

Then there's the sixth sense veteran targets develop that enables them to quickly and accurately detect unfamiliar stalkers and unnatural cognitive changes. This sixth sense cannot be underestimated and should not be ignored without a cautious appraisal when a dangerous person, dangerous situation, or brain intrusion is intuited.

Gavin de Becker's book *The Gift of Fear* explains the importance of using intuition, and other skills, to assess and stave off impending affronts and violence. I highly recommend it. It's reasonably priced.

Sometimes the telltale signs of a mind-control brain intrusion are subtle. We discussed that whenever I have wishful or pleasant thoughts they are replaced with painful beams or gloom-making frequencies. No one but me recognizes the coordination going on, that a positive mood is punished.

Speaking of thoughts, the time is right to tell you that they can be transmitted into a mind. Whether this is done by remote hypnosis, subliminal v2k, brain meddling, or something else, I can't tell you. The targets who perpetually experience this say they often realize when their thoughts are not their own and say they feel mind-raped and crushed, having lost every human freedom, including thinking.

These torture subjects are forced to mistrust each of their thoughts and mull over every one that seems important before deciding whose is whose. Half say they can hear the bogus thoughts, including a handful who say their thoughts are in the perpetrators' voices, which may or may not be v2k. The other half say they often know when thoughts are introduced without hearing them because thinking, "I should stick my head in the toilet for the evening," is not how their minds normally work. Transmitted thoughts are usually more serious than toilet talk and can have disastrous consequences. Hence the need for an internal dialogue that non-ti's cannot imagine: "Did my controllers just make me think I need to move to Haiti or was it my own idea?" or "I don't want to hate my sister, so why is my mind telling me I have to?"

Sometimes head-interloping is glaring. For example, if a ti goes kayaking and hums a sea-faring tune, either in his thoughts or out loud, the stalkers will hum the same tune to him on the phone, or by v2k, or in person. They will tell him that he snorted back to the sea lions. For a lark, either over the phone or into his head, they'll re-play his snort and hum, or even the scuffing noise of pulling the kayak ashore, for every sound a ti emits is automatically recorded in OS's logs by the remote-control office staff and can be played back.

This office staff transfers audio and visual recordings, along with data, to the in-your-face harassers. That's how the kayaker's perps knew to hum and snort behind him on the sidewalk. The kayaker was not alone on the ocean. Far from it. He had a cranium full of criminals. He even has a handy barcode.

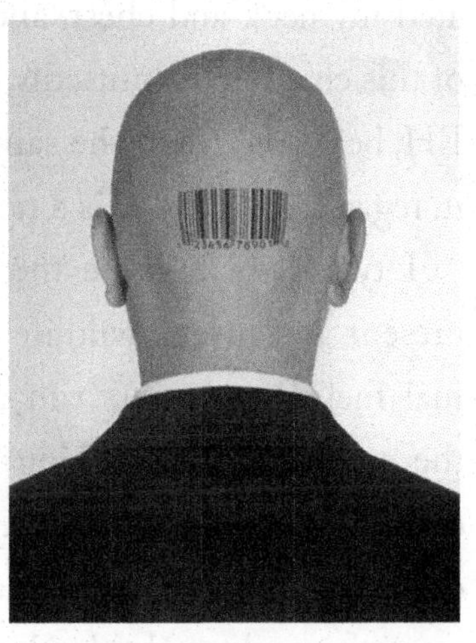

When you swipe the barcode of a Picasso print with either your smartphone or the store's scanner, whatever information the broker wants you to see will be displayed. It's the same thing with humans. Targets', loved ones', and rescuers' filed codes (no matter how they are tracked) are retrieved by perp-technicians (office staff) who are thought to be operating the surveillance computers. Whatever information was previously entered is immediately available. An OS technician can access a code, read that a person is allergic to shellfish, and then tip-off the on-heels stalkers.

It's doubtful that the street-level squad have access to high-tech, high-dollar equipment, for all the remote EH is covert. They own computer-hacking and phone-tapping tools, break and entry tools, mobile voice to skull transmitters, mobile energy weapons, see-through-wall human-detector devices, chemical dispensers, and spy store goodies. Still, street-level stalkers are kept informed by the armchair remote staff and make good use of whatever gems are handed down as this conversation shows.

Stalker on a campground path: "Hey, do you always go through your boyfriend's pockets?"

Target: "How did you see that? I was in the tent."

If remote surveillance happens to you and you do not adjust to zero privacy, you will not psychologically survive.

With a victim scrupulously watched, heard, mind-read, and assailed through airwaves, can you see why I didn't run around looking for the fricken hit-man who put a hole in my hand, lacerated my neck and chest, and punched in my face at the beginning of this chapter? Admittedly, even though there is no eluding remote EH, being visible in the same window hour after hour is asking for it, regardless that this is a nowhere cove.

I type here because the sea view is relaxing. With a doomed present and future, wildlife watching has become each day's spiritual fuel. River otters run across the lawn; and seals lumpety-up the creek in front, looking for salmon. Last spring, a large group of white-sided dolphins raced into the bay my little cove is in. I didn't know what they were at first, for all the splashing. Around the same time, a humpback whale swam in, taking refuge from his long migration: feeding, and snoozing, and drawing a whale-watching tour boat that used my cove for a lunch break and an all-together-pee-in-the-trees. (Did they know I could see them?)

It's my soft spot for great blue herons that routinely interrupts the writing, for I am entranced by a beauty who searches the meadow for frogs while his pals are fishing nearby. It's something that I'd never thought of—that a fish-eating heron wouldn't like fish. There are a lot of bald eagles this summer, and my little companion bird has learned to mimic them. And then there are kingfishers and loons and a reddish hawk that swoops after the sparrows.

Mink come right up to the house; and once a beaver waddled by, finding a pond beside the kitchen inadequate. Most delightful is that the carport is a deer short-cut. They saunter through, and I'm beginning to wonder if it is a game of deer-dare, seeing who can stand by the door the longest. Last summer a doe, somebody's pet, followed me down to the beach and dozed at my side while I read. For excitement, the island black bears converge on the property at apple time and look in the windows.

The loudest of the creatures are the ravens who have been doing today what ravens do best, hopping up and down on the branches and yelling at their kids. Turkey vultures have been gathering under my typing-window, so there's probably something to eat there. Or maybe they are having meetings. I'm not going to look. Night stalkers could be leaving dead animals. Not bothering to investigate will make it unlikely to happen again. Harassment is all about getting reactions.

The wildlife here has become critical in keeping me composed. The hummingbirds that hover in the windows and sparkle, the laughing duck—they make the days tolerable. Moving to town would emotionally be my demise. Moments of solace keep me rational.

Disappointingly, the non-bird critters haven't been around as much this week. It could be that animal-scaring frequencies are being discharged. Or maybe the night stalkers are up to no good in the woods. In my last two countryside homes, both furred and feathered animals deserted the area.

Targets who experience sentimental boosts, such as I do by watching nature, are less inclined to commit suicide. If the wildlife is frightened off to hasten mental collapse, the sea will remain. Salvation, for I am barely hanging on, as are so many.

A thread-hanging target from Seattle, Washington State, is asking to visit. She is originally from Alaska, so the solitude appeals to her. That might be nice when I've finished writing. Another Seattle ti is asking me to find her a Canadian home despite having flown to Holland. She likes Holland, but the large perp population won't let her keep a job. Canada will be the sixth country she's fled to hoping to lose the stalkers.

Two American ti's I know were injured in staged accidents last month. One, a MKULTRA survivor, is in a wheelchair with a head injury from a perp running her down on the side of the road. The other is raging, her car forced into a ditch for the last time. She's giving up driving.

To heighten anxiety, perps will craftily tell or show their victims what kind of accident they've planned and that was the case with these two. Some stalkers' full-time jobs are to move around and cause *accidental* injuries and deaths. With so many careers to choose from, they chose that.

Targets who have intentional accidents as their primary harassment theme cannot trust that their house stairs are safe. Or their bicycles. Or the chains on their chainsaws. Angry stalkers will definitely tinker with a vehicle's brakes and steering. Even my sawhorses were sabotaged. That's how far these guys will go. Remember, victims are made to know that the accidents were stalker caused. If they attribute mishaps to bad luck, the control would be negated.

A slew of American prison inmates are writing and asking where to find attorneys who know about OS. Targets find themselves framed and in jail or prison, or they end up incarcerated from self-defence measures. Several imprisoned men and woman claim they are tortured with v2k and pain beams yet are certain they were not targeted before being sentenced. Each one feels experimented on in a MKULTRA-like project. Such claims are dicey to substantiate as weeding out perps and misguided people who pretend to be targets is somewhat makeshift without the benefit of conversation. I've decided to begin forwarding the prisoner mail to a trusted ti society as delegating my time has become urgent.

More ti's than usual are brawling with each other this week, something I stay away from. They are really going at it, hating each other as much as they hate their enemies, believing their own pitches will be the blueprint to freeing us all.

A Vancouver, British Columbia, perp got irate at me last month and slandered my name throughout North America's human rights associations. He had assigned me to an activist group he set up and then demanded a bunch of favours. I politely refused his requests, based on him being a total stranger. Perps are always creating activism groups to draw in fraught targets. They then do wicked things. Anyhow, he publicly called me a useless old lady who deserves to be tortured and killed. Ho Hum. Some ti's get riled over this kind of thing. I did the first time. But these jerks aren't worth getting steamed up over. Targets eventually learn to decide what they're going to get upset about. Otherwise they will have no minutes of mock relief.

Opening my emails this morning to "u r ......TI SCUM!!!!" couldn't be more ordinary. The sender, Knight Mare, has been insulting me for years. Last week she wrote that I was unmotivated crap. What? You want me to put her on the email's "do not accept" list? No way. Some enemies I keep close. It's the only way to study them, and besides, this woman's local. Not that I respond to hate letters. I don't. Just the same, a lot can be garnered through quiet observation.

Organized stalking in Canada seems to be on an ominous rise. Troublesome is that more folks in cowboy towns are getting hit lately, mostly in the western provinces, including a young guy in a mining camp. A married pair near the Yukon border called several times last week about losing their hearing and vision from electronic harassment and losing their livelihood to OS chicanery. Then the perps stopped our communication altogether. Nice couple too. She was crying—sounded like posttraumatic stress disorder had taken over.

The bulk of new rural targets, however, are single women wondering how they were chosen and why in blazes they'd be victimized in such uninhabited areas. One such lady, from a small town in Alberta, is fraught with religious constrictions that are hindering self-protection.

It was a call this afternoon from a Halifax, Nova Scotia, mom that that has me in knots. When kids are involved my heart sinks. Recently targeted, the single mom's voice was strong and angry at the beginning of the conversation. After a few minutes she burst into tears, apologizing. She said her hair is falling out and that her car's electrical system and gas pedal have been tampered with. She said she can't go out the door without being mob-stalked and feels "lit up," believing that her kids and her home are under a high energy dose. Vibrating and vomiting, the woman is sick. She knows her seventeen-year-old daughter is in danger and asked me how to keep her family safe. My reply of target-tailored coping tactics was not the response she wanted. The police have characteristically turned their backs.

Another crying ti called today, from Japan. She lived on British Columbia's coast for several years to attend university. Upon returning home to Japan she found herself targeted. Because some calls are scams, during our first conversations I hammered the poor woman with more questions than usual. She certainly knew about coastal university life but was unable to explain the ins and outs of harassment which is the way it should be for a new ti. During these authenticity quizzes the answers don't really interest me. I look for trauma, confusion, and loony-tunes reasoning. She passed. This new ti believes she was targeted in Japan. She could very well be right. There's quite a few ti's there. I suspect though she went home already harassed because mob-stalking apparently began immediately upon arrival. Once a subject is chosen, there is no letting go. Regrettably, she had been staying in Vancouver, a city crawling with OS. Vancouver Island, a boat ride away, isn't any better. Even the little nearby islands like mine, jewels of the Pacific Northwest, have OS.

At the rate organized stalking is growing in British Columbia, the impact will soon be noticeable by the non-targeted population. Perpetrators vandalize the immediate area around their victims' homes. Scratched cars, flattened or softened tires, maimed pets, smashed-down fences, hit and runs, sunken boats, you name it. It's a blot on a beautiful province. God's country as tourists call it.

Speaking this afternoon to the Nova Scotia mom made me notice that my demeanor has changed. Non-emotional encouragement to despondent victims doesn't happen anymore. The advice remains the same, but I cannot control my sadness and find my voice cracking and the tears rolling no matter how hard I try to disguise myself as sensibly composed. When targets cry now, I cry with them. My psychological resilience is failing.

Suicide calls are up, as I mentioned, and all are Canadians. Two are in Vancouver; one is in New Brunswick; another is in Manitoba; and the others are in Ontario, Canada's other OS hot spot. Targets from Ontario swear that the Ontario Provincial Police are following the Royal Canadian Mounted Police's seeming example of lies and corruption wherever OS is concerned. Seriously suicidal targets comprehend that there is no chance for police assistance.

If I didn't have confidence in activists ending the crime, which would allow my children back in my life, the will to endure would be tenuous.

The tragedy is not what has happened to me. The tragedy is that my youngest children grew into adults wondering how their mother could abandon them. And the eldest who was newly independent must have felt truly unloved. The worst thing a mother can do is abandon her children. Yet, in order to save them, that is precisely what I did.

It's not like I packed up and ran off one day. For almost three years I moved in and out, over and over, to see if the kids were safer with me gone. They were.

Realizing that complete separation from my family was compulsory, I wanted the men to murder me, unwilling to live childless. I wandered in the woods with the night terrorists and parked down logging roads hoping for that one psychopath to finish me off, not understanding they were disallowed to deviate from my planned suicide. Of course, my children were all alive. But, I felt childless. Far worse was their plight, forever wondering how I could do such a thing—to seemingly love them so little.

For many years my children did not get any acknowledgement from me. I was certain they would be tortured, raped, kidnapped, or murdered should we connect.

Today, my kids and I speak just enough to keep me from suicide and just enough that they know I love them. They don't perceive the consequences of our scarce exchanges, sometimes experiencing the same energy strikes and harassment I get, in the same moment: a common isolation ploy. They blame irregular setbacks on atypical health issues, atypical events, and rotten luck; and I have to wonder if they've been targeted all along. They do not believe that the stalkers who endangered them in 1998 would still be at it. They don't want the past discussed.

My enemies force me to acknowledge that speaking to my children is irresponsible. I question if they would be free of OS should I die or disappear, knowing that if I were gone there would be nobody to help should they become full-time victims. Hopefully, when this book is published, my children will be safer. It's likely that the perps won't bother them so as to make me look like a liar. I am more than okay with that.

The hurt I've caused my children is unanswerable and unforgiveable. The youngest had their teen years ruined when I took off for good. They all felt unwanted. And here I am still hurting them.

A target's sorrows are endless. A target's family's sorrows are bewildering as well as endless.

At least I had the opportunity to enjoy my kids for a while. For men and women who are heavily targeted at a young age, dating, falling in love, and having children are lost dreams. It discourages and depresses them.

I guess this is a book of sadness. I need to dig myself out of this hole.

* * *

I've covered a lot more in this chapter than I'd intended. At least now you know the basics.

So that's it for tonight. While typing the last few pages both legs have been scorched, and the radiation is making me puky. A library documentary and a couch overlooking the moonlit sea are going to be my refuge. Pearls in the quicksand.

CHAPTER NINE

ELECTRONIC HARASSMENT IN SIMPLEST TERMS

ELECTRONIC HARASSMENT (EH): Energy aimed at people, animals, objects, or areas that is intended to do harm.

REMOTE STALKING: Tracking and monitoring a person with advanced technology from afar.

MOBILE ELECTRONIC-HARASSMENT WEAPONS: A variety of limited-range weapons, each with its own capacity to cause harm. They can be disguised and handheld, disguised and put on a table, box-sized and hidden, box-sized and out in the open, large units in buildings, or large units out in the open. These weapons send energy that deters, harms, incapacitates, or kills one person, multiple people, and animals. They are also used to malfunction or destroy electrical and non-electrical items.

REMOTE ELECTRONIC-HARASSMENT WEAPONS: Weapons of any long-range technology that beam energy at one person, multiple people, animals, vegetation, electrical and non-electrical items, buildings, and land tracts. These weapons are used to wound, incapacitate, permanently disable, control, kill, malfunction, damage, and destroy.

TYPES OF KNOWN ELECTRONIC HARASSMENT: Microwaves, radio waves, lasers, particle beams, ionizing rays, infrasound, ultrasound, and voice to skull beams.

MICROWAVES: Common. Emitted by carriable weapons, and by larger ground-based weapons, and assumed to be emitted remotely.

VOICE TO SKULL (v2k): Common. Beam which sends sounds and voices that are silent while they travel through the air to a head. As the beam seeps through its targeted head, hearing mechanisms are triggered and the sound is heard by that one person. The sound is not heard by others unless the beam is sent to them also. Voice to skull can be emitted vast distances remotely and can be emitted short distances by limited-range devices.

LOW- AND HIGH-FREQUENCY SOUND WAVE TORTURE: Common. Emitted remotely, and by carriable weapons, and by limited-range ground-based weapons. Defined as torturous inaudible sound waves that send harmful frequencies to a head and body for the purpose of causing physical and psychological damage. Death is possible.

IMPLANTS: Microchips put into people to control them and to cause physical and mental harm.

NON-MEDICAL TRACKING NANOSENSORS: Nanoscale systems manufactured to allow tracking of objects. Nanosensor people-tracking studies are ongoing.

NANOROBOTICS FOR HUMAN USE: Nanoscale systems put into people to change their physiology (still in experimental phase). They can be absorbed, swallowed, or injected and can have an energy field. A method to remotely control them is under development.

MYSTERY BEAMS: Unidentified energy types emitted to cause fear, harm, death, and destruction.

PHENOMENA: Bizarre moving of objects and other unexplainable OS-produced events which are perhaps caused by energy-matter-space physics breakthroughs.

CHEMTRAILS: Universal aerial spraying of barium, aluminum, and unidentified toxic chemicals that may or may not be linked to remote electronic harassment.

Please note: there are no courtroom-confirmed definitions of the remote energy types used by OS. Of the limited-range energy assaults that have gone to court, several have been publicized and can be found online. Look up "electronic harassment court cases."

Should you want to learn more about the effects of OS's known weapons, tech and trade schools offer courses that explain the science behind everyday and atypical energy devices that, besides being useful, can cause harm or death.

CHAPTER TEN

JOURNAL

Journal: Fall

Last night I was hit for four hours with what I believe were remotely sent microwaves. Standard energy-shielding materials had zero effect. My present condition consists of difficulty breathing, shaking (not vibrating), nausea, irregular heartbeat, a nosebleed, dizziness, stinging eyeballs, burning lungs, coughing, and a headache that is making me vomit. I'm pink-hot, yet compared to last night feel much relieved. I can't stop crying but cannot put a reason on it other than trauma. Although my entire body was cooked, it was my legs, brain, eyes, chest, and throat that were hit the hardest.

My thoughts reflect on tortured prisoners, wondering how they stay sane or if they do go mad for the duration. For a couple of hours I felt outside of myself and could not stop visualizing a mouse frenziedly swimming in a boiling black cauldron, though I've never seen such a thing, own no such pot, and am fond of mice.

If my tormenters have done permanent damage, as you already know, I shall not seek medical care, unable now to cope with doctors, questions, and remedies. Years back when perps seared my windpipe a surgeon sent pictures of the lesion worldwide. No physician could explain how such a serious burn could suddenly appear like that in one spot, and I was told that without intervention my ability to breathe unassisted would stop within six days. (I've never smoked.)

Revealing that injuries are energy caused is not something I will do until after EH gets publicly recognized. Too many targets have tried and ended up with compulsory psychiatric meds. That would finish me off. No one could withstand microwave torture like I just had while doped up. Wrongful medical doping is indisputably responsible for ti's quickly disappearing or committing suicide. We can't handle psychological and physical torture unless we are mentally strong.

Perhaps due to shock, letting myself die soon seems like a good idea. It was comforting last night to know suicide was an option. Plainly, doing so might hurt my children even more than I already have, and besides, soldiering on is critical, for some of us have to live to tell. Having an "out" plan relieves the mental burden of lifetime torture.

For the record, remote microwaving, if that's what I experienced, is accurately aimed. My companion bird is having a good day.

They've cut off my phone again, just now. Tapped-phone static has turned to tapped-phone silence.

It's frustrating that recovering will interrupt the writing.

Journal: December

While standing in the living room looking at the cove, my ribs broke. They popped. I looked down expecting to see my guts spilling out.

A pressure beam had been on my chest for days, feeling like when my horse fell and trapped me underneath, so long ago. Whether my torso was cracked on purpose or if my body gave out is unimportant.

I couldn't breathe when it happened and thought my lungs had collapsed, but it was the effect of the pressure beam.

Something else happened when I was cracked, and my body is out of whack. While shuffling forwards, my right half wants to go sideways, crablike.

Journal: January

An energy rod has been trained down one side of my skull every night for the past week. It's excruciating and has kept my right eyelid closed since it began. The left eye won't properly open until lunchtime. Both eyes stream, burnt and sore.

Baseball batting beams have been striking me for a second here and a second there, all over my body, for days. I am exhausted and will be glad to die. My inborn character has always been positive minded: an optimist. The pre-targeting me had infinite zest. Ongoing thoughts of giving up are out of character.

Journal: Late April

The remote-beaming staff compressed me in half mid-March when I was dropping a library slip into the kitchen's wastepaper basket. Obviously, being in half is impossible. That's the only way to describe how it felt, for my ribs were re-broken, my innards felt bulgy, and my back had trouble holding me up, as if my spine was jelly. This time it seemed I would not survive, for until last week, getting off the couch made me scream, yet here I am back at my desk. It's a game. If they wanted me dead, I'd be dead. My suffering is keeping my owners entertained.

Torture subjects need a reason to live and mine is to finish this book. Targets' kids—my kids—can only be saved if OS is exposed. So here I go, giving it another try.

CHAPTER ELEVEN

COPS

Raise your hand if you think there are bad cops. Alrighty, we've established that policing isn't perfect. Nonetheless, an ordinary citizen dealing with a crime, say, stolen antiques, expects a small measure of law and order. OS victims, on the other hand, expect disrespect. Most officers mock not only the vulgar gags played on targets, but they mock OS's graphic violence.

Let's begin with the way cops backpedal by slapping on a delusional marker when they realize they are dealing with a ti. "Delusional" and "may have psychiatric problems" will decorate each subsequent file the cop fills out. The fact this happens from one ti to the next is preposterous considering that every victim I know is well-grounded, which is who perps go after, including choosing individuals with a chronic illness or limited mobility. Stalkers prefer their prey to have sound minds, and other than for sexual exploitation, what's under a mind is strictly a vessel to be hammered.

Exceptions are people with a visible debilitating psychological disorder, or a severe learning challenge, or visible brain damage, all of whom can be regularly or irregularly harassed to punish or isolate the actual target (see Chapter Six). A cognitively impaired person who is not used to intimidate or isolate a target is unlikely to experience critical OS setbacks, though he could experience a strike or two, even as a bystander, for the sole purpose of egging on a ti's stress.

The real glory, of course, is in watching prototypal Anns and Andys break into unsalvageable pieces. This does not imply targets fit into a cookie cutter. Their foibles are as embodied as in any random crowd. Yet, someone whose thinking is recognizably divergent will not be heavily harassed and tortured unless he is a mentally disabled child or other mentally disabled loved one of a ti, particularly a ti with an isolation theme.

In contradiction to this, a mildly mentally disabled lady who as a child was a MKULTRA (government mind-control experiment) subject declares she is continuously electronically harassed as an adult OS victim. She can't be the only one, for MKULTRA doctors experimented on countless children, some of who are now elder ti's.

For the sake of not excluding anybody, recent legit accusations of ritual abuse, OS/EH sexual abuse, and illegal medical experimentation on ti's and non-ti's autistic or developmentally delayed children, (also, typical children) have been documented.

Finally, getting to the point, what I'm trying to say is that folks who have pronounced mental or developmental disorders appear not to be chosen in the grocery store as the next OS insect.

I know you know that OS victims have to adapt to gang stalking and electronic harassment and that these adaptations can be misconstrued as personality aberrations. For instance, I hang bells over doors that are blocked by chairs. Dense as I feel doing this, it's reassuring to know that other ti's are equally embarrassed over misunderstood safeguards, as well as feeling mortified over shell-shocked or needless exploits. An underwear-clad dash outside after hearing what turned out to be a v2k explosion will not be shrugged off by all who saw. Even so, irrespective of OS's creed to turn ti's into fools and androids, every confirmed victim I've spoken to has got all his marbles.

Notice the word "confirmed." Perpetrators posing as targets say dippy things like "I've a drawer full of metal stars that flew out of my neck" or "OS is run by rock bands." As perpetrators go public, they manage to combine the seriousness of targets' assertions with their own circus clown remarks.

Imposters aside, if you assembled a hundred ti's together, about eighty of them would be defined as exceptionally kindhearted. I used to believe this disproportionate demonstration of grace was attributable to being humbled from torture. In part that may be true, but in speaking with the same victims over many years, their pre-OS characters have been revealed.

Here's the rundown: targets are generally an empathic, competent, mentally healthy lot who render aid to the others even when their own circumstances are dire, for altruism is mutual. To avoid OS pitfalls, they learn to think in detail about their intentions, actions, and statements. It's this forced practical thinking to save oneself that has created an astute bunch.

My ti friends have also proven themselves to be honest. I've left them alone in my house and not worried. Could it be that courteous and principled folks make better candidates?

Allowances are necessary for new targets who express confusion, fear, anger, despondency, and panic in copious amounts. They are certainly reacting appropriately; however, because they haven't caught on to OS, they cannot unravel the chaos. Floundering victims are as sane and intelligent as the rest and are particularly vulnerable to being called mentally ill by perp-cops. Long-term victims have off-days, too. Feeling crabby or blue is the right response to being a gang's plaything. I'm going to go ahead and speak for targets: "Our lives are so abnormal you wouldn't believe it, but we really wish you'd try."

It's insulting that a number of non-ti's, and even unenlightened ti's themselves, presume that victims have done something to deserve OS's tirade. They think targets must be rotters. People holding this drivel assume that perps are employed to curb society's menaces. Such rubbish—that ti's are a bunch of misfits—is a convenient excuse for cops to deny assistance.

Still, it would be difficult to portray the cast of targets as defective since the majority are treasures. I feel honoured to be considered a friend and gain courage from them.

Their collective integrity is admirable despite unspeakable cruelty. Between torture sessions, they hold their heads high, support the spent, and determine to conquer. When thresholds are exceeded, they endure for as long as is humanly possible. It's these traits—sanity and decency—that OS victims hang on to no matter what is thrown at them.

So why is it that the majority of long-term, new, or secondary ti's who ask for police help are called delusional, or schizophrenic, or as having a paranoid or drama-seeking disorder? Why instead does a splinter group of perp-cops prefer to deem a respectable ti as a liar, trouble maker, con artist, criminal, airhead, or as mistaken? Why is a laudable scholar called cuckoo for telling police that he's stalked?

Well, let me fill you in. In my opinion, most, or all, Canadian and American senior-level police headquarters know about organized stalking and electronic harassment as do other developed countries' law enforcement commissions. For whatever reason, they are covering it up. I've examined countless ti histories, watched their videoed exchanges with cops, talked with targeted and non-targeted lawyers, researched, and tried to gain the Royal Canadian Mounted Police's attention. Not only do most police not want to assist targeted individuals, they exacerbate each victim's demise.

In my view, without an ounce of doubt, shameless OS-informed officers intentionally depict targets as either bonkers or crooked. These officers seem to deliberately support the stalkers' campaigns to fell ti's by writing profiles with contrived felonies or bogus claims of mental disarray. Who else but a dirty cop could persuade a dozen folks into conceding that a fit person suddenly needs to be sent to a cracker factory.

Let's look at these, perhaps, bought-off cops' handiwork. If a man tries to run over a little girl, an officer should make the effort to jot it down. And if strangers come to the little girl's school with pictures of her, asking her whereabouts, then that also should be worth a scribble. Not so with targets and their loved ones.

It's occurred to me that OS is another version of MKULTRA, and the officers who end up responding to a ti are paid, or elsewise bribed or coerced, and then coached to be remorseless. Other than that, it eludes me how so many victims' children are threatened, injured, or murdered after the parents have demanded that police intervene. When a targeted parent wails, "My children are going to be killed!" he is pigeonholed mentally ill. It happened to me, and it happens to all ti parents. It makes me sick.

My misadventures with Constable Satan are so typical I feel justified telling a personal story to represent what ti's go through trying to get police help.

At the crime's onset, night terrorism on my hobby farm was extreme. As soon as the sun went down, OS took control over the road, woods, and property. Besides my complaints, an outlying neighbour spoke to the police about night-crawlers, traffic, and multiple counts of vandalism. The fellow got so frightened he erected tall posts with spotlights around his house. Separately, we lodged enough grievances that a lying Royal Canadian Mounted Police constable was assigned to shut us up. The Mountie told the neighbour that my household was to blame and told my family we were imagining it. Keep in mind that that the neighbour and I shared a dead-end forested gravel lane. (Mob stalking in my case is uncommonly brazen and noticeable.)

After relentless nattering from my partner and me, the assigned constable, Satan, begrudgingly dropped by to inspect how vandals had buckled and disassembled our farm gates. Funny thing was, we had to coax him to walk over to the first gate, and once there, he exuded an unchanging expression that can only be described as Mr. Potato Head on a bad day. Stranger still, he refused to look at the gate, swiveling his head this way and that. When we pointed to a crumpled rail and a pile of drilled-out bolts lying on the ground, he saw something in the trees. As soon as we started talking about the night terrorism and the second trashed gate, he walked away; so we followed, telling his back that men were hiding in the feed- and woodsheds and that the horses had been beaten. We vainly tried to steer him to the broken rose trellises and the black circle painted on the house. Baffled with his lack of interest, I told the police car window that after it got dark men knocked on the house walls. Having to shout through the glass at him about how the phone always went dead at 9:00 p.m. and how scared we were was discouraging. It was the only time RCMP (Royal Canadian Mounted Police) came to the farm when we asked that an officer check out the night raids or see a raid's aftermath. It was the best we got.

The license plate numbers my family submitted were ignored as were the dozens of tokens (items left by stalkers) I handed over to the detachment. I repeatedly pleaded for a lie detector test after being called deranged, and Constable Satan pretended each time not to hear. In fact, he pretended not to hear, or twisted, everything my partner, parents, friends, witnesses, neighbour, and I said, even when the children's safety was at risk.

Yes, it was my daughter who a man tried to run over, a tactic mentioned while discussing that assaulting loved ones is a common coup to make a ti leave home, and it was my daughter who a perp sought in the schoolyard, showing photos of her to students and asking where she'd be. (The perp-woman bolted during questioning by a teacher.)

Unbeknown to my family, OS had taken over another property less than two miles away. No one can tell me the RCMP didn't know that both households were experiencing the same onslaught in a community of three thousand country bumpkins. The nearby target was called deranged too and, like me, tried to sue the RCMP for not doing their job. But he said they broke his neck and he won a sue case for that. My neck stayed intact because when I sued they did other things, like hire motorcycle meanies.

There were five targeted homes within a short drive from my farm and a large population of victims within two hours' travel. We were all called delusional. I'd like that explained as each of our families was destroyed.

It took me longer than any of the other local ti's to figure out the RCMP are the enemy. I liked the police, figured Constable Satan was sub-par, and soon set about on Plan B. Plan B was that by appealing to different Mounties in the detachment the matter would be resolved. I kept getting referred back to Satan, so I constructed Plan C which was mobilizing the staff sergeant. This is where ti's call me a dim bulb.

It was one incident that convinced me the RCMP are in cahoots with OS. "Sir," I implored on Satan's answering machine, "the kids and I were walking the horses to the mailbox, you know—same as you walk a dog, and a stalker aimed his car at my daughter. You've been to my house. It's in an untravelled road. This wasn't an accident. The driver looked right into my eyes—fiftyish, big guy—crossed the road, and drove straight at her. I dropped the horse I was leading, ran ahead, and pushed my daughter so hard that she pushed her horse. The car scraped my coat. It turned around in my driveway and took off. There was mud on the license plate, and I only got a partial number, but I can identify the car and the man's face. You've got to do something. My kids are going to get killed. If you don't believe me, talk to my daughter."

Constable Satan would not return the call, so I handed a statement to the front desk personnel who told me Satan's work schedule. I continued calling and going to the detachment, talking to various cops who were equally useless. It took weeks before Satan agreed to speak to me, but only in the RCMP foyer.

Reciting to him once again what happened, he turned his head away. When I stepped around so that we could talk eye to eye, Satan's barefaced contempt hit me as if he'd confessed his OS involvement through a loudhailer.

For filing formal negligence charges against Constable Satan, I was called mentally disturbed and told my hand-written letters detailing the incident, and other serious incidents, were mislaid. Three years later I was still haggling with the Complaints Commission. There's an old box of their replies in my closet, telling me to stop. I knew that the RCMP never admit misconduct. Even a unit's corporal told me that. But I sure as hell couldn't quit, not with the stalkers still threatening to hurt my kids. Cooperation in all levels of the RCMP was declined, and I was told to see a doctor.

Pretty well all noisy targets are trotted off by police for a psychological exam with the objective of being branded insensible. Constable Satan did that to me twice. The first time, he said he'd take me to the hospital about my failing health. When we got there, I was stuck in a shrink's office. Soon extorted into another trip, only a patient offered to prop me up when I keeled over from probable radiation poisoning in a waiting room chair. Satan, in his workaday dark-blue and grey uniform, sat unmoving an arm's length away. As no medical care was offered either time, it was evident he had deceived the hospital staff with a yarn.

Taking me home after the second try to declare me loco, Satan snapped. Seething that the hospital shrink again declared me normal, he raced towards every red light, braking hard at the last moment. He took corners so fast that crashing seemed inevitable. Halfway home, nearing the countryside, he pulled over, told me to stay put, got his shotgun out of the trunk, and stuck it between my legs. Driving on, he spoke in gibberish, wanting me to think I was hearing crazy-like. When he pretended to be lost in the dark on a lonely wooded back road, my lips remained sealed. Satan was unstable, and speaking or getting out, in my mind, would have been dangerous.

Shortly after, to separate my kids from the crime, I was forced again to amscray and find refuge elsewhere. Squeezing the cops had not gone well. Worried about residual intimidation on my family, I took the children's little boat along, knowing how easily OS's men could drown them. While asking around at my new hamlet's marina for a place to stow the truck-box dinghy, an elderly fellow named Otto looked at it and said, "Oh, sure. You follow me home. I'll take good care of it." Although he lived nearby, the stalkers managed to stay out of sight until we got to his house where they converged as a pack.

"Are you in trouble?" Otto whispered, his driveway filling with motorcycles and work trucks as we slid the boat onto his veranda.

The old soul convinced me to talk to police as the community was not RCMP territory, but protected by an outskirts municipal force nationally renowned for its competence. That's where I found a super cop, making me the only ti among thousands who has had an ongoing, earnest police investigation into her stalking and harassment.

Super-cop called and interviewed family and friends at the farm. He visited reachable relatives. And, without me knowing, he and another undercover officer watched. He couldn't understand what Constable Satan had been up to and reiterated wonderment at why my situation had been spurned by the RCMP.

Ever-communicative, Super-cop preferred to meet and talk at Otto's house, if for any reason, to see Otto's latest vandalism, for night stalkers had waged reprisal on the old fellow. Pretending not to notice that every coffee the pensioner brought him was in a chipped mug, the detective listened to our latest harassments with unhurried interest. When he handed me his pager number, saying, "It's important you don't hesitate to use this," I felt both frightened and relieved. Rape was used as intimidation from day one.

Otto, for his generous offer to store the boat, had his workshop rifled, found glass shards in his cookie jar, and had his car engine trashed three times. He could not sleep until he'd boarded up easy-entry doors and windows, and after he did that the men threatened to burn his house. When he caught a stalker on his roof, he strung wartime wire-traps around the yard. "Don't you worry," he said. "When Finland was invaded I learned what to do."

Amazingly, in the middle of all this, Constable Satan got rather productive, determined once and for all to label me psychotic despite us being in different cities. He made up stories about the old Finn and told everyone he could think of that the two of us were schizophrenic shysters who were conspiring together to agitate the police. He constantly called my partner and my parents trying to brainwash them that I needed to be institutionalized. He even called my brother, Brian, and convinced him I was a pest for over-worked officers. Brian came to my home and yelled at me, which was useful as he repeated everything Satan had said. Still, it was unnerving for a nerd like me.

Unlike Brian, Super-cop wasn't going for any of it. He gave me hope. What I did next defies stupidity. Super-cop took a holiday, and when I couldn't connect with his replacement, retributive terrorism became unmerciful, and (being younger back then) I ran for fear of being gang raped to death.

Running from place to place doesn't really work in OS. It's only good for heading off a vicious stalker or two and soon milks a person of his last financial, psychological, and physical reserves. After learning that lesson, I recoiled and prepared to confront Constable Satan in court. I sent for my RCMP files, municipal police files, and medical records through the Freedom of Information law. Actually, I sent for the RCMP files several times trying to get withheld papers. My fourth unsuccessful attempt resulted in a nasty conflict.

Out of a folder full of RCMP reports, there is no mention of the attacks on my children. The stalking, harassment, maimed pets and livestock, night terrorism, witness accounts, and tangible evidence aren't mentioned either. Two of the dozens of vandalism complaints are on file, but there are no details, just the word "vandalism" and the date. There is not one written-up RCMP statement about the crimes over the years my family or I were in contact with Constable Satan and his uniformed accomplices. There are, however, pages that imply I'm delusional, two mentionings of schizophrenia, and a false file saying I had mistaken my friends' vehicles for stalking vehicles, complete with a list of their penciled-out license plate numbers. The pages I like best show when Constable Satan may have been partying at Christmas. The report he wrote is a mess of arrows, doodles, crossing-out, and grandiose comments. Gotcha.

I appealed to five community's RCMP detachments while moving around on Vancouver Island. In one town, a neighbour called the RCMP after seeing a man squatting in the bushes outside my door and then again after seeing two men hiding in the underbrush beside my truck. Those records were rapidly purged (so they say) as were all the RCMP files from two other towns, along with a 911 call from a man who thought the mob stalkers converging on me were rapists or abductors. My own 911 calls were "purged" as well. Satan said I made no such calls.

Super-cop's municipal police files tell the true story. His reports declare me sane and stalked. He wrote of mob harassment, deadly vehicle vandalism, and collecting black hair out of my bathtub where intruders left a sexy top. (I'm blonde.) His many witness interviews, including talking to several truck-vandalism repairmen, verified my dilemma, and he was on to the "we're watching you" phone calls. I was a dunce to run when he went on vacation. He was trying to free me.

The lawyer representing my court case against Constable Satan offered to do so on contingency. He said that based on the credible cop's reports there was no way he'd lose.

Constable Satan knew he was in trouble. He, or the RCMP execs, hired bikers to impose around-the-clock scare tactics. Then Satan called the charities in my newest little town and told them I was a con artist. One church-run charity was so angry at me that the clergy came to the door demanding an apology for exploiting their services. Telling them that the cop lied backfired. This severed my food supply and other basic needs as I was recovering from an acute EH'ed windpipe burn and had been relying on handouts.

It was humiliating to see people cross the street or leave a building because they'd seen me. The slander left me on the brink of destitution, never mind hungry. So, the lawyer added defamation to a growing suit, having also learned that Satan instructed other RCMP detachments to tune my crazy-ass out.

My one friend, Joanne, disappeared at this time. The bond we formed at a women's safe house was unwise to maintain, so at the end of our stay we went separate ways. When a hospital nurse called me as Joanne's only contact, saying she was ill, I was asked if it would be okay for her to stay with me for a few days.

Joanne fell apart in my rocking chair after a biker's death threat. She cried and decided to spend our last money on milk for tea. As the threats were meant for me, we felt the posse would ignore her. Joanne went missing at one-thirty in the afternoon between my scabby apartment and the store six houses away. She left my place with two dollars' worth of coins in her hand and a balm for chapped lips in her pocket. She was wearing my Salvation Army cable-knit sweater, and we looked somewhat similar.

For weeks afterwards, two RCMP officers made unannounced visits with an audio recorder trying to pin Joanne's disappearance on me. Unfortunately, the lawyer, through no fault of his own, was no match for high-caliber intimidation. Defenceless from the cops' framing ploy and the bikers' arm-twisting, withdrawing the court case was imperative. Disappointment from dropping the suit plunged me into mourning, for my dream of safely reuniting with my children was moving further away. Hearing from a constable that Joanne's name had been found on the registry of a distant United Church hostel was no comfort. Every word the RCMP had said was a lie. It took ages to buck up.

Eventually, staying quiet about RCMP corruption seemed immoral. More importantly, I was determined to see justice over having to flee my children. The next idea was to tell government heads what Constable Satan and his collaborators had been up to. Two years later, my petitions reached the Deputy Prime Minister (McLellan) who wrote letters to Constable Satan and me. Satan was flabbergasted. I know because his and his sergeant's comments are on the police files. What happened is no surprise. The RCMP detachment "proved" I was mentally scrambled with a portfolio of fabricated insulting documents. Then the bikers came back to town.

I am not finished with the RCMP.

My struggle with perp-cops is dull compared to other ti's. They didn't break my neck like they did to the ti down the road from my farm, and they didn't commit me to the psych ward five times as they did to a ti mom who lives across the narrow strait from my present home.

She too is going to be separated from her children through isolation tactics. Remote electronic weapons are grilling and disabling her eight-year-old. Yesterday, the mom came home from her daughter's doctor appointment to find the living room rearranged. She emailed me a photo of the door frame where intruders had chiseled out chunks, disengaging both burglarproof locks.

Appallingly, the woman dare not call police. The last time she called about men crouched in the shrubs, responding constables committed her to a psych ward. As with my family, the RCMP would as soon see her and her children dead.

The only reason I got off relatively easy from police wrath, unlike the nearby mom and the broken neck guy, is because of my quiet nature. My responses were never verbally or physically confrontational. Perp-cops detain ti's whenever possible whether it's in jail or the psych ward.

Furthermore, as I am an avid bird watcher, remote v2k bird chirps were occasionally transmitted to my head at the beginning, but usually where there could be no birds. Had I mentioned hearing tweets in banks and beds, a psychotic diagnosis would have been immediate. The fact is, I never did mention EH, not one word of it to anyone, including my partner, and only complained of endless stalking, harassment, threats, violence, and vandalism that would have been obvious to a blind person.

The barefaced obvious OS bullying I received requires explanation because it defies the usual day-and-night harassments that only the ti sees as menacing. A sprinkling—a slim few—of selected heavily harassed targets is on an agenda that at times includes transparent witness-drawing vandalism, stalking, mobbing, and threats. Could it be that in some areas or situations perps feel they won't get arrested? That they're above the law? Do police protect selected ti's perps?

Flaunting of criminal acts is quite rare. All the same, it happens.

Anyhow, back to the story. I spent seven unproductive years politely asking the RCMP to do their job, but do not consider the time wasted. Learning that Mounties will, apparently, commit heinous crimes rather than have organized stalking or its perpetrators exposed is important to know. It's occurred to me that as the RCMP and other police forces seem to be covering up OS, a country's intelligence network could be covering it up as well. Worldwide, most police will not investigate OS crimes, not even when children are used as pawns. Don't be swayed by cop-school smiles.

To be fair, it must be said that a handful of ti's received police help for the first few days they asked for it. When the officers retracted, with or without using the delusional pretext, OS's blood-thirsty retribution put these ti's and their loved ones at grave risk. If a ti manages to get police help, it's imperative that the cops (and the ti) follow through.

No matter whose side an officer or his/her detachment is on, OS impedes all actions that involve authority figures, unless, that is, a target has already been slated a queer duck and is exacerbating his own demise with starkly unorthodox self-saving behaviours and declarations when appealing to jeering law enforcement.

Here are a couple of tips for new targets. Don't take jeering cops' remarks personally when they laugh in your face or insult you. Stay calm and focus on saving yourself. Don't try to persuade or educate a cop who is mocking you, and avoid further contact with him. Although for a few of you, avoiding a bad-mannered cop, or even a good-mannered cop, will be impossible.

There were times, lots of times, when I felt that the RCMP were following me and keeping tabs on everything I did, well outside of hoped-for protective or investigative measures. But I dismissed my feelings as silly even when the stalking was blatant. RCMP harassment prior to my charges against them made no sense. Why would cops bother an uninteresting woman after she asked for help? I was so confused.

Life experience and exhaustive research change everything. I am now positive that selected ti's, particularly the outspoken or justice-seeking ones, are monitored by appointed police officers, constantly. For some targets, it is their primary complaint. These ti's take videos, go public, and get framed.

Having mentioned videos, I am reminded that I missed a good video-taking opportunity when an RCMP officer knocked on my door recently with the pretext of asking about a lady down the road. I was preoccupied with other harassment at the time and just wanted the officer to leave. But he wouldn't and tried to weasel me into talking about OS, all the while telling me things about myself that he had no business knowing and no reason to bring up without an ulterior motive. I said nothing about OS and waited to see where the farce would lead, which was nowhere. I think it was a scare tactic, for the cop was enjoying the charade immensely. Out of politeness, I was going to describe him to you as crass. But it cannot be done, as if I do not call him an arrogant jackass, I'll explode.

Anyhow, for the sake of ti's who think police are stalking and harassing them, who might have initially thought the police were being intrusively conscientious, I've copied, with permission, a part of a PIVOT Legal Society newsletter. It's about police using Stingray surveillance in the U.S. and probably in Canada. The Stingray is a device that can simulate cell phone towers for the purpose of tracking phones' locations and for intercepting voice and text communication. Here is the quote from the PIVOT Legal Society.

> The Stingray is a surveillance device that has been put into use by police only upon agreeing to a non-disclosure agreement that prohibits the department from even acknowledging its existence. There are a lot

> of reasons for police to use this type of surveillance device. Some of them are legitimate . . . However, we know from experience that when police have access to powerful surveillance tools . . . they are prone to misuse and abuse. In British Columbia, the Office of the Police Complaint Commission admitted to receiving a couple of dozen cases a year where officers breached an individual's privacy rights by illegally accessing databases. The Stingray device, which could potentially be used to create massive stores of meta-data on citizens to be searched at a later date by any officer, raises those same concerns.

The PIVOT Legal Society asked the Vancouver Police Department if it uses Stingray surveillance, and the department refused to answer. Hmmm

Police and targets, with few exceptions, do not get along. Yet to the credit of a few hard-working victims, a California city mayor and police department made a promise to assist ti's. The victim community was elated. A foot in the door. Then the mayor and the police department changed their minds. They began asking people who claimed to be stalked and harassed by OS to find their way to mental health services. What? Were they saying that many thousands of people are suffering from the same "I'm gang stalked" mental disorder? Or maybe stalking and harassment are no longer crimes. What an awful thought.

Today, the city is reconsidering and is again meeting with OS activists. My guess about this back-and-forth is that when electronic harassment complaints started coming in, the complexity, oddness, and power of the crime overwhelmed the city's original good intentions. Other victims believe that the U.S. government told the city and its police force to stop ruining another MKULTRA-like experiment.

To the cops everywhere who are aware of OS and intentionally take part in destroying lives: "You've sunk low on the scale of humanity. A criminal yourself."

Well, that's the scoop on cops, but what about the doctors they scam. It's unusual for a doctor to dispute a perp-cop's persistent renditions of why a victim should be committed to a psych hospital for observation and drugging. When a perp-cop is pitching falsehoods to a doctor, the victim should not mention OS and EH to medical staff. He must concoct an acceptable reason for having high anxiety.

I prefer to think that ethics keep doctors honest, but when you look back on MKULTRA, the whole horrendous experiment was supervised by medical professionals. Some targets swear that doctors are employed by OS—far more than those accused of implanting victims with microchips.

We're going to close this chapter with the fate of the old fellow who stored my kids' rowboat, for Otto's wretched tale is a good example of the impact targets have on innocent others.

The Finn became a secondary target and had to move into an assisted living complex. It broke his heart to leave his tumbledown house on the beach. Gone are early-morning sausages on a deck that overlooks a spectacular bay. Gone are ambles on the dock out front asking layover mariners if they'd like to use his bathtub and join him for lunch. I am unsure if harassment drove the gentle fellow out of his home or if it was Satan's slander. Satan made the same remarks about the Finn as he did about me. It's possible he convinced Otto's family their ageing dad needed to be put away.

It haunts me that although I quickly caught on to OS's impact on my children, harassment towards acquaintances and bystanders didn't sink in until several folks were terribly hurt. Stalkers must get rid of everyone around an isolation-theme target, particularly helpful people, and the selfless Finn had to be quashed. His future was kaput the minute I said, "Thanks, your veranda would be perfect for a little boat."

As for the little boat, christened the *Bullhead Princess*, it fared all right, at least after I repaired substantial vandalism and after Satan tried to charge me with stealing it. I hauled it, or had it hauled, from town to town, finally returning it to one of my sons, who by that time was an adult and would recognize stalker-drilled holes. The *Bullhead Princess* was the only link to my kids when it seemed they were lost to me forever. I'd sit beside it remembering summer days of the kids playing "ferry," rowing back and forth across a tiny cove, collecting clamshell fares from pint-sized passengers. It's what kept me alive sometimes.

CHAPTER TWELVE

THE ANIMALS

Let's take a detour to victims who are clean forgotten about. The critters.

Steel yourself. Attacking animals is a powerful tactic to control humans. In other words, every time Ms. Teedoff investigates a stalker, her best friend Doodles pays an ungodly price.

By any method, hurting or dispatching the pets, livestock, and wildlife in a victim's world hastens his psychological breakdown.

Let's look at how the creatures suffer.

Mobile Microwave Weapons

- A perp with a see-through-wall human detector who is outside your house or in an adjoining apartment can locate Good Dog snoozing on his blanket. He will then plant a microwave weapon. (The diagram on page 160 applies to pets as well as people.) Microwaves flow through walls, so unless your pet has been alerted and is roving, he will be nuked in his sleep. Perpetrators who know that the pet's owner is afraid to take offensive or defensive actions may plug a weapon into a home's outdoor outlet or, if necessary, bring along a power source.

According to the thugs' snickering, they find the job sportive, so toting equipment to nuke your pet is not an imposition.

- If a stalker has been in your home, he might not require see-through-wall equipment, having seen Good Dog's blanket or basket. See-through-wall (radar) devices are handheld and usually use AA batteries
- Perpetrators often run adapted microwave ovens or other microwave wares behind a shared apartment or condo wall for days, weeks, or months in order to sicken a ti (see diagram on page 160). Animals living around-the-clock in this ti's adjoining apartment or condo will succumb.

Sound Waves

- Perpetrators emit noxious inaudible infrasound (sound waves) continuously through a shared wall situation in order to sicken a ti. Animals' hearing spectrum is different from humans', yet a pet's physiology could still be adversely affected.
- Ultrasonic animal repellent gadgets that are bought or home-built (with electrical aptitude) produce an unbearable high frequency to deter creatures big and small. A powerful one could be lethal over time to a pet who cannot escape its effects. Even a low-powered one would eventually make him ill. Ultrasound is silent to people and cannot flow through walls.

Intruders

- Intruders electronically zap, heat, burn, and blind house pets. The weapons, disguised or not, fit in big and little pockets. What's more, Kitty's food and water might be poisoned; or she could be injected, beaten, or cut; or her face could be sprayed

Bump keys

with a corrosive chemical. Unless a lock or door is burglarproof, intruders can enter using a bump key. Bump keys look like regular keys, except the teeth have been filed down. You can buy a set of them online for less than a haircut, or you can make your own. A bump key is inserted into a lock, lightly tapped, and the lock opens. There will be no sign of illegal entry and no damage to the lock. The intruder's mission may be to injure or kill the pet and do nothing else. Kitty's owner, besides being crestfallen, is never going to come home again without feeling nervous. The intruder's mission was successful.

Outdoor Trespassers

- Night stalkers and daylight trespassers boot, bat, cut, cripple, blind, and electronically wound outdoor animals. The animals may be sprayed or injected with chemicals. Water and food poisoning is entirely possible.
- Trespassers often bring stomped, poisoned, or road-hit vermin, wildlife, and pets and place the dead or dying animals around a home, vehicle, or workplace. Nests of dead baby birds are popular springtime omens for ti's to find near their front doors.
- Night stalkers will set up a microwave weapon against an outside wall and nuke whatever pets are inside.

Remote Electronic Harassment

- Remote electronic harassment can track, injure, and mind-alter anything with a brain: animals and people.

- Remote stalkers send energy beams to pets, livestock, and wildlife if the animal's distress or death could affect a target. This is by far the most common form of OS abuse on creatures. The animal will sustain temporary, permanent, or fatal internal or external damage, just as with humans. If Good Dog is a target's primary comfort, every tail wag is watched remotely; thus, the owner can be controlled by incessantly assaulting the dog through airwaves. An isolated or lonely pet owner will do anything to keep his pet safe.
- All the animals in a kennel or herd can be EH'ed simultaneously, although it's more usual for selected animals within a group to be struck.

When Good Dog is injured by remote EH, mobile EH, or another form of abuse, the owner understands he is not allowed to have anyone in his life, not even a dog, and is susceptible to serious depression.

Organized stalkers are not fussy about what kind of creature they exploit. They will tamper with a child's hedgehog if it will concern the parent. Moreover, children's pets appear to be prioritized when stalkers are trying to force a parent to leave his family. When a target discovers that his son's puppy is plastered with scorches, he's going to live in terror that his son will be scorched by remote means. Stalkers will bludgeon a horse as they did mine or pour a box of moth balls into your youngster's aquarium of angelfish.

Barbarity towards pets and livestock takes a noticeable toll on ti's, making it a favourite strategy. Grief, vet bills, animal replacement costs, anxiety, and fear further destabilize an already overtaxed victim. Subsequently, it's no surprise that pet or farm animal mutilation can be on a ti's "send her over the edge" list.

When Good Dog is an isolated ti's only consolation and he's killed, there is no one to survive for. Getting a new dog is not an option.

I'll never forget a phone call from a van-living Quebecer whose black Lab was being remotely tortured. Our previous conversations had centred on her devotion for the dog. On this day, his legs were too rickety to walk after suffering the same overnight EH leg-blitz as the woman, who was also struggling to walk. As the woman had lost her children, extended family, home, and job to the crime, the situation was critical.

"Should I put him down?" she asked.

"Can you come to my house and we'll figure it out when you get here?" I asked back.

"I don't think Comet would make it. He's going to die soon, and then I'm going to die. I can't lose him, too."

That was in 2010. The woman has not been heard from since that call.

When a ti asks if he should euthanize or re-home a pet, I never answer yes or no, and neither should you. Only an owner can gauge the situation. Listen up. Attacks on Good Dog might not stop after he's been re-homed. If there is a chance that a ti will see his pet or hear how it's doing, the pet will continue to be remotely harassed. This reaffirms a ti's isolation: that everybody he befriends is doomed.

So, how can you tell when Kitty has been struck with energy weapons? Oftentimes you can't. Kitty is ailing. That's clear. You have a hunch she's been EH'ed, but really, with the language barrier, and with many energy wounds being internal, you're guessing.

As a target, your most reliable indicator of what's happening to Kitty can be by assessing what is happening to you. Do you have an isolation theme? Are you being pushed to suicide? Are you heavily

EH'ed? Did you insult, expose, or worry your perpetrators and they are picking on Kitty to punish you? Is there a new rotation of OS staff? Did you sneak some pleasure and must be disciplined? Are you a secondary ti who after three perp-free weeks is entering another round of OS torment? In any way, whether you are a target or not, are you assisting one and, therefore, braving retribution?

You may never know why Kitty is sick or why she died. It's not your fault. Undoubtedly in the beginning, there must have been days when I asked my animals to do something when they were ill from remote energy or had been roughed up. When I was a child, my dad said, "Before you get on that horse, make it a habit to ask yourself if he has a headache." It was Dad's way of teaching me to be considerate. For targeted animal owners to be considerate, they need to ask themselves macabre questions: "Was Mittens stuffed in a gunny sack and swung overhead?" Or, "Is Daisy Calf unsteady because her noggin was clubbed?" Or, "Has Ruff been lying down for two days because he's slowly cooking?" Well, Mittens could be quaking from being "it" in any one of a hundred devil's games. And, yes, the calf may have been clubbed. If Ruff won't get up, my first thought is remote energy, in spite of multiple credible reasons, as pretty well all ti's pets and livestock do get remotely EH'ed occasionally. It's just too easy.

Remote and nearby microwaving will depress, fatigue, and weaken an animal and possibly overheat him. A high dose of microwaving results in conspicuous symptoms, and an animal undergoing this treatment is going to be grossly feeble or dying. When his eyes are energy-assaulted, they will smart, and he may develop the same blurry vision or blindness as his targeted owner.

It may take minutes or it may take weeks for aspects of your pet's physiology to be disrupted or totalled from up-close or far-off radiation.

Now, let's examine remote strikes that an EH-educated pet owner can easily detect.

Good Dog could be having a great day at the park and suddenly act like he's been shot. In fact, he has been shot, but with a bullet of energy that can be lethal or non-lethal, depending on the computer operator's wishes.

Later on at Uncle Bill's cookout, Good Dog's going to blame Bill's wife for thumping his backside, and so might you. I wasn't joshing that EH can feel like someone smacked you or beat you with a bat. Tenderness from a clublike pressure beam can be lasting, especially when one region is focused on for minutes, hours, or days. Pressure beams result in broken bones, irregular heartbeat, heart and other organ failure, and pounding pain. This is true torture. Due to internal injuries, the animal might feel limited or no relief when the operator pushes the off button.

Perfect holes from a straw-sized beam may go unnoticed by an animal, can be deep, and will need to be kept clean. Slices, on the other hand, might be sore. Slices can also be perfect, as if a computerized razor made the cuts, often in parallel lines. Hang on, I'll check my heel where I got incised a few nights ago. Yup, the row of cuts look mathematically machined. Neat slices, jagged-edged gashes, hole-boring beams, and burns are likely to focus on Good Dog's less furry areas, maybe his snout and pads. There's no point in remote stalkers burning and carving up your dog unless you notice.

Then there are the pinpoint EH hits that feel like electrical jolts, stings, or fiery cinders. Good Dog will overextend his neck, legs, body, and energy trying to bite and scratch these split-second strikes, for he will be prickled on different parts of his back where he can't reach, or from side to side. He could feel on fire if they are sparking him, as I did the first time. Maybe he'll think he's covered in bees.

A particularly annoying energy-type causes excessive all-over itching and, like stinging blitzes, strikes successively in difficult to reach places. Again, Good Dog will scratch and snap at his skin, for these irritating beams feel like burrowing insects. Alternatively, itching in one spot can be eternal and is something that both owner and pet might tussle with at the same time. Patches of skin can become raw from scratching or the energy itself. No medical reason will be found for Good Dog or his human's energy-caused skin problems.

Restraining a frantic EH'ed pet could be disastrous. Survival instincts are strong, and you might get bitten. Moving your pet is unlikely to help as remote beams can be programmed to stay on a travelling target, but it is always worth a try if teeth and claws can be avoided. For some people, Mylar blankets deflect a beam or two, so maybe you'll want to keep one handy to throw over Good Dog in the rare event his beam can be averted. (Mylar blankets have a foil coating, are under $5.00, and can be found in the first aid or camping aisles. They are also called space blankets.) What will probably work best is the opposite of what you're going to want to do. Walk away if the creature's squirming is exhausting him. OS's intention is to upset you while you watch your pet struggle. Beams are often turned off when they will not get the desired result. If it's any reassurance, it's unlikely that successive or single-shot stinging or itching beams are striking Good Dog when nobody is around to witness.

Instead, they could be striking the pooch next door. Let's assume you are a heavily harassed target and your neighbour has a dog. That's all it's going to take to start a rivalry, for that dog is going to yelp from remote zaps every time you and the dog are outside at the same time. At least, that's what happened to me in one of my runaway homes. The neighbour, a short-tempered man, accused me of throwing rocks. I ended up obsessed about Ripper's whereabouts, coming and going according to whether the terrier was on the front or back lawn. Had Ripper's owner called the cops, because I'm a ti, a charge of animal cruelty would have been laid.

The terrier was struck by remote weapons because remote stalkers watch and control everything flanking their victim. This includes wildlife.

Wildlife racked with energy harassment is a nature-loving victim's predictable comeuppance. Birds and squirrels will flop in front of this ti or go into contortions from those split-second strikes we just spoke about.

A victim who impacts wildlife will find writhing, dying, and dead creatures along trails and sidewalks, as well as around his home and car, more than can be considered even partway normal. "Looking like a knacker's yard" sums up designated ti's properties during a retaliatory phase.

It's troubling under normal circumstances to see a crippled animal. When you feel responsible, it's a whole other emotion. A couple of summers ago, while sitting at the picnic table in front of my beach, the second broken-backed river otter of the afternoon dragged himself across the grass, this time inches from my toes. In trying to rescue him, the poor creature rightly panicked. All that was left to do was watch as he dragged his useless back-end to the beach where he vanished into a log pile. His death would have been slow, what with wildlife centres being too far away for a "catch and care" mission.

That episode left me in tears, realizing my impact had gone up a notch. I still feel culpable for not realizing the first mashed otter was OS work. Had I known, I'd have withdrawn inside. A handful of ti's cannot look at wildlife at all. Lucky for the critters, writing has kept me housebound; and as much as I miss long hours of sharing the cove with them, watching from the windows relieves me of guilt.

You needn't get the impression that targets suppose all ailing wildlife is their fault. It's common knowledge that a predator's dinner sometimes gets away. Then there are accidents, disease, and recognizable inhumanities. A victim, though, is made to know in one way or another when his presence is responsible for remote electronic assaults on others, for perps demand that their feats take a toll. As for my broken-back otters, there were no shooters and no trappers in the cove, nor have there ever been.

Because I find otters comical, they are used to reaffirm the no-joy rule, as are the laughing ducks and other life, especially in cycles of punishment. Let's be honest. When an isolated, heavily harassed ti finds a few moments of happiness, or is under penalty, someone's going to get viciously hit with energy, and it may not be the target.

Remote energy does much more than snap a Clydesdale's neck, fry a parakeet's feet, or electrocute a fawn. That's because of the mind-control beams we've discussed in previous chapters. What do you say we ease back into the discussion of electronic mind control by revealing its influence on animals.

You might recall that OS's brain beams are capable of reading what's going on in a brain at that moment. If Good Dog is eager, his eager frequencies will be seen on the computer operator's equipment. If Good Dog is sleepy, sleepy frequencies are what the operator will see. Think of a targeted brain as an interloped phone. Information coming in and going out is monitored and manipulated by interloping criminals, who in this case are OS's computer staff.

For you to better understand brain-altering energies, I'll use a demonstration: Natural occurrences strongly change how people and animals think. A cat caught in a thunderstorm is going to be expressing hurry-up frequencies in his noodle. On the other hand, a mind-controlled cat can have hurry-up frequencies sent in a beam to his head where they seep through his skull. The feline will be streaking home and not know why.

Like music to your radio, you can't see the frequencies coming. The difference between a radio and Kitty is that Kitty cannot turn off his receiver, which is his brain. When artificially produced frequencies are forced into a creature's head, he's lost the freedom to be himself.

This is why targets' pets behave peculiarly sometimes, even responding to v2k. There's one thing that happens periodically that no one will be able to understand unless animals learn to talk. Good Dog and Kitty will not be able to go near their targeted keeper. Likewise, the critters at a petting zoo might crowd into a corner as soon as the ti shows up. It's as if a cloud of evil surrounds the person and repels animals. For example, my three dogs would bound toward me with their usual exuberance, stop, and then run away. Sometimes they swerved as if they'd come to a wall. The horses and sheep did the same thing. My animals didn't instantly hate me. There was something else going on, and it was either a mind-changing frequency or a painful frequency akin to an intolerable ultrasonic device that is used to repel dogs.

How, you ask, could energy beams control three romping dogs' brains at the same time? I'm going to refer back to phones. Three cell phones, each with a different number, can receive transmissions through space at the same time. If the phones are bouncing on a trampoline, they will still ring.

It appears that every brain that is useful to OS has been scanned and coded and can catch OS-sent energy wherever the body under the brain goes. To reiterate, Good Dog's and Good Target's electrical heads are antennas. Furthermore, if a creature crosses paths with a ti just once, maybe a stray cat in an alley or a bear at the garbage cans, it can still be remotely beamed. Everyone and everything a remote stalker wants to meddle with can be honed in on, from a bunny, to just its tail, to the part of its brain that makes it hop. You shouldn't be surprised then that five-year-old Benjamin who's stroking the bunny might have his loving thoughts replaced with sudden EH'ed head pain.

Personally, I wouldn't be surprised at seeing Benjamin's mind controlled, as well, for a moment or two. In my world, a muddled-with brain is normal, be it yours, mine, Benjamin's, or a bunny's.

Here's a thought. From bunnies to beagles, are any animals safe from OS staff? Do OS's perps become so accustomed to hurting targets and targets' animals that they'd think nothing of hurting uninvolved animals and strangers when they're off-shift? Think about it; working for OS is not a job for the average good-tempered Joe Blow. So can all perps be psychopaths? I doubt it, for assumedly somewhat-decent folks are coerced into occasionally acting like OS psychopaths. Some of these fallen-from-grace patsies even commit themselves to hurting honest folks and defenseless animals day in and day out, for decades. Let's look at that, inasmuch as it's a departure from our EH-controlled animals topic.

It seems to me, despite having no proof other than eyewitness accounts, that once a novice perp is thoroughly immersed into OS, there is no turning back. It would be like a Mafia member saying, "Aw shucks, this isn't as much fun as I thought it'd be. I don't want to see you guys anymore." In my situation, it's doubtful my current perps would quit if they were given a choice. Their faces exhibit smug satisfaction. A handful of ti's say they feel that one of their stalkers has come to hate the job and looks ashamed when confronted. Out of my hundreds of stalked, harassed, and tortured situations, two of my enemies looked sorry, one time each, so I'm assuming remorse or self-loathing in the perp population is rarer than rare.

Would that apply to mutilating pets, wildlife, and livestock? Could these people feel no pity when they break an otter's back or fry a bunny's brain? It's something I think about a lot, considering that OS injures and kills an unspeakable number of creatures.

Although I know of no research that examines if someone can be coerced into harming an animal, there are two famous studies that examine the paradox of decent people who can be easily talked into hurting a person. The first is the Stanford Prison Experiment which was a study of what happens when average people are put into simulated roles of prisoners and prison guards. Remarkably, the study had to be abruptly stopped ahead of schedule when the (role-playing) guards began acting savagely. *The Lucifer Effect* by Philip Zimbardo explains it all. The second famous study is the Milgram Experiment which examined ordinary people's obedience to authority when asked to electrically shock a person they've just met. Gina Perry discusses the results and the participants' emotional aftermath in *Behind the Shock Machine: The Untold Story of the Notorious Milgram Psychological Experiment.* Should the participants in either of these experiments have had the opportunity to hurt people and animals long term, would they have? Because that's what the vast majority of the cajoled perps do, and with enthusiasm.

This brings us back to OS.

Unlike the coerced and perhaps lied to perps, an informed individual who volunteers upfront to engage in any capacity of electronic harassment and torture would have to be in the tiny percentile who drives around on Sunday mornings looking for cats and dogs to run over.

These pathological operators have access to such a strange animal-constraint science I hesitate to mention it for fear of sounding like the village idiot. It turns creatures into statues. A raccoon will freeze on a branch and appear fine but is either in a trance or is paralyzed. It will not so much as blink or twitch, no matter what commotion is going on under its nose. How is that possible?

My first hunch is a mind-control beam, maybe hypnosis, for animals can stay frozen from minutes to hours. It's also occurred to me that stock-still creatures are a result of that phenomenal energy no one can crack.

There's another outlook, and it's a lulu: researchers at George Washington University sent frequencies to a patient's claustrum—an area of the brain—and turned her off repeatedly while she was reading aloud to them. She didn't move, speak, think, or remember the lost time and carried on reading as if nothing had happened when she was turned on again. The *National Geographic* documentary *Decoding the Brain* shows this experiment. As EH manipulates brains remotely, it is disturbing for me to think of this revelation, but it's one more theory for the frozen animals.

These animals are not holograms, or taxidermy figures, or scared stiff. At least, mine aren't. I threw dirt on two transfixed raccoons to get them further up a tree, afraid that dogs would get them. They couldn't budge, so other folks and I took turns guarding them until they scurried off. Then there was Henny Penny on my old farm who went rigid on the truck hood on a summer day. Oh, I mustn't forget the "can't move" black cat on a fencepost and, lately, a sprinting mink that turned into a statue under the kitchen window.

If EH can paralyze animals, what would be the repercussions of paralyzing people? Is this what happens when ti's lose time? When I lost two hours this afternoon, was I a mannequin? Can this be caught on film? Will somebody with perps who let him keep a surveillance camera running please try? (I couldn't resist asking—this book is a handy podium for pooling evidence.)

We've just discussed total electronic mind control—when a human or animal head responds according to electronically sent commands.

And so it is that heavily harassed ti's, including me, are convinced that the creatures in their lives exhibit the unmistakable signs of being EH'ed in the same way as people: mind control, v2k, energy-caused injuries, and phenomenal events. Who would know better than those who experience these things?

Remember, creatures are picked on in order to sadden or fluster the target. Animals are tools to OS—tools to bring the ti down.

One last thing . . . Please, if you associate with a ti, watch for changes in your pet's behaviour and health. Not all targets have a high impact. I, however, am bad news.

I'm going to pause here to pack a suitcase. The guys in the white smocks are sure to come-a-knocking, and I want to be ready. It's contentious enough to declare that animals' brains and behaviours are manipulated by EH, but I've gone and tossed in the living ornament trick. You're going to have to trust me. These things take place.

CHAPTER THIRTEEN

TOTAL ELECTRONIC MIND CONTROL

I've been brooding over how to write this chapter since the book's inception. Asking a non-targeted person to appreciate what it's like to have a beam penetrate and change his mind felt greedy when I first brought it up—that too much was required from the reader.

"Half of Chapter Thirteen has to go," I figured while reviewing a draft. Determined to emulate a real author whose crossing-out pens run dry, my pen lost no ink at all. That didn't seem right, so after harumphing through a checklist of pros and cons, my decision to keep the whole caboodle was relieving. Even inspiring.

Time has a way of souring what was once a good idea, and weeks later a reevaluation was sorry business. The section still felt overly jam-packed. And it sounded flat-out weird. Clueless about which passages to drop, a former lady friend's tip came to mind. She had nine kids and said that when you are stuck choosing what should be done next, change pace. Unruffle yourself and the answer will come. Impersonating nonchalance, I made a peek-a-boo cardboard house for my bird. Peek-a-boo's his favourite game.

The answer of what to do did not come through little girl cut-outs. Nonetheless, it was time well-dallied. The bird got a toy, I cleared my head, and the phone rang.

As has often happened during the writing, a distressing conversation put me back on track. You're going to hear it all. The cross-out pen is back in its flower vase.

"Can my computers give me headaches?" he asked.

"Describe them," I said.

"They're strange. It feels like a steel rod is being driven through the right side of my brain. That's the only way I can explain them. My eyes are sore."

"Like a migraine?" I asked.

"Not at all. I don't even know if they *are* headaches."

"Moe, yesterday morning you emailed me a copy of an affidavit. How did you feel in the afternoon?"

"That's why I'm calling you. The pain after that got so bad the kids had to make themselves cereal for dinner. It's because my computers are hacked into, isn't it? The creeps can make an energy field come through them."

How could I do it? How could I tell this man that a remote beam is pouring through his skull? "It could be something else, Moe, but I hate to say just yet. How are you sleeping?"

"Funny you'd ask. When the headaches began, weeks ago, I started waking up every hour—every twelve, one, two, you know, all night, always the same exact time."

"All right, what about your dreams?"

"I swear last night there was a ghoul with a cartoon face beside the bed. It's not the first time. They're part of the nightmares. That's another reason I'm calling. I know who runs organized stalking. A satanic cult. They're making demons."

"You're not the first person to tell me that. However, the most common explanation for targets' apparitions is scientific, based on your brain being electrical, meaning you can receive electrical transmissions. What's probably happening is that OS's technical staff is using revolutionary science to direct energy at you. These beams send mind-altering energy types to a head, and they also take information back. In other words, targets' brains are mucked with. It's simple, really. Perps are sending painful beams and scary pictures into your head, and at the same time they are reading your mind to check for reactions. My guess is that since they couldn't close your resort, they're rampaging."

"What about my kids? Why aren't they getting headaches and seeing ghosts?"

"Moe, if the staff want to send brain beams to your kids, they will. Different emissions do different things. Some broadcast over miles. Others focus on one head."

After too long a silence it seemed wise to jump in. "It's okay to be upset. You should be upset. I'm telling you right now that most ti's fall apart when they realize they've lost the freedom to own their own minds. Many of us get PTSD. It's important you keep in touch."

Poor Moe still couldn't speak, and like a blabbering fool I couldn't stop. To have him hang up in mental disrepair was worrisome, so on I went. There was much to say, yet the less said the better.

"It breaks my heart to tell you about this part of organized stalking. Maybe I seem blunt, but if no one told you, you'd think you were going crazy. Some of the things perps do to our minds are supposed to make us think we are schizophrenic or possessed by the devil. If you weren't already a full-fledged victim of OS harassment, I'd say stress or an illness could be causing the headaches and ghouls. Take a head exam anyhow. It would be awful if you were sick and went untreated."

"I was always healthy," he said, "before this started."

"Don't you find it uncanny, Moe, that almost every ti says the same thing? That it feels like a metal rod is being driven through his skull? And we all suffer from timed wake-ups and nightmares. Those are telltale signs."

"Does anybody know?" he asked.

"No. Everybody we tell thinks OS is crock. Well, our country's leaders know."

"That's not it, June. I already read about targets being microwaved from space. The headaches are because they've tampered with the wiring. After they broke into my garage, all the appliances started blowing up. I think the hackers can make my computers kick out dangerous radiation now."

"That's part of the crime. Electrical problems. You need to hire an electrician to do an inspection that includes detecting compromised energy output."

"What you're saying," the fellow replied, "is the perps are totally demented 'cause if they want to mess with my brain they've no reason to keep lighting my resort on fire. Last time, two fires in one night, the store and a barn. The time before, the hotel went up, and before that, a grass fire. All ruled as arson. What's next? The house?"

"You're new at this, Moe. Organized stalking has a goal. It's to get you—all of us—on our knees. That means they have to attack your home, resort, and everything in between, including your brain."

"June, I've got to get back to work. Can we meet somewhere tomorrow? I need to speak with you in person."

"They won't let me have a car; the vandalism is unsolvable. But, yes, we will get together. For now, tell a doctor about your headaches, and ask for a scan. Don't mention the ghoul or whatever it is. One other thing, you might not want to dump this on your kids. At their age, it wouldn't be fair."

Moe and I will meet after the book is finished even though, yikes, his stalkers are fire-bugs. He is, after all, only a ferry and a forest away. Not having a car was an excuse, for I could have given him my address. Call me a lily-livered cad as you wish. It's too big a gamble that should Moe drop by, the manuscript, never mind the old cedar house, would be charred crumbles before backwoods volunteer firemen jumped in their truck. Of course, the hotelier's stalkers already know about me. They or my own perps could burn down the house with me in it any time they want. Nevertheless, it would be reckless to invite over the tycoon and his entourage of arsonists right now.

So that's what it's like to hear a criminal gang has taken over your noodle. I'd better declare that if Moe hadn't already spoken at length about stalking, vandalism, break-ins, slander, document tampering, financial theft, mob harassment, night terrorism, arson, and interloped privacy, it would have been cruel to convey that his mind is under siege.

Perhaps my spiel was impudent. Maybe noodle looting is better explained in person or even not at all. At any rate, and I'm willing to be wrong, it seems best to tell a bewildered confirmed target about electronic mind control. Had Moe naively sought solutions, this is what could have happened.

He would probably have stopped using his computers and other electronics rather than checking his buildings for an output of avertible noxious energy, which if present would still not give him the pain he describes.

He might have resorted to excesses of sleeping sedatives or booze to get through Mothman nights, or he might have tried not sleeping at all.

If Moe told friends and family about inexplicable skewer-in-his-brain headaches, nightmares, and devil-creatures, a well-meant suggestion such as snake oil, witchcraft therapy, or clerical counselling could steer him on a course that might be hard to reverse. (Counsellors who are unknowledgeable about organized stalking's EH complicate a ti's ability to cope with it.)

Telling a doctor about demonic hallucinations, and that he'd been seeing them for weeks, would put the compliant greenhorn in the usual revolving door of prescriptions trying to find a magic pill when we all know that nothing cures electronic mind control.

Comparatively, because standard headache remedies are vastly inadequate for relieving energy-polluted skulls, Moe could have treated himself for a syndrome he doesn't have.

The abbreviated version to this rant is that when psychological and physical maladies stalemate medical knowhow, and they are symptomatic of EH's brain and body invasions, it's better for an established target to consider his new reality rather than struggle with falsehoods.

You may have thought Moe was squirrelly for believing his computers are making him sick. He's not alone. A small clique of ti's state much improved health after they took computers, cell phones, TV's, and even electrical power out of their homes. That they all have acute electrical sensitivity, a calamitous disorder, is dubious based on what they tell me.

This group holds two guesstimates of what's going on. The least popular idea faults up-close electricity for activating in-body nanorobotics. The second idea declares that dirty electricity from tampered wiring inside or outside the building is causing illness. Tampered wiring and hacked computers are what Moe mentioned.

Other than the nanorobotics and tampered-wiring hypotheses, it's feasible that the remote staff are sending nausea-, fatigue-, dizziness-, and headache-producing beams as deterrence whenever specific ti's use electronics for communication, information gathering, employment, or entertainment. Most victims who have lived without phones, computers, and TV's, along with those who have lived without electrical power, including me, state they are EH-sick with or without household appliances.

A home's breached electricity is considered by many as a means to enhance snooping and as a means to cause hard-to-solve electrical worriments that exacerbate unrest.

Electrical mischief, which includes wrongful wiring, causes problems with appliances, security systems, electric heat, air conditioning, pumped water systems, and personal electronics. Without exception the results are disastrous: fire, nixed private communication, no communication at all, nixed surveillance and alarm equipment, drained pocketbook through repairs, inconvenience, and tremendous stress.

Most targets can tell you about a long-standing and inconvenient electrical problem that vanished for a repairperson. "Well, ma'am, it seems to be fine. But I still have to charge you for the service call." Electronic harassment's tomfoolery, involving everything from a TV remote to a home's power source, is annoying, which is why it's a common occurrence. A tip for ti's: when a wireless item suddenly stops working, consider that signal jamming, from near or far, is to blame. Don't throw it out. Try it again in a few weeks. Another tip: when an electrical item sprouts magical qualities, think remote EH. Again, don't throw it out. Not yet.

The following letters from ti friends speak of electrical problems that are quite serious. (Copied with permission)

> It seemed like the electricity was too strong: sparks when plugging and unplugging. I had to replace the microwave, toaster, fridge, washer, and dryer, to mention a few. Before the ground wire fell off the plug-in for the dryer, it was smoking and burning in the socket. I had to repair the furnace connections/electronics three times. The baking element in the stove snapped in two. Utility companies for both cable and Internet had to come out and replace wiring going to the hydro pole on the street. The wall beneath my landline phone was screaming with RF (radio frequency) when I used a detector. I moved across country, and it's starting all over.

This is friend number two's letter:

> My take on it is that they absolutely use the wiring in our homes to deliver some of the EH, as well as the "pops," "snaps," "crackles," and other sounds in the ceilings and walls. Sometimes the appliances turn on and off. On different occasions, repairmen spent entirely too much time in my attic doing things that were unrelated. As a retired phone technician, it bothers me that I didn't jump on them, but it seems that when repairmen are here, I get zoned-out.

(Author's note: the sounds could be v2k.)

Now that we've discussed electrical hassles, you can see why Moe is conflicted about why his head hurts every time he uses his computers. I'm betting his pain is not from the hackers and tampered wiring he spoke of. In my view, it's likely that remote EH is attacking his brain.

Once Moe gets EH savvy, he will begin a private self-saving path, as all ti's do, and that could include chucking his computers and selling his home while he's sorting out his own brand of attacks. Targets are disposed to distrust advice from those who are more experienced, feeling no one understands. I am guilty of this as well.

As a closing note regarding my conversation with Moe, you won't find me opposing anyone's belief about who the stalkers are unless those beliefs are getting him into trouble. Based on demon-creatures, arson, cryptograms, nightmares, sinister comments from strangers, and sexual innuendos, Moe has decided all OS stalkers are Satanists. In the beginning, I thought all OS stalkers were white supremacists. Clusters of Satanists and white supremacists may have been inducted, but OS's army of riffraff is a conglomeration.

* * *

The ramifications to having an overtaken brain are all-encompassing. I know you can't grasp that yet. You might be asking yourself, "How can she write a book after saying the enemy is in her head?"

It takes practice and doggedness. Veteran targets are conscious every second that their thoughts, emotions, moods, senses, words, behaviours, physical actions, and physical functions can be influenced or one hundred percent overridden. People who hear v2k around the clock have zero moments to be themselves, for the voices sent into their heads can comment without pause on their thoughts.

Let's expand on that, beginning with what you already know. You've learned that remote stalkers monitor how a mind and a body function and feel; and you've learned that remote stalkers can put thoughts into a head. All this is done by reading a brain. You've also learned that remote stalkers critique what a person says. This again is possible, at least in part, by reading a brain. Here's the new bit: remote stalkers monitor what each ti is thinking, then choose feedback at will, be it by v2k or a matching clever deed.

Consolidated mind reading is what I call having thoughts and emotions analyzed by electronic harassment. Other names for it are unprintable, but better, and in Canada usually begin with "Bloody useless Charter of Rights and Freedoms . . ." American ti's, being less reserved than buttoned-up Canadians, loudly denounce their Constitution's duplicity, whereas quiet Canadians instigate a protest with pens, paper, the odd poster, and a gathering here and there. Cultural differences aside, the message is universal with each country's targeted citizens demanding that the physical and mental freedom obligated to them be returned. This isn't to say that OS and EH are government crimes, ceding that it's tenable.

Should OS and its energy weapons be run by a Josef Mengele fan club, or a political cabal, or a banking cabal, it's always a government's duty to protect its people from having their minds stolen. Kingpins in Interpol, the United Nations, and developed countries' governments are aware that EH interlopes ordinary individuals' thinking.

Mind activity emits energy.

This is where ti's loved ones are surely speechless, afraid to ask, "Are my thoughts being read too?" followed by, "She must be joshing." Nope, I'm not joshing and, yup, your thinking might be getting plundered.

Thought-reading is an elusive OS inhumanity to vindicate, for it has to run amok in a person's head a while before the enormity—the staggering realization—sets in. Not even prayers said in one's own head are private.

v2k voice: "Stupid bitch. We know what you're thinking. But hey, pray to God that you'll get your diploma. You'll see."

My brain is read without v2k verbal interruptions as v2k for me is usually noises, not words. The remote stalkers, though, respond to my thoughts with mood-altering frequencies or immediate EH pain when they don't like what I'm thinking. Then there's the usual intimidating harassment when thought-about plans have been relayed to the perpetrators on my little island. Gees, there's also sense manipulation, cognition impairment, and controlled sleep, all of which are often coordinated with my thoughts.

Saying it takes practice and resolve to live under total electronic mind control is a wishy-washy remark when, really, I want to circulate your thoughts to the Global Louse Association for a month so that you'd see how crippling it is to have your mind unceasingly critiqued by an organization of wannabe psychopaths.

It smothers my personality. Moreover, three or four times a year I fall apart for a few hours, overwhelmed that my head is owned. There are ideas to mull, dreams to dream, and nirvana moments to relive in my mind, but when I think about disallowed topics, the repercussions are dour. After so many years, what's allowed and what's not have become sharply defined. In every respect, even partial thought-stopping success requires an endless dispiriting process of self-persuasion.

A ti who is trying not to stress, anticipate, plan, yearn, remember, be emotional, or leak whims of satisfaction or relief will still have random uninteresting thoughts acted upon. In this way, his mind's auditors have control over minutiae, over all elements of his life.

A victim thinking, "Hmm, a roast beef sandwich would be great right about now," might be precisely the kind of opportunity his remote stalkers have been waiting for. You're wondering, "What could go wrong with a roast beef sandwich, and why would OS staff even bother?" The answers are this: anything could go wrong and it's all about power.

When a person's anticipatory, "Yum, roast beef," thoughts are read, remote perps could emit something off-putting into his cranium: maybe the smell of rotting carcasses or a snapshot of skinned cattle, for mind-control beams dominate a brain's every human sense, notably olfactory (smell) and visual systems. If the meat lover is a full-time v2k victim, he might hear, "The roast beef is poisoned. We were in your fridge."

Coincidence you say? Not a chance. Brain invasions don't happen without a tactical reason. Every time hungry Harry thinks of a sumptuous sandwich, he's going to be beamed with a rancid smell, disparaging words, or a slaughterhouse mind-picture. He'll get the point, all right.

For you to tumble to electronic mind control, compare losses of free thinking to losses caused by the on-heels stalkers. On Sunday, Harry could lose the freedom to think about sandwiches and also, thanks to slander, lose his tennis partner. On Monday, he will have to stop thinking about desserts, and because of unsolvable harassment, he'll have to stop using his sundeck.

Harry, however, is quick to catch on and concentrates on not letting any words, images, or thoughts about food slink in. He knows that if the computer staff want to keep a revolting smell, picture, or slur in a head, they can.

All heavily EH'ed victims live the same way. Granted, they might not have food on their no-no list. Pam's thought restrictions might be mulling over hair styles. Sam's might be fantasies of being rescued, and Cam's might be a restriction that stops her from studying for final exams.

For most, it's insects. Unspoken fearful or "that's icky" appraisals of insects equals an infestation. Targets are conscious not to look at, think about, or internally react to a spider in the bathtub, knowing that ants, spiders, flies, bedbugs, crickets, and cockroaches, among other crawlies, are OS's calling cards. Ask five heavily harassed ti's to tell their bug stories and you'll hear ten different methods of how OS can riddle a home by either deploying EH razzamatazz, which we'll be discussing, or by breaking in. Veteran targets know that any passing thought or instinctual reaction can be used against them. This loss of free thinking is the nucleus of ownership.

Ruminations about money often have lickety-split repercussions: "Hello, this is the homeless penny drive" and "Hey there, is this the charity that gives tents to bums?" will be calls within hours of a ti's thoughts about how he's going to pay the rent. A ti who is in a dither about money is not going to answer his phone for a while. Plus, he's going to be deleting personal and flippant emails from perps pretending to be money lenders for as long as he frets. It's probable, too, that stalkers will come to the door as debt collectors who got the wrong address. All this transpired because the fellow is rightfully strung out about keeping himself off the street. He didn't utter a peep about his woes to anyone, nor was online activity a tip-off. Doubtlessly, and I experience this myself, pensive thoughts are swiftly handed down to a victim's street gang.

Also on the list of non-thinkable topics is concern over loved ones and pets. Wise targets try not to think about loved ones and pets other than in humdrum aspects. Stewing over doddery Grandma could bring consequences to her, providing the ti will hear about it. Synonymous with feeling unrest about Granny is punishment for mood-cheering reminiscences of her. Recollecting a sunny afternoon together picking strawberries could cost both her and the target if, that is, the ti exudes bliss or peace. By nature, memories come, and for safety's sake, ti's make them go.

Foreseeably, there's a kink to this. The remote stalkers will beam an unstoppable remembrance when they know it will make the victim cry. Don't ask me how they know what people's memories are or how the scenarios can be repeated in a head several hundred times. Do ask me how many ti's experience this. The answer is—all heavily mind-controlled victims are sent emotionally evocative sad or bad recollections. Every single one. If fond thoughts of picking strawberries with Grandma will eventually induce tears, an isolated target could be forced to pine this particular loss until he's beaten down hours, days, or weeks later. Nothing else will be allowed in his head, only the equation of Grandma + reminder of loss = psychological decline.

This is not a stress disorder symptom even though poignant reminiscent-reruns are part of PTSD. This is a display of mind control, for the next round of unwanted memories could be as inane as a childhood swing set or yesterday's face-off with a clogged vacuum cleaner.

To discerning people, an overtly trounced brain feels altered by an outside source, meaning seasoned ti's can detect when their moods, attitudes, reactions, and thoughts are appointed or amplified. An energy-injected EH mind transformation can take seconds, minutes, or hours to complete. Usually it's instant.

An analogy for unmasking this mode of an enemy-occupied mind is mistakenly doubling the sugar in your coffee. It's not supposed to taste like that. It's too much. Something went wrong.

The same fallacious impression is repeated when the remote crew abruptly smacks a head with frame-of-mind frequencies. A blast of artificial-feeling happy frequencies after the person's long forgotten the emotion is about as mean as it gets. It happened to me once while grieving the death of a parent, and the devastation of pure joy continues to chip away at the hang-in-there backbone that ti's must have. Lasting under a minute, on and off, it was a rough reminder of a life now over. It was also confusing to be force-fed with elation in the midst of being brokenhearted. A happy-mood irruption is exceptional in that only two others in my circle have mentioned this deviation. Being flooded with pseudo anxiety, fear, dread, panic, and despondency is the norm. Either way, whether it's extravagant gaiety or dark doom that is doled out, like the too-sweet coffee, there's a sensation of surplus and fabrication.

I'll further explain fabricated-feeling mentality with another comparison, as foisted thoughts and moods jockey for position with what's natural. Envision a bouquet of fresh white tulips. Now poke in red plastic ones. Together, they're still called a bunch of flowers, although the naturalness of fresh tulips (genuine thinking) would prevail as what's real over factory-made tulips (EH mind control).

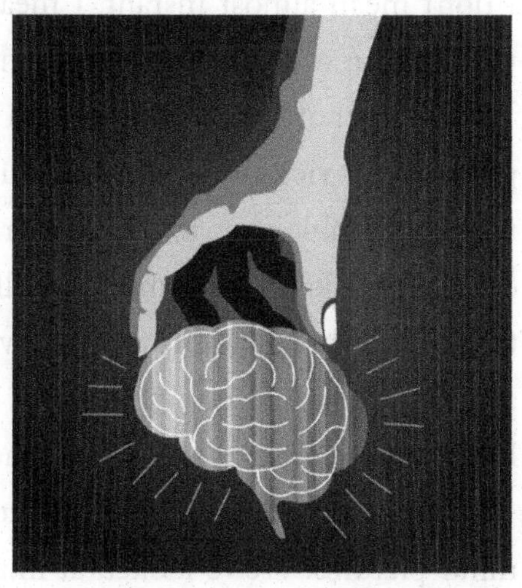
Thoughts are not private.

Having thoughts read converts a person differently than emotion- and mood-making infusions. The mind does not feel transformed, but revealed. It's rather like knowing a wretchedly nosy neighbour is staring in the windows all day with binoculars. You're putting on a performance and are not at all yourself, for you don't want the busybody to reach even further into your personal affairs.

While typing this, my brain is filled with gravestone heaviness, weariness, and a v2k squeal. I know "they" are in there, reading my thoughts as I type. It's not supposed to be this way. My head should not feel like it's going to fall off, and I shouldn't be struggling to stay awake having just gotten up. I shouldn't be afraid to think certain things. There should not be an unstoppable noise in my head. Something's gone wrong.

Every mind's managers have the same intent, yet each brain intrusion is custom-designed. Simply put, each ti's technical crew reacts according to its victim's thoughts, emotions, moods, words, and actions. As soon as Ms. Timid worries that a prowler could slip past the storage shed's alarm, v2k staff will send a knocked-over-bicycle noise to her head, and she'll be certain her bike is being stolen, which it isn't.

The remote stalkers' response time to thoughts is usually instant. I don't mean almost instant. I mean bang-on instant. It's as if the technical crew are ahead in time and have their responses prepared. The prospect of that sounds asinine until you think back to the other phenomena victims' experience, such as a ledge of potted violets taking a ramble over to the spice rack while a ti is mixing a batch of pastry. (Okay, it was me.) For all the theories that exist, I prefer to believe the paranormal-like events are attributable to covert advances in military or intelligence sciences. A whack of smart analysts finger advanced physics, engineering, and space programs.

What else is there? Hmm. How about the taboo subject of mind-pictures. We've looked at images sent into two minds: Moe's demons and hungry Harry's snapshots of a slaughterhouse. They're not exactly as you read. I didn't lie. It's just that you weren't quite ready for the unabridged take on them, as the images that OS emits into a brain can incite suicide or at a bare minimum induce fears or phobias.

There are various kinds of mind-pictures, so let's get started, beginning with the vision of a horizontal pole that was flashed into my head. "Ho-hum," you yawn, "big deal." That's true, which is why the mind-film was of a sparkling blue pole jerking up and down a hair's-width from my face. Under closed eyes, it dazzled brighter and jerked faster seemingly on the backs of the lids. It was better to see it open-eyed. Discharged into my head, my cranium was a TV set, and someone else was holding the remote. Should this or a similar mind-film be kept up, a person could not survive the incessantly lurching or pulsing figure sent through his visual pathways. He could not block it out, it would make him ill, and he would die.

A mind-film feels so real it's as if the projected scene is actually happening. The usual response is to be shaken and stunned or to disengage from society while sorting it all out. A victim who is plagued with mind-films could develop a sleep disorder; or PTSD; or, as I already said, pick up a phobia or kill himself. There is something freakish about them. More than that, they warp a person's past, present, and future. Mind-films warp minds.

In order to understand an in-head movie we need to affirm what EH is capable of. Remote electronic harassment can tickle, thump, cut, bruise, sting, itch, burn, and seriously injure a person. It can also generate the senses: a computer-operating brain manager can make a ti smell anything, from roses to rubber. Now don't forget voice to skull. So, while an OS video is rolling through a head, the victim, besides seeing the movie, could be hearing, feeling, and smelling it. Maybe even tasting it.

Mind-films are one of OS's most lethal weapons. Thresholds are exceeded when one or more senses are taken over in a death-grip or piteous scene that the victim has no hope of ending.

As a non-target, if that's what you are, it's important to acknowledge mind-films' existence; for folks around ti's are afflicted with nonviolent emotionally-staggering dreams, psychedelic dreams such as being squished between animated walls, and violent sensory-filled nightmares. A non-ti who experiences wild dreams is usually, but not always, asleep. If the dream or nightmare was sensory-filled, he may not know if he was awake or not. After a few, it becomes apparent something is going on as even mild induced dreams and flitting glimmers of illusions are so abnormal the person is distracted for hours or days afterwards.

One of the reasons it takes time to recover from a disturbing EH'ed dream, or an interactive mind-film, or a projected image is because overwhelming emotions can accompany it. Sure, any bad dream or experience can evoke bad feelings. Nonetheless, EH'ed dreams, images, and mind-films are not any old bad turn of events. I'll explain using a mundane, yet unsettling, induced dream I had. In my dream I had moved to an apartment that had bare concrete walls inside and out. It was noisy there: highways on all sides and no trees. I despised it.

Knowing me as you do, you're not surprised that I would detest living in such a place. The clue to this being an induced (EH'ed) dream is how I emotionally reacted both during the dream and upon waking up. I felt devastated, and I remained devastated till nightfall, although my day was really very good considering that I'm a ti. The bottom line is that mood-making EH was in my head through the dream, and after the dream, and there was no getting it out.

We've discussed this before: emotions sent through mind control can be so strong that a person will realize that what he's feeling is unnatural. Even so, trauma-causing dreams, glimmers of illusions, and mind-films can leave a person feeling blue, ratty, out of sorts, panicky, or weepy. For hours and hours.

A person whose mind has been taken over during the night can wake up with an unusual headache in the front of his brain. The pain is hard or impossible to get rid of, resulting in the person being sickeningly queasy, weary, and perhaps dizzy and sweaty. Eyes might be sore, eyesight might be blurry, and nose might be runny. This kind of brain pain is the aftermath of disturbing dreams or interactive mind-films for some ti's. Other ti's experience emotional trauma along with drop-dead fatigue, and no pain.

In sum, overnight EH'ed brain pain, emotional trauma, and fatigue do not result in a typical-feeling headache or migraine, or a typical day of sadness, agitation, or tiredness. Oppressive mental or physical conditions after a night of being EH'ed are byproducts of mind control.

At the end of this chapter (page 373), we'll discuss how to dampen the inevitable trauma EH'ed dreams and mind-films evoke. Note that I lump EH'ed dreams into the same category as mind-films; both of them, mental images and mental stories, are artificially produced in a mind from an outside source. Mind-film (or mind-movie) is the overall term I use.

It would be brazen to relate other victims' visual transmitted encounters as they are told to me, in spite of knowing full well that their episodes are invariably as vile, and conceivably more so, as my own. A torturous mind-film can only be explained by the person who experienced it, so you are stuck with my accounts. A real writer would have asked for submissions long ago; it didn't occur to me until today. My apologies.

A visualization that stands out is when I was particularly hard hit with frequencies of sadness. In other words, synthetically produced sadness was pouring through my skull with the usual remote beam that stays in my head. I wept nonstop. It wasn't depression. It was directed energy. Targets can tell.

By the end of week four, I was beginning to feel that the only way to quit crying was to die. That's when a suicide-urging mind-film was played.

Waking up with a start, eyes wide open, I saw a paved road. On it, in the dusk, was one of my sons. He had been run over and was dragging his flattened body towards me, inch by inch. When I looked closer, it was not his clothes that were shredded, but strips of skin that looked like patterned clothes, bloodied and blackened.

Responding as if I was in an actual tragedy, I saw that my arms were stretched forwards, but not in the air as you'd suppose. They were stretched across a gravelled roadside. I knew I was still lying on the couch. There's no doubt about that. Yet I saw and felt myself lying belly-down in the gravel, straining with all my might to grasp my son's clawing fingers. It was like being in two worlds at the same time.

Amid my confusion of what was and wasn't real, the mind-movie took a merciless twist, for not only did my hands and wrists hurt from leaning into the gravel, but the overwhelming smell of tinny-gore and asphalt made me woozy—of having the love for my dying son in my nose.

Then he was run over again in front of my face. The tires made a bump-bump sound as they went over his back. Feeling the insufferable mourning of a mother who has just lost her child, I watched the back end of a 1940s sedan leisurely travelling on, as if my son was nothing, down the straight road until the plink plink from stone-filled tread grew as faint as the greyness it faded into.

When the mind-film ended, the computer operators kept the gagging bloody smell going. And for days, thanks to a sensory beam, I scratched at simulated gravel-scraped palms and wrists. Anyone who's fallen off a bicycle and had his hands embedded with road grit knows the prickliness. That's what it was like, minus visible scouring.

This same interactive horror show is played into assorted brains worldwide. Remarkably, the characters, vehicles, and lingering effects are changed to suit the person wearing the EH'ed head. Another Canadian who had the run-over-child movie took time away from her job so that she could accompany her adult daughter everywhere, foreseeing the visualization as a warning. The morning she relaxed her vigilance, the daughter was mowed down on a street corner by an, apparently, distracted hit-and-run driver.

Although the versions of mind-movies are infinite, films that guarantee tears or fears are dominant. Tuesday night Baby will drown, and Wednesday night will be spent in an electric chair. My last two were back-to-back beginning with a tabby cat looking out the glass door of a rocking, clattering hot-smelling woodstove. Then upon recovering and going back to sleep, the next movie showed my wonderful dad looking lonely on a rocky shoreline, complete with the sound of splashing as he fell in. How I miss him.

Upping the carnage- and sadness-replicating technique is a class of brain-invasion pageantry that defies what ti's think mind-movies can do unless they are inducted. On hearing about clashes with apparitions, I understood the victims' shock, but not at all what they were telling me. Close encounters with phantom people did not begin for me until the fourteenth year when a fragmented man pulled me off the couch one night as my head hit the pillow. I saw his hairy hands wrapped around my wrists and saw his masculine arms straining as he yanked me up. There was no body. No head. This vision actually did pull me to my feet, then let go fast, sending me tumbling to the floor. I giggled and must have been hysterical. My wrists hurt. That's how hard he had pulled me. While I was giggling, slumped on the floor, the drama ended, and I instinctively replaced the laughter with hyper-acuity. Listening for footsteps, floor creaks, and the sounds of someone leaving, there was only the silence of a house in the woods.

Rationality dictates that a man had come into the house, and my brain, gridlocked with a muted scream, failed to compute seeing all of him or hearing him leave. I refuse to accept that happened based on several factors. One, the house is barricaded; two, if I believe a man is getting in, terror would exceed my already maxed out threshold; and three, my brain felt the same as during the mind-movies.

It was weeks before I would lie down, preferring instead to sit bolt upright on the couch each night and nod off in stints. The lapse, however, hadn't deterred a further visit. The first time I got confident enough to sleep horizontally, the same hairy hands protruded through the gloom and grabbed my face. Again, there was no body or head, but then my concentration was on prying his fingers off my cheeks. His hands, by the way, felt entirely real. Once more, I giggled hysterically when he, or it, let go.

It made a third entrance not long ago, but early in the evening whilst working on the book. I told it to fuck off, which is potent language given my strait-laced make-up. So, what is that? Are the hands and arms a mind-movie manipulation? Or are they something else? Given that typical sensory-filled visualizations do everything except grab, an attacking apparition is unorthodox even for this crime, although it's happened to several others, along with a nurse-friend who, like me, ended up on the floor, but after her mattress was tipped, twice.

Righto then, aside from the fragmented man and his cronies, how do computer perps make sense-filled, lifelike mind-movies? Targets don't know. Well, some think they know. A few credit holograms beamed outside or, somehow, inside a head. Only two things are for sure:

- Simulating senses and producing emotions by electronically accessing a brain was fine-tuned in laboratories a long time ago.
- Streaming movies into a head is doable, according to university brain-study labs, but is not ready for mainstream use in the same way v2k is. Streaming movies into a head is supposed to be in the drawing-board stage. In the opinion of hordes of ti's, transmitting pictures into a brain has been covertly accomplished and is being used for universal torture. With proof in head, I agree.

Much of a ti's persecution is shrouded in compulsory ignorance. This does not negate that cerebral butchery is underway. Nor does ignorance dull a victim's suffering when his brain is seized. It just means that OS's personalized construction of mind-movies is an enigma as is how someone can be made to interact with the film. As far as this chapter is concerned, the value is in recognizing that each raid on a brain is assault with a deadly weapon. Netherworld Cinema and its human-head screen top the arsenal.

Not all mind-movies require the victim's involvement, thank goodness. The majority of them are meant only to be observed, such as my jerking blue pole, Moe's demons, hungry Harry's slaughterhouse snapshots, and graphic dreams, all seen inside or outside a noggin.

I'm going to presumptuously state that all heavily harassed victims see not-supposed-to-be-there objects and scenes whether they recognize them as facades or not, especially early on when mental splintering is eagerly sought. A ti might catch a glimpse of an unfamiliar dress in her closet, and within a couple of seconds its picture is deleted from her brain. She knows what she saw, but now that it's gone, logic triumphs, and the woman decides that there was no dress.

The reverse can also happen:

Target: "Where did the car go?"

Spouse: "What do you mean where did it go?"

Target: "It's not in the garage. Come see."

Spouse: "You're losing it. It's the big white thing with the tires."

Target: "Well, it wasn't there a second ago."

Many ti's are certain that black ops physics breakthroughs not only send mental imagery but can make items appear and disappear. When you stop laughing, consider that from 1968 to 1972 the U.S. government purportedly tried to make things and people do just that. According to witnesses, this top-secret project in teleportation and time travel was conducted by DARPA (Defense Advanced Research Projects Agency), which is an agency of the U.S. Department of Defense.

The story goes that the people who were used as lab rats came forward, and with credible evidence of their involvement, they declared that teleportation and time travel are possible through quantum access technology. A couple of these ageing lab rats are determined to reveal DARPA's secret projects to the public and say that "disappearing" and "reappearing" tests continue today.

More to the point, a number of ti's blame DARPA for all the remote harassment.

What a government's covert science escapades are is not for me to say. I'm just a messenger with an open mind who hopes that this information reaches the ti who couldn't see her car, for she'll be less frightened if she ponders "science" rather than "not science."

Aside from DARPA's alleged magic acts, there is another explanation for a ti not seeing a car that her husband says is there. It's a poor excuse at best and involves pattern recognition loss, which is a medical term for when the part of the brain responsible for recognizing objects is damaged. It goes like this: "Mabel, everyone can see the kettle except you. The chunk of firewood that beaned you has busted something in your head."

Although EH manipulates brain centres to simulate brain damage, EH-imposed pattern recognition loss, should it be possible, contradicts Mabel's targeted son momentarily seeing his ukulele up a tree.

I'm concerned that you, poor reader, are getting bogged down with inconsistencies. Stop thinking, take a deep breath, and relax. You are befuddled because as of this writing few elements of OS's remote EH make sense. Yes, bits and pieces of the technology are known; yet how EH gets to a head and how exactly it meddles with a head are debatable. You're not slow to catch on, as only the enemy can answer your remote-EH-based questions, and they're not talking. Don't be dismayed. You are learning about remote-EH's effects and overall impact, which are the topics you need to be versed in. Feel better now? Shall we continue?

My insinuation that all heavily harassed victims see not-supposed-to-be-there objects and scenes, and don't see supposed-to-be-there objects and scenes, could be viewed as an indiscretion; for a few folks claim to be stalked and not electronically harassed.

The vice versa is also true. A spattering of targets claim they are not stalked and instead bear a disabling, high-level stand-alone energy such as v2k, microwaving, or mind control. My opinion is that these victims cannot allow themselves to believe remote surveillance and spotters are on their tail, for all targets are watched. Either that, or they are mistakenly calling themselves ti's.

It's probable that stand-alone low-level EH is widespread and not recognized (or diagnosed), particularly among a ti's EH-naive loved ones. Tinnitus, visual impairment, unrelenting itchiness, and mild heart aberrations immediately come to mind. So does fibromyalgia. Whole-body EH causes every inch to throb and makes climbing even one stair really, really hard. After days of pain and twenty-four hour fatigue, the ti begins to feel despondent. Does that occur to any of you who are around a ti? Does it sound like fibromyalgia? Or maybe you've got chronic unexplainable pain in just one place.

Then there's Morgellons disease, or something like it, where people experience the skin-crawling sensation we've talked about, or itchy sores. Often described as an ailment that cannot be, a delusion, the ti's who have it swear that their disbelieved skin problems are genuine and linked to electronic harassment.

I am not implying that most of the general public's usual and unusual health problems are EH caused. That would be silly. I am suggesting that once a loved one is OS/EH educated, he can begin learning how to tell the difference between EH and normal afflictions and that will raise his antenna (pardon the pun) to mind-control strikes on himself and the target.

Perhaps you disagree with my statements affirming that all heavily stalked and harassed subjects and all heavily EH'ed subjects are mind controlled in some way. EH is pretty darn sneaky—sneaky enough that unenlightened victims can be hoodwinked. My firm stance is that EH is in every OS victim's head whether in readiness, or inconspicuously, or raucously, even when energy attacks on the body seem absent or are possibly being misinterpreted. The same can be said for close loved ones who regularly engage with the ti in their life.

Anyhow, the images seen inside or outside a head are, perhaps, advanced test-room ruses to mess up a well-functioning person and are not necessarily DARPA related. Nazi and MKULTRA experimenters also messed up well-functioning people and their brains, but by using psychological abuse, poisons, drugs, direct-contact electricity, and elemental remote electricity instead of today's exceptional from-afar energy assaults.

The mind-imagery situations in the following two lists could be caused by brain muddling, quantum access technology or other advanced science field, mind-movies, paranormal phenomena, or something else. No one knows. Personally, I lean towards science and believe all EH will eventually be explained by physicists and engineers, but I'm willing to be wrong.

It's important to remember that the people who experience OS ruses are not mad. They are crime victims.

This first set of EH'ed pop-up imagery, as reported by targets, can be statue-still or moving:

- Dark silhouettes of objects, men, other people, animals, demons, and unidentified shapes

- Entirely realistic men, women, and children who are strangers or who are familiar
- Entirely realistic animals and objects
- Demonic creatures
- Glowing white or beautifully coloured light in circles or wide rays
- Glowing white or beautifully coloured narrow light beams
- Indoor flashes or indoor clouds that are white or black
- Snapshot-type photos inside or outside a head—usually stationary, but can have motion
- Objects or scenes that seem to have moved a substantial distance after the person blinks or looks away for a second, for example, a lamp, puddle, mountain, backyard, person who is walking, and a crib with a tot in it. During another blink or glance away, the object or scene returns to its normal position. Or it could vanish.

The following EH-made imagery is always moving:

- Movies played inside or outside a head
- Translucent trailing gusts of black, white, or another colour
- Slow waves of ethereal (ghostly) air or similar waves of white light
- Large stationary objects or sweeping scenes that slide sideways, melt, or tilt as they are being looked at, for example, a boulder, building, floor, orchard, and a hillside. They return to normal in a blink.
- Scenes with movement that slide sideways, melt, tilt, or reverse direction as they are being looked at, for example, a rushing river, horse race, and leaves falling off trees. They return to normal in a blink.

Daytime and nighttime mind-pictures are regularly relayed to some ti's with the goal of frightening them into psychological collapse.

One gentleman who watched a mythological beast dart through his house went bonkers, fled, and did not return for months. Back home now, he is preoccupied with how he'll react if he sees it again, shrugging advice to relax and forget it. The first demon that OS's staff emitted to me was a brown blob with beady eyes and a spikey head. It zoomed out of the floor in my parent's basement at the crime's onset. The second and final one (to date) was a red devil's face the remote staff flashed in my head for a few afternoons.

As legitimate as the technology of mind-movie transmission, mind-snapshot transmission, and other mind meddling is, the natural reaction after seeing a "that can't exist" semblance outside a head, even for veteran ti's, is to leave the room or area, or at least want to.

Before you determine that you'd be the one person who'd keep his cool, imagine being stalked. Being stalked exacerbates fear responses. The last thing chronically skittish people need is the willies.

A hundred or so targets that I know of, along with the innocents around them, acknowledge seeing people, objects, and scenes that shape-shift. There could be many more witnesses. It's something that's difficult to admit to. Shape-shifting sounds warlocky until you remember that the electronic mind-controllers' job is to inlay a brain with bedlam. I recall someone rearranging the numbered flags at a mini golf course and then putting them back in order after feeling guilty. (Yeah, it was me again, but this time I was young.) Pandemonium reigned on the little course for those few minutes as the perfectly working system had been altered. The golfers were not playing in sequence. The course stopped making sense. When OS revises a head, it, too, is out of sequence until the person under the head sorts the anomaly out or the assault stops. Shape-shifting, I'm sure, is incorporated into selected ti's mind-control theme.

A counter to the favoured EH'ed-brain theory is that occultism is being used as a mind-control weapon. It may offend you to read about fringe viewpoints. That's alright. The crime fits no paradigm; therefore, I need to show all sides of supernatural-like EH. Me? I think (and hope) shape-shifting, sudden appearances, sudden disappearances, and mind-movies are illegally-used spearhead sciences. Thus, the science of energy (electronic) harassment is examined in this book.

We're going to leave the how-it's-done perplexity behind for the moment as the toll on "you're it" peons—you, me, and our families—is the present issue. Above all, a bravado attitude is advantageous during OS's scarier pitches, the reason being that a victim receives a lot of what he's most afraid of. As a rule, it takes years to develop an "oh well" attitude towards the spookier marvels. Please, if the mind perversions are unravelling you, know that your fight, flight, or freeze reactions are normal and then speak to those ti's whose trials sound like yours. It helps.

To illustrate an "oh well" response, let's look at Wednesday evening. While setting up the next day's book-work, a young fellow dressed in 14th-century garb popped into my eyesight as if he were standing beside the fireplace. Just for a second. That's twice lately with this guy. Excelling in craftiness, the mind-reading crew fabricated the historical figure because, in working my way through Shakespeare's plays, I'd been thinking about ordering the library's 1968 Romeo and Juliet DVD. The men's costumes in the film remind me of a Joker in a deck of cards, so my thoughts were inquisitive, trying to associate a Joker with Italy's Renaissance.

Certainly it startled me to see a comically-clad Romeo in the living room. Mind-pictures always startle me. Nonetheless, I thought, "It's gone. I always survive show-off tactics." My only residual emotion was intrigue, craving to get wind of revolutionary wizardry and the miscreants behind it. Lord only knows what will pop up tonight, for I'm also thinking about adding Appalachian bluegrass music to my library order. To recap, thought-reading can prompt one or several senses to be artificially employed, as Romeo's guest appearance proved.

Yet thought-reading is unnecessary to tap into someone's senses. Whatever sensory gig the technical crew finds amusing is delivered at an apropos or preplanned moment to a person who will see, hear, smell, taste, or feel a not-real turn of events, from a snippet of what appears to be a hallucination to being cast in a full-out illusory stage production. If electronic mind-control perpetrators want you to ride a perfumed zebra in the rain, across a field of yodelling daisies, while you're chomping toffee, that is what you will seem to be doing.

I know what you're thinking—that the rain wouldn't be noticeable in the midst of the whole zebra-daisy kafuffle. Surprise. You would definitely feel wet. Rain or a thorough dousing is faked really well as my former apartment roommate found out.

Leaping out of bed, Whatshisname found me in the kitchen where he proceeded with a string of cussing. Peering into the sink and opening the cupboards, he yelled, "Where is it?"

"Where's what?" I asked.

"The bucket."

"What bucket? What's wrong with you?" I demanded.

"You threw water on me. Cold water."

"What? Why would I do that? You dreamt it. You're dry."

I'm no doctor, but in my opinion Whatshisname was in shock, unable to find water, yet feeling soaked. He stood naked in the tiny living room trying to sort himself out, having removed pajamas that should have been wet. He then took the bedding apart and, exhibiting mental disintegration, checked under the mattress. Asking the upstairs tenant if she'd had a flood would have gone better without mentioning the dry ceiling.

As someone who crossed my path as a bystander, Whatshisname had been chosen as a secondary target straightaway. This led us to shack up for a short time during my years on the run. The sensation of being wet was his main electronic mind-control harassment.

I remember waving to him from the patio wondering why he was always patting his head and looking up.

Unlike having a single sense taken over, which as you've just learned can cause acute disorientation, multi-sensory brain movies are apparently comparable to the poison-laced drug states that result in colourful townsfolk. Judging how traumatized victims are, it sounds about right.

Before determining once and for all that the book is a hoax written by a twit, which you undoubtedly have been contemplating for ages, consider this. Most heavily harassed targets have on par paranormal-type experiences. They seldom publicly talk about them, except for simulated sexual attacks, which are status quo for some.

Faux rape and other faux sexual assaults are oftentimes attributed to the remote mystery energy-beams that can be felt irritating, poking, and wounding all areas of a body. This means victims don't have to say, "It felt like an invisible person groped me," or, "Rape-reproducing frequencies were sent into my head," or, "My brain centres were manipulated to make my genitals feel manhandled." They can simply say, "An energy beam did it," because short-range transmitted energy and direct-contact energy on a brain or genitalia can do all those things, which is why ti's can talk about remote electronic sexual assaults, assuming that new-fangled technology with far-reaching energy is to blame, be it mind control or a felt-on-contact mystery beam.

You might have seen a documentary clip that showed a wide-awake surgical patient's brain being touched with a tiny electrical probe. He may have said his leg tingled. That's what some synthetic assaults are like, except in this instance genitalia are affected instead of a leg. Remotely operating staff can make a victim experience anything by invading a brain with pinpointed energy or precise frequencies, presuming EH is to blame.

If you're having trouble following along, remember the quip of a fellow falling off a ladder and then smelling burnt toast. When a brain is disrupted, there can be a mental or physical response or a mental reshuffling. A person can feel sexually mauled by his own invaded mind.

Many ti's claim their brains are not being managed during a sexual assault. They say their genitals and bottoms are truly being assaulted and penetrated by a beam or heaven knows what. A ti I know can explain it better. Our conversation began with how he assumes microwaves are heating his head to near-death states and ended with his confession of being raped.

"I spoke to Ms. R," he said, "about something personal they're doing. It's hard to bring up. I don't want to be judged."

"Don't say anything that makes you uncomfortable," I replied. "Ms. R is my dearest ti friend. You can trust her. You may want to keep this between you two."

"No," he said. "I need help with it."

"Alrighty, shoot."

"Sometimes when I go to the bathroom or have a shower, they poke me in the rear end. Are they trying to make me homosexual? Or afraid to take my clothes off?"

"I don't know why they do it other than to upset you," I said. "Most ti's get raped or molested by EH in intervals, and a few women get EH-molested every day. Please understand that I believe you."

"It's sadistic," he said. "I pretend the perps are aliens. It's easier to believe aliens are raping me than men behind computers. This must sound crazy to you."

"Not at all. There's no harm imagining aliens are raping you. Humans need rationality, and as the attacks are invisible, you've come to a rationale that works for you. A few ti's do blame aliens or evil entities. The rest think sexual assaults are from beams on their genitals and rear ends or from brain-centred EH that makes their private areas feel attacked."

"Remember when I called two weeks ago?" the fellow asked. "And you didn't get to the phone? I was tying an extension cord around my neck. Being nuked and raped at the same time . . ."

"We've talked about suicide before, and thank goodness you're smart enough to be honest about it. It's something all heavily tortured ti's confront. Try to talk to Ms. R more. You need support, and I can be hard to reach sometimes. They're always cutting off my communications. You know, there's another raped fellow not far from you, who would be empathetic. Actually, I can think of two more on the West Coast. I'll ask if they want to connect with other rape victims. To speak to another man . . . It would be a relief for you four to not feel alone, helping each other out. Oh, before you go—the imaginary aliens. Be careful who you tell."

"June, I don't want you to take this the wrong way, but you sound awful. Are you okay?"

"The way I'm talking? Like there's a sock stuffed in my mouth? It's something new—woke up with it. Yup, I'm fine. It's better than the stutter they gave me. And the lisp. And when they made me sound like I was talking into a fan. No worries."

To a non-ti fly-on-the-wall, that conversation would have sounded like a screenplay dialogue between a psychotic mentor and a psychotic sci-fi junkie. Welcome to my world of life and death discourses about electronic raping and other remote electronic harassments.

If remote raping or remote sexual manhandling happens to you, stay as composed as possible to reduce the number of future attacks. Then, no matter what you think the source is, try stuffing or securing a harm-free material, perhaps a room-temperature gel pack, Mylar, or a wet or dry towel, tightly against the area. This works, somewhat, for a few, as does a thick layer of natural or medicated cream that's safe to use on a bottom half. Crannies will still be affected.

On a similar subject, overwrought ti's adhere salve, bandages, tape, Mylar, and damp cloths to their genitalia and bottoms for days or weeks at a time, striving to dampen hour after hour of skin-crawling discomfort. For those of you who have never experienced EH's skin-crawling molestation, imagine bugs and sand roving all over your private areas. A bath or shower is effective for some and not for others. A cool shallow bath, though, is quick pain relief for EH-burned genitalia, bottoms, and legs. A large EH'ed patch of skin that has unstoppable itchiness might be temporarily soothed by one of the above-mentioned remedies. Cling film, with or without a layer of salve, is supposed to be good for itchy limbs.

Veteran ti's, for the most part, learn to distinguish between EH hitting their innards or skin (expressly genitalia) from EH hitting brain centres that trigger bodily pain and sensations. To a non-ti, this sounds as easy as telling the difference between a stubbed toe and a tension headache. However, unless there are visible wounds, differentiating strike types is a wee bit sticky and not infallible.

In addressing now the targets who are reading this, identifying whether an EH'ed brain centre is why an intimate area or your palm (for example) is aching takes strenuous concentration. We took a peek at this before. While imagining the pain as a positive event, perhaps that a missed loved one has accidentally hurt you (good luck with that), or while mentally trying to block the energy as it enters your head, you feel the pain suddenly stop, or stop and return ten times worse, or move somewhere else, then a brain center is being evoked. Fallibility comes in when the EH perps treat your test like a game or punish you for self-saving and deploy energy hits like a machine gun on one spot, oftentimes on genitalia or eyes. We'll be exploring a brain-beam reversal exercise shortly.

Recognizing a solo strike, no matter what the EH weapon is, can allow a target to mobilize established stamina ingenuity. This is what the energy-raped chap did by pretending aliens were poking him. He has since learned to mentally resist each rape, mollifying prescribed indignity. Adopting an on par coping attitude during intense head-cooking, he learned to divert his attention with a movie and, despite claiming irreligiosity, by reading the Book of Psalms to allay disconnection from hope. The chap wants to survive. It doesn't matter that his family is uptight about the Bibles strewn around his apartment or that they criticize his large DVD collection. It doesn't matter that they saw his self-help guide for rape victims. This whipping boy is still here whereas one of his raped friends isn't.

When several energy types are attacking at the same time, or the attack is lethal-bearing, the ti has been conquered, and there's nothing to do but dredge up the primal oomph to stay sane and alive. A person whose genitals are being electronically injured may somehow be enduring a meticulous line of remote energy, along with "I feel raped" brain invasions. A double-dealt assault victim like this will bear a mishmash of pain, penetration, crawling skin, burns, cuts, scrapes, long-lasting internal or external tenderness, faux emotions, genuine emotions, unwanted memories, and replicated smells that range from puke to lavender.

Artificially produced experiences, from rape to rain, must be addressed so that disbelieved folks can come forward and be treated as crime victims. So we will continue along in this vein.

Stimulating brain centres to simulate sexual assault is just one mind intrusion out of an open-ended number and combinations thereof. It appears that EH may be manipulating two brain domains to mock the senses: sensory brain centres and the energy they absorb (frequencies).

Imagine dribbling purple goo into a big clear bowl of water. Maybe in the middle. Maybe off to the side. It's your choice. Where the water is brightly coloured is where the mind will be influenced or entirely taken over. If the water were alive, it would feel the change. Whether the purple has coloured this (brain centre) or that (brain frequency) only matters to the person who dribbled the goo. To the water, it's all the same.

In other words, the senses can be forcefully produced, or erased, through remotely manipulating brain centres or by sending frequencies into a skull; and the person wearing the skull will not know which method was used. Consensus among EH investigators is that frequency-filled emissions prevail. In plain English, much of a victim's mind control could be caused by frequency-filled signals that are sent into his head.

The spectrum of remote mind control has generated a diversity of theories about how it's done. The aforementioned occultism is only one out of an ideas' cache. As stated, I happen to agree with numerous scholars' conservative scientific hypotheses based on their (and my) private and collective research, education, and personal experiences; so that's what I'm relating in this book. Until OS's technology is proven in a courtroom, it will benefit both you and me to keep an open mind about all aspects of electronic harassment.

This is not a science text. It's a rudimentary look at OS and its tactics' effects on individuals. Let's break down mind-altering sensory stratagems (tricks) into their havoc-wreaking formats.

A. Sensory stratagems can be momentary and non-violent. In one day a victim could smell mown grass in a skyscraper, use an iron-heavy toothbrush, and eat eggs that taste like cookie dough. These types of sensations scare or confuse. A momentary EH'ed sense can also have major consequences, such as smelling smoke in a skyscraper instead of mown grass. Many individuals can experience the same sense(s) faked at the same time: a class studying whales could feel, smell, and taste a salty ocean mist.

B. Sensory stratagems can be long-lasting. A person could taste soap or smell gasoline for weeks. One or many individuals can be affected.

C. Sensory stratagems can be violent feelings of rape or other type of assault. Faux sexual assaults occur in the daytime as well as in the night hours. Women, men, and teens are subjected. As well, there is concrete evidence that targets' young children and grandchildren are sexually, or otherwise, abused by remote EH. The psychological trauma of EH-assaulted victims is misunderstood by those who have not experienced such an attack.

D. Sensory stratagems of being gently patted and fondled result in horror or, in some instances, hope that divine intervention is trying to provide comfort.

E. Sensory stratagems include snapshot images flashed into a mind. Eyes can be open or closed. The individual can be sleeping, almost asleep, or wide-awake and active while seeing an image (or several) inside or outside his head. Anyone who is with, or involved with, a primary or secondary target could see a mind-snapshot.

F. Sensory stratagems include mind-movies. These are the faked sensations that create seeming reality in a prolonged film sent into a brain. A victim can spend a night feeling, seeing, hearing, and smelling the casket he's apparently buried in. A different victim who's hiking a West Coast trail will see and hear a pack of wolves ten feet in front of him that his companions won't see and hear. Mind-movies are experienced inside and outside a head. Anytime. Any place. Asleep or awake. A non-ti who is with a heavily harassed target could see a mind movie. It could be the same one the ti sees or one that only the non-ti sees.

G. Sensory stratagems include voice to skull (v2k).

H. Sensory stratagems are often combined with OS's other crimes. A mob-stalked teen might be flashed an image of being thrown down a ravine. A parent under night terrorism might hear v2k gunshots in the children's bedrooms. And an elder could smell his cherished dog long after intruders killed it. For a last example, sexual threats made to a woman over the phone may include a night-long mind-movie of being hung from a rafter, or hearing a v2k rape, or tasting semen.

I. Sensory stratagems can nullify sense of smell, taste, hearing, sight, touch, and every other human sense. Fireworks or an alarm clock might not be heard. A bus or red light might not be seen.

This is rather a protracted segment of the book. Sorry about that. You could probably do with a break having been tossed in over your head. Howbeit we push on anyhow and get this difficult chapter behind us.

Because I work with victims seeking assistance, they eventually develop enough trust in me to relate their bizarre tales of mind control. Remotely conjured human senses and remotely intercepted human senses, which you have to admit are phenomenal achievements, are the zenith of brain-chaos as they simulate paranormal events and psychosis. Of all the ti's secret common denominators, sensory control is the most critical. No target, according to my bias, escapes sensory management, yet few want to talk about its wackier side for fear of being ostracized or hospitalized. Notwithstanding public condemnation, never mind being labelled an asylum candidate, I've decided to accept the kickback for exposing hushed issues. Knowing that more and more of my friends are hoarding suicide drugs is intolerable when the crime can be stopped. Canadian government, where are you? Where are all the countries' governments?

Till this book, I've sidestepped speaking about electronic mind control except with other targets. Outspoken victims fare poorly, not just because they sound nuts, but because it's accepted among the ti community that OS's stalking, on-heels harassment, and v2k must gain public acceptance before total electronic mind control should be introduced. I've blown it.

In other respects, to write about OS crimes and omit the most heinous feels deceitful: that half of the story is missing. Only you can judge whether telling all has been the right decision. What needs no second guessing is that living under electronic mind control eclipses the sum of atrocities against human beings.

My lovebird is sitting on my shoulder right now. His weight is less than two ounces (about fifty grams). Sensory control in my head is making him feel heavier than a three-pound tub of margarine. (If you call me *especial* for putting a margarine tub on my other shoulder to compare, we'll have something in common.) In itself, a lead-weight lovebird isn't galling. What's troubling me is losing sole access and authority over my own brain. The bird, by the way, is his chipper self: unaffected.

Sensory and thought-reading invasions are infinitely varied, swinging from petty, to viperous, to mystical. You, ti or not, may hear victims speak about supernatural-type curiosities not mentioned here. It's conceivable that these personal confessions resonate to you as witchcraft or psychic power. Please be patient. The instigators of organized stalking have tapped into classified genius-equation breakthroughs that are run behind closed doors.

"They're seeing through my eyes" is a recurrent catchphrase in victims' conversations. With everything in a target's environment dissected by the enemy, "They're seeing through my eyes" is a legitimate statement. Maybe they are. Who knows what can occur when criminals and their computers take over an indefensible brain?

A ti who is conscious that his predators are watching everything right along with him, and also reading his mind, is going to edit what he looks at, as well as edit what he thinks about. He'll not look at a baby stroller, nor allow sentiments to envelop him, having lost an infant daughter to an isolation theme. He doesn't want to remind the henchmen that he misses her.

Oh dear. After denying you a break, determined to mush on, a supreme case of butterflies has taken hold, and it's me who must stop. All this talk about puppet-brains has been over-taxing, interrupting the rhythm of explanation with what's really on my mind—what's always on my mind. How on earth do I atone for bringing OS into my loved ones' lives?

You may as well learn something from my despair. Here I am grovelling for clemency, yet am consciously trying not to emit any distress frequencies, knowing they will be artificially stoked by more of the same, along with varying harassments to myself and the loved ones I must atone to.

* * *

Maybe my objective is greedy, wanting you to swallow the complete mind-control package. But then again, maybe it's not. We've come to a juncture. To tell you or not to tell you.

On the grounds you've a right to know, in spite of how disturbing this is, here goes. Disdain, lust, jealousy, obsession, hate, greed, revenge, recklessness, yup, the whole shebang of quarrel-making, tight-spot-inducing, and perilous emotions and traits can accompany a beam aimed at anybody, meaning you, anywhere. So, if a ti in your church group is sharing a box of chocolates, war could break out among the others.

Although it's accurate to say anyone can be electronically mind controlled, we'll review who besides targets are most at stake. A person who persistently rescues or backs a ti is probably going to be affected. So might a person or animal who loves, knows, interacts, or stands near a ti.

That means it's likely that Carpenter Cal and his dog Chisel will have emotion- and sense-changing energies seeped into their skulls while they're at heavily harassed Tilly's house. Cal could drop his fence-building tools and march right into Tilly's kitchen horny as all get-out, insisting on a slice of the nonexistent apple pie he's smelled baking for the last half-hour. Mutually falling prey to EH, Chisel will for the first time in his life bite someone.

With regard to amorous Cal, remote perps have the ability to make an individual, of any age, sexually needy to the extent of deviant, aggressive, flaunting, dangerous, or submissive behaviour. In Carpenter Cal's case, my opinion is that specific people around targets are mind-managed to crave sexual activity for, you guessed it, perp jollies. And though wanting to engage in sex all day sounds like fun, the men and women ti's who are mind controlled this way hate it. They say they never feel satisfied and get into trouble. Too, EH sometimes numbs these eager folks' genitalia at crucial moments.

Savvy targets recognize flagrant electronic mind control. Innocents, having never heard of it, do not. I've had to step away from good folks for this reason, which is absurd as it's me who is the real ti. For instance, glamorous secretaries might blankly stare at a ti and then pick their noses. Or scratch their bums. Or make crude remarks. Mind control on innocents happens when a ti will be perturbed, inconvenienced, confused, saddened, embarrassed, frightened, made to worry, made to look dumb, made poorer, or further isolated. If a bystander, acquaintance, or loved one detects his impropriety, he is left wondering, "What possessed me to do that?"

As you'd expect, families, friendships, jobs, admissions, and opportunities are severed because of a loved one's, the public's, or the target's unintended rudeness, dishonesty, comments, and gestures.

An irascible v2k remark sent into only one head has the same effect: "Did you call me a donkey?"

The topic of EH-caused difficulties with gullible outsiders will thread in and out of the rest of the chapter because it's an OS practice you'll want to recognize when it pops up.

Mind control on innocents is sometimes done as a display of power to intimidate the real mark. I've seen bystanders wobble from dizziness or reveal a zoned-out look. Others talk in syllables that aren't words or are unable to execute a simple maneuver, like putting on their glasses. With every bystander who feels the brain control, there is a single commonality. The person is upset. Something's gone wrong with his head, and he knows it.

Most innocents, though, don't know. My grocery delivery lady thinks her pleasant small talk is dandy: "The baker packed fresh unbaked rolls," she says, "that are still warm from the oven. Here they are. They're unbaked. They're still warm. They're frozen." (In truth, she says it every time.)

When sentences are out-to-lunch, the speaker will not hear the discrepancy. He'll think it is you who is the goofball if you repeat the blather back. After all, he has been forming composite passages in his mind and then correctly saying them since he was three.

In the case of my delivery lady, she appears spellbound and not at all herself. It isn't just nonsense talk that is obvious. Her physical actions are governed to be speedy and choppy. Plus, she's uncouth. Rummaging through my groceries until the obsessed-about bag of buns are found, she moves the bag from place to place in the kitchen like an automaton on amphetamines, seeking a showcase surface. Never finding one, she opens the freezer and throws them in. By that time the buns are dented after being jabbed repetitively in an effort to make me pay attention to their hot and frozen history. As a methodical, responsible mom with a high IQ, the remote stalkers must find transmuting her a blast.

Upon leaving my house, her next delivery is to boat-dwellers at the marina. "Walk slowly along the middle of the wharves," I say, "and use the wheelbarrow if it's there." Her eyes betray amusement at my little-kid advice, yet I say it anyway in the event residual control makes her giddy. Away from me she's all-together.

New ti's might be calling me a dope right about now for not spotting a perp's spoof when it's in my own home. Be careful with assumptions. Not everyone is the enemy. The crime is designed to cause discord.

Please, if you are a target watching a sideshow like my grocery lady performs, say nothing about mind control. Do say something cautionary when it's necessary even if the innocent doesn't like it.

While admitting that I appear careless to have deliveries made to my surveilled house, there is no way to buy groceries here without human interaction. I tried. As my impact on others has increased lately, insulating innocents has become a perpetually irresolvable stressor. Perhaps the book's repercussions are affecting more than just me.

We're now going to dissect haywire speech as it causes a lot of friction. Innocents and targets insult and confuse each other all the time, but it's not their fault.

You've just learned that when brain infiltration forces a full-length eccentric conversation, a person can be made to sound like an idiot, which is what you'd think if you heard the bun lady. Alternatively, a beamed person who is construed as offensive may be told to "Stop being so mean" or, "Stop talking to me like I'm five!" or, "Come back when you're having a better day."

When just a few words or a sentence or two are off, the remote perps could be restructuring the ABC sequence of speaking:

A is thinking about, or knowing, what to say.

B is saying it.

C is recognizing what you said – which is missing in this type of mind control.

Disjointed ABC sequences take us back to the mystery of instantaneous transactions.

How can OS masters change a person's words between thinking them and saying them? Imagine hearing this from a classmate: "Tomorrow's seminar was fantastic." Now imagine hearing this from a lifeguard: "I'm going to take a nap."

In these cases, the speakers' mouths matched the misleading words that came out of them. With v2k, the mouth is not involved as the words are sent into a head via a perpetrator's v2k equipment.

Presently, because my newest owners humour themselves differently than the former, everyone, including me, sounds dysfunctional.

"I'll stick on some birds and label them," is what I allegedly said to an electrical repairman. The sentence should have been, "I'll stick on some tape strips and label them," referring to labelling switches he replaced (twice in one month). The fellow repeated what I said, wanting to be sure he had heard right. He had. But I didn't tell him that.

We should go over this again. In my mind, I said the correct words, yet the electrician heard the wrong words. Of the two of us, I believe it was me, the speaker, who had the controlled head. In the same respect, I believe it is the grocery lady (also the speaker) whose mind is controlled, since I feel normal while she's talking nonsense at length.

I'm going to ask you a favour. Please remember that the speech-substitution trick can occur anytime. Consequently, when your chinwag goes off the rails, you'll understand why, to a degree.

Phone conversations crumble under the same word-substitution and word-addition game:

"No, I said the reservation is for Smith. Two people at seven o'clock tonight. A quiet table if you don't mind."

"That's right, Mrs. Newton. That's what I have written down. Saturday for eighteen people at five o'clock. You'll have the party room to yourselves."

Many ti's blame the science of electronic voice conversion (replicating a voice) for phone call mix-ups like this. That seems doubtful because OS's voice-mimicking sham can happen to anyone at any time, abruptly and flawlessly. As it stands today, using known methods, it is an intricate process to replicate, say, your mom's voice, and then script her voice to carry out, or interrupt, a conversation.

Worth a second look are the mind-control sensory deceits where statements and sounds are voided rather than added: vamoosed from the listener's hearing. A ringing phone, siren, or instruction—anything important that the person needs to have heard won't be if the remote perps are seeking a troublemaking opportunity. In my humble opinion, this happens to all ti's and the people around them from time to time and goes unnoticed due to self-blame: "I didn't hear him say to be at work early" or "He said he rang the bell and then knocked five times. Maybe he came when the tap was running."

I'll say it again. Predominately, as in jabberwocky (nonsense talk), flip-side behaviour, and revoked sounds and words, brain incursions on innocents are surreptitious. A beamed person can be oblivious to being negatively changed, as a video of my grocery lady would show.

To further demonstrate jangled speech, along with the gamut of electronic mind control, I'll recount a bad Saturday that began with three invaded brains in a book store: the book store owner, a friend, and me.

It was my first summer here, and predictably, my secondarily targeted friend, J, and I found ourselves at the island's "kind-of" bookshop. Kind-of is a merited moniker, for the decaying timbered attic is a hangout for old hippies who bring their writing to hand out, where no one buys anything. While I was perusing a shelf, J and the book store owner were chatting in the store's armchairs. They were discussing that poetry interpretations are subjective. It was an interesting dialogue. Then my mind vacated and time stopped. Yet I was still standing and, apparently, absorbed in my search.

My consciousness returned to the men shouting at me, puzzled why three times I wouldn't respond to their askance of a viewpoint. Curiously, each fellow recalled an entirely different debate and transpiration of the warped minutes. Despite talking across from each other, they had lived the past several minutes separately. The store owner was querying why a Canadian author would romanticize bamboo, and my friend had wanted me to agree that the best poets had miserable childhoods. They looked at each other surely thinking, "This guy's not all there."

As for me, I was preoccupied with what OS does with a stolen mind and how an unconscious person can stay standing so answered neither question other than to smile when the shop owner said, "She's still deep in thought." The men recovered, whereas I did not. The mind control remained and took away my ability to descend the store's steep staircase to the street.

What to do with my feet was like taking a quiz on Martians: no answers were forthcoming. Nonetheless, as a veteran victim, the occurrence was neither unusual nor unnerving. Long-term targets get used to such moments. My pickle was in explaining sudden dementia to J. Feigning pain in my recently broken foot (having fallen down a staircase from an earlier brain-block), J took one arm, and I slid the other arm down the long wooden railing, taking one slow step at a time. My brain had no concept of the necessary legwork, so I copied my friend. At the bottom, J was still talking about the odd book store visit, and I was trying to understand the word "sidewalk." When we drove away, my head felt like it should be on somebody else. J, it seemed, was fine. We both commented on the trail of cars following us to the mini-mart that islanders call town, where a bowl of dog water and a box of help-yourself dog biscuits are at the door, where the forest has to be cut back every year.

Shopping for lunch and dinner stuff, I could think again, but J had been beamed with cranky frequencies. His temper erupted over my choice of salad greens, not once, but in spurts up and down the counters, despite my attempts to appease him. He even raised his voice in front of an employee. This was unsettling. J's profession is assisting disabled folks. He is unyieldingly courteous.

After a quick trip home to put the food away, on to the seaside park we went, stalkers and all. "Aha," I thought after a few minutes, "we're back to normal." But we weren't. J criticized me at length for using a term coined from my university days, saying it was prehistoric. When we got home, he grumped again about the salad greens and, also, about a 1970's rock band album that was in the CD player. Then he gave me a curt lesson on slicing tomatoes, insisting the house reeked like a dump. It didn't. It was immaculate.

"You've got a raccoon on the roof," he said, "or a bear. Something's growling down the chimney."

"That's country life for you," I responded, unwilling to explain to a skeptic that the growling was in his v2k'ed head and only he could hear it.

"Aren't you going to scare it away? Don't be so lazy. It sounds right in the house." Scowling at me, he continued, "I have to keep stirring."

That's when EH began sparking my eyes. Between the pain and fretting over permanent vision loss, my patience over J's disapproval plummeted, and I felt like bopping him. As a bonus, mind control began compelling me to sing "The Teddy Bears' Picnic," which is a song the EH crew regularly harass me with anyhow. The problem this time was that I was physically unable to stop, and J, who was already crabby, got thoroughly frustrated with me. Here I was blinking, ouching, and holding a metal pasta sieve over my face trying to block the eye-sparking beam, all the while singing, "Picnic time for teddy bears, the little teddy bears are having a lovely time today," right through to the end, finally getting stuck on, "Their mommies and daddies will take them home to bed," which I sang continuously. Have you heard of a gong show? 'Cause this was the kind of ridiculous performance that defined the term. (It is common for ti's to be harassed with an exasperating tune, in one way or another.)

Our much-anticipated day together was a train wreck, just as OS planned. Weeks later, when I recalled to J how eerie it was at the book store, he had no memory of it. Pressing for recollection, I said, "Well, you know, it was the day we argued about "The Teddy Bears' Picnic." But that was gone too. All he remembered was feeling completely unwelcome. Telling him we'd been mind controlled by directed energy would have resulted in a chuckle-fest about flaky islanders. As a prototypal secondary target, J scoffs graciously offered explanations about EH and OS.

Although most ti's can tell far more incredulous stories than that of J's and my bad Saturday, it was an instructive debacle to relate as, frankly, it irreversibly spoiled our relationship: another silver star for OS.

I don't want to give you the impression that every ti and everyone around him are walking around mesmerized. Self-evident mind-control tactics usually befall heavily harassed targets a time or two during a mundane day. That's enough to have total power—reminding the head that every one of its functions is OS's business. However, a full cerebral overthrow can be unabating when a potentially good day needs to be destroyed, or when a victim is seeking freedom or justice, or when a loved one or rescuer needs to be taken out of the way.

Rescuers, close loved ones, and targets ideally need to be ready (informed and alert) so that they can try to oppose control over their thoughts, emotions, and behaviours. You'll hear me prompt you about this again, not because I don't know what superfluous writing is, but because shrieking at you isn't possible.

You may be thinking that electronic mind control is impervious: unopposable. For the most part you're right. Nonetheless, some interference, namely bold cognitive wiles, can be wrestled out of a head once the individual catches on. Take note—a person cannot think, "Now that I know intruding energy is what made me neurotic over which pen to buy, the next time it happens I'll wish the energy away." Wishful thinking, on its own, is not enough. Reversing a mind beam takes concentration and determination as the following standoff shows.

While looking online for companies that sold beaded journals (blank books to write in that have covers decorated with beads), remote stalkers decided my quest for the perfect gift was a fine mind-management opportunity. They made me obsess about them. Tearing away from looking at screen after screen of mail-order journals made me agitated. "I have to see them all" versus "No I don't" went on for weeks. Seashell beads on wavy covers, wood beads on bark covers, pearly beads on shiny covers—my heart is pounding while describing them, for the control remains. Buying a gift certificate at a specialty stationary store was not the hoped-for solution. The only way today to repel the draw is to tell myself, "It's *them* again, trying to waste my time."

A fair standpoint is that anyone can go overboard about finding an ideal present. That's correct, except an EH obsession feels mentally and physically fake and after quickly grinding a person to burnout, continues to drag him under. As you already know, a profusely adulterated brain feels intruded into. It's impossible at times not to notice, rather like not noticing that a cauliflower has had mustard squirted into it.

Victims who can feel antagonists' fiddling around in their noggins strategize countermeasures when they are up to it. Most often they learn to ignore the very minor agitations, for no one can devote all his time and energy to mind care. To keep one's awareness on constant guard is truly grueling and will not stop a strong beam; or a "get him while he's asleep" assault; or the ever-present head-embedded "ready for action" fusion that ensures humans are wind-up toys, ready to dance to a contract killer's tune.

Generally, conspicuous mind interferences feel vague and muddy, although the analogic mustard-squirted cauliflower still applies. Not being able to index the mustard's overall toll is unnecessary to know that unnatural emulsion is going on. I should also mention that now and then an EH brain hit can be felt as a slight jolt that lasts for a quarter of a second or so, maybe just as long as a blink, and can only be compared to tuning to a different radio station. The person detects a switch in awareness or consciousness: a signal break.

Infrequently, there is an accompanying noise: static, buzzing, a high-pitched whining, or a dull roar. A few ti's say their signal changes are denoted by a pop, beep, click, a flicker of silence, or an adjustment in EH-made tinnitus or EH-made static. I've heard beeps, clicks, silence, and fluxes in tinnitus and static.

Given how convoluted EH is, the noises could be v2k scare tactics to enhance the process of entering a brain. And losing hearing during a signal change, which is a sensory omission that makes the world go silent, could be a substitute tactic. Nobody knows. Perhaps the noises and silences are effects of brain-pummeling or the operation itself.

It's feasible that changes are felt or heard when an in-head computer program is "looping" or is being revised. Full-time v2k sufferers speak of prerecorded monologues, noises, and songs that stop for a second or two when the recording is done and then loop back to the beginning. Could interruptions in consciousness and awareness denote adjustments in head-sent computer programs?

Consciousness transitioning and consciousness tuning can occur any time and as often as not leads a sharp mind into wooly thinking for seconds, minutes, or days.

Alternatively, and scarcely ever, ti's (including me) encounter a captivating zippiness in thinking but only whilst doing an important, complicated, or time-sensitive task. The controlled person will be elated at getting the work done at bionic speed, and so well. And though this sounds advantageous, everything she did will be ass-backwards. This type of control is easy to detect, for the person feels like she's overdosed on caffeine that's laced with smart-making chemicals. When the control abruptly stops, the overall response is "Holy crap," followed by hours of fixing the errors, or starting all over.

It's necessary to add another condition of contrast to wooly brains, for assorted victims declare rare states when their skulls' insides give the unimpeded impression of bright blackness. That in itself is not unpleasant. But wait. Right after assessing "my head feels like a black crystal ball," a mind picture could be flashed, or a v2k voice could resound, or a short-run obsession or moment of incomprehension could have a ti reading the same line in a magazine thirty times. The flashed image in this dark, stark state, as I've been told by several people, can be snatches of a tiny person inside the EH'ed head. It's as if the victim can see a miniaturized remote stalker in his own noodle, a reminder of being parasitized. The little-man photo image has only happened to me once over the years, and I hated it as my first thought was "someone's in my head." I cope better when not dwelling on the psychopaths inside me. The most prevalent snapshots are of a devil, a demon, and a close-up of a strange man's face.

Of course, photo flashes, obsessions, incomprehensive moments, and v2k can happen any time. But when a head is filled with blackness, look out.

There is also a seldom-borne brain beam that tangibly feels like a beam; that is, a brain ascertains that hardball energy is streaming in. Gosh, it's hard to describe. When it happens to me, I'm afraid to think—afraid of what a powerhouse electrical outpouring is capable of. It lasts too long for my liking and results in hours of aftershock nervous trembling. I'll compare a head that's experiencing this to a balloon that's over-inflated with radio waves and ready to burst, for the beam completely fills a skull with revealed pushing energy that can communicate with the mind and damage a brain's circuit board.

The painless surge is so strong in my head that I visualize my face is growing plate-sized. Thankfully for targets, it strikes rarely, lasts under five minutes (usually), doesn't seem to do much other than take over until it's finished, and disappears as fast as it hits. This particular strike would leave innocents and novice ti's rattled for days.

Most often, though, painless smoothly transitioning control, which is by far the most common, goes undetected until it's too late. Naturally, there are exceptions. A v2k voice may tell its head of a change. Also, some folks are expertly perceptive.

It's important to at least try and recognize routinely EH-altered states, as noticing a quick-fire strike, no matter how it checks in, can occasionally stave off being captivated by folly. Counting the leaves on a tree or writing a fifty-page letter can be skirted—this time.

Different people receive different treatments even though the same result is sought: that of psychological control. This is what drives many to assume they are being experimented on. One thing that is for sure, when an EH'ed fascination, phobia, or compulsion does take hold, or when a mind is forced to take a little vacation, a ti's body and brain are servants to the defect until that eureka moment: "It's them, not me." Accordingly, non-targets lack "aha" insight.

"Wow, what brought this on?" is an uninformed obsessing person's response if he realizes his fixated brain is hog-tied, foggy, or scrambled. (Thought-unresponsiveness, fogginess, and scrambled thinking accompany all sorts of head-sent EH.) The real giveaway to binding ruminations, especially for a primed ti, is the immense power the control has. Have you ever been so thirsty you couldn't stand it? How would you have felt refusing a drink? That's akin to me avoiding pictures of beaded journals or another ti oppressing newfound fanaticism over pen varieties.

A commonly unrecognized obsession is over a stalker, neighbour, friend, colleague, or relative. The riveted ti will be consumed by real, perceived, and v2k-tattletaled wrongdoings that he sees as antagonistic, even after he's demolished a central part of his life to create a distance. Marriage, home, rescue, or employment could be forfeited. A ti proscribed to be suspicious, fearful, or hateful towards a particular person might not catch on for years, if at all. He will sabotage a potentially good situation if he doesn't take stock of what's going on. Regrettably, it is easier to walk on water than alter the thinking of someone who is mind controlled in this manner. The attitude will change only through self-awareness. What's not mind control is when a heavily harassed ti accuses almost every victim and nonvictim he comes across of being a perp.

Be assured, targets need to be hawkeyed when it comes to their stalkers. Vigilance saves lives. But to lose sleep night after night fussing about what shady Uncle Paul is doing, regardless that he's in another city and probably not involved, has zippo pay-off.

Innocents are not absolved; a mind-controlled loved one or co-worker can develop obsessive hatred, disgust, or distrust towards the target in his life, with little reason.

Innocents, new targets, and secondary targets who are allowed by OS staff to notice a temporary cognitive shakedown, or who are discerning enough to detect and abhor a mental change (which is often obsessing; blanking out; or being inordinately confused, angry, anxious, stupid, or sad) usually take their anomalous thinking in stride in the same way they do if their thinking is amiss from alcohol or drug intake, being upset, tiredness, or a chaotic lifestyle. They will never oppose the distortion by concentrating or mentally pushing it out of their heads until their eyes cross, as veteran ti's do.

Perpetually managing self-recognized reversible mind control is not always as artless as telling yourself "no" a thousand times. Wishing it gone, as I've already pointed out, is not enough, even for someone with stanch will power.

Ridding a head of electronic harassment is an exercise like no other: concentrating and mentally boosting invisible foreign matter out of a skull. Based on my prostrating misadventure with the following exercise, as previously professed, how about if you just pretend to do it, unless, that is, you are an experienced ti.

Okay, picture your brain covered in yellow dots. Now by thinking, urge the dots off your brain and through your skull. It sounds preschool-ish. It's not, because EH's dots are sticky—like gummed price tags. Think harder. Oh-oh, there's more incoming. Pushing EH back is uphill work with no guarantee of success. Win a few, lose a lot. No one can do this exercise recurrently, and many ti's can't do it at all because of retaliation, physical and mental aftershock, or weakened health. Pushing back will never stop v2k.

As a rule, low-dose electronic mind control and subtle gradually increasing control won't be opposed by anyone except sage gifted victims. Drinking a tad of arsenic in your orange juice every morning is analogous to being unsuspectingly overcome by slick mind control, for the greater number of brain breaches are incredibly elusive. Whether slow decline is from arsenic or energy, the victim can initially bear the symptoms, the murderer goes unopposed, and in the end the victim is a nonfunctioning shell or is dead.

A major intractable hit to a brain is missile-like whether it is causing pain, or is impairing or terminating vital areas of cognition, or is a sensory project. Fury, dread, surrender, limitations, handicaps, or death ensues. Always.

We're now going to look at a grim category of EH that ti's try to counteract, namely a tough brain-brawl with beamed shots that direct physical movements.

Foremost, you need to sympathize that fighting mind control can hurt. The brain becomes overwhelmed with "yours versus theirs" stimuli with "theirs" having the advantage: machine-made energy is more powerful than human energy. For starters, a victim disputing mind control can get jittery. Not just jittery in a head, but can't-keep-still jittery. If you're familiar with restless legs syndrome, then you know exactly what I'm talking about, except this is restless brain, body, legs, and arms syndrome. Rivaling electronic mind control by opposing it or concentrating it back can result in a splitting headache, nausea, vomiting, shock, psychological trauma, overall physical pain, angst, depression, exhaustion, and the fidgets.

Having learned that it can hurt to oppose control, we can carry on, keeping in mind that physical movements begin in the brain. For instance, someone who has a blood clot in his brain can suffer stroke-impaired limbs.

Every evening around 11:00 p.m. my arm would forcibly wrench behind my back in one of the pretzel positions used on suspected terrorists. It was excruciating. Grabbing and pulling the stuck arm with my free hand was impossible as it was contorted too far behind me, and the slow intense process of mentally compelling it frontward resulted in a chilly, queasy sweat that took the next day to recuperate from. Sitting or lying on my hand so that it couldn't be bent behind me was unsuccessful as the control

Torture museum photo

would be upped until it seemed my head would burst. Sure, the pretzel bit only lasted three or four hours, but my shoulder was hooped by morning, every morning.

After months of living one-armed, my only recourse was to again challenge the EH. "I'll wear a too-big coat," I thought, "and have better luck if my free hand can yard on a floppy reachable sleeve." It was an ordeal. The arm, which felt tied and broken, resisted. It was like dragging a cylinder of cement and made me sick to my stomach. I had to do it every night for weeks before the perps went on to something else.

This story does not appropriately represent OS-requisite postures and actions that prevent walking, or accelerate suicide, or kill outright. It bothers me terribly that my showdowns with EH are told when other victims are much more deserving of being heard. Moreover, recounting my handling of the crimes is uncomfortable, for torture is ever so private. Yet, for some of the travails to be understood, they need to be told firsthand.

One hassle I don't get, that I'll attempt to describe anyhow, is having limbs violently jerked: arms and legs flying every which way. These people are true live marionettes. They say it goes on for years and is debasing in all facets of life. Plenty of these folks blame implants.

Contrary to what you might think, the smaller the jerk, the more serious a situation can be. Ma's hand can be jerked while holding a boiling pot. Or a chainsaw, knife, or steering wheel. According to my data, a short jerk is always an attempt to cause a critical accident, often right before a welcome project or pastime.

Under similar mind control, with the same catastrophe-causing intent, an in-motion or stationary hand, foot, or limb can become rigid, unable to budge in spite of all the victim's efforts. A few ti's experience jerking, flailing, and rigidity constantly.

Anyone in OS's sights can get his foot pressed down on the gas pedal. There is no lifting the foot off until crashing seems certain. This shakes the bejesus out of drivers who breathlessly re-enact a "thought it was curtains" jaunt into town. Personally, I believe a brain centre is taken over in the same manner that my arm was fastened to my back. Many folks think otherwise—that an energy beam is pushing the foot. Given the evilness of this gas pedal game, some survivors see a link to archfiend tagalongs, so they blame the devil's little helpers. No one has ever blamed the pedal or the car. The foot feels held. By the same method, whatever it is, a hand can lock onto the steering wheel.

You have to wonder how many ti's, loved ones, rescuers, whistle-blowers, and activists are seriously injured or killed from this type of prank. As you'll recollect, it is immaterial to perpetrators if children, oldsters, pedestrians, passengers, or passers-by are involved in an arranged accident or in any other attack. People are things. Maybe they're ants.

For information's sake, a vehicle's computer can be disabled by a directed-energy gun that allows police and militaries to bring a speeding or suspicious vehicle to a halt. More relevant to OS, car-computer functions such as accelerating, braking, and steering can be controlled or affected by an extremely skilled hacker with a lot of spare time.

In getting back to over-powered physical movements, what's largely ignored because it's unexceptional is mind-controlled stumbling and ankle-turning. Ti's are no clumsier than the rest of the population in spite of bungling a jaunt to the fridge twice in a row. Still, many don't catch on unless they speak to a full-time v2k victim who can set them straight. When a v2k voice tells its head, "We're going to make you trip right NOW!" there's no way to prevent a bumble or turned ankle. The victim trips on "NOW!" To think that non-full-time v2k sufferers and the people around them are expunged is idealistic.

Earlier, we talked about a beam that feels like a steel rod (or spike) is ramming through flesh and bone. Then there are the baseball batting and cooking energies, plus a pressure beam that squishes or caves in body parts. What I'm getting at is that transmitting agony into a head, testicle, or anywhere else is indisputably slave-making but is dissimilar from directing thoughts, emotions, speech, behaviours, and physical movements through brain manipulations. They are two separate types of control. The list of OS's dictatorial techniques is long. Nevertheless, pain and brain-mucking are mainstays.

Inasmuch as you are stuffed with anecdotes that demonstrate zany or deadly mind meddling, even stranger mental deceptions will wind up this corner of electronic harassment.

We're going to expand the broad topic of sensory manipulation by furthering our discussion on OS's ability to rig smell and taste, and then we'll take a quick peek at OS-rigged temperature, balance, direction, time, weight, ailments, and kinesthetic sense. (Kinesthetic sense is what your body should do in relation to its environment, like spontaneously turning sideways to squeeze between closely parked cars.) We'll also take a quick look at day-to-day forced cognitive losses, misleading mannerisms, decoying, and target populations.

To re-introduce the sense of smell forgery, let's say you are a non-ti who is with a targeted pal. "Pew," you say holding your nose. "Been rolling in pigeon shit?"

"I thought it was you," the target says back. Sniffing one another like a couple of stray dogs, each of you makes a decision. "It's not me, it's him." Few victims, along with their friends, relatives, clothes, homes, cars, and workplaces, escape this stinking gag. It is just one of OS's humiliations that is mentioned in whispers, and hardly. A few pages back you read that my friend, J, said my house stunk like a dump. I initially deleted the remark, not wanting to sound like a lazy housekeeper. That's how effective the smell caper is. Be warned. The tang of an unwashed wanderer could seem to be coming from you.

Worse than reeking of urine, feces, sweat, mold, garbage, shellfish, mouse pee, or maggoty meat are the chemical fumes EH produces. Though this might not impact a social life, it will make the victim ill from what he presumes is a bubble of toxic air, somehow, stuck to his face or upper chest. On listening to pleas for help from chemically asphyxiated people, at the onset I was unconvinced. Then it happened to me. Several times. The vapour's clout matches the wallop that suffocates anyone dumb enough to empty a bottle of ammonia into a jug of bleach to make room in the cupboard for on-sale copy paper. (The gas from combining bleach and ammonia is lethal.)

Every ti who undergoes an OS synthetically produced chemical odor declares that it lasts from days to weeks and burns his eyes, lungs, and nostrils. In all cases, the victim is distraught. This criminal achievement has me stumped. How can mind control form a caustic haze? Is the stunt taking place entirely in a brain or is there something else going on?

A few victims declare that oxygen-less and airless pockets cause them to collapse, keeping them in a petrified standstill state. This is an authentic complaint, for targeted doctors treat these folks. Whatever the technology is, it can also simulate or activate influenza, colds, bladder infections, and chronic or acute diseases, turning them on and off as if by a finger snap. Medically unstoppable and medically unexplainable bleeding, coughing, choking, salivating, twitching, itching, tooting, burping, sneezing, and pain are more finger-snap on/off paradoxes.

As for me, I get choked, but usually while assisting a devastated ti on the phone. My owners won't let me breathe until I end the call. Any one of a hundred targets will tell you she heard me coughing, then croaking, "They're choking me. I'm hanging up." This is more than a scare tactic. A couple of times while trying to calm a person undergoing torture, the remote-weapons staff didn't let me breathe until I was blacking out.

As hard as all this must be for you to conceive, these conditions really do happen and sometimes as often to a ti's loved ones and acquaintances as to himself, particularly if the ti has an isolation theme.

There are three principal hypotheses for remotely generated health maladies. The first is that OS has identified brain signals that are naturally occurring during a physical ailment (see photo) and, by covert EH transference, activates or replicates those signals to cause the sensation of, say, a virus, or the reality of, say, bleeding gums, but at the perps' will: an energy-beamed (EH) flip-switch ailment. Another theory is that skilled psychics have achieved the ability to transmit the correct brain signals for any health problem at all, again turning the signal on and off at

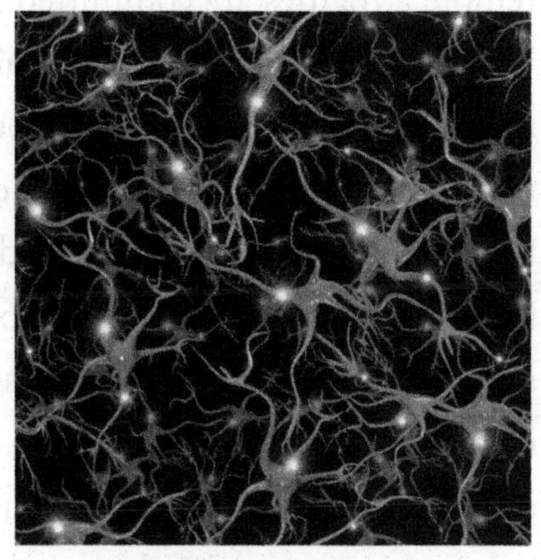

Brain neurons transmit information by electro-chemical signalling.

will. The last idea credits OS with tapping into demonic or alien operational systems or of commissioning the entities themselves.

Supporters of the psychic, demonic, and alien hypotheses decree that from-space weapons and land-based weapons are unnecessary for remote stalking and transmission. They say that invisible stalking and remote attacks are a matter of walkie-talkie-type brain-signal relays from perpetrator to victim or entity to victim in order to produce a sensory feels-like-real affliction or an actual affliction, wherever the victim is. Do any of these left-field theories explain the milepost antichrist hijinks? Could one of them be responsible for all remote harassment?

If you feel bewildered by it all, that's good; you're getting the hang of the crime, as backwards as that sounds. We've spoken about this before: you're not supposed to be clear (yet) about how all the remote atrocities are committed. Neither am I.

Both legal and illegal electronic instruments and energy weapons that anyone can research and sometimes buy or build are currently used on humans to burn, cook, cut, break bones, electrically shock, bruise, blind, stalk, send v2k, deafen, mentally incapacitate, read brains, influence brains, cause ionizing and non-ionizing radiation sickness, destabilize nervous systems, and slowly or instantly shut down a heart and other organs. A similar class of weaponry fouls electrical and non-electrical non-living matter. The elephant in the room, as you appreciate by now, lies in how the weapons find, follow, and harm their marks from great distances (assuming weapons are to blame).

You also appreciate that man-made long-distance energy transmission coupled with the well-investigated mode of brain wave tracking is what's considered in this book as a possible answer. Yet the other methods and angles presented here could be correct. I've said it before and I'll say it again: in no way, at the time of this writing, can someone bang his fist on a table and proclaim long-range EH is this or that, for there are areas of OS that baffle the most brilliant educators, never mind the regular folks who are stuck with it. The population that's awake to electronic harassment are doing their best to understand it with the best information to date, particularly the ace activists whose hard work and "open sesame" pleas have rooted out damning evidence from government agencies.

What you can have indisputable confidence in is that the consequences from being stalked, harassed, tortured, and mind controlled have been told here as accurately as possible, as have victims' descriptions of the diversity of attacks.

My point is, don't beat yourself up over thinking, "I don't get it." Getting to the moon was easier to figure out. Its calculations can be put on a blackboard. For the electronic mind control we've just discussed, there are no equations to show you, no clarifying schoolbooks, and no technicians except for the enemies.

There are, however, hundreds of thousands and possibly millions of victims worldwide. The agreed-upon estimate of reported ti's is 30,000 in Canada and 300,000 in the U.S. The number who are unreported, being confused, scared, or hiding, is thought to be double that, at least. Also unreported are the deceased first victims from the 1980s (or earlier) when home computers and the Internet were not the standard information and communication tools they are today. And what about the secondary targets who choose to believe they are the unluckiest people on the planet? There's a whack of those.

There is also a whack of unhappy people who suspect they were young children when they were chosen for the crime, but they aren't sure. Some of these unhappy people are grown-up bona fide ti's, and the rest don't know if they are ti's today or not. What these undecided folks do know is that they had terrible childhoods and continue to be plagued with nonstop atypical and often unexplainable health and life problems, enough so that they feel suspicious something unnatural is going on. I've spoken to a lot of these folks. They call me to learn about the crime and to ask if I think they're targeted, which is impossible to determine in a phone call.

Could certain children be picked for ongoing OS/EH studies in the same way Project MKULTRA picked certain children for ongoing studies? I can't really say. If this is happening, though, you can add thousands more to the victim population. It's possible that some of these undecided folks have been secondary targets since childhood and thus live the life of all secondary targets: confused and, by degrees, oppressed. The only facts I can offer to you about this group is that they are sane and sincere. The exception is a man who wanted to be a target because it sounded exciting. He hoped that after telling me his litany of problems I would label him a ti and get him involved in thrilling adventures. Good grief.

At any rate, the futures of could-be targets, OS-ignorant targets, and silent targets—all of whom are not resisting the crime—are dependent upon the droves of hopping-mad OS-savvy victims who devote their lives to answering the who, why, and remote-EH questions. Aggressive truth seekers may look like all the other bull's-eyes in OS's shooting gallery, but they are determined to take down both the shooter and his bullet if it kills them to do so.

And often it does, especially the victims who finger their government. It bothers me when researchers and activists are smeared for looking under every rock to find the answer to free us all, even when the rock doesn't look like a rock.

My outlook has not always been so objective. For a long time I could not conceive the quirkier adversities EH elicits and did not validate shellshock from victims of ala kazam hoo-hah. To each one I apologize, notably to the woman below.

"They're coming in at night and gluing my eyes and nose closed," she said.

"Wouldn't it wake you up?" I asked.

"They must be putting me in a trance. I'm scared to death and no one believes me. Not even you."

Well, woman-from-Ottawa, they weren't coming into your house. They were doing it with the same remote technology that fills my Vancouver friend's hair with gook—the same gook that dribbled from the backs of my ears after doubting you. It's glue-like all right. A few ti's get glued, slimed, powdered, or caked in crusts regularly.

The woman from Ottawa spoke of mutilations. "They're filing my teeth at night," she said. "The side teeth look like a vampire's, and the molars are like razor blades."

"You're sleeping through that?" I asked.

"Someone needs to believe me," she cried. And she cried a lot.

It turns out, a lot of ti's wail over filed teeth. They can't talk or eat without cutting their mouths and tongues to shreds. The woman was right. Teeth sharpening can be slept through, same with a haircut. So can waking up with healed-over gouges or healed-over physical modifications (mutilations) on genitalia, face, thighs, hips, or elsewhere. In all cases, no trace of hair, bone, flesh, or blood will be found. At a loss to explain this, I once suspected that a highly advanced remote laser was to blame, although such a laser struck me as a science fiction weapon. And I don't like science fiction. So now I don't know what to think.

Overnight and on-the-spot conditions are not exceptional symptoms of extreme anxiety. I used to think most of them were as the stress ti's live in creates a free-for-all of infirmities. EH'ed anomalies are in an entirely separate category. A study on a single ti, never mind hundreds or thousands, could be pretty darn telling, and I suggest that university-level harm-free scientific studies on the effects of OS's various tortures begin today. Yes, I volunteer.

Oh, before I forget, flip-switch EH sometimes attacks pre-existing physically weak areas. The difference between a person's flip-switch EH-caused ailments and pain, and his usual ailments and pain, is astounding: "Dude, I had the weirdest asthma attacks of my life yesterday. One minute I felt like I was going to die, and the next minute I was totally fine. Happened about ten times. I don't know what's going on. Last week my bum knee was like that too. On off on off."

It appears that the technology involved in remote EH can see and study a person's insides the same way medical imaging and medical testing can: a feat that implies EH is very high tech. Thus, a victim's internal weak areas, such as an allergy and a bad heart, are as prone to flip-switch management as a finger that's swollen from squishing it in the door. Indeed, I understand how insane this sounds. Listening and speaking to victims, and asking questions, will resolve your justifiable doubt.

You needed to know about flip-switch and overnight health disorders and mutilations, and as some of them do involve the senses, adding them to this section seemed reasonable.

There are two sensory anomalies that defy categorizing, so I'll stick them in here.

Specific musical notes and specific sounds from nature elicit pain, disorientation, or panic into selected ti's brains. They say that a "trigger" note resounds in their heads as if a super-loud vibrating tuning fork was embedded.

The second sensory anomaly is visual. A subset of ti's see only the colour grey after a remote strike on their eyes. They say the greyness lasts from minutes to months after the attack. One credible woman claims that she's been seeing grey for years and that her eye attacks are perpetual.

Returning to fundamental sensory control, it anesthetizes body parts. It deadens the back of my head, the top of a friend's, and benumbs fingers, limbs, limb patches, and genitalia on myriads. The impression is that of a dentist's anesthetizing injection.

Of all OS's little ploys, power over taste is one that catches ti's by surprise. Once a victim gets past blaming stalkers in stores, perps working in restaurants, and roommates or intruders he thinks are sabotaging his food, he'll tell you that EH's taste alterations are annoying. These comments are typical:

1. "I blew the last of my money on mangoes. They may as well have been cardboard."
2. "Everything tastes like garlic. I'm worried others can smell it."
3. "The birthday cupcakes I bought? There was something wrong with them. We wondered if the baker had sprinkled citric acid on the icing."

Is taste, too, entirely managed by deploying a brain centre?

Along with the antics of manipulating taste, smell, touch, ailments, vision, and hearing, the remote stalkers distort temperature. You or the ti you're with could be shivering on a hot Mexican day. There is no changing a mind-controlled temperature. When an energy beam is transmitted to make the victim freeze darn near to death, no amount of clothing or heat will help. It happens instantly.

A number of ti's claim a right-left disturbance, for example, constantly heading in the wrong direction or trouble turning doorknobs. See here, I may not be the sharpest tack, but it's odd, don't you think, that being liberated from behind closed doors was in the beginning an ordinary part of going out. Other women speak of their own mind-controlled humiliations.

Mademoiselle might find her purse has gained sixty pounds and is going to need help getting it off the floor, yet the obliging monsieur will detect only a make-up-filled handbag. Physics-types attribute EH force fields for the sensation of added weight and also for why a few folks feel like they are walking into a hurricane, minus the wind, pushing against a barrier of nothingness as they trudge onwards.

Oppositely, targets with a push-pull theme are, you guessed it, literally pushed and pulled all over the place. Is this the same energy that knocks ti's off their chairs? Maybe.

While granting respect to the physics-types' force-field theory, the fact that targets' EH-heavy purses and whatnot are light to others, and that close onlookers around the push-pull and hurricane-walking folks are unaffected, and that my two-ounce lovebird can feel like three pounds and not notice tells me that perhaps brain tunnelling—meddling with the human sense of weight and the biology of momentum—could be responsible. Both the force-field and the brain-penetration hypotheses have merit, yet either, neither, or both could be correct.

There's also the stair incomprehension we've skimmed over. This is a must-know affair because scores of ti's and the innocents around them break or otherwise injure their legs, ankles, and feet.

With no thanks to electronic mind control, a particular step or staircase, even if it's familiar, can be dodgy to descend, making bum-bumping from one house level to the next a degrading act when no one's looking. Targets often set up props to hang on to before stepping into their bathtubs, sunken living rooms, or balconies. I've pretended to pat a dog's head in order to walk off a curb, needing something to steady myself, for curbs can be nail-biters. A ti could skip through every pothole and bit of roadwork for years only to find himself in a fluster one day while stepping into a depression where a street-tree was planted.

The medical term for feeling dizzy and disoriented when taking an uncertain step, usually a step that is forwards or down, is "broken escalator phenomenon," named for folks whose brains get muddled when stepping onto a broken escalator. It's a perfect term. You won't see targets with this don't-know-where-to-put-my-foot theme on rail-less staircases, rocky beaches, rutted trails, ladders, and sometimes not even on striped or checkerboard flooring. You will see them walking up and down wheelchair ramps, and you will hear them asking other people to replace ceiling-high light bulbs.

Victims who lose balance while they are standing, sitting, or walking on level ground experience cerebral muss that's similar to the broken escalator crowd. Wobblers hang on to a wall while showering, hate being next to windows and edges, and they fall a lot. As several brain and aural aberrations cause unsteadiness, identifying what region in a head EH is hitting is impossible.

What's more, perception can be altered to make a floor look tilted, requiring a hands 'n' knees venture to exit a bizarro-world kitchen.

A mind-controlled kinesthetic indignity is not knowing where to position one's chair in relation to a desk or table, or where to put oneself comfortably on it. When a victim has been successfully sitting for decades, it's distressing, not to mention embarrassing, to repeatedly rearrange his chair and bottom, only to find that he's never going to get it right.

Time sensory loss is altogether different from losing time in an EH trance. Time sensory loss is a state of total confusion relative only to dates' names; dates' numbers; and the passage of time, such as not knowing if it was one week ago or four weeks ago since you fell in an icy crosswalk. Calendars can look like gibberish. The concept of time is gone; thus, reading or hearing "May 22, 1901," renders no comprehension. Maybe that doesn't adequately describe it. Targets who are occasionally controlled this way, including me, look at the calendar squares and think, "Hmm. I'm supposed to know what those mean." If it was not for the photo of the puppy on top, we'd not bother. One of my ti friends calls her ally every bedtime trying to get the date straight. Otherwise, she can have two Fridays in a week.

Most ti's lose specific cognitive skills momentarily, or for weeks, or for years. First in line of cognitive losses, and maybe the most devastating, is reading incomprehension. Although a sentence or two can be managed, books and long articles cannot. Sometimes reading incomprehension occurs because certain words don't make sense; for instance, a victim might suddenly, and temporarily, forget what the words "oak" and "shade" mean. More often than not the problem is that concentration and memory are blocked but only whilst reading. I originally thought targets' high anxiety or PTSD was the causation of their reading incomprehension, and in some cases that will be correct. Yet so many love-to-read ti's complain of this particular loss, saying they haven't been able to read for years, that I have to declare that reading incomprehension is on the list of EH'ed brain attacks. Reading aloud is helpful in slowly overcoming this dilemma.

Following suit is the inability to count. In public I have pretended to be brain injured. In fact, I had to say it so often at one store's tills that the clerks treated me like a mentally disabled person, which was okay as the service was fantastic. The cashiers smiled a lot, counted my fistful of money out loud, slowly tallied the change into my hand, and carried my bags to the cab. (Canada is famous for its polite citizens.)

This is a conversation I had with a friend who also feigns a damaged noggin.

"You know I was a math professor, right?"

"I do."

"They've taken away my ability to count money. I may as well as be looking at carrots. Actually, I understand carrots. I don't understand money or numbers. They've also taken away my piano playing. I look at the music and think if I sit there long enough it'll come to me—what to do with my fingers."

Each of the mind-game artifices cannot be mentioned here, yet no victim should feel snubbed. I know that every target is subjected to regularly and irregularly employed individualized gimmicks geared to make him feel or look mentally ill or to cause a loss. I know that new ones are introduced, sometimes weekly, until the victim is cognitively straitjacketed. There is no end to them. All are designed to reinforce domination, and they will stop only after death. Not having each of them listed in no way demeans a person's struggle to endure. One that's worth addressing purely because it's communal is tic-like mannerisms.

Electronic mind control forces faces and limbs to twitch or gesticulate as often on innocents as on ti's. When a ti sees relatives, bystanders, and stalkers demonstrating identical affectations, such as a darting tongue or jumping eyebrows, he concludes that all these people are perpetrators. The same precept applies to gestures. An innocent will never know why he tapped his forehead. He may not even notice. A ti surrounded by tappers is surely going to notice, for every person he speaks to, from the pharmacist to the farmhand, taps his forehead, which you have to admit is peculiar.

You may as well know, too, that innocents, whether they are loved ones or strangers, can be controlled to snarl or to make expressions of disgust at the target. For new ti's, this is a startling introduction into brain-hacking.

You learned a while back that stalkers might point, stare, sneer, laugh, retort, wiggle, or jiggle right in their prey's face. They need to be validated as enemies. Stalkers also use hand signals, facial signals, code words, and body language to communicate among themselves. Nonetheless, the unnatural comments, physical movements, and expressions foisted seamlessly on innocents through mind control are entirely different from the stalkers' intentional conduct, even though they look and sound the same.

This extremely simplistic prank of gestures, twitches, grimaces, and trigger words makes a ti suspicious of everyone who is inadvertently doing them, especially loved ones who are mind controlled to copycat the stalkers. You can see that this affects families:

"Grandpa, you keep touching your ear. Why are you doing that? My stalkers are doing that. Did you join them? Are they paying you? Maybe it's best to stop coming over."

Here's another example: "Sunshine? You said 'sunshine'? That's my perp-neighbour's code word that I'm on the balcony. Give me your phone. I want to see who you just called."

One more: "I've told you a million times that my stalkers use the number eighty-eight as a fear-response trigger, and here you are doodling eighty-eights in front of me."

To jog your memory—colours, patterns, clothes accessories, and everyday articles are used in the same way as numbers, words, and gestures. My own stalkers used ladders and striped shirts to identify themselves for the first five years; thus, whenever I saw a truck with a ladder or a fellow in a striped shirt, I felt unsettled. If a trustworthy loved one wore a striped shirt, I would still feel my anxiety rising despite all my efforts to quell it. This is called a conditioned (learned) fear response, which is involuntary and can cause ti's to be antsy around well-intentioned people who are accidentally displaying the victim's learned triggers.

Weeding out familial foes is a cagey mission. Loved ones, along with best friends and friendly associates, do join organized stalking on very rare occasions. Yet, to accuse guiltless individuals of double-dealing could cut family ties, sour a relationship, and end a job—self-propelling a nosedive into the "poor and alone" trap.

As a last forewarning on this subject, a couple of new ti's whose limbs are made to gesticulate in the same way their stalkers' limbs (purposely) gesticulate are positive they are being stealthily trained for a New World Order's military. They're not.

This brings me to the topic of decoying, which I'd clean forgotten to explain. I'll use a victim's recent misadventure with decoying so that you'll get the idea.

Targeted Miss Led was seated at a restaurant and kept falling asleep as if on demand. She overheard a woman at the next table talking to her husband: "George, you've got to tell her that it's you who is putting her to sleep with your phone. It's not fair if you don't." That night, Miss Led called police because of night terrorism, and when an officer took out his cell phone, Miss Led grabbed it, screamed "Psychotronic weapon!" and accused the officer of trying to put her to sleep. The officer then interviewed Miss Led about her mental health status.

Here's my opinion: Miss Led was likely forced to sleep by a far-off weapon. The next-table woman who spoke about a magical phone, likely didn't. I'm betting it was v2k. There's a possibility that the magical-phone couple were perps who were told what to say while Miss Led was being EH'ed from miles away, but I doubt it.

And that's the short version of what decoying is. The long version, due to the infinite variety of decoying ploys, would fill another hundred pages. Note that a slim few victims are certain that OS-adapted cell phones, or devices that look like cell phones, can manage a brain.

Honestly, it would be okay if you remember only one element of this chapter: anyone's brain—yours, Good Wife's, the bank teller's, and Good Dog's—can be overtaken. It's not hooey. It's progressive technology. On the same principle from-afar energy directs Internet-sourced information in and out of an electrical laptop, energy from afar can direct OS-sourced information in and out of an electrical noodle.

Shrewd now to organized stalking, you as a non-ti have figured out that encounters with primary targets, secondary targets, and perps are inescapable. In the belly of the book, that meant you could suffer from stalking, vandalism, phone and computer interloping, harassment, mob terrorizing, single-stalker scare tactics, pet and livestock mutilation, idle threats, genuine threats, document tampering, electrical and plumbing tampering, financial theft, slander, voyeurism, break-ins, arson, being framed, false imprisonment, false psychiatric confinement, poisoning, rape and other assaults, attacks on your loved ones, night terrorism, vehicle and machinery tampering, physical harm from planned accidents, physical harm from nearby and remote energy devices, v2k, isolation, homelessness, perps holding you prisoner, and murder. Add having your mind trammelled, for the likelihood of your brain being managed to reinforce OS's control over a ti is colossal.

After one of OS's harassments impacts you, consider yourself a ti candidate. You have been useful: watched during a role. If the staff takes a fancy to your reaction, appearance, or usefulness, you have been catalogued. As a proponent of positive thinking, an optimist myself, it dismays me, for concerns of well-being, that ordinary folks believe they can't be targeted because they're ordinary folks. This is la-la land reasoning. It's like saying you'll never be robbed because you're nice. So, knowing that cognitive monkeying is probably going to happen, which of the changes would you prefer in the following settings:

While you're out drinking beer with your pals on the weekend, what eccentricity would you pick? A three-hour obsession about finding a perfect peanut or fussing about loose shirt buttons until your friends rip them off. Far worse, what function are you willing to lose in front of the boss on Monday? Would it be remembering how to write? Understanding what those darn levers are for? Or maybe you'd rather spend the day wondering if you're even in the right place. Come Thursday, now that Mr. Manager has ordered you to take a medical exam, would you prefer clapping your hands at the doctor's or hearing crows recite the national anthem on the ride there. Finally, on Friday evening, having asked Girly-girlfriend if she's noticed anything unusual, which of these would be the easiest to pull off—calling her by her dog's name all night, missing your chair three times, or squeezing into her high heels because in your EH'ed mind they have transformed into your loafers.

The questions are sarcastic. Do give them some thought anyway because when electronic mind control is dispatched a part of your brain has been encroached. It could last a minute, a week, or a lifetime. You'll never get the time back: never get the chance to retract the raid. You might never be the same. Life could take a bad turn. Consequently, given a choice, which function would you choose to lose first, even for a little while. Memory? Swallowing? Coordination? Sleep? Freedom of thought? Maybe you'd prefer to lose a capability like reading, speaking, counting, or descending stairs. And of all the things you could tolerate having added what would that be? v2k? Fake smell or taste? A speech impediment? Forced physical movements? A fear? Interactive mind-movies? Fake emotions? Pain?

You may be wondering if Chapter Six, "Impact of Harassment and Unconventional Weaponry on the Bystanders, Acquaintances, Loved Ones, and Rescuers in a Target's Life," applies to electronic mind control. Part of that discussion was on which innocents do and don't suffer OS's wrath. We've established that folks around ti's get brain-beamed, so Chapter Six's sections of who is impacted are applicable, but to what extent? There's no way to study electronic mind control on innocents, meaning that a roadblock of tree huggers, a cruise ship of merrymakers, or a brother and sister could be influenced or under total mind control; and they wouldn't know it, and the ti might not either.

Could OS's plan be to electronically alter the minds of masses for a political or financial take-over? It sounds farcical. By the same token, speaking from a controlled head, who is witness to umpteen other controlled heads, it's definitely possible. If that's the case, what's with the stalking and harassment? Are they smokescreens? Wouldn't it be easier to beam us into obedient robots in one go? Or is OS multifaceted because it's a continuation of the MKULTRA experiment? Perhaps OS is, as an array of people are convinced, a maniacal high-tech elimination sport for either capital gain or jollies.

I won't tiptoe around on this subject. If you're a mentally healthy innocent and have experienced acute psychosis, unreal dreams, or believe poltergeists are messing with you, there's a chance electronic harassment is to blame.

Remember when I denied you a chapter break and then I had to take one? Now that we're nearing this section's end, permit me to tell you—

Unable to write, upset over dragging loved ones into the crime, I sat down with my proverbial tea and library documentary. A few sips later, up the tea came in projectile vomit. That's not unusual for any EH victim, so after scrubbing the carpet, back to the documentary I went. Here's the wrinkle: as Scotland's art history was being told, the narrator blared, "She thinks it's the milk!" Yes, I know an on-screen narrator can't speak to me. I do know my thoughts were read, wondering if somehow the milk I'd put in my tea had been poisoned. "She thinks it's the milk!" could have been v2k. It could have been something else.

Calling me a studious bore is correct. Calling me a lunatic is not. That's simply the way it is to live under total electronic mind control. Had this happened at the crime's onset, my reaction would have been a new hang-up. Instead, I laughed at such nonsense and finished the tea.

Watch Alice in Wonderland, for her adventures look rather tame compared to mind-control adventures. Still, I wouldn't trade Alice's articulate doorknob for a magical narrator unless my fragmented man was thrown in.

Let's neaten up this over-stuffed chapter. Electronic mind control is responsible for the following and oh so much more:

- Altering a brain by manipulating brain centres and by emitting destructive frequencies and other noxious energy
- Hazy thinking—described as having a wooly-feeling or sluggish brain
- Stopped thinking—a trance-like state or blanking out during an activity
- Dizziness, nausea, vomiting, diarrhea, blurred vision, tiredness, headaches, sadness, dread, fear, anxiety, and panic
- Drop-dead fatigue
- The agonizing feeling of a metal rod or spike being driven through one or both sides of a brain
- The agonizing feeling of a head being smashed in
- Being awoken every night at a predetermined time, for example, 3:02 a.m. or every forty minutes
- The victim's emotions and moods being read, analyzed, and acted upon by OS staff
- The victim's emotions and moods being erased
- The victim's brain being seeped with frequencies that produce negative emotions and moods
- The victim's brain centres being evoked to produce negative emotions and moods
- The victim's thoughts being read, followed by OS's cruel responses to the thoughts
- The victim's necessity to monitor all of his thoughts
- The victim's necessary cessation of many thoughts and emotions

- Beamed thoughts that alter behaviours such as a new obsession over having the perfect pen or a new fear of being struck by a falling tree
- Beamed bad, sad, or inane memories that cannot be stopped
- Cognitive impairment—a victim may not understand or remember how to do a simple or standard task such as tying his shoes
- Cognitive impairment—a victim may not recognize numbers, simple words, or familiar images
- Cognitive impairment—a victim may lose a honed skill such as playing an instrument, dressmaking, driving, or repairing engines
- Overall memory and concentration impairment
- Forced repetitiveness
- Loss of eye-hand coordination
- Loss of coordinated or smooth speech
- Altered words and conversations
- Beamed physical behaviours such as twitching, singing, or involuntary movements
- Uncontrollable flailing or jerking of limbs, hands, feet, head, or the entire body
- Paralyzed or held-down limbs, hands, feet, other body parts, or the entire body
- Numb body parts
- Problems with momentum
- Loss of coordinated walking or loss of maneuvering stairs and uneven ground
- Hearing voice to skull (v2k)
- Movies and pictures that are transmitted into a brain, which can be seen inside or outside a head

- Induced dreams
- Instantly occurring genuine health problems
- Inability to wake up even when shaken or moved, as if unconscious
- Waking up and being unable to move for a frighteningly long time
- Sensory changes as described below:

Electronic mind control is responsible for sensory manipulation which simulates, activates, alters, or vetoes touch, smell, and taste, along with vision and hearing. The victim will seem to be hallucinating if artificial senses have been emitted into his brain. When senses are vetoed, the victim can appear blatantly unobservant or neglectful. Mildly provoking energy that accesses a brain centre may alter a sense just enough that the victim appears only somewhat confused or having made a mistake. Sensory manipulation that interferes with temperature, balance, time, pain, kinesthesis, sense of direction, sense of illness, and sense of weight are also part of mind control. A brain can be entirely overrun by sensory control.

COPING WITH MIND-FILMS

As promised, here are suggestions on how to tolerate mind-films, flashed images, and induced dreams. For the sake of brevity, mind-film (or mind-movie) is the overall term I use. You might find the procedures helpful for other brain invasions as well.

To refresh your memory—secondary targets, rescuers, loved ones, and acquaintances are occasionally impacted by mind-movies. Heavily harassed targets get them frequently.

This is the film: picture yourself kneeling in the living room after a bomb has exploded. Your kids and spouse, maybe your friends and the dog, are hanging in pieces from the walls.

As a victim of beamed visualizations, for the seconds or minutes between experiencing the scene and wondering, "What happened?" or "Was that real?" you must get in the habit of telling yourself, as soon as possible, that you are okay. What comes next sounds ludicrous. No matter how shaken you are, you must tell yourself, "I can do that again and survive," because it probably will happen again. Perhaps soon. Frightening mind-takeovers often run in bunches.

The daytime wide-awake films and photo flashes are life altering, but the ones that catch you at night are deadly. Sooner or later, as much as you don't want to, you are going to have to sleep. Adapting is critical.

1. "I'm okay."

2. "I can do that again and survive."
3. Turn on the TV or the computer, or put on some music, or do whatever will immediately pull your mind away from the inevitable after-effects. You won't be able to comprehend anything for a few minutes, so distraction must be a simple visual or audio deflection. The quicker the better.
4. Note any lingering mind-control smells, tastes, sounds, images, and sensations on your skin. Tell yourself they are not real. If your "how it's done" theory is psychic interloping, parallel dimensions, aliens, or demonic malevolence rather than black operation brain sciences, tell yourself that the sensations are not meant to kill you outright.
5. The trauma you are feeling is normal. So is thinking, "If I commit suicide, I won't have to go through that again," or, "I'll never be the same," or, "No one can survive such despair," or, "No one can survive such fear."
6. Never, and I mean never, feel silly for taking reasonable harm-free coping measures if you are regularly tortured with mind-movies or other brain assaults.
7. If you sleep under a spotlight with every light in the house on, surrounded by EH shielding materials, with the TV or radio on, in your clothes, with a phone in your pocket, and there's a camera pointed at your head, that's okay. If you don't do what allows you to sleep, your recovery resilience will diminish. Over time you will adjust. However, you will never find electronic mind control easy to endure. You are being tortured.
8. Tell trusted ti friends what happened and how you are managing. They can give you the foothold you might need.

9. If you are entirely isolated, please comfort yourself. It's essential that you do, as staying in post-mind-film shock is dangerous and can lead to suicide if mind-films are your primary form of torture.

CHAPTER FOURTEEN

DOCTORS

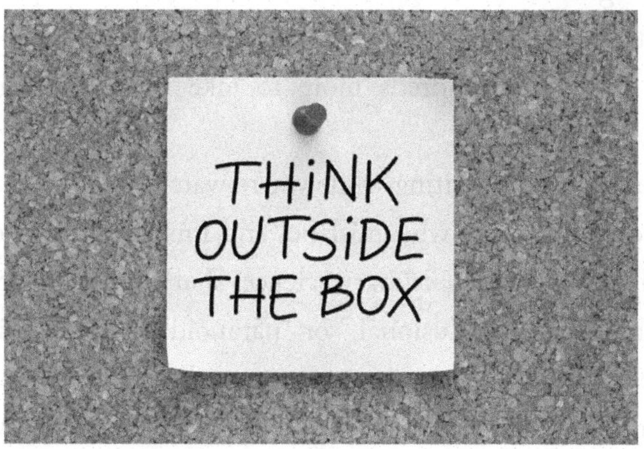

I can't think of a worse place in the book to discuss doctors' roles in OS, yet I can't think of a more honest place.

* * *

Doctors who disregard targets' health problems from legitimate extreme fear and legitimate extreme sadness disappoint me. They're not doing this because they can't grasp electronic and non-electronic mind control, for ti's almost never bring these issues up with non-targeted professional folks. It's because overworked or disinterested doctors can't or won't spend the few moments online that would teach them something about organized stalking's other schemes.

There are plenty of targeted professionals whose videos, radio appearances, and research are on the Internet. These heroes have even been on primetime TV trying to alert their country's citizens.

If you are a doctor or anyone else who's new to the crime, watch this video: www.youtube.com/watch?v=cmNOuRKINJ4 The speaker is a medical doctor, author, and targeted individual. He explains organized stalking and electronic harassment quite neatly in seventeen minutes. If the video disappears off the Internet, no worries. There are hundreds more to take its place. This video, however, is concise.

I'm going to keep writing while you're watching it.

To the psychiatrists who mislabel and mis-medicate victims of mass bullying and extraordinary science, shame on you. Scribbling "schizophrenic," or "delusional," or "paranoid" in ti's medical files shipwrecks them.

In plain English, targets with damaging undeserved psychiatric charts are stranded. They are afraid to seek help for EH- and stalker-caused conditions, never mind standard health problems that crop up. Going unattended are ti's burns; fractures; PTSD; suicidal ideation; energy wounds; regular wounds; strokes, heart attacks, and other you're-going-to-die emergencies; infections; EH eye injuries; illnesses; injuries from rape and other stalker assaults; and poisoning from radiation, tainted food and drinks, and gas. Many ti's sit at home and risk a preventable death, a permanent impairment, or a suicide attempt rather than risk complications stemming from having their "schizophrenic," or "delusional," or "paranoid" patient history read.

Targets' terror of doctors is valid. When strong psychotropic drugs are forced into a victim, his ability to ride out electronic mind control and other EH is vanquished. A wrongly medicated ti is a prone ti. Doctors are hurting targets by not treating the unremitting stress that any contestant in a killing game would feel and by instead treating nonexistent mental disorders.

Yes, targets, especially new ones, can display significant mental disarray. If they didn't on occasion, they wouldn't be targets. Even those who don't have posttraumatic stress disorder (yet) could be wilting, hostile, or distracted and erratic due to bona fide fear of themselves or their children being raped, mangled, or murdered by unfathomable methods. It's a compulsory duty to save oneself and one's family. With nobody listening, a ti gets pretty damn inventive to secure help, followed by temporarily shattering into pieces when assistance is denied and his thresholds are overloaded.

A veteran ti who is mentally broken for a short phase is still reacting accordingly. Torture and intimidation do that. The few who claim that their superior mental strength has prevented them from ever caving have not been at it for long, and if they have, are neither tortured nor heavily harassed.

As a heavily harassed torture victim myself, I've a question. How normal should someone behave while an inescapable beam is cooking her to death? What attitude is considered acceptable? And when a v2k device has emitted dueling banjos into a senior's hearing for ten months without pause, what exactly should his public persona be? Should he smile more? Should he look casual at the swimming pool while stalkers pile up around him? Really, it's important information because if victims can get their paws on a guidebook of appropriate torture and stalking reactions fewer would suffer at the hands of their doctors.

I'm not bs-ing you that in spite of relentless mind and body torture my friends remain tuned in and defiant. Still, as you know, it's unavoidable that through no defect of my co-captives and I, we fall on our asses from time to time from any combination of pain, ill health, mind control, fear, sadness, hopelessness, guilt, living in isolation, night terrorism, extreme poverty, accumulated distresses, accumulated losses, and overwhelming harassment. That's when doctors see us and refuse to learn something new. Why is that?

Please, if you are a doctor and a practical patient is speaking of stalking, harassment, v2k, and afflictions from energy emissions, kick around the notion that your textbooks are incomplete. If this same patient is expressing obvious trauma, then perhaps he's traumatized.

When your patient says, "I get sore spots on my head, like I came up under a kitchen cupboard. Sometimes they're hot," add EH to the list of possible causes. (One particular beam wields the same pain and tenderness as mistakenly standing up under a low roof.) If your patient says he's being radiated, then perhaps he is. Look outside the box.

The following man's gone-wrong visit to the doctor is only one representation of the enormity of ways a victim's askance for medical help snowballs him into the adversaries' trench for easy pickings.

"Why, Doctor, would you say I'm schizophrenic?"

"Your dad came in. You don't want to be alone at night? You're staying at a hostel? The voices—are they girlfriends?"

"I'm twenty-eight years old. You've no business discussing personal issues with my parents. They called me loco when I said my superintendent was stalking me. What about the documents I gave you? Did you even look at them?"

"Your dad said you'd tried to contact the prime minister about turning off reconnaissance satellites."

"Tell me, Doc, why you won't consider the crime of organized stalking and electronic harassment."

"I'd like to hospitalize you. There's a bed waiting."

That's how it goes for scads, especially the full-time v2k'ed individuals, the full-time mob-stalked individuals, the full-time harassed individuals, and those whose limbs are EH-controlled.

When a ti gets out of the hospital, his stalkers are tickled pink to get back to work gutting their disheveled lamb-person, having efficiently annihilated multiple areas of his life, with the support of doctors.

Amid "yahoos" and psychopathic jabber, the celebrating maniacs will be preparing the next level of violence: unyielding psychological and physical torture with no chance of rescue. Target Donefor has a crazy-label.

Can you now understand the role doctors play in OS?

I can see how the kookier accounts sound psychotic or paranoid when victims are not given the chance to elucidate. I really can. Admittedly, some of the ti remarks sound weird to me too, despite knowing that my own top the lot. "Doctors, for Pete's sake, if a self-proclaimed victim is in your office, type in 'organized stalking' or 'electronic harassment' and press Enter. Dare yourself to explore a new medical field. Better yet, dare yourself to consider that your patient is a crime victim and not a nut."

What floors me is that national medical federations are bypassing a defined epidemic after hearing recurring sagas and recurring complaints from human rights associations, as well as from thousands of targets with histories of good mental health. More perplexing, how is it that physicians everywhere are missing a wholesale extermination program?

Could it be that neither the government offices responsible for health care nor the physicians are missing a thing? A lot of ti's believe doctors are being manipulated by government bureaucrats through lies, bribes, extortion, or threats. That being said, OS would have had to infiltrate health bureaus or, at the very least, have persuaded top officials to convince doctors that a covert program would benefit the country's future.

A subset of ti's believe nations-wide professional-scale gaslighting is underway. Gaslighting is the term used for conning someone into questioning his own sanity. Gaslighting is largely unsuccessful on ti's although a small quota of perps devote their lives to the task anyhow.

Another theory about doctors is that potentially helpful academics are mind controlled to treat victims shoddily.

My Pollyanna stance is that despite the depravity of MKULTRA's homicidal practitioners, exceedingly few present-day physicians could promote physical and psychological torture on children, allow them to be murdered, or sanction their disappearance, seeing as attacking children is a popular tactic to isolate or devastate targeted parents and grandparents. That does not stifle my ire at the closed-minded or cajoled professionals of who the bravest could rally against OS or offer aid were it not for their own delusions that criminal despotism cannot exist in their culture.

If I'm wrong and do-no-harm oath-takers are willingly abetting OS executives, an iceberg must be located for their exile.

Before doing any more doctor-bashing, we must applaud a scattering of mostly targeted folks in the medical field who care for as many ti's as they can. The victim community leans on these Supermen and Superwomen for hope and survival, all the while appreciating that the humanity and courage of each one is unparalleled. How do you thank people like that?

Should you want to see these Superfolks in action, look up the Covert Harassment Conference, which is a seminar where doctors, scientists, and experts in various fields talk in depth about OS and

EH. Much of what's in this book is discussed, yet because crackerjack speakers come from around the world, there's a lot more to be learned from them than from me. The doctors who speak at the conference, as well as the doctors who listen, are saving targets' lives. Videos of the event and excellent information about OS/EH can be found at www.covertharassmentconference.com

Unworthy of praise is the targeted physician a puddle jump from my house who is closed-mouthed about the crime. Is this a situation of reputation and money versus ethics? Was he threatened with harm and medical-license revocation like one targeted doctor I know? Or maybe he thinks he's protecting loved ones by staying mum: another forgivable conundrum.

The only reason I know about this man is because we accidentally hired the same private investigator who intermingled our plights while snooping for clues. According to the PI, the Vancouver Island doctor and I were harassed nearly identically, so it's presumable we still have twinning EH and obstacles. He couldn't solve his vehicle tampering either. I'm betting that for the brief periods he's well enough to work he is useless to victimized patients, and maybe even detrimental, afraid of exposure.

Across the board, the types of health practitioners ti's would rather avoid comprise a laundry list, with dentists coming in at number three. Targets worry that EH will strike during and after surgical and non-surgical procedures, as EH-strikes on physically weak or prone areas are predictable. Targets also worry about being implanted with a microchip and worry that a doctor or dentist could be mind controlled to do something stupid. The concerns are legitimate. We've already discussed that many ti's steer clear of health care altogether to avoid awkward questions and wrongful psychiatric treatment.

You may have guessed that ti health care is a personally hot issue. Two pending suicides are making me tense. The first is a Saskatchewan athlete whose stalking, harassment, and v2k threats have rendered him housebound. The other is a former British Columbia university student with the same stalking and harassment but who hears v2k insults and machinery squeals instead of "You're a dead man." Each fellow was chosen by OS hunters five years ago, and each has been involuntarily institutionalized for schizophrenia in the last year. Today, they are afraid to seek help for roaring PTSD, probable radiation poisoning, and suicidal ideation, having been told that the next time they are admitted they will be injected with antipsychotic drugs and put under government care. These men do not know of one another, have dissimilar lifestyles, and are simultaneously done-in.

As I know the men so well, I spoke to their abandoning relatives as a last resort. Both family units believe that denying support and contact will compel the victim into admitting that his stalking and EH allegations are inventions from a schizophrenic mind.

"What else can I do?" each parent asks.

"Believe your son," I say.

The men presume their loved ones are mind controlled to be indifferent. To imagine their families would forsake them is unthinkable.

* * *

Addendum

The Saskatchewan fellow died after a series of heart problems.

CHAPTER FIFTEEN

LONG-TIME TARGETS

This is a piece directed at the non-believing loved ones in targets' lives. It depicts typical veteran ti's unspoken reality: mine and multitudes globally.

We've given up talking to you about anything except the weather and cleverly turn the conversation towards yourself, for we cannot think, speak, and act as you expect us to.

You, as a non-believer, often view us as closed-off nobodies and in murmurs call us strange. Do you understand that although we may care deeply for you, in order to cope, there are phases when we no longer care what you think about us? We've done our best to explain, and as veteran ti's we're tired. We're finished justifying our actions.

It's understandable that our worlds may look small to you, for we are held hostage.

In contrast, there are days when your worlds look small to us. We don't see worth in all that may be meaningful to you, which could be as conventional as natural enthusiasm over self-image, luxuries, and special days. Likewise, we're not bothered by many of the little things that annoy you.

It's not that we find your life trivial, because it used to be ours. The conflict is that we are far, far removed from freedom. Uppermost to us is getting it back. Frills, celebrations, and ho-hum sniveling will not help us.

Surely you recognize that much of what used to be important to us isn't, now that our lives are condensed into blocks of attitude and time: staying cool and resolute through terminal hopelessness. Within the few hours we're allowed to function, despite poor health, we've plenty to accomplish; thus, our precious little mental and physical strength is conserved for the battle. We're not going to waste it by being affected over events we now find insignificant. We're not going to waste it in unrewarding pursuits. Resilience is gold.

Therefore, it's conspicuous to us, as targets, that the commonalities we once shared with you have changed. Take compromising. It's something no one likes doing—something you, personally, don't think about. Compromising is all us worn-out ti's have. We think about it a lot. When mind control erases a capability, we find conciliation and compensation not in drugs or booze as you might expect, or maybe as we once did, but in diversions that others might find inconsequential. A sunrise. A song. Researching. Writing. The wind in the trees. And when harassment erases a freedom, we make do. With no external assistance or comfort, we get by in ways that would surprise you with their simplicity. As I said, compromising is all we have.

You as a non-believer see our false-fronts of well-rehearsed optimism and normalcy. What you will never see is our loneliness while we sit at thrift-store kitchen tables, with cruddy meals and a headache, speculating what the nighttime mind beam will bring.

Yet, we speculate with composure. The night will bring something. For a moment we might want to die. But we are tough enough now.

It sneaks up—this heightened mental position we hope you never attain, for our form of intellectualism is gained only through torture. We learn to be bigger than our masters, reaching into our souls for buried instincts.

Too, we are humbled. The homeless among us hold even ground with the movie stars among us, equally trapped in the same burning building.

The funny thing is, quite unintentionally, we became better people. Our plight has made us spiritually enlightened: not airy-fairy with superiority, but with a grave sort of knowing.

For that reason we sympathize why you could feel shunned, hurt that we've withdrawn. Maybe it's you who has done the abandoning. Either way, losing you haunts us. Every day.

Our sadness at losing you is visceral. It makes us heartsick. We don't know what to do with the love and the memories, in part because we're not allowed to express ourselves, not even in our own minds. We are afraid to mourn lost loves, lost children, lost years, and you. Our owners get excited when we do. Terrifyingly, it's those very memories that are keeping some of us alive: of children, and lovers, and relatives, and friends, and pets. We mourn anyways, prepared for the consequences.

If you want to, reconsider our last conversations together and see what you've missed, for what we offer is valuable. Our core potential is enormous. We are experts at staying sane despite pathological efforts to render us mad. Should OS stop, the last standing victims would be outstanding leaders.

Along these lines, it will surprise you that in spite of it all, targets get smarter. We study science, governments, law, criminology, policing, military and intelligence regimes, human rights, covert operations, health, psychology, sociology, human experimentation, historical crimes, and current affairs as if our lives depend on it. Because it does.

Less flattering decrees can also be said. A few of us older victims have rare moments when we wonder if we're still all human. Our brains buzz, ding, and rattle. Our vision pixelates into dazzling cubes. Some of our minds go black and blank, and we don't know where the time went. We wonder if our heads are computerized and if they have an on and off switch. It's natural to ask ourselves, "Am I the same person on the inside since being targeted?"

The ti that you as a non-believer know may be on a different emotional seesaw: maybe about ending his life. Or perhaps he's forever reviewing the moments when he was unkind, hazarding that he deserves to be crapped on. Whatever he's pondering will be unthinkable to non-tortured people, yet he hashes through these issues with absolute clarity.

The fact is, each target has serious unique scores to settle within himself, that he keeps to himself. Nevertheless, he's dependent upon his fellow hostages for the incentive to slog on and for infusions of new information.

We're rather like prisoners of war forever planning a collective escape, except that rational science must be defied before we can slip through the bars.

CHAPTER SIXTEEN

JOURNAL

Journal Entry #1

The hackers wrecked my laptop royally this time, all because of a mistake I made. A broken TV across a lengthy living room is my new computer screen, connected to the broken keyboard by a long HDMI cable. Binoculars are necessary. That's not a joke. Moving the TV closer will require muscle and an extension cord. Both are absent.

"How's your book coming?" a driftwood salvager asked at the door, having sought permission to pick oysters off my beach. (No one owns the beach. She was being polite.) Inquiring about my writing was not the lady's intent. Either v2k or electronic mind control was responsible. Regrettably, the trick eluded me.

"Pardon?" I stammered, upset she knew about the book, as I'd told no one except an apparently blabbermouth accountant when asking if he could print out my latest draft, seeing as my copier was broken. (He didn't know what the book was about; nor would I have asked him a favour if there were other options. Being an affable villager, who had not blabbed, he gave me an old printer.)

In any case, my mistake, which became a nightmare, wasn't in the five EH'ed words the lady and I exchanged about my writing. The mistake was in being Canadian and afraid of offending an innocent islander who lives in the tiny cove around the rocky point from my own tiny cove.

"Would it be all right," she asked, pleased she had permission to get oysters off my beach, "if I called you sometimes to see if any interesting driftwood has washed up? I could give you my website so you'd know what to look for. You've probably seen my gnarly chairs at the Farmer's Market."

"Nothing personal," I said, "living as a recluse, I don't hand over contact information."

"Oh," she replied looking down, unsure how to respond.

This was awkward. "Okay then. Let me get a pen. I'll give you my email." Before you, the reader, judge me, envision forever being belligerent to the nicest of folks when doing so chips away at your decency. On saying goodbye, noticing how pretty and happy the young seawoman looked, my selfish, wimpy act of needlessly exposing her to OS hit me.

Weeks passed before the woman emailed: "Do you mind if I row over tomorrow and get some more oysters for dinner?

My reply was based on believing she'd come to no harm: that a row to the beach and a yen for shellfish had nothing to do with me. "Help yourself," I wrote. "Nobody else is picking them. I only like clams."

She soon emailed again, but it wasn't her. I should have caught on having noticed her ID change from Sea.gal to Sea.gals. The message read: "You should call Mack at the Islander Weekly. He could help with your book."

My hasty, unthinking reply was, "Thanks for recommending Mack, but I'm going to keep plugging away on my own. So far, publishers have been complimentary."

Minutes later the computer screen went black, the keyboard went wonky, and my mistake was realized. Communication was knocked out for two days: both phone and email.

Whoa there. I just read your mind. You're thinking: "She's become obsessed that everything that goes wrong is OS's fault. Everybody's stuff breaks."

Indeed, everybody's stuff does break. Yet, in charging that all of life's glitches are OS caused, the opposite is true of myself and other timeworn ti's. We excel at cooking up reasons why it's not "them" when our seasoned hearts are screaming, "I'd like to ring their ruddy necks." It's easier that way.

Just the same, please don't think me snooty by saying you'd have to be a victim to understand the quick exchange between a slip up and OS's punishment. A ti telling himself, "Drat, I've gone and broken it again," only goes so far, only so many times.

As correspondence with publishing companies has been with (safer) typewriter-written letters sent through Canada Post, the book's pending publication, evidently, was news to certain interlopers, which begs the question, why didn't all my enemies eventually come to know this? Why didn't the remote-monitoring team bother to hand down this publishing tidbit? Other than expected retribution for chronicling OS, the rest of the scenario makes no sense.

Nevertheless, it seems the uninformed hackers, of which several live nearby, never imagined my drivel would get so far, thus prompting an immediate parade of back-and-forth cars outside the house, which in my case is a rare ploy due to being nosed out by homesteaders and true-blue hermits who travel the otherwise deserted road, who investigate everything that's out-of-order in their never-lock-the-door paradise.

It's presumable the moron ensemble didn't hang around for long. You'd have to ask them. I closed the blinds. The fact is, my place is walled in by bushes, and the road is so far back that were it not for a small shrubby section they cleared themselves one night, and hearing them shooting in and out the driveway, the impact of vehicular pestering would be confined to the mental illnesses they surely must have, for mentally healthy people don't, for fun, dedicate their lives to the ruination of ordinary folks.

Remotely frying the TV, which I was watching to get my mind off the cavalcade, may have already been on the remote workers' agenda. Yet by all accounts it looks like a retribution breakage. It's hard to tell. Since beginning to write, all of my money, other than what's required to scrape by, has gone on replacements and repairs. Regardless, the scrambled-audio, yellow-blotched TV is only good now as a defective yellow-blotched computer monitor.

That was six days ago. The flux of harassment since then has surpassed my coping threshold. Most of the targets who contact me are in this category; nonetheless, my ability to express their psychological buckling has fallen flat. This afternoon, slavery is personal: raw and savage. I can't stand it anymore.

It isn't only the broken computer, broken TV, accelerated EH, accelerated daytime harassment, accelerated night terrorism, and the new round of financial tampering that tipped my threshold. It's guilt. To all appearances, the perpetrators leapt on the angelic-looking driftwood salvager in a big way. It's not like she and I are chums. We don't even know each other's name. Decimating a bystander, like her, is exceptional and is what happened to Whatshisname, the always-feels-wet guy who crossed my path as a courier.

My guess is the wood salvager's beauty could not be passed up by the summoned other-side-of-the-strait perps and that harrying her would have sexual appeal while reinforcing my isolation theme, assuming her streak of misfortune was not a fluke of coincidence. When stalkers ferry-over for a mob attack, bad things happen.

"Someone dragged my skiff down the beach," she emailed, "and sunk it. Who would do such a thing? If my life jackets or buoys float in, would you let me know?"

"That's terrible," I replied. There's nothing right now, but the tide's about to turn. Cross your fingers."

"Thanks," she wrote. "My truck won't start. My boyfriend will pick up anything that's found."

How do I live knowing the woman's catastrophe could be my fault? An explanation would have her digging into the island's OS stranglehold, locking her in as prey when she might have been let go. A wait-and-see strategy is the most cautious approach, yet non-disclosure corks self-defence if her life continues to go downhill.

There's something else. The community centre held an unscheduled public meeting last weekend on adult bullying. Obviously it was considered necessary, but seemed out of place, squeezed in between the talk on fish farms and the yoga class. It feels incompatible, is all, with the love, peace, and flowers philosophy that the hamlets in the Salish Sea are famous for. I was disappointed to have missed it and have to wonder if there are other ti's on the island.

Anyhow, a cardboard "Do Not Disturb" sign will prevent potential door-knockers from being hurt, eradicating temptation to be sociable: a too little, too late attempt at redemption.

Also worrisome is what may have happened to the computer repairman for his pop by to say, "You need a new one." When organized stalkers are steamed, they become Nazi-like, committing inhumanities in droves.

On account of my mistake in mentioning publishers, my enemies coordinated a widespread campaign of swamping my email and voice mail with childish messages from bogus book companies and editors. Some of the callers pretend to be targets in crisis or local handymen looking for work and interject their spiel with, "I wrote a book, and some bastard stole the manuscript." It's all quite easy to ignore, in part because I turned the ringer off and in part because stronger than usual beams are pressing on my ribs and leg bones and my mind is preoccupied with being laid-up.

Adding to the misery, remote staffers are deploying tortures I've heard of but never encountered. My joints, all of them, feel mashed—that I am no longer stuck together. Every three hours the beam is turned off, and the agony suddenly ceases for a spell. My owners require a suicide, not an assassination. Life is nothing more than an on/off button.

Right now, along with the internal EH, a seeming electric current is sparking my outsides from neck to toe; at least, that's what it feels like. It's racing my heart. Shock is setting in yet is not severe enough to override the soreness of a crunchy scalp, over-scorched and bleeding.

There are other burns, far more serious. While finishing off the last of a forgotten mug of tea, the remote stalkers nuked it. Raising it to my mouth, it spewed out like a volcano, as hot as a volcano, and my front is covered in penny-sized red and yellow holes.

How long has it been since I wrote the last sentence? An hour? Two? While dabbing my bloody head at the bathroom sink, a flip-switch energy paralyzed me: activity, coherence, and memory were vetoed.

Finally back at my desk, a frequency is filling my brain with a funereal dread that has me weeping in gasps. The moment feels non-survivable, which is satisfying. I truly want this over. Most heavily hit targets have a private "out" plan. Mine has steps.

"Sweetheart," I said, calling a secondarily targeted loved one, "how are you?" What I wanted to say is, "Please look after me. If you could finish sealing the leaky pipe in the basement . . . If you could make me a sandwich . . . Everything's too hard."

"You sound tense," he said.

"Yeah, my laptop is barely working again." Tears streaming, turning my face away from the phone, he did not hear, "My will is on the fridge."

The mental toppling of targets is as distinctive as the crime. We don't always commit suicide from sadness or physical torture. Desperation can come from needing someone to look after us for a day when we're overwhelmed by a surge of crimes. A small measure of rescue.

If someone could say, "I shall do for you what needs to be done," the psychological crisis I am in would have been avoided. But nobody's going to say that. The crisis workers who are in a position to aid, don't believe. Not that I should accept help from innocents, due to the "impact on others" factor. It's just consoling to think someone would offer rather than let me die.

What every ti's skeptical loved ones can't fathom is that the victim in their family, despite being transparently handcuffed to captors, must maintain life supports of food, housing, and communication yet is further harassed and tortured for doing so. That's what's got me hung up today. I must do everything non-targets do—what regular people do—but in dignified PTSD, with a stolen brain, in the midst of violence, in the midst of guilt, and I can't.

Begging God and my deceased dad for the strength to look after myself was not relieving, for backlash to prayers always occurs. It was sloppy to ask.

While telling a ti friend I wanted to die, she prudently didn't advise me to run to a hospital. "Me too," she said. "The voices are as loud as they've ever been, and now they've added screeching machinery in my ears. Green sine waves are coming out of my head, a mindfuck to make me crazy. Plus, my landlord wants to kick me out for something a perp said. My son has been missing for twelve years, and I can't stop thinking about him. I'm sick, and I'm scared of the stalkers. It's our new owners. They've gone too far. You can't die. You've always been my rock."

"Maybe we should rent side-by-side cabins," I said, "to look after each other. It's not the stalkers I'm scared of. It's of killing myself. It would hurt my kids."

So that's something we'll discuss: sharing our lives but not our homes. Targets who are heavily harassed and/or heavily tortured can't often live together within the same walls long-term, not unless they have ground rules and ample private space. Voice to skull, electronic mind control, and extended periods of distress make for incompatible close-quarter roommates, as the house-mood develops an edginess that builds over time.

Admitting frailty clashes with my goal to establish a countryside full-scale ti centre. Such an achievement might be better suited for a stronger person: someone who isn't so often grovelling for mercy. Where did my confidence go?

I've got to pull myself together.

No amount of fortitude, though, will sort out this week's madness. Any military leader will tell you that prisoners are more controllable when they are in a constant state of confusion, which describes the mindset of my present tottery foothold. Creating confusion, as you know, is a mandated OS practice.

For that reason, why all my perps weren't aware that I'd corresponded with publishers and why the driftwood lady may have been viciously attacked is conjecture. Could it be that the volunteer Citizens on Patrol (community watchdogs) who are asked to harass ti's are not kept wholly in the loop? Could the driftwood lady have already been in OS's sights, as are all folks who live near a target's home?

As I type on a wonky keyboard, the broken TV that I'm using for a computer screen is going dim. The paragraphs are being switched around, words are being changed, dotted lines are popping up everywhere, and white space cannot be filled. An aggressive hacker has taken over.

When the wood lady emailed about gathering oysters, not so long ago, I was touching up a chapter outline that explains EH's accurately dubbed razzamatazz. Razzamatazz is the remotely generated impact on bank machines, medical devices, and all sorts of useful amenities. That chapter is going to be written on my vintage manual typewriter.

It's raining. I've always loved the West Coast's grey and wet. Here in the ancient trees, earthy sogginess harmonizes into a romantic scent I tried to replicate when the kids were little. We put on our gumboots, filled an old pot with red-cedar bark and Nootka rose hips, and left it on the woodstove to simmer. "Let's spin some wool," I said. "If we can't get a good smell, maybe we can get a good dye."

Watching the forest drip into the cove is not enough to pull me out of crisis. It's a genesis to revive.

Journal Entry #2

Time has passed since the last journal entry, and the crisis is gone but not forgotten. It was unnerving to be on the edge and impelled the creation of Plan B backup resources, having accepted that psychological fatigue will occur again, no matter how meticulous Plans A and B are.

As predicted, the wilds salved my funk, reviving optimism, which is something OS has not been able to altogether eradicate. More importantly, the driftwood lady and the computer repairman contacted me about oysters and computers, which indicates they feel lively enough to be busy.

My "Do Not Disturb" sign was stolen on the same night a perp plugged a long, long extension cord into an outside electrical outlet that's under the kitchen window. There's no telling what was on the other end. I try not to play their games. So I unplugged the cord and threw it into the bushes after deciding not to take scissors to it. Then I duct-taped the outlet, but they tore the tape off and wrote a note on it thanking me for—hang on, I'll grab it. It says, "June, have a good day!! You've taught me so much, I don't know how to thank you." I found it in the driveway.

No, it wasn't someone being nice. A nice person would have left a paper note in the message box beside the door, not a piece of duct tape ripped off the house and thrown on the ground.

Did I say that the crime is designed to confuse?

More recently, a couple of Sundays ago—

Knock Knock

"Sorry, I can't open the door. My bird's out."

"I'm out of gas and need to use your phone."

"Shout the number, and I'll call for you."

"It's ——, my mom, Yvonne."

I called Yvonne whose voice mail greeting said Yvette, put the bird away, told the young fellow I'd try again, and offered him a seat on a cement planter.

"Your brownies smell great," he said.

"Really? No baking here. I'll try your mom again."

After a five-minute lapse, I found the fellow hovering over the notorious electrical outlet, assumedly by happenchance. "She's still not answering," I said.

"What a pain in the butt," he replied. "I'll have to walk to the ferry."

"That's quite a ways," I said. "Maybe someone will offer you a ride."

Here's where it gets weird. Having seen some weeds that needed pulling, I went inside to get my old gardening shoes, went back outside, and watched the fellow climb into an SUV parked behind the storage shed. He started it on the first crank and drove off smiling, flaunting his performance.

I called the alleged mom in the evening, and her name had changed to Adrian. My guess is the number was one of those anonymous on-the-spot disposable phone numbers. They have all the features of regular service. Scammers use them.

So what the hell was that about? Is it naive to hope a garden-variety robber was checking to see if anyone was home?

As for the fellow smelling brownies, many of the people who come to my door smell something that isn't real. Sometimes it's bacon. Twice it was freshly sawn wood, in the kitchen.

Moving forward, on the next afternoon my husky perp, the one with the rip-your-head-off scowl, parked his truck and trailered boat halfway down the driveway, climbed into the boat, put a blue tarp over himself, and flailed around under it making a heck of a racket until I went out to look. "He's fixing something," I told myself the first time, knowing that islanders are pretty laid back and would think nothing of using someone's driveway to attend a problem. But he did it for days—stopping and flailing under blue plastic. And it's targets who get called crazy.

Can you see a pattern of harassment here? Can you imagine what the city-living targets go through if this is what happens to a ti on a sparsely populated island?

Journal Entry #3

I couldn't get up last night despite wanting to several times. Something was amiss in the house, and there was no way to crawl off the couch. On awakening and telling myself, "Better check this out," I'd feel myself being forced back to sleep. Over and over.

This morning, my strewn-about dime-store reading glasses had been neatly folded, and one pair had a crab beside it. It's only a scare tactic. One of a jillion.

In fact, for a number of mornings over the last few months, I've woken up to find newly dead beach crabs in the sinks, on the counters, on the foyer rug, in the shag carpet upstairs, and in assorted other places. You know the kind of crab. They're the dark-red ones that you won't pick up for fun because they are big enough to hurt when they pinch. No, they're not scuttling up from the beach. Anyhow, I looked. It's a nighttime OS prank. I'd forgotten to mention it before as it's beginning to feel normal.

Saving up for surveillance cameras is an ongoing priority, even though they'll probably be fried. The book, research, legal files, and door blocks are undisturbed, and that's unsettling for reasons we'll cover in the razzamatazz chapter.

Whatever's going on at night lately, it's making me too weary to get the vacuum cleaner out of the closet. It looks heavy. The bird's molting, so I'll hands 'n knees the feathers.

My eyes and throat were also burned last night. It's hard to swallow or read: spitting blood and seeing fuzz. The underside of my right arm and the topside of its hand were burned and laser-holed as well, and some form of EH is preventing me from getting a full breath.

On the bright side, my internal and external burn scars are accumulating and will be useful to prove EH torture, especially with the accompaniment of my video diaries. Whenever my camera works, I record the burns, slices, holes, vandalism, and night goings-on, along with the razzamatazz you haven't learned about yet. Videos of the many untended EH-caused bone fractures are useless and only infer that I'm a klutz. I record them anyways.

I'm not whining. This book is to teach you about OS and EH. A lot of my comrades woke up in far worse shape, and some didn't wake up at all. Torture does that—the whole pain and death thing. Optimism still reigns; it's not a bad day. I can still write.

I'm going to end the chapter with this:

If the ti in your life is speaking about odd vehicles, odd people, finding odd things, and odd medical concerns, which admittedly can happen to anyone, please ask yourself if maybe—just maybe—this person, who says he's a target, is in danger. Believing a ti is critical to his well-being. Let's play out a scenario:

You: "Gees, a semi in the wrong lane almost hit me head-on. I'm still shaking."

Skeptic: "Don't be ridiculous."

You: "But it did. I feel sick."

Skeptic: "You're imagining it."

When a ti has an exchange like this, except over his stalking, harassment, and torture, he feels like garbage.

CHAPTER SEVENTEEN

RESPITE HOUSE

Orcas near respite house

We're going to take a look at why private-residence respite houses are difficult to maintain and why staffed and sponsored relief accommodation is the best way to tend heavily hit ti's.

This is not to say that a person who takes in an ailing ti is wasting his time. Just the opposite. An extended hand saves lives. What I'm saying here is that someone who consistently assists an ever-changing roster of victims is in danger of high-powered retribution, emotional exhaustion, and monetary loss.

Although we're beginning with the worst cases from when my home was open to ti's, from before writing the book, you will leave with the impression that helping targets has been rewarding. It's unfortunate that relating only the times when giving aid was wonderful won't teach you anything.

The panicking lady we're about to discuss was in fight-for-life mode, a natural reaction that for her went sideways and is comparable to being obnoxious towards the person who's trying to get a sharp-toothed otter pup out of your wide-leg pants. Maybe that's not quite it. A better comparison is if you shouted, "You're ugly and stupid!" to the stranger who's wrestling a mugger off your back.

"Do you have room?" she asked on the phone after explaining her targeting.

"Unless there's a cancellation, probably not for a month," I said.

"My family are perps. I have to leave. They're planning something."

"If you're in immediate danger, go to a women's shelter. I can make arrangements for you this minute. Tell me the town you want to be in."

"The women's shelters here suck. I'll call you next week and see if there's space."

Indeed, the woman did call: "Give me your address," she said. "I'll be there in twenty minutes."

"I'm sorry," I answered, "you're going to have to tell me who you are."

"It's me from San Diego. You said you'd have room."

"Are you sure? We only spoke a few days ago. There won't be a bed available for a while."

"I took a stinking bus ride from California and you're saying I can't stay? What kind of respite house are you running?"

"A busy one. Let me book you into the women's haven. They are really very nice in Canada. I've stayed in plenty. You'll be okay until there's room here."

"I'm beginning to wonder if you're a perp."

When the woman called from the shelter the following day, she was beyond furious at me. "I don't know why you made a big deal out of getting me admitted. I didn't even need your name. What did you tell the staff? Did you say I am a victim of organized stalking?"

"No, and you shouldn't either. I said you are escaping a violent situation and needed protecting until you could stay with me."

"The staff are perps. They're using hand signals and trigger words. They put acid in my shoes and burned my feet. You tipped them off, didn't you?"

"If you think I'm the enemy, you shouldn't stay with me."

"I'm not going to use the phone here anymore. The whole place is bugged."

"Please, Tara, go onto the Internet and learn how electronic harassment is following you. The remote perps are playing pranks to make the shelter look involved."

"Oh, I know all that. I also know when people have been paid to abuse me. Once the perps know where I'm going, they get there first and buy everyone off. You're one of them, aren't you? Telling them my plans."

"Tara, my phone's tapped, and the shelter's probably is too by now. Nothing we've talked about is secret."

Legitimately, I was worried about welcoming the woman into my home. Fleeing ti's who don't understand the crime turn other people's lives upside down. Although her plight and behaviour were characteristic of new or uninformed victims, attacking my integrity wasn't.

Tara openly despised me. She was incensed that I couldn't seem to grasp that the shelter employees had been paid to harass or kill her and was equally livid that an unexpected visit landed her outside of my home.

"A worker came in my room last night," she said from a pay phone the next day, "and poisoned my bra. I heard her bragging about it. There are welts all over me."

"The staff are delightful ladies," I replied. "You're probably getting energy burns and voice to skull. Make a doorstop anyways tonight. You'll feel more secure. The good news is you can come shortly."

"The girl who checked in yesterday put something in the coffee maker. She's signaling to the workers. The place is a deathtrap."

"Okay, maybe a stalker's slipped in as a battered woman. That's pretty common. There's a haven an hour away that takes in only one woman at a time. Let's try to get you in there."

"All these places are the same, run by perps, and you won't give me your address. What a fucking waste of money. You're a fucking perp, fucking bitch, and I'm going to tell every fucking person what you're fucking up to."

And she did.

In case you're wondering why I didn't offer the woman an empty corner to curl up in, it is imperative for a ti to have her or his own private room in a respite house. In emotionally volatile cases, or when the lodger is an imposter, a rescuer that has no barrier can be (figuratively) climbed on top of and drowned in his own home. Exceptions are suicidal victims who must receive emergency intervention.

Tara was unorthodox in that almost all the frantic targets who cross my path are truly considerate people just trying to survive. Whether she suffered from an anxiety disorder, which may have explained her snappiness, is unknown. When someone's detonating from across the channel, it's hard to tell.

Generally, targets' unique stress symptoms engender problems I can handle: first, because I've experienced them and second, because of my training. Fury and sadness stemming from the losses are also manageable, but when contempt is directed at me, finding middle ground with the individual is nearly impossible.

Everyone who assists ti's will tell you that a small sector of refuge-seeking victims, perhaps five percent, expects unconditional help and unconditional accommodation, as the following misadventure shows.

Craig visited me many times before I moved to my present Discovery Islands' home. Solid, blond, and handsome, the building contractor had expressed surprise when we met. For some reason, he'd thought only Hollywood-looking young people were preyed upon.

From his first impromptu stay at my former logging-town duplex, he demanded my total everything. Telling him I was also a ti, and might be ill or busy, had no effect when asking him to call ahead. Even so, knowing a panicky victim's mindset, constantly dropping by would have been fine if he hadn't been inconsiderate.

"I missed a mortgage payment," he shouted in my duplex over the moving boxes, for shouting was often how he spoke. "Well, it's my mom's house. I built it for her." Rolling on to his side, the fellow was being hit with baseball batting beams, one after another. "I'm living with her," he moaned. "They harassed me out of my own home on the weekend. It could be trashed for all I know. I'm afraid to go back."

"Gees, Craig, I've got to pack. We'll have to discuss this at my new place on the island. I'll call you in a couple of weeks when I'm settled in."

Craig rolled into the carport the day after I moved, having told someone a lie to get the address. "You can stay overnight," I said, "and we'll hash out your troubles, but you'll have to go tomorrow."

"Aren't you opening a respite house? I'm a ti who needs respite."

"You've got to let me at least move in, Craig." And off he went the next morning in a snit.

Two days later he was back. "I have to stay. I can't take it anymore. The rays won't get me here in the bush. Isn't that why you moved into the boonies? To get away from the rays?"

"No. The rays are everywhere," I said. "What about your dog? My lease says no dogs. And you're going to have to smoke outside. You know that EH trashed my throat. The beers have to go as well. This is a drug- and alcohol-free home."

"Aw, come on," he said, "be reasonable."

"Look, stay the night, but I'm not set up yet. This is a really big house, and I'm doing it all by myself, with a badly broken foot, and a headache that won't go away. It's going to take a while. Besides, the furnace, the plumbing—everything's on the fritz."

Craig and I talked about his harassment until 10:00 p.m. Well, he was shouting, and I was listening.

"Did you see a light blinking?" he bellowed, covering a moonlit cove with the blinds. "In the trees. They're watching."

"No one can see us, but did you think you wouldn't be followed?"

"You took this place to keep ti's safe. This isn't safe at all. The rays are still hitting me. God, I'm in so much pain. Mom too. We're always puking. Come here, I want to show you a video."

Flipping open his camcorder screen, the video began with Craig's mom begging him to stop doing whatever was making a gang retaliate, and progressed to her pleading with police.

"Sir," she said to an RCMP officer, "they are throwing shit onto the sundeck at night. They fill the fish pond with it and stand outside the windows and laugh. And someone's breaking in—turning on the taps." Tears streaming, she shrieked, "Son, tell the officers what you did to make a gang so mad at you."

"I fucking did nothing!" Craig yelled. The clip ended with him swearing at both his mom and the cops, declaring innocence.

Craig appeared on the doorstep three weeks later. "Look at this," he said after a long day of grousing. One thing the fellow had going for him was proof. Every time EH fried a camera, he bought another to hang around his neck. On the camcorder screen, the video roamed between his mom's house and the neighbour's garage. "Am I nuts or are those energy waves?" he asked.

We watched the clip together for a second and third time. Airborne ripples, like ghostly lapping sea waves, were emanating from the neighbour's detached garage, crossing a narrow patch of grass, and seeping into his mom's house. I'd never seen anything like it. Unnoticeable to a naked eye, the camera had picked it up: the mystery being that this kind of electromagnetic energy is invisible. So whether we were seeing the "effects" of the energy waves or were being visually tricked is anyone's guess. EH tricks, or decoys, make ti's sound, look, and feel goofy when they tell others what they've witnessed. I can tell you with certainty, though, that I saw what looked like energy waves, one after the other, about four feet off the ground.

"This is what's given my mom terminal cancer," he said. "The waves went right into her bedroom. The doctor thinks I'm home looking after her. Fuck, to get cancer too? Her pills and a commode are beside the bed, so she'll be okay for a while. We're moving here. You're like a nurse, aren't you? You could look after her."

At my request, Craig left to sign his mom into the hospital. He popped up again within the week. "Mom's in pain," he said, "and the nurses won't give her enough morphine. I went apeshit, and now they won't let me visit without security guys in the room. Fucking put them through the wall."

The final time Craig visited, his mom had died just hours before. He'd gone home from the hospital and thrown an array of belongings into his truck box so haphazardly that much of it fell onto the highway. He wore one sandal and was hysterical. On opening the passenger door to let his dog out, a closetful of shoes and clothes tumbled to the driveway.

"I'm not going back," he said, "not even for the funeral. I'm staying here. The perps won't let me work, and I didn't want to sell anything, so mom's been supporting me."

Craig always carried a wad of cash. Relying on his mom was news to me. A successful contractor until OS took over, Craig owned a new Harley, truck, and sports car, yet had asked his mom to keep up the mortgage payments on both the houses. Plus, he had a large inventory of tools and equipment and a good relationship with a close-by sister. Now there was an inheritance.

What Craig couldn't say is that OS had pushed him to commit a crime at the hospital, and it meant losing everything. Oblivious to the felony, I dismissed his irrational behaviour, presuming the stalkers had worn him thin enough to override losing his mom. But unbeknownst to me, the burly builder had cracked with the added stress of evading police.

"I need a bowl for the dog," he said.

"We'll have to find a dog sitter, Craig. Are you expecting to move in permanently? Your house is in the truck box. The barbecue is more out than in."

Craig was so agitated—really quite out of his mind—that reasoning with him about the dog, his smoking, and his intentions would have to wait. Watching him rush around closing the curtains and blinds, it was clear that the situation required some thinking. "I'm going to have a nice long shower and put my foot up in the den," I said, needing privacy. "It's not healing."

Taking advantage of the moment, Craig transformed the kitchen into a pigpen. Not just a little pigpen, an out-and-out sty that included ketchup blobs on my clean floor. "Turn it down," I hollered, on entering the mayhem. "If you want music that loud, go sit in your truck. Hey, what did you do to my computer? And my camera?"

"I'm trying to set them up for a video stream from the kitchen window."

"What if I want to use them?"

"You've done nothing to defend me. I'm doing it for you."

"No way, Craig. This is my home. I try to live as normally as possible," I said, putting my computer and camera back.

"Well, I'll set up my own then. I'm going to have to cut a hole in the blind for the lens."

"Forget it."

"You don't care if I get murdered, do you?"

Craig had become unpredictable in his desperation to stay hidden. Calming him down would have taken knocking him out. "Can I touch your boob?" he asked, while brushing my breast with his hand.

"Get back. You're scaring me."

"Let's have sex. Why not?"

"That is never going to happen."

Craig got busy aligning his own camera on an entryway table that was covered in knickknacks and jasmine plants. "I'm not helping you," I answered after he asked multiple times. "Have you seen my foot?"

Pushing me over on the couch, peeved at my apparent indifference, he had a tantrum about being targeted until dark. That's when things really got interesting.

"Did you hear that?" he yelled. "They're tapping on the walls."

Telling him it might be voice to skull would have started an argument. "I'll go look," I offered, limping outside. It's true that a night stalker was up the driveway. It's also true he didn't need to know.

"Get some sleep," I said, and up the stairs he went to the main ti suite, a previous ragtag layover for whale watching tours.

He soon came down. "The wind chimes on the deck are playing "Twinkle Twinkle Little Star," he said, not understanding v2k. "Some safe house. My stalkers are in the driveway coughing. Let's have sex. It always makes me sleep. Don't you want me to get any beauty sleep? Everyone says I'm cute."

"This isn't a safe house. I never said it was. It's a place for ti's to take a breather. Do you want me to check your truck again?" When I came back in, Craig was more aggravated than ever. He kicked the umbrella pot in frustration, saying his inevitable murder could be prevented by setting up my computer and camera in his bedroom. With cold eyes, he confessed to the atrocity he'd committed, which resolved why he needed my place for a hideout. No one knew to look for him here.

"Water under the bridge," I said, feigning nonchalance over his wretched deed. "I'll keep guard, and you get some rest." My words had been a gut response.

Stand guard I did. Not from lurkers or cops. From him.

Knife in hand, I called a local ti. "Sorry to wake you, but someone needs to know I'm in danger here from Craig. He's totally lost it."

"Oh my God, June. What can I do?"

"Nothing. I'm going to get him up early and tell him he has to get on the first ferry. He's committed a terrible crime. He's capable of anything. Call me in the morning in case he goes ballistic."

At 5:00 a.m., Craig's stomping could be heard from the patio where with purse, knife, and phone in hand I waited to see his truck leave. "Thanks for fucking nothing," he yelled in the carport, dropping a twenty-dollar bill on the ground, as we'd agreed that because of his abundant assets he could not empty my fridge without compensation. That I was abjectly poor, had no car to get groceries, and was left eating only toast after he stayed, never entered his mind.

The fact is, I would have given him twenty bucks to leave.

Craig is in the tiny percentile who expects the world from a rescuer. So is a ti who emailed, "You always say you are busy. I deserve to be treated better on the phone and when I ask for support." This ti believes I'm obligated to satisfy her every whim and expresses only criticisms for my efforts. She gets angry that I cannot talk for hours and gets angry when I cannot immediately fulfill a request. No, she's not a perp pretending to be a ti.

"Find me a woman target I can befriend," she said, "around my age and in my town. Someone that you've known a long time and who's never been homeless. Homeless ti's get bought off by the perps."

Not only was this a tall order, but because she was ill-tempered, I couldn't refer her to anyone at all. Two weeks later she blew up at me for not producing a target-friend that fit her specifications. Reminding her that I'm a volunteer made no difference. Ms. X is one of five victims whom I've had to deny further contact with. Two others had the same scolding sense of entitlement that discussions and patience would not resolve. And two were grossly demeaning other targets.

Desperate people can, forgivably, act out of character; and some people are rude, regardless.

Now that you, the reader, have decided only a fool would assist ti's, we'll do a U-turn and check out why offering care is almost always awesome. Very few victims are ungracious.

Plunking her purse, keys, and bags on the hall table, the fifty-year-old woman said, "All I want is a nap."

Pointing upstairs, I said, "Consider it home, but take your things with you. I get the paranormal EH. It's a freak show around here." Her eyes conveyed utter comprehension. She lived like that too.

When she came downstairs hours later, she said, "Do you know how many years it's been since I felt safe enough to have a nap?"

"I do," I said, over tea and warm scones.

V was a quiet guest, soft spoken, and simply needed to rest up before beginning her next sojourn of survival. "I got a job," she said, "teaching woodcarving at a Pacific arts school. I've given up on Eastern Canada. The stalkers won't let me work. I've been living in my van."

We didn't talk about the crime much. We talked about trees, collecting wild edibles, and our childhoods. "I want to give you something," she said, dashing up to her suite. The tattered black suitcase she opened in the cedar living room held treasures that made me sigh to think she wanted me to have one.

"Take your pick," she said.

"I can't," I replied. "You must have spent a million hours on them."

"They're only spoons and bowls."

"They're masterpieces."

"I've been living off them—selling to galleries."

"Are you a renowned carver?" I asked.

V napped a lot, walked on the beach, matched me cup for cup of tea, and preferred to talk about hope. We're still great friends. My own hope is that she will visit when the book is done.

Being offered a carving was better than accepting one. And having her in my home was better than not having her in my home.

V left rested and stalked, knowing she had nearby support. I was sincerely sorry to see her go.

The next lady we'll look at was reacting oppositely, but also typically. Given a choice, she preferred not to use a chair, and although that wasn't typical, her angst and grief certainly were. Sitting cross-legged on the floor, staring out to sea through a massive window, she rocked and cried all day, every day.

"I don't know how it happened," she said. "I was studying religion in India and got targeted after coming back to Canada. My friend didn't know what to do with me and brought me here. She thinks you and I should be committed for thinking we're stalked. That we're too old."

This woman now lives on a nearby little island, having fallen in love with mine. She still cries and rocks but doesn't want to die every day. She sent me a picture of herself, and gosh I was pleased. She's lost the terror-struck look, which means she's probably learning to cope with the worriments and the isolation. Like so many, her OS theme dictates zero lifestyle: no curricular studies, no outside job, no outside interests. Needing companionship, she wants to get a pet, but is hesitant to. Yet the loneliness is suffocating her.

In spite of this woman's psychological pain, or perhaps because of it, she gave me an accidental lesson in humility. I am a better person for having her stay.

There is a piece of the soul that OS cannot infiltrate, a closeness of the heart with others who are suffering. She gave me that.

So did the woman who recently left this message on my answering machine when I sorely needed a bit of humanity: "Don't call back. I know what you did. Thank you."

I would never have called anyhow. The process to help her had been far riskier to me than to her, and she knew it. We'll probably never meet for that reason.

You see, much of my work in assisting ti's is cloak and dagger. Sure, the remote perps see everything and pass information along to the appropriate street thugs. Still, trying to secrete the comings and goings of ti's from their violent on-heels stalkers for as long as possible is worthwhile and can mean life or death when a victim, who cannot help himself, has a brutality-filled theme.

Clearly, it's not just other people's lives I'm protecting by closeting rescues. It's my own. To some folks, it might sound ever so exciting—all this spy-thriller sneakiness. Please step into my shoes.

"I need to get to Point B," a hidden Quebec ti said from a public phone.

"Check the Point A post office," I answered.

Work like this is tedious and far from exhilarating. Mostly, assisting distant, fear-paralyzed victims, like the Quebecer, is a lot of covert research, a lot of covert communication, and keeping multiple copies and records of whatever action has been taken in case the target dies or disappears. Of course, OS might have foiled the Quebecer's plan or made her too sick to go anywhere, yet amazingly, targets who are foiled, sick, fear-frozen, or broken manage to eventually pull themselves to higher ground, much of the time, if they've a rope to grab.

As you know, the hardiest of victims are unable to help themselves at intervals. Being terrorized by stalkers or levelled by EH, never mind the effects of PTSD, can make even a trip to the mailbox a nerve-racking or physically impossible feat. Without a favour or two, some will die. Naturally, there are repercussions to the person who throws the rope.

The day after one ti left my home, the carpeting on the second and third story filled with long, fat healthy earthworms. (No, it was not the ti who did it.) The night, predictably, was harrying. Doodads, like my dad's old fishing lures and a stained glass hummingbird, were placed beside my head while I slept. The den downstairs had been completely rearranged, and a locked, blocked door was ajar.

Usually, though, highly specific punishments for assisting a ti begin while the person is still here or while I'm wholly entrenched in a long-distance rescue, meaning there's no second-guessing that retribution is taking place when the same we're-teaching-you-a-lesson offences continue for days afterwards. Scare-tactic incursions are expected and can be sort of lived around. EH's horrendous pain and brain-entrenchment, however, make for slow writing.

Did I mention that after last week's slippery rescue, my legs—well, they're not broken—they just feel like it. I was already seeking a secondhand walker and cane as the EH attack on my joints after mentioning the p word—publishing—seems to have done some damage. It left me laid up for a stretch, only to be crippled again by this newest round.

The problem with seeking used merchandise is that once the perps catch on they flood the local online papers with ads for the item I need, or they answer my own ad, and cause me nothing but trouble. I learned that trick the hard way when the bottom fell out of my birdcage, and I needed a replacement pronto. It surprised me when they wagered a strong harassment attack to prevent me from getting a secondhand cage, and I ended up ordering a new one. Of course, I expected them to be annoying, for they are always annoying, but their creative cruelty over my attempt to find a house for Little Bird was unprecedented. "What could possibly go wrong with buying a used birdcage?" you ask. It would take a chapter to tell you what happened. And although you'd learn a lot more about stalker harassment, I'm going to pass. You probably have the gist of stalker-harassment by now, and besides, I'm unwell. Retribution against me is becoming severe. Activists get it much worse. Let's face it, they can get murdered.

One last comment about a respite house: it should have rules of disallowing alcohol, nonprescription drugs, and illegal goings-on. This isn't being prudish. It's being smart. Drunk or drugged ti's, and ti's acting out from fear or revenge, can unintentionally pull their rescuers deep into the pit with them.

A well-run ti centre would ideally need, as I said at the chapter's beginning, to be sponsored (funded) and staffed. On- and off-site victims must be offered counselling and medical care that focuses on living with capture, psychological and physical torture, and mind control. Accommodations, each in his own self-contained unit, should extend for a year. Too, victims must receive help to regain financial stability and housing, providing their stalkers and owners will allow them to recover any of the forced losses. A centre would need to incorporate extreme forms of security and, most importantly, instigate thorough follow-up care and communication with each person who asks for continuing support.

"Ya, ya, ya," you say. "Tell me another story." I think centres are possible even before OS goes to court. Furthermore, when the crime does receive complete public recognition, and it will, OS- and EH-aware governments will be exposed for perpetuating or ignoring the crime, meaning help centres and financial compensation will be mandated by the survivors. If you think my fellow targets and I will be satisfied with an apology, you're on the wrong planet.

* * *

My hackers are now deleting the letters "un" (for example, usual versus unusual); scrambling MKULTRA's spelling; and generally playing with meanings and spacing. I've done so many rereads to fix the perp errors that I'm about ready to snap.

Sometimes I use my old manual typewriter, yet the finished material still has to be transferred to my laptop.

The period between the final edit and publication is in enemy hands. They could leave the book alone, or they could distort passages. It's keeping me up, worrying.

CHAPTER EIGHTEEN

LETTERS FROM TI'S

These letters are verbatim except for the names. They connote the emotional states and diverse conditions of countless others and represent what I get in the mail. Perhaps the ti in your life wrote one of them.

Letter #1

Really not doing so well…

Hi June this is Crystal again. I was wondering if you are able to hook me up with another individual in similar circumstances as I. I was wondering how others would know I wasn't just trying to infiltrate to cause them more grief. I gave my son your phone number so that he can get a perspective on this. I am losing all sense of love for life and look forward to nothing. It seems to take too much energy to do anything outside of this property. I don't want to go anywhere because the feeling of being invaded is everywhere. I see the same stalkers everywhere I go, so it's easiest to go nowhere. My fear is as strong as the circumstances that are truly going on and I know that I am emitting negative energy all the time... I feel as if they are winning and controlling my thoughts. Forcing any type of positive reinforcement for myself is fading daily. I don't feel very strong. At any rate I would be so encouraged if you could maybe explain some of this to my son and answer some questions he may have.

Letter #2

If you get this?

I am looking for support and a community. I was born very sensitive so my abilities to cope are of a spiritual nature. I do meditation and healing. However, I do this alone. Those whom are very dark that are stalking me that live close by have used thought reading combined with surveillance and stalking. I am basically afraid for my life at this point. Just yesterday I was mobbed by vehicles that were using intimidation tactics to give the impression that they were trying to hit me. The cars were less than inches from me. Combine this with being massively socially ostracized and I am pretty much at a breaking point. I do not know where else to turn. I believe there are tracking and surveillance devices in me or in my home. I just didn't know that it would be so many people and close to home. They have taken pictures of me. I am perfectly sane however these things are happening. Literally my every move is being watched.

Letter #3

June, I'm still forgetting to breathe since the last time we spoke. What worries me is if it's them messing with the breathing centre of my brain. I'm worried my breathing instincts won't kick in and I'll die. I'm definitely very panicky about this and worried it could even be medical. But if I go to a doctor he'll think I'm crazy. I guess they've found something that cranks my anxiety up and this really upsets me. Do you know anybody who can help me?

Letter #4

I am pleased you wrote back. Yes, I've been worried about my eyesight. Everything is fluorescent, or loose colour, or black and white, or grey. Sometimes I have pixelated vision, or coloured little stars, or like TV snow. They often beam holograms into my head like spiders, monsters, butterflies, dragons, bears, mazes, chains, all kinds of odd things. Monarch mind control. I just got off the phone with an international ti broadcast and a few of them said they had the same vision problems as me. I'll send you the number so you can participate. I have Morgellons too.

Letter #5

I am rather at the end of tolerance. I was wondering if Mormon country had more honest cops, you know Mormon cops. I need to find the device on my truck. I put Mylar inside the truck doors but for some reason I got severe vibrations and I think someone parked a vehicle near with one of those machines that look like portable radios. It's hard to find a spot to park and sleep. I didn't go to sleep until about 5 a.m. I'm going to drive to Utah and check out the cops there. Has anybody you know had luck with an honest cop? If Utah doesn't work, can I live in my truck at your house?

CHAPTER NINETEEN

THE WOMAN

Whilst much of the following story parallels my own countryside targeting, it is an account of one of the many other forest-dwelling women who are tormented after dark in Canada's Pacific Northwest. It appears to me that night terrorism aimed at lone rural females has been standardized to cause maximum fear, as the resulting distress, which could be years-long, is guaranteed.

It is vital that loved ones, along with folks who are working in health services, acknowledge that targets who suffer nights (and days) of extreme horror suffer lives with extreme consequences. Many of these consequences could be avoided were it not for the disbelief and undermining of others.

Suicide attempts are high in the perpetual nighttime-daytime harassment group. Such a desperate person is not mentally ill; we've all seen films of a wolf pack chasing a weakened deer until it is too exhausted to go on. It's like that. Lone women are among the most viciously attacked and are habitually ridiculed, year after year.

Please keep in mind that targets terrorized by stalkers are undergoing mind control of a different nature than the electronic mind control we've been discussing as of late. A mind controlled by fear and grief or a mind controlled by energy weapons—either one—is what OS is all about. In sum, OS involves manipulating and maintaining control over a person's thinking and behaviours by whatever method is necessary: stalkers or weapons.

Moxie aside, the woman in this story was easy to control, as her self-sustaining lifestyle, without Internet, kept her blind to OS. She only knew she was hunted.

At the end of the chapter, you'll learn how the woman could have quite simply lessened the attack: the key word being "lessened."

The Woman

The homesteader did not understand what she'd done wrong. Whatever it was, her husband was angry. He'd become the feared actor in a horror flick, a lover whose vulgar contempt chills his subordinate to the bone. He viewed the woman as vile, a rat to be expelled, especially after losing her job. She was as afraid of him as of the strange men who had watched her all summer sawing, and splitting, and piling next winter's fuel, who took pictures of her swinging an ax, who masturbated in plain sight.

On this August morning, hiding from the husband behind a tool shed, between rolls of barbed wire, she waited to hear him leave for work. He knew she was there, for the horses poked their noses over the fence at her.

The woman had her own work, beginning with rebuilding the firewood lean-to. Prowlers had sledgehammered it just hours before, by moonlight. There'd been a thwack and another and the rumble of her neat stacks tumbling.

Although the husband had dashed outside one night with a two-by-four, he left it up to the woman to defend the property. It was, after all, her fault. With police making up stories, unwilling to help, the woman had tried, and failed, to stop the gang by herself.

She also failed at something else—to get the tall lean-to back up that afternoon, a two-person job, and worried excessively about the husband's wrath upon his return. She hoped his roving eye would keep him away until late, but he came home early and ripped into her.

When his conniption was over, while she was washing the dinner dishes, he said, "The kids and I will be at a hotel this weekend. There's a concert. You'll be fine."

The woman knew, in truth, what her husband's stoic expression meant. She knew he'd smile as soon as he looked away, for he always smiled after delivering upsetting words. The fact was, he hadn't been to a big city or a concert in over twenty years, and wanting to go now, with the farm under attack, was no coincidence. And for him to take Friday off when he worked through celebrations, even their wedding day, was no coincidence either. So it wasn't paranoia that told her he hoped she'd be killed on the weekend, alone in the firs. He wanted her gone for bringing chaos to their home. He'd been plenty clear about that.

Kissing the children goodbye that warm Friday morning, wishing them fun in the city, the woman got busy with chores. The soil, and shovels, and gardens were prized; the woman was proud, living honestly in the bush. But this day felt different, like waiting to be executed. She thought about how a husband should not give his wife to brutes.

When the prowlers came early, double the number, along padded-down footpaths, the woman presumed she would not live much longer. Yet, she wouldn't have left if there'd been a thousand, at least not at first. The livestock had been solace and sanity when it seemed the whole world hated her. To each animal she owed a debt of gratitude.

From her window seat atop a washing machine, the woman watched the horses trotting nervously up and down the gate in anticipation of being cornered and clubbed. She had not got the dogs inside in time, for the men always came after dark, except for this evening, and now the dogs were frantic, unwilling to come in, unable to protect their home from a swarm of predators.

She watched a man on the sundeck jump on a picnic table she'd built for the kids, and from there jump to the sundeck rail, and from there to the roof, pulling a wisteria vine down as he clambered. She wondered if he could fit in the chimney and what he was doing up there, if others would throw gas cans to him.

Crawling under the windows, from room to room, a magical spot eluded her—the one not to get shot in, the one to disappear in, the one with an uncut phone line. She realized the hunters were playing: thumping the walls, and rapping the windows, and jiggling the doorknobs when they could smash a glass door and step in.

Hearing the hosepipe running, the woman screamed at the thought of another hen being drowned, of cats being drowned, and the man on the roof whistled and stomped. She screamed as loud and long as she could, hoping someone would save her. But she'd bought the place because of the forest. The silence had been a religion to her. No one would notice.

Cursing herself for leaving the truck in the orchard, they'd caught her off-guard, collecting windfalls; so she crept inside a cupboard to see if a claw hammer could rip the floor up and drop her into the crawlspace. Then she heard the men in there too.

With a farm mutt now yelping, thoughts of retreat evaporated. The woman, who was going to die anyways, crawled to the nearest door, put her mouth to the crack she bared, and pleaded for the dog to come. When a black snout appeared, she grabbed it and hauled him in, fastened the deadbolt, and dragged her friend into the bathroom. Wrapped in towels, he looked at her and stopped breathing, only to begin again.

They sat together on the bathroom floor while lines of men slapped the frosted pane with their palms. Examining the blade on her pocketknife, the woman imagined tearing to the truck with King on her shoulder. She imagined piercing the face of whoever grabbed her, and tried to find the courage.

Hesitating, and despising herself for it, the moment of reckoning came and went. There'd be no getting away. The men, proving themselves to be lock pickers, were telling jokes in the house. They were on the roof, in the crawlspace, at every wall, at every window, and in the kitchen.

Placing one hand on King's lovely head, the woman stared at the knife again, relieved that it was long enough to slice far into a heart. She poked her chest hard, and again, and again, making a blood map through her pink cotton blouse. She practiced all night and through the first glimmer of dawn, prepared to fatally stab herself when the time came. She thought about her bareback rides along the lake at sunrise, until she'd done something wrong to make the countryside unsafe, and prayed her old horse was okay.

In the brightness, the men were quickly leaving. The game was ending, and she waited to be taken, waited for the moment to stab her heart. She watched a man-shape descend a tangle of wisteria vines by the window, for the plant engulfed the house, and wondered if he would be the one to open the bathroom door, wondered if more men were on the vines. She listened to cars crunching on gravel, retrieving the men, readying to whisk her to the butcher they'd promised. But the car doors banged, and the crunching faded.

The gang was gone, but not really. Some would be in the firs, and some would be driving by, as always.

The woman with a bashed-in dog sat on the bathroom floor until the silence she loved revived her enough to consider the horror of what her husband would do if anything was broken.

Confused to be untouched, and surprised to find the kitchen as neat as she'd left it, the woman was forced to replay the night in her mind, trying to—hoping to—make it a dream. But her shirt was ripped and she was wounded.

Still clutching the knife, the woman dared to go outside, where she stood among the hazelnut trees, unable to think straight—unable to think at all—as she gazed at the aftermath.

Pulled-off siding from the tool shed lay in jagged pieces in the grass, and paint was spilled on the porch. The old horse looked dead on his feet and the other dogs were missing. She wished the men had taken her.

Cleaning up and fixing up as best she could, the woman wept as she'd never wept before. Burning her bloodstained clothes in the woodstove, and the dog's bloody towels, she tried to make it all look fine. She considered life without her kids, leaving them with a miserable father. So she stayed.

As soon as the husband got home, he tore into her for letting the men take over while he was having fun at the concert.

"I couldn't help it," she said. "There were so many."

The husband stopped speaking to the woman. He did not want to hear what happened, and he did not want her to eat, or talk, or be seen, expecting that his loathing would make her bolt. But she couldn't. Not even for an hour. Not yet. Not empty like that.

Her spirit left when the men came in the kitchen. Or maybe it was her soul that cast off. It was a sensation from the heart, of essence flying, vacating its shell, a surreal feeling of being hollow but alive. She could only speak in a whisper. Every noise made her panic, and she stopped sleeping.

After one full moon, sick from something, the woman did go. Opening the vegetable garden gate, she stumbled her way to the red plastic tub that held her peach-tree seedlings, dumped it, and keeled over. Grieving for all she was about to lose, she wondered if the seedlings would die and wondered if all her hard work had meant anything. Rolling the tub to her big truck, she stood on it, slowly pulled herself up to the steering wheel, and drove off, unwilling to put the children through her final decay, tired of being despised for whatever she'd done wrong.

* * *

Author's note: The sound of men in the house was likely v2k. Nothing inside had been disturbed and the woman had not been approached. Voice to skull is commonly used in conjunction with other crimes to exacerbate a victim's fear, especially during terrorizing. This ploy is responsible for many cases of PTSD, as capture or death seems unavoidable. Stalkers are not known to break into a home when the target is there and alert, not even in ti sex crimes, for the victim is always mentally incapacitated first. Nor have I heard of a large group of stalkers taking over a city-dweller's yard, although it appears to be mandated for those who are rurally isolated.

New and off-grid targets, in particular, experience crippling psychological distress from both nighttime terrorizing and misunderstood v2k schemes.

Terrorizing, with or without v2k, changes a person. Ongoing extreme terrorizing, such as what the woman went through, inevitably leads to a mountain of losses and too often leads to a lonely death.

It is unusual for stalkers to be as aggressive at an occupied house as the woman's stalkers were. Obviously they were not afraid of being seen, filmed, and identified. Fifty miles away, I experienced parallel stunts, so I'm guessing the woman and I were assigned the same trained crew who knew we would not take pictures of them.

Looking back, and speaking only for myself, I question why I couldn't muster the courage to photograph my attackers in the beginning; for the opportunity presented itself repeatedly. Yet I'd collected an excess of other evidence.

My reason seems weak, now that it's almost two decades later, and this is it: by the time I realized the RCMP were useless and that I needed to be filming to prove my case, I had become useless as well. And the men knew it.

It was during my fear-paralysis stage that the men trapped me, a lot. Of course, this stage didn't last long, but the damage was done. I'd been entirely traumatized through trapping.

The truth is, I made a lot of mistakes and let the intimidation and retribution take over my self-help-thinking for a while, believing that clicking on a camera and showing someone the pictures would have been disastrous. I wanted to take pictures. I had a good snapshot camera. But I was afraid of the stalkers, both for my children's safety and my own.

Indeed, there is retribution for filming stalkers, yet in my opinion, it is the best way to prevent up-close terrorizing, particularly if the victim is hooked up with social media, which the woman in the story and I did not have access to at the time.

Many ti's post their harassment videos on Youtube accounts, in spite of retribution. Should you take a look, you'll see that many of these videos show regular-looking people doing regular things that only the target and the stalker see as significant. Yet it is these very videos that are saving the victim's skin.

Now, don't get me wrong and begin a crusade of picture-taking on the bus, in the cheese shop, and at the sidewalk cafe. Doing so will get you into trouble, even after you declare "It's legal," which it might not be. Nonstop picture-taking can also become an obsession that will impede any sense of normality in your life. For your own sake, you must live as normally as you can.

But the indisputable fact is, when you are known to take pictures of bare-faced harassment, prowlers will tone down their scare tactics. And they will stop using pretenses to knock on your door.

Need I say it? A camera, for a ti who can keep one running, is the most powerful deterrent.

Nevertheless, camera or not, every neighbour-less female ti I've spoken to has experienced trauma-causing elements of the woman's harrowing story; yet few are actually trapped in their homes by visible mob-stalking men, except on Vancouver Island, British Columbia, where I was living. Nationally and globally, there must be other pockets of trapped rural ti's that I'm not hearing about.

CHAPTER TWENTY

QUIRKY REMOTE HARASSMENT
OR
RAZZAMATAZZ

If reading about the can't-happen wonders puts you in a foul mood, as it does for so many, consider skipping this section. Here and now we'll be discussing phenomena where objects, animals, people, and natural elements change in ways that cannot be explained.

To reiterate a previous comment, beyond suggesting theories, I have no intention of eliciting how these deviances from rationale occur. My own theory that covert beyond-university physics is to blame is best illustrated by astute ti's who no longer ask themselves, "Is my place haunted?" or "Do I need an exorcism?"

It's these people you need to speak to should you want to learn more about quirky remote harassment. I am a person of one, and they are persons of thousands. It would be wonderful if the razzamatazzed folks could amass their experiences for a first-ever in-depth study.

In any case, according to my view, it's presumable that some—not all—of the mysteries in this chapter will one day be proven as brain meddling: EH outstripping human cognition and human senses. And still other mysteries may be attributable to EH management of electricity. The remaining curiosities appear unsolvable, yet everything in life can be explained when the right rocks are looked under.

Targets who are plagued with phenomena (razzamatazz), such as disappearing and reappearing soup, are disbelieved by targets who aren't and by many who are but don't know it. It's plausible that the small number of victims who claim their items get stolen and returned may be experiencing this obscure harassment. Except for articles that can better a ti's future, disappeared items can materialize months or years later right in front of the victim.

"June," a collaborator said, "do you remember the octopus sculpture someone stole off my wall a couple of years ago? I was watching TV last night, and there it was lying on the hearth. A perp must have been in the house and snuck it there when I was looking down changing channels."

I believe this victim is being honest, having had similar unsettling moments, but predict that a sculpture-returning perp was nowhere near the house and was instead running an advanced energy-matter-space computer program.

Ample credible reports, most of which are spookier than a returned octopus, dictate that razzamatazz can be a ti's primary or auxiliary theme.

In my opinion, both new and heavily harassed targets are shown bewildering paranormal-type marvels as a gaslighting tactic: a step-by-step plot to make the victim think he is going insane or losing a particular mental function. At the very least, when a ti is describing paranormal-type events, he will sound dippy. For those of you who have forgotten, gaslighting is when an evildoer manipulates words, actions, social situations, or objects to make a person think he's become mentally unzipped. Gaslighting is unsuccessful on ti's in the long run, but initially creates self-doubt and emotional disarray.

Because remote phenomenal hoodoo is disbelieved by about half the ti population, even those racked by it, dissension occurs. Contrariwise, most everyone agrees that OS's variety of energy attacks stirs up bickering between victims with different viewpoints, assaults, handling, and conditioning. Victims also agree that having no consensus among the ti community corrupts all attempts at cohesive activism, which ensures the crime's future.

For example, Jack says, "I get puddles. Don't ask me how they do it, but all I do is blink and there'll be a puddle on whatever's in front of me."

Jill's response is usual for someone who doesn't experience razzamatazz. "Jack, that's lunacy. I hope you haven't told anyone else."

Some ti's discredit others' accounts to the extent of being downright rude, simply because they haven't encountered all the techniques but think they have or because of a strong stance. We can all agree to disagree, but let's do it with restraint, respect, and willingness to educate ourselves about opposing sides.

Despite my backhanded lecture on keeping an open mind, delving into OS's wizardry is rather a precarious situation, for every ti who talks about OS's abstract doings is subject to labelling. For me, the moment is long past for redemption. The cracker box was opened chapters ago.

Charging ahead, to illustrate remote phenomena, I'm going to put witnessed incidents into narratives, as well as in a list. So let's begin with Deb, whose main theme is razzamatazz.

Third in line at the help-yourself coffee counter, Deb chats amicably with the person behind her. It isn't that she's happy. Deb needs an ally: someone to render a hand. Placing her cup under the spout and pressing the red button, she has to pretend to try, even though nothing ever comes out for her. Never. When the ally becomes concerned that he's not going to get a coffee either, he presses the button and, voila, coffee dribbles into Deb's cup.

This ti realizes she's living in Poppycock World, for she has the same problem with bank machines, debit and library cards, vending machines, well, pretty much anything computerized or automated. It's a tactic that ruined her life for a while as she worried excessively about everyday tasks, like withdrawing cash and getting her morning brew at the cafeteria.

Deb is lucky, though, in that targeted cohorts believe her. A few of them have the same problems, but not incessantly, as she does. She's fortunate there is a victim meet-up group nearby that discusses mysterious harassment. Some blame the devil, and some blame an energy beam that can turn electrical appliances on and off. Then there are theories about interdimensional travel; interdimensional non-humans; cloaking (military technology that makes people and objects invisible); and new findings in the combined study of energy, matter, and space. The support is helpful—the act of being believed—but for the most part the others are clueless how this phenomenon impacts her. Frankly, she's jealous of targets who can get things done. What she hasn't told her pals is how depressed she is, inconsolable with guilt from bringing OS into her daughter's life. During their last get-together, the daughter complained that programmed transactions aren't working for her either: gas pumps, checkout tills, and elevators.

Howbeit we leave Deb and her daughter and look at Whosis, whose harassments are so outlandish she's only told her best friend for fear of being stuck in a hospital.

"Every time I charge my phone," she said, "the cable tangles itself into granny knots that are hard to undo."

"That happens to me too," her friend said. "Cheap cords will do that."

"Really?" Whosis asked. "Isn't that impossible without someone actually tying the knots? Maybe then you can try to explain this to me. I took my pizza out of the oven last night, and someone had scraped the toppings off. It was just a red-smeared crust."

"You probably didn't see that you'd been ripped off when you stuck it in," her friend reasoned.

"This morning," Whosis confided, "when I dressed for work, my clothes were too small, even the ones that can't shrink. I stood on the scale, and the dial was bouncing around, so I tried my blouse and skirt again, and they fit like they should have the first time."

"You were just having a bad wardrobe day," her friend said.

"When I got to work, my key didn't fit either. But it did for my boss. No matter what I tried, it wouldn't turn. By noon he was calling me a witch lady. Every light I went under went out and then came back on when I was a few feet away. All day."

Talking now to you, the reader, we're going to keep on this track until you get the idea of quirky harassment.

Remotely altered keys, clothes, contraptions, furniture, lights, hardware, and food cause some victims to believe a burglar's been busy pranking. As you'd expect, these victims live with persistent suspicion that a stalker is around every corner waiting to play a gag. Thank goodness targets like Deb and Whosis eventually learn to accept that their OS theme is covert innovative deception. They can calm down and take necessary precautions.

Don't ever think that ti's are at peace with their quirky harassments just because they have accepted what they can't explain. Ti's hate every minute of quirky harassment, believe you me. They are only better off because acceptance beats walking into traps or panicking over shazam events.

Keys and locks are the most common objects to be remotely altered. "They changed the locks while I was sleeping (or shopping)" is what targets say until they catch on to razzamatazz.

As a ti, if that's what you are, look around your home and identify something you definitely don't want a stranger fiddling with. For a diabetic victim, this could be a blood glucose meter; and for a victim with an arson theme, this could be a smoke alarm. Whatever the object you've picked is, I'm surmising your worriment does not so much lie in the item being remotely broken, but in the item being remotely controlled.

A ti's blood glucose (blood sugar) test result will be whatever the remote perps want it to be. In fact, medical test results can change before, after, or while a ti or doctor completes an analysis. A negative test result, which has been noted by one or more people, can change to a positive. Or vice versa. And a test result of 5.0 can change to 17.2 in a blink. Witnesses generally claim surprise, scratch their heads, and blame the equipment or their aptitude.

When puzzling changes constantly happen with a variety of devices, services, and non-electrical items, to ti's or to the people around them, it's OS's razzamatazz, meaning there's going to be a lot of head scratching.

What's reprehensible, and I've seen this happen, is that a functioning smoke alarm will not ring when stalking arsonists begin a house fire and the remote perps want it to get out of control. Moreover, and more emblematic, a target could find that every flashlight and match is nonfunctional during a power outage. You get the idea. If it's critical to a razzamatazzed or other targeted person's welfare, it will be remotely meddled with.

If it's not critical, but is important to the person, that's enough for the razzle dazzle team to wreck the moment. A ti might not be permitted to open his Friday night treat of canned shrimp, finding that his electric and manual can openers are faulty. When he borrows the neighbour's, it doesn't work either, at least not then. After saying, "Hey, Fred, thanks for the loan, but it's broken," Fred will open a tin, ribbing, "Try it again, Einstein."

Notoriously, as already mentioned, ti's who can't accept that there is no definitive answer for how, in a blink, the drapes open or close, how the bed makes itself, how the armchairs turn upside-down, how the door chains grow six inches, or how a cherry pie turns into lemon meringue tend to believe stalkers have superhuman sneakiness. When these targets' pack-around bottles of water turn brown or smelly, they think a perp is absconding the bottle, then altering or poisoning it before returning it their carryall, all without being noticed. People in this group may return to a cashier who handled a purchase, claiming tampering or a switcheroo.

Absolutely, ti's can have scads of stalkers sidling up to their backpacks and handbags. And absolutely, perps muck with victims' food. It's true too that targets are put into mind-control dazes and have no recall. But for sidlers to taint the same ti's drink dozens of times in crowded areas and not be caught is incredible. On-heels stalkers are not omnipotent sleuths nor are they capable of Merlin sorcery. The spectacular achievements are done from afar by God only knows what science. Anyhow, that's my perspective.

Oh, and this is pivotal, onlookers, acquaintances, loved ones, and secondary targets are definitely impacted by quirky phenomena. They usually dismiss an episode, such as seeing a street sign change from Alpha St. to Eagleview Rd. and back again, believing they've made a cognitive mistake in the time it took to blink. They rarely share their so-called error and often don't need to. A "knowing" ti can look at an awed innocent's wide eyes and horrified expression and realize that Ruff may have changed into Kitty for a split second. Or done something else.

"What do you mean you put Ruff out? He's right here."

"That's what happens when you let him in."

"I didn't let him in. He still wants to go out."

"Then put him out."

"I'm doing it now . . . Hey, stop playing tricks on me. I put him out and here he is."

To people who enjoy occultism or science fiction, having razzamatazz as an OS theme might sound neat. It's not. Affected victims cannot believe a thing they see and cannot trust that anything they do will be exempt from troublesome changes.

Razzamatazz victims seldom bother with doctor-ordered non-emergency medical tests, pharmacy and home tests, EH-detection tests, implant-detection tests, nonessential measurements including scales and size tags, and employment and hobbies that involve precision. They find such activities pointless and frustrating.

For bewitched ti's, on-paper financial statements receive the same in-a-blink alterations, as can personal letters, orders, invoices, resumes, and applications. A handwritten "Happy Anniversary Mom and Dad" can change in a millisecond to "Unhappy Anniversary Mom and Gladys" with no change in handwriting style. Then there's money that disappears out of a hand in the same way gravy vanishes from mashed potatoes while you're wiping your chin.

Razzed targets would like to say that a robber has stolen their evidence of OS, because it's both possible and believable, but sometimes they can't. Vital documents, data-storing gadgets, and printed photos of stalkers, gees, what can I say . . .? Poof. Unlike a returned octopus sculpture, disappeared material that pertains to proving the crime will never reappear. Neither will money, medical needs, security equipment, and important papers.

Victims with a razzamatazz theme are screwed. There's no recourse. "Honest, Rob, I didn't spend the rent on shoes. It's just gone. No, I don't know where. I was putting it in my wallet to give to the landlord and it disappeared. That's all there is to say." A grievous phenomenon only has to happen once to understand the levity of OS's black ops crimes. Still sound like fun?

Razzamatazz victims ask themselves, "Can I be dematerialized?" My answer is, "Yes."

Targets and loved ones who think they've evaded OS's black arts, or disbelieve in them, are in my eyes subjected to bizarro yet explicable remote harassment, for it's not normal to go through two or three batteries or light bulbs a day, all the time. Or be dumbfounded all the time.

"Honey, what did you do to the printer? Every time I go past, it spits out my teaching schedule."

"I know. We need a new one. We're tripping it somehow. Yesterday, whenever I walked past, it printed sex ads. You can put a new stove on the list, too. It's turning itself on all the time. Maybe we should disconnect it."

What Honey doesn't know is that the next printer will be really quite possessed, same as the new stove that seemed to come with an invisible hand that adjusts the burners, as well as the oven dials. Furthermore, the put-together desks and pole lamps the couple ordered are going to be non-constructible, and they will conclude mischance on all four purchases. When the couple's Chinese ceramics rearrange themselves every evening, they say, "That's weird," then drink a bottle of wine and again avoid facing a new reality.

They ignore their new reality even after their celery sticks turn into chewed-up gobs on their plates. They know neither of them did it, and they know it isn't possible, not in a blink. So they drink another bottle of wine, decide to work on their home business, and find that none of the new pens and pencils will write. When the lights start to flash, they quit.

With Honey's theme having evolved to include razzamatazz, she and her hubby are going to go through a lot of booze.

A personal dilemma with phenomenal harassment is that it often coincides with a ti's thinking, as this conversation between two victims shows.

Ti #1: "Last night I was looking at my Venus painting, thinking how much I loved it, and it fell off the wall and smashed like someone lifted it up off the hook and dropped it."

Ti #2: "That happens to me too. I think about something and the freaks wreck it. How do they do it?"

Ti #1: "Gordie says it's Satan. He even put it on his website. I told him a New World Order has got some weird science going on, and he lectured me about Satan taking over our minds. Got real mad when I said he and the alien crowd should have an end-of-days party."

Ti #2: "Whatever it is, I'm afraid to think. Or look at anything. Even then the freaks know what pisses me off, so they use that too. Have you ever had bugs appear out of nowhere?"

Ti #1: "All the time. I'll blink and there'll be a bunch of flies on my knee. Or a spider. They even covered the car headliner with wood ticks one time. Must have been a hundred."

Ti #2: "You know what else? They can turn off a whole city's electrical grid."

Ti #1: "But they wouldn't. They'd be caught. It's better for them to torment us one at a time, like changing the size and shape of stuff."

Ti #2: "What stuff?"

Ti#1: "All stuff. Doesn't that happen to you? You take your fridge rack out and it changes dimension and can never fit again?"

Ti #2: "So that's what that is. Do you know how many times that's happened and I never caught on? I've broken so many things trying to get them back together. I mean, why would all the shelves suddenly not fit anymore?"

Ti#1: Here's another one for ya. The buttonholes on my favourite shirt sealed up. It's like there were no holes."

Ti #2: "I believe you 'cause all my jeans are too long now. Or maybe I'm shrinking."

Ti #1: "Gotta go. That choking beam's on me."

As a veteran ti, conversations like these still astound me, yet they're an ordinary part of my and other victims' confidential dialogues.

This is the tail end of a chat I had with a targeted doctor:

"Doc, can you believe how we must sound? Rocks that appear midair? Rivers that run upstream? Did you ever think you'd be talking about such things?"

"No, but if we don't talk about these matters, targets will think they have mental disorders, when space tech is altering their brains."

"To be honest, Doc, I always feel a little cuckoo after discussing phenomena."

"If you didn't, June, you wouldn't be normal."

This doctor declares that covert satellite operations infiltrate a mind and that all paranormal-type events are figments. I think tangible energy-matter-distance physics is at fault for certain obscurities, so I disagree with the doctor on a couple of hot topics, especially this one: a lot of the spontaneously appearing insects, animals, people, inanimate objects, and natural elements can be interacted with and are not a brain's figments. Eerily moved or altered living and non-living matter aren't always figments either.

However, brain incursion has been proven and is responsible for mind reading, mind control, sense manipulation, mind-movies, mind-snapshots, and physical and mental torture, so the doc's assertions are partially correct, according to my interpretation of OS.

Practicing professional folks, it seems, will understandably only go so far when it comes to talking about unexplainable hoo-ha and fall short of admitting to, or investigating, the reality of supernatural-looking harassment. Perhaps they are fearful of being lumped in with the Satan and alien theorists.

In returning to the subject of OS-devised gaslighting, mentioned a few pages back, I'd like to further explain this psychological conspiracy to brand someone mentally incompetent. It's a ploy that loved ones should be familiar with.

Razzamatazzed targets have OS themes geared to make them look and feel utterly loco. In the beginning, a perfectly sane ti can be pushed to tell himself, "There's something wrong with me," when there isn't. Razzamatazzed targets are particularly prone to doubting their own sanity when OS-disbelievers get involved. If you are a loved one, don't be hornswoggled by a psychopathic agenda against your targeted spouse, child, or parent.

Discouragingly, the majority of relatives merge with the enemy by buying into the "he's nuts" con. The consequences are tragic. The very people who could be helpful end up inadvertently greasing a ti's slide into hell.

"Daughter dearest, there is no possible way a spoon vanished out of your hand. Listen to me. You need to see a doctor. Last week, you said you woke up with your make-up already on. And the week before that, when we were having lunch, you said the storm painting beside us was getting you wet."

"Mom, have I ever said things like this before? Have I ever made up stories? It hurts me that you think I'm lying."

"Oh, I don't think you're lying, dear. You are suffering some kind of mental breakdown. It's nothing a few pills and a hospital visit won't fix."

"But, Mom, I really don't think there's anything wrong with me. Those men that are always following—I think they are playing a sick game."

"No one's following you, dear. Let's get you to the doctor this afternoon. We'll tell him everything that you're imagining so he can sort it out. It's probably stress from losing your job, then breaking up with Scott."

"Maybe you're right, Mom. Isn't your cousin schizophrenic?"

As a victim with a razzle dazzle theme, "Yikes!" is my immediate response to a conversation like this. Please, please, please, if you are the loved one of a ti who has always been mentally healthy, how about if you try and keep him or her that way. Don't add to your loved one's nightmare. Don't let a gang of miscreants deal you in. If you do, you may as well hand arsenic and shovels to them, for they are slowly killing your loved one right under your nose, with your endorsement. Don't be the invisible member around the gang's card-table meeting of "We got her good this time, thanks to her mom." Don't support a gaslighting scheme. Don't hang the victim. Don't support a gaslighting scheme. I said it twice because you need to hear it twice.

Listen well. Think well. Research well. If you do all three, you'll find that genuine mental illness is altogether distinct from the psychological effects and the psychological toll that OS, EH, and phenomenal harassments engender.

While we're on the topic of gaslighting, I can't imagine fully grasping the concept without discussing the intriguing name.

The name comes from the 1938 play *Gas Light* and its 1940s movie adaptations called *Gaslight* (or *Gas Light)* where a two-faced husband needs his wife to be out of the way, so he stages ruses to make her think she's demented enough to be committed. Gas lights, the dimming of them, are central in exposing the husband's endeavor. The story may be old, but its plot echoes the life of a ti with a gaslighting theme that may or may not include razzamatazz.

Gaslighting is a recognized medical term in the psychological field because trying to make someone look and feel confused or insane (gaslighting) occurs often enough in the mainstream that it warranted classification.

To the victims of gaslighting, know that the people doing it to you are the ones with the mental disorder and that your best tools are to stay cool and ignore as much of it as you can.

Okay readers, here is a list of the razzmatazz which I hear about often enough to consider standard. Included are a few of the remote-EH wonders that we covered in earlier chapters simply because they are phenomenal. Every one of these tricks is done in a blink. They are in random order.

- Overtaken and manipulated senses
- Mind-movies
- Mind-snapshots
- Phenomenal events coinciding with thoughts
- People and animals being flipped or tipped over

- People being invisibly picked up and thrown where an injury will occur
- Being invisibly pushed or pulled
- Invisibly jerked or held limbs
- Stock still (paralyzed) animals and people
- Vehicles being pushed over while parked or in motion
- Words being changed as they are spoken (speech manipulation)
- Voices being spontaneously replicated to produce problem-making statements
- Words, letters, sentences, numbers, designs, and pictures that are on objects or paper that change in a blink, such as train station signs, advertisement signs, signatures, price tags, stripes on vans, album covers, instructions, legal documents, and patterns on fabric
- Items that instantly change colour
- Items that instantly age
- Words, numbers, and letters being changed as they are handwritten, or after they are handwritten, with no change in handwriting style
- Windows, furniture, and objects that suddenly shatter or crack
- Exploding light bulbs and other objects
- Furniture and objects that shake, move, fall, flip, or tip
- Chairs, beds, walls, and other surfaces that are aggressively and loudly thumped with a strong invisible force
- A seemingly invisible person sitting, lying, or standing alongside that may thump something beside the target, or touch the target, or make an impression on a chair cushion or bedclothes, or otherwise make itself known
- Heat-supplying systems and exhaust systems being invisibly blocked by "blackness" thus causing carbon monoxide poisoning

- Instantly rearranged or moved plumbing, wiring, dishes, books, anything at all
- Multi-component articles which have one or more of their parts shifted or altered
- Engines and all other mechanical items, electrical items, and lights that change operations or operate by themselves
- Automated, computerized, mechanical, and encoded items that instantly stop working for the target, but may work for other people
- Things that do up or undo when it is impossible to do so, such as fasteners; buttons; ties; knots; latches; locks; chains; zippers; envelopes; packaging; and items that are taped, glued, nailed, or screwed
- Things that change size or shape—may or may not return to normal
- Flying, melting, and reversing of natural elements, scenes, and objects
- Perfect mounds, shapes, outlines, and pictures made from "bits" or small objects when no human could have been responsible. An example is the sudden appearance of a dirt-drawn helix on a lawn chair. Bit-made formations can be huge or tiny and can be found anywhere, even under vehicles.
- Puddles of water and leaking water, or other fluid, that instantly appear without cause, often in unusual places
- Indoor spontaneous gusts of wind
- Indoor hot or freezing air pockets
- Pockets of asphyxiating gas or chemicals
- Pockets that are seemingly airless or oxygen-less
- Thick clouds of instantly appearing powder that cause choking or sneezing

- White or coloured light beams that stream through roofs and walls
- Overnight physical mutilations such as an enlarged nostril; cut hair; filed teeth; shrunken, enlarged, or reshaped hand, nose, eye, ear or foot; completely altered face or body structure; altered genitalia; healed-over gouge on hip, buttock, face, or genitalia; cuts and holes
- Gooey slime, gluey slime, powder, and dry crusts appearing on body and things
- Instantaneous and on-and-off health maladies
- Blunt objects that are instantly sharpened: furniture edges, teeth, objects
- Contents (solid and liquid) that are invisibly taken out of containers and placed elsewhere, or disappear altogether, or reappear at a later date
- Instantly appearing insects, people, animals, things, and natural elements that may or may not disappear or shapeshift
- Instantly disappearing people, animals, things, and natural elements that may or may not reappear and that can shapeshift if they do
- Instantly disappearing money, OS/EH evidence, medical needs, security devices, and documentation that will not reappear
- Shapeshifting, such as a cement truck that changes into a golf cart, for seconds or minutes

Gosh, there's probably a million more. I apologize if a particular razzamatazz that's not mentioned is destroying your life, as your struggle needs to be recognized.

Could all remote EH be razzamatazz?

CHAPTER TWENTY-ONE

FOR TARGETS: GETTING BY

1. You didn't do anything to deserve organized stalking. If a work or social connection, or whistleblowing or activism, or a skill is why you were targeted, please keep in mind that you were enjoying your individual rights when a perp recruited you.
2. Forgive yourself for unseemly behaviour while figuring out the crime or while saving your life or your loved ones' lives.
3. Your loved ones may now be targeted. It's not your fault.
4. You may have had to abandon loved ones. It's not your fault.
5. You may be too sick, scared, or threatened to do activism. It's not your fault.
6. You have no privacy. You do not own your own head. You are tortured. Nevertheless, decide on areas of the crime that you will try to ignore.
7. Ignore others' ridicule or abandonment. They don't understand.
8. If you are in an abusive situation, ask yourself if you would be better off with or without the abuser(s).

9. Stay as calm as possible. Still, it is normal to fall apart or feel suicidal sometimes.
10. You may feel shaken for hours or days from OS-caused ups and downs, as well as feeling shaken from non-OS-caused ups and downs, however small. This is normal for a seriously traumatized person. Read books about coping with trauma and experiment with the suggested coping methods until you find one that works for your personality. The simpler, the better. Self-talk works for many: think or repeat a personal statement that will calm you or put your thoughts into perspective. For example, you might tell yourself, "I've survived the worst kind of torture; I can certainly handle a grumpy neighbour." Alternatively, you could repeat a prayer, such as a serenity prayer.
11. *Living Through Personal Crisis* by Dr. Ann Kaiser Stearns may help you endure your losses. Both the book and DVD offer doable, empathic advice.
12. Meeting with other ti's can help you cope.
13. Educate yourself about OS and EH. To learn OS's and EH's full scope, listen well.
14. Put a routine or daily ritual in your life, however simple or small.
15. Find something relaxing to look at or listen to as often as possible, even when you don't feel like it.

ACTIVISM FOR TARGETS

1. Be a good listener.
2. Be respectful to opposition.
3. To get the word out, prepare a short believable statement about OS, EH, or both. Stick to it. Keep it simple. Talk about OS and EH as a crime.
4. Do not insist that others agree with you. It will turn them off.
5. Do not give definite answers to the who, how, and why questions, and do not say you know which remote energy weapons are in use. Do not state possibilities as facts. (You wouldn't say you saw a tiger in your yard unless you were sure.) Everybody is saying something different and this discredits the entire ti community. We will never be heard or believed if we don't all begin saying, "We've got theories that are close to being proven. We're preparing to take this to court." Do not hesitate to speak up and say that it is not your job to know or explain the criminals' intentions. Say that it is your job to explain the criminals' impact.
6. Renditions of EH mind control should be avoided until the other parts of the crime are understood. There are better EH startup topics, such as v2k and other provable directed energies, along with their harmful devices.
7. With EH being difficult to describe, you might choose to educate the public about the stalkers and their harassment and avoid the harder-to-believe topics, at least until a listener is open to "heavier" discussions. From my experience, OS's stalking and harassing is the best place to begin a talk.

8. Get your city's flyer-distribution bylaws in writing. Distribute flyers that contain only sensible-sounding information and credible references. Stay away from left-field topics. When educating the public, put yourself in the shoes of someone who's never heard of OS and EH.
9. If you place a poster in a public place, keep the message simple and believable and add a credible reference for curious folks to look up. For example: Stop Organized Stalking and Electronic Harassment www.——.com.
10. Drawing from your prepared statement, speak and write to local health and help centres. Most times, the less said, the better. Offer common-sense references: nothing flashy. Don't fret if a meeting did not go well. You planted a seed, and that's an accomplishment in itself.
11. Do not sensationalize OS and EH. It's the saddest crime going.
12. If you have PTSD and it's through the roof, put off public speaking until you're feeling better, unless, that is, you can stick to your short prepared statement without causing yourself more emotional pain.
13. Expect retribution for your activism efforts.
14. Writing or speaking to your government about directed-energy weapons can get you put on a "watch" list that could result in an unwelcome knock at your door. If you are concerned about repercussions from your government, keep your discussion to OS's gang stalking and gang harassment, which inevitably leads to EH in one way or another.

Activism to stop OS and EH is unlike any other activism you might be familiar with. The public is unaware of OS and EH and is resistant to its very concept. Let's do a comparison:

Activist: "Good morning, ma'am. Here is some information about our area's last forest being cut down. Would you like to read it and sign my petition?"

Ma'am: "What are you talking about? Forest? Who ever heard of forest?"

Activist: "The trees, ma'am. We only have one park and the trees in it are being cut down. The wildlife will die and there will be no nice place for us to go."

Ma'am: "You're talking nonsense. I've never heard of any of those things. Look, my husband's coming. I'll ask him. 'Vic, have you ever heard of forest or trees?' He said no and that I shouldn't interfere. But I think you should talk to your doctor."

So there you go, fellow targets. Activism for us is an unpleasant upstream-effort. It means taking a strong stance about an intensely personal yet inconceivable issue, which is why I refuse to offer much advice on what basic areas of OS and EH to focus on (for example, v2k versus isolation tactics). Only you know your passions and strengths. Use them wisely. Please, though, do not talk about subjects that make targets sound unhinged. Besides, some of us (finger pointed at me) are pretty good at sounding like idiots without any help.

Forming a local ti group benefits all involved. On a bigger scale, a well-managed confederation of like-minded groups would have collective power.

As for me, activism did not go well due to retribution against my children, hence the book. Anyways, I'm a born and bred Canadian. I'm overly apologetic; disproportionally docile and polite; and showing true Canadianism, am prone to (sometimes unwelcome) humour despite it all. An aggressive spokeswoman, I am not. Still, there are ways that I and other quiet or invisible targets can help get OS and EH recognized by the public and by the courts: write books; write to governments, human rights associations, crisis centres and shelters; support the visible activists; and record your own targeting so that it can be used in a class action suit. Better yet, summon the courage to construct your own class action suit based on getting organized stalking's harassment legally noted. Go after the local and national offices that turn their heads instead of assisting. Once recognition of the stalking and harassment occurs, recognition of EH will naturally follow. It has to.

You are an exceptional witness to one of the world's most heinous crimes. You are important. Your story is important.

Thank you for your time. I appreciate it.

THE END

APPENDIX

Below is a document which discusses destroying MKULTRA records. Remember, MKULTRA was a CIA mind-control experiment on ordinary citizens in the U.S. and Canada.

This document is in full-sized print on many websites. Here is one: www.druglibrary.org/schaffer/history/e1950/mkultra/appendixb.htm

APPENDIX B

DOCUMENTS REFERRING TO DISCOVERY OF ADDITIONAL MKULTRA MATERIAL

22 June 1977

MEMORANDUM FOR: Deputy Director of Central Intelligence

THROUGH : Deputy Director for Science and Technology

SUBJECT : Request for Guidance on Handling Recently Located MKULTRA Material

1. (U/AIUO) This memorandum is to advise you that additional MKULTRA documents have been discovered and to obtain your approval for follow-on actions required. Paragraph 7 contains a recommended course of action.

2. (U/AIUO) As a result of John Marks FOIA request (F-76-374), all of the MKULTRA material in OTS possession was reviewed for possible release to him. Following that review, the OTS material in the Retired Records Center was searched. It was during that latter search that the subproject files were located among the retired records of the OTS Budget and Fiscal Section. These files were not discovered earlier as the earlier searches were limited to the examination of the active and retired records of those branches considered most likely to have generated or have had access to MKULTRA documents. Those branches included: Chemistry, Biological, Behavioral Activities, and Contracts Management. Because Dr. Gottlieb retrieved and destroyed all the MKULTRA documents he was able to locate, it is not surprising that the earlier search for MKULTRA documents, directed at areas where they were most likely to be found, was unsuccessful. The purpose of establishing the MKULTRA mechanism was to limit knowledge of the sensitive work being performed to those with an absolute need to know. If those precepts had been followed, the recently found B&F files should have contained only financial and administrative documents. (In retrospect, I realize that

Declassified by 187475
date [illegible]
29 JUL 1977

The following MKULTRA document discusses experimentation on humans. You can find it in full-sized print by going online and typing "MKULTRA Subproject 119."

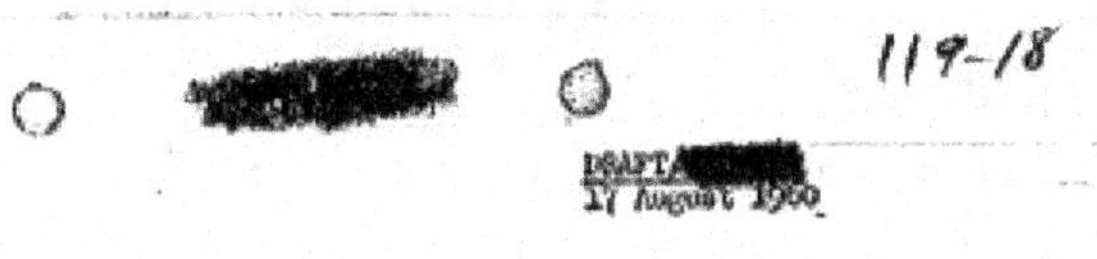

MEMORANDUM FOR: THE RECORD

SUBJECT : MKULTRA, Subproject 119

1. The purpose of this subproject is to provide funds for a study conducted by [redacted] to make a critical review of the literature and scientific developments related to the recording, analysis and interpretation of bioelectric signals from the human organism, and activation of human behavior by remote means. When initiated this study was being done on a consultant basis by [redacted] The reason for converting this into a Subproject is to provide more flexibility in the disbursal of funds for various kinds of assistance and equipment needed.

2. As indicated in the attached proposal this study is to provide an annotated bibliography and an interpretive survey of work being done in psychophysiological research and instrumentation. The survey encompasses five main areas:

a. Bioelectric sensors: sources of significant electrical potential and methods of pick-up.

b. Recording: amplification, electronic tape and other multi-channel recording.

c. Analysis: autocorrelators, spectrum analyzers, etc. and coordination with automatic data processing equipment.

d. Standardization of data for correlation with biochemical, physiological and behavioral indices.

e. Techniques of activation of the human organism by remote electronic means.

Project MKULTRA
The CIA's Program Of Research In Behavioural Modification

The transcript below discusses a CIA how-to manual that was given to MKULTRA staff to help them sneak drugs into innocent citizens. To the CIA's embarrassment, a copy of the manual was discovered many years after it was thought they had all been destroyed in a cover-up. To read the manual online, or even to buy a reprinted copy, simply look up MKULTRA Trickery.

MKULTRA Trickery

[document begins]

November 11, 1953

[deleted]

[deleted]

Dear [deleted],

This is a memo in regard to expansion of the manual on trickery.

The manual as it now stands consists of the following five sections:

1. Underlying bases for the successful performance of tricks and the background of the psychological principles by which they operate.

2. Tricks with pills.

3. Tricks with loose solids.

4. Tricks with liquids.

5. Tricks by which small objects may be obtained secretly. This section was not considered in my original outline and was suggested subsequently to me. I was, however, able to add it without necessitating extension of the number of weeks requesting for the writing. Another completed task not noted in the outline was making models of such equipment as has been described in the manual.

As sections 2,3,4 and 5 were written solely for use by men working alone the manual needs two further sections. One section would give modified, or different, tricks and techniques of performance so that the tricks could be performed by women. The other section would describe tricks suitable for two or more people working in collaboration. In both these proposed sections the tricks would differ considerably from those which have been described.

I believe that properly to devise the required techniques and devices and to describe them in writing would require 12 working weeks to complete the two sections. However, I cannot now work on this project every week and would hesitate to promise completion prior to the first of May, 1954.

I shall await you instructions in the matter. Sincerely yours

[deleted]

[document ends]

PATENT FOR MICROWAVE VOICE-TO-SKULL TECHNOLOGY

United States Patent 4,877,027 Brunkan October 31, 1989

Hearing System

Abstract

Sound is induced in the head of a person by radiating the head with microwaves in the range of 100 megahertz to 10,000 megahertz that are modulated with a particular waveform. The waveform consists of frequency modulated bursts. Each burst is made up of ten to twenty uniformly spaced pulses grouped tightly together. The burst width is between 500 nanoseconds and 100 microseconds. The pulse width is in the range of 10 nanoseconds to 1 microsecond. The bursts are frequency modulated by the audio input to create the sensation of hearing in the person whose head is irradiated.

Inventors: Brunkan; Wayne B. (P.O. Box 2411, Goleta, CA 93118)
Appl. No.: 202679 Filed: June 6, 1988

PLEASE MIND
YOUR HEAD

RESOURCES

There are enough informative websites, videos, books, radio shows, and articles to fill a separate resource guidebook. This section lists just a few of them. Note that every person and group speaks and writes about organized stalking and electronic harassment according to subjective beliefs and experiences. You will not agree with everything you read, see, or hear. I certainly don't. But you will acquire a lot more knowledge if you keep an open mind.

Do be cautious when you are doing casual willy-nilly research. Misguided people, and the perpetrators themselves, have published videos and websites that in my opinion are just plain goofy. And then others claim to have answered the who, why, and how factors of remote stalking and remote harassment.

Horse-sense reasons that until the ti community gets OS's and EH's motives and technology legally defined and criminalized, no one should be saying "I've figured it out"; yet it's a common occurrence, which is made all the worse because everyone's saying something different. Simply put, during your hit-and-miss research you are going to come across both hogwash and truth.

Anyhow, I recommend the following well-respected resources, each of which has educated or supported me in its own way and might do the same for you.

In Random Order

1. People Against Covert Torture & Surveillance, International. This active group offers support, networking, activism, and news.

   www.pactsntl.org
2. Dr. John Hall's books *Guinea Pigs* and *Satellite Terrorism*. His many interviews are online.
3. Elizabeth Sullivan's book *My Life Changed Forever: The Years I Have Lost as a Target of Organized Stalking*
4. ICAACT International Center Against Abuse of Covert Technologies

   www.icaact.org
5. Peacepink – Worldwide Campaign to Stop the Abuse and Torture of Mind Control/DEWs. Peacepink has groups worldwide and is based in China.

   www.peacepink.ning.com
6. European Coalition Against Covert Harassment

   https://eucach.org
7. Covert Harassment Conference

   www.covertharassmentconference.com
8. Brochure: Citizens Against Technological and Community-Based Harassment (C-A-T-C-H). You can find the brochure on several OS websites.

   The C-A-T-C-H group is now inactive, but their brochure is still a good resource.

PACTS
INTERNATIONAL

JOHN HALL
GUINEA PIGS
Technologies of Control

International Center Against Abuse of Covert Technologies
got chipped?
www.icaact.org

EUCACH.ORG
European Coalition Against Covert Harassment
Save our children from electronic slavery

International Center Against
Abuse of Covert Technologies

PeacePink™
Worldwide Campaign to stop the Abuse & Torture of
Mind Control / Directed Energy Weapons

A Project Camelot
Live interview with Melanie Vritschan
Covert Surveillance
Covert Harassment and
Non-consensual Experimentation

Foundation

STOPEG

STOP ELECTRONIC WEAPONS
STOP GANG STALKING

WHAT IS HAPPENING IN NANAIMO?

The city of Nanaimo, on Vancouver Island, Canada, is a major organized stalking hot spot.

IMAGE CREDITS

#1 Welcome to Hell

feverpitched@123RF.COM

#2 Mind games

Samantha Craddock@123RF.COM

#3 Magnetron

Pixabay rgouveia

#4 Silhouette head

Dima Lomachevsky@123RF.COM

#5 Electrical brain

majcot@123RF.COM

#6 Head rays

Adrian NiedehAouser@123RF.Com

#7 Hand holding camera

Open 24 Seven Co. Ltd.

#8 Screw head

Denys Prokofyev@123RF.COM

#9 Jammer on building

istockphoto.com@flyflyis

#10 Handheld jammer

istockphoto.com@lebazele

#11 Girl at car door

Ion Chiosea@123RF.COM

#12 HAARP

HAARP archives

#13 Satellite dish

Patinya Indrawoot@123RF.COM

#14 Electrical waves through head

Rosella Apostoli@123RF.COM

#15 Electrical impulses in brain

abidal@123RF.COM

#16 Homemade microwave weapon

Anonymous

#17 Electrical nervous system

blueringmedia@123RF.COM

#18 Man with antenna on head

dedmazay@123RF.COM

#19 Directed sound

Audio Spotlight https://holosonics.com

#20 RFID implant on finger

Vitalily Kytayko@123RF.COM

#21 Close-up of implant

Albert Lozano@123RF.COM

#22 Door in brain

Slaven Devic@123RF.COM

#23 Head with barcode

Dimitriy Shironoscov@123RF.COM

#24 Zippered whistle

lightwise@123RF.COM

#25 Bump keys

www.lockwiki.com

#26 Mind activity emits energy

Bruce Rolff@123RF.COM

#27 Hand grabbing brain

artqu@123RF.COM

#28 Manipulation

Dirk Erken@123RF.COM

#29 Arm behind back

Joshua Kristal

(Permission granted to crop photo)

#30 Electrical brain neurons

mikekiev@123RF.COM

#31 Hand reaching for rope

ktsdesign@123RF.COM

#32 Think outside the box

Ivelin Radkov@123RF.COM

#33 Orcas

Philip Stone Photography - Wild Isle

#34 Please mind your head

Pawel Opaska@123RF.COM

Cover photo taken by the author

NOTES

NOTES

NOTES

NOTES

NOTES

Lightning Source UK Ltd.
Milton Keynes UK
UKOW06n0457291217
315172UK00007B/41/P

9 781460 271391